Readings in Social Research Methods

Diane Kholos Wysocki, Ph.D.

University of Nebraska at Kearney

WADSWORTH

TM

THOMSON LEARNING

Australia • Canada • Mexico • Singapore • Spain • United Kingdom • United States

For more information, contact
Wadsworth/Thomson Learning
10 Davis Drive
Belmont, CA 94002-3098
USA

For more information about our products, contact us: Thomson Learning Academic Resource Center
1-800-423-0563
http://www.wadsworth.com

International Headquarters
Thomson Learning
International Division
290 Harbor Drive, 2nd Floor
Stamford, CT 06902-7477
USA

UK/Europe/Middle East/South Africa
Thomson Learning
Berkshire House
168-173 High Holborn
London WC1V 7AA
United Kingdom

Asia
Thomson Learning
60 Albert Complex, #15-01
Singapore 189969

Canada
Nelson Thomson Learning
1120 Birchmount Road
Toronto, Ontario M1K 5G4
Canada

ISBN 0-534-57915-9

DEDICATION

To my parents, Rona and Norman Kholos
and
my children, Eric and Jonathan Wysocki

Contents

PART IV ■ ANALYZING DATA   281

Chapter 11: An Introduction to Statistics   281

Preface

I have been teaching research methods and working with students on their own research projects since I began teaching. I love working with undergraduates, just like you, to help guide them as they make sense of the world in which they live through research. However, I know that sometimes research can be difficult and that some students might even be a little hesitant to take a research methods course. I worry about that and want students to understand that research can be a lot of fun.

There are some very good textbooks available about research methods. However, it is my experience that students like to hear not only about the concepts they need to learn but also how those concepts have been used in original studies. It has also been my experience that the more interesting the research topic and the more closely it connects with student's lives, the easier it is to learn the material. My intention is not to cover everything there is to know about research methods in this reader. I believe that would be an impossible undertaking and would just replicate what you can learn from a textbook. Instead, I have compiled a series of brief readings that can be used to support the terms and concepts you will learn in your class. You will find that these concepts parallel Babbie's *The Practice of Social Research,* ninth edition, organization, making this reader a perfect companion for Babbie's widely used text. However, you may also use this reader with any research text because the concepts this reader illuminates are central to any course in research methods. *Readings in Social Research Methods* is intended for undergraduate students who are taking their first research methods course. The goal is to provide an introduction to important issues and topics while supporting those ideas with interesting original research articles.

Many people helped make this book possible, and they deserve thanks. First, I must thank Shelley Murphy, my book representative from Wadsworth Publishing. A few years ago, Shelley sensed my frustration with teaching research methods classes during her visits to my office. My students were just too overwhelmed with the subject and the huge textbooks. While I still needed to use the textbooks, I wanted my students to be able to read the original research that I was talking to them about in class. Shelley listened carefully, suggested I send in a proposal for a reader, and introduced me to Eve Howard of Wadsworth who supported the idea for this reader and told me to start writing. Shelley's work didn't end there, however. Shelley "jump started" my writing, encouraged me when I became frustrated, read numerous drafts, made suggestions, helped me format the manuscript, and never lost sight of what the end result would be. Shelley, this reader would not have happened without you. I am very thankful for both your friendship and your help.

Second, I would like to thank Earl Babbie whose textbooks I have been using, and will continue to use, in my classes. Earl supported the idea of a reader to compliment his textbooks, and I value the support and encouragement he gave to me.

Third, I must thank my outside reviewers who made numerous suggestions. Having been a reviewer myself, I know that a constructive review requires time away from other activities that are important. To Theodore C. Wagenaar, Alisa Potter, Matt Sloan, Joseph Fletcher, Zhenchao Qian, and Jeffrey Burr, I appreciate the time you took to make comments on the drafts of this book. I also would like to thank my copyeditor, Robin Gold. Robin, you were thorough, kept me on track, and made the process of finishing a book a really good one. Thank you. I would like to thank George Wysocki, John Parish, and Ruth Pigott for reading proofs of various drafts and making comments. I would like to thank Daryl Kelley, my chair, for supporting me and allowing me time off committee work to write. This reader is also a result of some of the wonderful students who have developed an interest in research and gone on to conduct their own projects with me. Having students who love research as much as I do is what teaching is all about. So, with that said, thanks to Andrew Conrad, Jay Wahrmund, Tobbie Doremus, Sheri Hink, Cyndi Crabtree, Rebecca Bauer, and Sandi Nielsen who have given me encouragement, checked up on me periodically, and told me when I needed to leave my office to do something else besides write. And I can't forget JT, my 3-pound poodle, who might have rather been out taking walks, but instead sat by my desk or in my lap without complaint the entire duration of writing this book.

General Introduction

Anytime you read the newspaper or listen to a news report you hear about some type of research study. I subscribe to the *Denver Post,* and in the last week alone I have read about the following research studies: over the next 20 years, the growth of the senior population is expected to increase dramatically (Vidal, 2000); AIDS may have evolved from a benign simian infection in the early 1930s, long before it was recognized as a human disease, but it stayed in remote Africa until jet travel, big cities and the sexual revolution spread it worldwide (Recer, 2000); a case study of an alleged gun trafficker, who managed to sell thousands of guns without paperwork, suggests that the Bureau of Alcohol, Tobacco, and Firearms apparently failed to thoroughly investigate and prosecute this man who authorities believe made hundreds, or possibly thousands of illegal gun transactions over a 20-year period (Olinger, 2000); and according to two studies, television "is no friend to women," because one study says women are treated disrespectfully and the other says women are treated unrealistically (Pulfer, 2000).

Readings in Social Methods Research is designed to help students, like you, learn about scientific research methods and how to decipher the studies that you hear about. While you will be learning about research methods to reach your goal of completing this course, you will find that the things you learn, the way you will be taught to think, your ability to gather information, and your capacity to draw your own conclusions will go beyond this class. I find that students are often quite fearful of taking a research methods course, and they come up with some preconceived ideas about how difficult the course will be. Sometimes they even *dig their heels in*, making it difficult for me to teach and difficult for them to learn. Furthermore, I have found that some textbooks are overwhelming for students and lack strong examples, primary sources, and exciting readings that will capture the attention of college students. Since my desire is to make research methods as fun for students to learn as it is for me to teach, *Readings in Social Methods Research* has been designed to create a reader with basic information, brief, stimulating, readings that will capture your attention, and a variety of questions to help you incorporate what you have learned with what you have read.

Readings in Social Methods Research is a reader suitable for students in basic research methodology classes who are just learning about research. The process of *reading* research is very important because most of us read much more research than we actually conduct. However, the ability to know how to read a research paper and understand it must be learned, be practiced, and is the basis for this reader.

Readings in Social Methods Research can be used in any basic course or discipline and has been written to provide the student with plenty of information about the most popular social science research methods currently used. Instructors can use this reader as a supplement to any methods text on the market, but I have specifically designed it to be used in conjunction with any of Earl Babbie's research methods books. You will notice that the table of contents is structured to match Babbie's books with only a few deviations. For instance, I have placed ethics early in the reader because I feel strongly that ethical research *cannot* be an afterthought, but must be learned up-front and thought about as research projects are designed and evaluated. This reader may also be used with any other textbook on the market or as a stand-alone text that is supplemented with class lectures and outside reading.

Readings in Social Methods Research provides a brief chapter introduction of methodological techniques and topics with the key concepts **boldfaced**. After each introduction there are a few questions that incorporate the subject matter with InfoTrac College Edition, so students can gain practice finding sources on their own. After each chapter introduction, there are least two articles that represent social science research—although sociology, criminal justice, and social work are heavily represented—which show the student how the method is used in research. One of the things I have found in teaching is that the more interesting or controversial the research is, the more interested and excited my students are about learning. In my classes I try to pick research to use as examples that will fulfill this goal. The same is said for this reader. I have picked the articles because I believe they are particularly interesting to students.

At the beginning of each article I have written a small abstract to help students understand what to look for while they are reading the article and to help them integrate what they have learned with the work researchers have conducted. At the end of each article there are questions that allow the student to demonstrate their understanding of the methodological technique and how it has been used in the literature.

ORGANIZATION OF THE READER

Readings in Social Methods Research is divided into 4 parts and has a total of 11 chapters. This book is organized to follow the format of Earl Babbie's ninth edition and can be used along with his textbook or by itself. What I have tried to do is gather articles that are relevant and that I thought would hold your interest. After each chapter introduction there are at least three InfoTrac College Edition assignments to help you use the concepts to work with each article. There are two to three articles in each chapter supporting the concepts discussed and three review questions at the end of each article. At the end of the book the Glossary lists important terms that appear in bold type throughout the text.

Chapter 1, "Why Do You Need to Understand Research Methods," begins Part One and covers the basics of research. It tells you that our ideas about the world around us might not be as accurate as our "commonsense" ideas would have us believe. You will learn that we all have two realities in our lives, one that is based on what we see and know to be real and the other that we believe to be real because someone else has told us they are real. In this chapter you will learn the how important this idea is to research.

Chapter 2, "Combining Theory with Research Questions," focuses on the how the data we collect is empty and meaningless unless it is combined with theory. You will learn about four different paradigms that can be used in your research and the difference between deductive and inductive theory.

I placed Chapter 3, "Ethics," early in this reader. Sometimes in other textbooks you will see it as a chapter toward the end of the book or as an appendix. This leads me to believe that ethics could be an afterthought. I believe that it is important to have a good grasp of ethic problems in research, so you keep in mind all the way through the reader and through your class how important it is to think ethically when you design a project. You need to understand why participation should be voluntary, why you should not deceive or harm your subjects, and the role of the institutional review board. It is also important when you are reading the research of other people to be able to tell if they conducted their research ethically.

Part Two begins with Chapter 4, "Research Design and Causation." In this chapter you will learn the purpose of research, how to think about units of analysis and the time dimension.

Chapter 5, "Conceptualization and Operationalization," is somewhat difficult for some students, but will tell you how to put variables into identifying concepts that you can ultimately measure during your project. For instance, if you are investigating religiosity, you can conceptualize that concept by giving it a definition. Let's say you define religiosity as someone who goes to his or her place of worship at least one time a week. You can then operationalize that concept and measure it, by asking the question: "How many times a week do you go to your place of worship?"

Once you know what you are studying, Chapter 6, "Indexes and Scales," can help you construct a way to measure your variables. You will also learn the difference between using an index and a scale and how to determine which would be best for your particular research question.

An important topic within research methods is in Chapter 7, "Sampling," where you will learn how you pick the group you want to conduct research on. Often it is impossible to pick the entire population because it is way too big. Therefore, you must somehow find a sample that represents the population. You will learn various sampling techniques and how to pick the best one for your project.

In Part Three, you will learn various modes of observations. The first few modes, in Chapter 8, are "Survey, Experimental, and Evaluation Research." Experiments are the easiest way to explain concepts that you need to know such as that the independent variable causes the dependent variable. This works well in controlled environments such as a lab, but when experiments are done on people, you have to think about other variables that can affect the dependent variable. Survey research is probably the most common method used in the social sciences and involves administering a questionnaire either in person, through the mail, or over the Internet. Evaluation research is used to find out how well programs are working to cause the desired change in either individual behaviors or programs.

Chapter 9 is about "Field Research, Narrative, and Interviewing." Field research involves going where some type of action is happening and observing it. This action can be on a street corner, in a public library, or on a grade school playground. Narrative research involves listening to people's "voices" and letting them tell their own story. As researchers, we sometimes are so busy asking questions that we forget to just listen; thus, we can miss what our subject is trying to tell us. Regardless, interviewing is important in research, and you will learn various techniques for asking questions.

In Chapter 10, "Existing Data, Content Analysis, and Historical Data," you will learn how existing data can support any type of research you are conducting. For instance, if you are interested in gender differences in sixth-grade math classes, you can go to the Department of Education data base which shows how the Department has been surveying large numbers of students about their feelings and beliefs about their own math abilities. This type of existing data can support and guide your project. In doing content analysis, you can analyze anything such as books, newspaper articles, pictures in magazines, or bumper stickers. For example, you might be interested in how women are portrayed in computer advertisements. What are their roles? Are they actually shown working with the computer, or are they helping the male who is working with the computer? Historical data provides an analysis of things that have taken place in the past. Diaries, journals, essays, and other types of literature can be used to find out about people's lives or compare their lives and situations with those of current people.

And finally, Part Four is about "Statistics" in Chapter 11. You will learn basic information about how to use univariate, bivariate, and multivariate statistics. This chapter is not to be a complete course in statistics, by any means, but, rather, a short overview to use in reading articles and understanding results.

And now with the overview complete, you are all set to learn about research methods. I hope you enjoy the journey.

REFERENCES

Olinger, D. 2000, June 5. Firearms charges uncover a mystery—Arvada licensed dealer sold thousands of guns privately. *Denver Post*, p. A-01.

Pulfer, L. 2000, June 7. More real life than we need. *Denver Post*, p. B-11

Recer, P. 2000, June 9. AIDS virus may date rom 1930s. *Denver Post*, p. A-06

Vidal, G. V. 2000, June 11. Facing the future aging population presents many challenges. *Denver Post*, p. I-01

PART I ■ AN INTRODUCTION TO INQUIRY

■

Chapter 1: Why Do You Need to Understand Research Methods?

Why are you taking this class in Social Research Methods? Is it because you are interested in the subject? Is it because you are required to take the course? Is it because you want to understand the articles that you have read for your school courses or for your job? You could be taking this class for the reasons already stated or for any number of your own reasons. However, I believe that an important part of learning about research would be to understand how the research was conducted and conclusions were found. The only way for you to understand the conclusions, however, would be to learn how researchers planned and conducted their research.

Just think about it . . . what type of questions do you have about the world in which you live? In March 2000, in Mount Morris Township, Michigan, a 6-year-old boy pulled a gun from his pants and shot a little girl to death in their first-grade classroom. This shooting took place in front of both teachers and classmates and resulted in the death of 6-year-old Kayla Rolland. As budding researchers, you might wonder what the motives and the effects of this disaster were on society. How could a 6-year-old carry a gun into a school, unnoticed by anyone in authority? Under what conditions were these children living and could those conditions, in any way, have affected the resulting death of this little girl? Why would a child so young believe that shooting someone was the way to handle his problems? Did he learn this at home? Did he learn this from television? Can school shootings such as these be prevented? How do you go about finding out some of these answers? We are all curious about one thing or another, and the key to our curiosity is to find out if our ideas are correct, to learn which ones are not, and to make recommendations for change.

Here is another important reason to learn about research methods. We often see TV sales pitches that say "75% of doctors interviewed prescribed drug X for relief of arthritic pain." Would you believe this? Would this make you want to purchase drug X? What questions might you ask about this claim? Understanding research methods will help you figure out what questions you should ask about these findings. For instance, how many doctors were interviewed? What happens if the 75% of the doctors they surveyed were actually based on four interviews? Would you want to buy a drug because 3 doctors stated they liked it? What kinds of questions were the doctors asked about prescribing drug X? If the doctors were asked "Have you ever prescribed drug X?," were they just as likely to prescribed drugs A, B, C, or D? Who interviewed the doctor? If the manufacturers of drug X did the interviewing, were the doctors compensated for their participation in the study? Could compensation sway their responses? As you can see, you might think you have the answers to the questions, but actually those answers might just be in order to get you to buy the product and have nothing to do with reality or truth.

DIFFERENT REALITIES

Research[1] is actually a series of steps, techniques, exercises, and events that can be applied to every sphere of life in order to help you understand the world in which you live. If you want to actually conduct research on doctors to determine how likely they are to prescribe drug X to their patients, you really need to come up with some sort of plan to help guide your research. Your plan of action can also be called **research methods** because the methods you use are an absolutely essential set of skills, insights, and tools needed to answer any kind of questions. If you still think about the drug X study, you might ask some questions about the types of methods that were used to conclude that 75% of the doctors prescribed drug X? Who did the researchers actually talk to? How did they find the doctors to interview? If, prior to conducting the study, the researchers had a plan about how they were going to do their research, you could actually go back and look at their methods if you had a question or a doubt. The methods the researchers used could help you decide if the findings were reliable and could be trusted.

Why do you think methods sections are so important to research? One of problems in research is that it is very easy for any of us to be uncertain about what is real and what isn't. How do you view the world around you? What kinds of practices, thoughts, values, and insights do you have about the world based on where you came from? Would they be different for someone who grew up in a different situation? Where do you get your ideas about different cultures, people, and countries? Let me give you an example. I just returned from spending four weeks in Asia with my 19-year-old son, who has been backpacking around the world for the last seven months by himself. I have been worried sick about him as you can imagine. However, some countries that he planned on going to were of particular concern for me because my reality about those countries was based on movies I have seen in the past. A very long time ago, I saw the movie *Midnight Express* (1978), in which a young American tourist was arrested by Turkish authorities after trying to smuggle hashish out of the country. This young man was sentenced to 30 years in prison where his realities were pretty harsh and his parents were unable to get him out and back into the United States. The things done to him in the prison were so terrible I had to leave the theater and couldn't watch it all, but the memory has stayed with me as my reality. In another film, *Return to Paradise* (1998), one American was arrested in Malaysia for a prankish misdemeanor. While he and his friends all shared in the prank, he took the rap for all of them and was sentenced to be hanged as a drug trafficker and had been held for years on a terrible Malaysian prison. In the most current movie, *The Beach* (2000), Richard (Leonardo DiCaprio) travels to Thailand where he ends up in grave danger on an island with some friends (I actually got to visit this island, and it is beautiful).

Even though I am a sociologist and understand there are different types of realities, movies like these made me more concerned about my son going to Asia by himself. My

---

[1] Words in **boldface** are defined in the glossary at the end of the book.

agreement reality, where the things I considered real were real only because I had learned about them through the media and people around me, took precedence. It wasn't until I actually went to Asia with my son and traveled all around, met the people, ate their food, and learned about the culture that I developed my **experimental reality**, where the things I knew were a function of my own direct experiences. I found that the things I had been concerned about originally were not as real as I had thought. The people were wonderful, they were helpful, I learned about new lifestyles that were different from my own, and my concerns were unfounded. When I left my son in Thailand and came back to Nebraska, I wasn't worried like I had been before I experienced the realities of these countries myself and found out these people were not out to capture young Americans and throw them into prisons never to be seen again. This doesn't however, mean that you can break the law in these countries and get away with it!!!

How then would two different realities affect the outcomes of research? Easy. It can blind you to things that might be right in front of your faces because you have preconceived ideas about the situations you are studying. You might also be looking at it from only one point of view and be completely blinded to other points of views. What do you think? Do you believe that your reality could affect the outcome of the research you are conducting? The methods used in research give us an idea about the perspective the researcher is using and the ways the data was gathered so we can understand the methods and interpret the findings.

HUMAN INQUIRY

While your own reality plays a big part in the type of research you are interested in and the conclusions you come up with, one thing you need to know is that you don't need to start over when you begin a research project. And your topic doesn't have to be a something no one else has ever thought about before. You already know some things for sure about the world around you. For instance, we all know that the world is round and if you drop something it will fall. These ideas are based on **tradition**. So, if you accept what everyone around "knows" to be true, then you don't have to start from the beginning. You could look at other research reports to see what other researchers have found. Those findings could give you a basis for your research. While tradition is good on the one hand, and saves some time and energy, it can also be bad. There is a good chance the findings might be inaccurate, but you might have stopped looking far enough to find another "truth." Similarly, judgement errors can be made because all of us tend to believe in people in **authority** and believe that authority is legitimate when, in fact, it might not be. Let's say you went to the doctor's office for a check up and you were told that something might be wrong with you and that you needed more tests. Would you question the doctor who seemed to be an authority on the subject? Or would you believe you had to do what you were told regardless of how you felt about the subject because the doctor was an authority and you believed the doctors' suggestions were legitimate?

STEPPING BACK

So, if you were reading about research, how would you be able to see beyond your own personal realities and tradition and authority of those who have conducted research previously? According to theorist C. Wright Mills, who in 1956 wrote *The Sociological Imagination*, we all have both **personal troubles** and **public issues** and must know the difference between the two. Personal troubles occur within all of us and within our immediate relationships with others. Public issues, on the other hand, have to do with the environments in which we live. If you get a job after graduating from college and the job doesn't pay enough money to support your children, it is a personal trouble. If you consider the fact that you might have been tracked in school to take home economics and shop classes rather than math and science and that it didn't happen just to you alone, but to many young people, then it is a public issue (Claus, 1999).

How can you know the difference between personal troubles and public issues in your own research? Mills gives some basic steps to follow. You must first *distance yourselves* because often you are so immersed in your everyday life that it is difficult to see things that are right in front of your face. You need to "think yourselves out of the immediacy." Second, you must *engage in a systematic examination* of empirical methods and observations. This means you must conduct research to help you find answers to your questions. However, to do this you must also work within your own experiences. Third, you must eliminate **ethnocentrism**. Ethnocentrism is prejudicial attitudes between groups of people where there is the feeling and belief that one group's attitudes, customs, and behaviors are superior to those of the other groups. Do you believe you are better than people who live in a different social class from you? Let's say you grew up in a rural area and your assignment was to go observe gang members in the inner city. Would the fact that you had never been to an inner city and had never seen a gang member except in the movie affect the conclusions you might draw about their behaviors? Fourth, you must *analyze the data* that you have collected. An analysis of your data may tell you that your commonsense ideas about a topic were actually incorrect. Finally, action should be taken. If you know something, you must do something about it. Improvements in society depend on this. Whether you take action by writing about your results in an academic journal or standing on a picket line, research works to help transform society.

REFERENCES

Claus, J. 1999. You can't avoid the politics: Lessons for teacher education from a case study of teacher-initiated tracking reform. *Journal of Teacher Education*, 50(1): 5.

INFOTRAC COLLEGE EDITION SUGGESTED READINGS AND DISCUSSION QUESTIONS

Cormack, P 1999. Making the sociological promise: A case study of Rosemary Brown's Autobiography. *Canadian Review of Sociology and Anthropology*, 36(3): 355 (Article A55397667). How does this article use C. Wright Mills' sociological promise?

Freud, S. 1999. The social construction of normality. (Knowledge Building) *Families in Society: The Journal of Contemporary Human Services*, 80(4): 333 (Article A55267776). Compare the way this author uses the social construction of normality to the way Berger uses the social construction of reality.

FROM THE SOCIOLOGICAL IMAGINATION

C. Wright Mills

C. Wright Mills believes that the "the fruits of [our] imagination is the first lesson of the so-cial sciences." Furthermore, he argues that while the social sciences are filled with what researchers have done in the past, the questions and conclusions that are found can be constructed differently depending on who conducts the research. Your own reality may in-fluence the ways in which you look at life and could blind you to other possibilities. By using your sociological imagination, you can understand the larger context and how it af-fects individual lives.

Nowadays men often feel that their private lives are a series of traps. They sense that within their everyday worlds, they cannot overcome their troubles, and in this feeling, they are often quite correct: What ordinary men are directly aware of and what they try to do are bounded by the private orbits in which they live; their visions and their powers are limited to the close-up scenes of job, family, neighborhood; in other milieu, they move vicariously and remain spectators. And the more aware they become, however vaguely, of ambitions and of threats which transcend their mediate locales, the more trapped they seem to feel.

Underlying this sense of being trapped are seemingly impersonal changes in the very structure of continent-wide societies. The facts of contemporary history are also facts about the success and the failure of individual men and women. When a society is indus-trialized, a peasant becomes a worker; a feudal lord is liquidated or becomes a business-man. When classes rise or fall, a man is employed or unemployed; when the rate of investment goes up or down, a man takes new heart or goes broke. When wars happen, an insurance salesman becomes a rocket launcher; a store clerk, a radar man; a wife lives alone; a child grows up without a father. Neither the life of an individual nor the history of a society can be understood without understanding both.

Yet men do not usually define the troubles they endure in terms of historical change and institutional contradiction. The well-being they enjoy, they do not usually impute to the big ups and downs of the societies in which they live. Seldom aware of the intricate connection between the patterns of their own lives and the course of world history, ordi-nary men do not usually know what this connection means for the kinds of men they are becoming and for the kinds of history-making in which they might take part. They do not possess the quality of mind essential to grasp the interplay of man and society, of biogra-phy and history, of self and world. They cannot cope with their personal troubles in such ways as to control the structural transformations that usually lie behind them.

Surely it is no wonder. In what period have so many men been so totally exposed at so fast a pace to such earthquakes of change? That Americans have not known such cata-strophic changes as have the men and women of other societies is due to historical facts that are now quickly becoming "merely history." The history that now affects every man is

Mills, C. Wright 1959. The promise. In *Sociological Imagination*. New York: Oxford University Press, pp. 3–8. Reprinted by permission of the publisher.

world history. Within this scene and this period, in the course of a single generation, one sixth of mankind is transformed from all that is feudal and backward into all that is modern, advanced, and fearful. Political colonies are freed; new and less visible forms of imperialism installed. Revolutions occur; men feel the intimate grip of new kinds of authority. Totalitarian societies rise, and are smashed to bits—or succeed fabulously. After two centuries of ascendancy, capitalism is shown up as only one way to make society into an industrial apparatus. After two centuries of hope, even formal democracy is restricted to a quite small portion of mankind. Everywhere in the underdeveloped world, ancient ways of life are broken up and vague expectations become urgent demands. Everywhere in the overdeveloped world, the means of authority and of violence become total in scope and bureaucratic in form. Humanity itself now lies before us, the super-nation at either pole concentrating its most coordinated and massive efforts upon the preparation of World War Three.

The very shaping of history now outpaces the ability of men to orient themselves in accordance with cherished values. And which values? Even when they do not panic, men often sense that older ways of feeling and thinking have collapsed and that newer beginnings are ambiguous to the point of moral stasis. Is it any wonder that ordinary men feel they cannot cope with the larger worlds with which they are so suddenly confronted? That they cannot understand the meaning of their epoch for their own lives? That—in defense of selfhood—they become morally insensible, trying to remain altogether private men? Is it any wonder that they come to be possessed by a sense of the trap?

It is not only information that they need—in this Age of Fact, information often dominates their attention and overwhelms their capacities to assimilate it. It is not only the skills of reason that they need—although their struggles to acquire these often exhaust their limited moral energy.

What they need, and what they feel they need, is a quality of mind that will help them to use information and to develop reason in order to achieve lucid summations of what is going on in the world and of what may be happening within themselves. It is this quality, I am going to contend, that journalists and scholars, artists and publics, scientists and editors are coming to expect of what may be called the sociological imagination.

The sociological imagination enables its possessor to understand the larger historical scene in terms of its meaning for the inner life and the external career of a variety of individuals. It enables him to take into account how individuals, in the welter of their daily experience, often become falsely conscious of their positions. Within that welter, the framework of modern society is sought, and within that framework the psychologies of a variety of men and women are formulated. By such means the personal uneasiness of individuals is focused upon explicit troubles and the indifference of publics is transformed into involvement with public issues.

The first fruit of this imagination—and the first lesson of the social science that embodies it—is the idea that the individual can understand his own experience and gauge his own fate only by locating himself within his period, that he can know his own chances in life only by becoming aware of those of all individuals in his circumstances. In many ways it is a terrible lesson; in many ways a magnificent one. We do not know the limits of man's capacities for supreme effort or willing degradation, for agony or glee, for pleasurable brutality or the sweetness of reason. But in our time we have come to know that the limits of human nature are frighteningly broad. We have come to know that every individual lives, from one generation to the next, in some society; that he lives out a biography, and that he lives it out within some historical sequence. By the fact of his living he contributes, however minutely, to the shaping of this society and to the course of its history, even as he is made by society and by its historical push and shove.

The sociological imagination enables us to grasp history and biography and the relations between the two within society. That is its task and its promise. And it is the signal what is best in contemporary studies of man and society.

No social study that does not come back to the problems of biography, of history and of their intersections within a society has completed its intellectual journey. Whatever the specific problems of the classic social analysts, however limited or however broad the features of social reality they have examined, those who have been imaginatively aware of the promise of their work have consistently asked three sorts of questions:

1. What is the structure of this particular society as a whole? What are its essential components, and how are they related to one another? How does it differ from other varieties of social order? Within it, what is the meaning of any particular feature for its continuance and for its change?

2. Where does this society stand in human history? What are the mechanics by which it is changing? What is its place within and its meaning for the development of humanity as a whole? How does any particular feature we are examining affect, and how is it affected by, the historical period in which it moves? And this period-what are its essential features? How does it differ from other periods? What are its characteristic ways of history-making?

3. What varieties of men and women now prevail in this society and in this period? And what varieties are coming to prevail? In what ways are they selected and formed, liberated and repressed, made sensitive and blunted? What kinds of "human nature" are revealed in the conduct and character we observe in this society in this period? And what is the meaning for "human nature" of each and every feature of the society we are examining?

Whether the point of interest is a great power state or a minor literary mood, a family, a prison, a creed—these are the kinds of questions the best social analysts have asked. They are the intellectual pivots of classic studies of man in society—and they are the questions inevitably raised by any mind possessing the sociological imagination. For that imagination is the capacity to shift from one perspective to another—from the political to the psychological; from examination of a single family to comparative assessment of the national budgets of the world; from the theological school to the military establishment; from considerations of an of industry to studies of contemporary poetry. It is the capacity to range from the most impersonal and remote transformations to the most intimate features of the human self—and to see the relations between the two. Back of its use there is always the urge to know the social and historical meaning of the individual in the society and in the period in which he has his quality and his being.

That, in brief, is why it is by means of the sociological imagination that men now hope to grasp what is going on in the world, and to understand what is happening in themselves as minute points of the intersections of biography and history within society. In large part, contemporary man's self-conscious view of himself as at least an outsider, if not a permanent stranger, rests upon an absorbed realization of social relativity and of the transformative power of history. The sociological imagination is the most fruitful form of this self-consciousness. By its use men whose mentalities have swept only a series of limited orbits often come to feel as if suddenly awakened in a house with which they had only supposed themselves to be familiar. Correctly or incorrectly, they often come to feel that they can now provide themselves with adequate summations, cohesive assessments, comprehensive orientations. Older decisions that once appeared sound now seem to them products of a mind unaccountably dense. Their capacity for astonishment is made lively again. They acquire a new way of thinking, they experience a transvaluation of values: in a word, by their reflection and by their sensibility, they realize the cultural meaning of the social sciences.

Perhaps the most fruitful distinction with which the sociological imagination works is between "the personal troubles of milieu" and "the public issues of social structure." This distinction is an essential tool of the sociological imagination and a feature of all classic work in social science.

What we experience in various and specific milieu, I have noted, is often caused by structural changes. Accordingly, to understand the changes of many personal milieu we are required to look beyond them. And the number and variety of such structural changes increase as the institutions within which we live become more embracing and more intricately connected with one another. To be aware of the idea of social structure and to use it with sensibility is to be capable of tracing such linkages among a great variety of milieu. To be able to do that is to possess the sociological imagination.

REVIEW QUESTIONS

1. What does C. Wright Mills mean when he says that "in this Age of Fact, information often dominates their attention and overwhelms their capacities to assimilate it"?

2. How can the fact that Mills believes each individual can understand his own experience and gauge his own fate by locating himself within his period affect the outcome of research?

3. Mills states that "no social study that does not come back to the problems of biography, of history and of their intersections within a society has completed its intellectual journey." Using a topic that might be of interest to you to research, how does Mill's statement apply?

THE REALITY OF EVERYDAY LIFE

Peter Berger and Thomas Luckmann

Peter L Berger and Thomas Luckmann explain that sociology involves the desire to under-stand the everyday social reality around us. We must understand the differences between our commonsense ideas about life and what is the "truth." While reality is interpreted by each individual and adds meaning to his or her world, that reality of everyday life is often taken for granted and may influence our research questions and conclusions.

Since our purpose in this treatise is a sociological analysis of the reality of everyday life, more precisely, of knowledge that guides conduct in everyday life, and we are only tan-gentially interested in how this reality may appear in various theoretical perspectives to intellectuals, we must begin by a clarification of that reality as it is available to the com-monsense of the ordinary members of society. How that commonsense reality may be in-fluenced by the theoretical constructions of intellectuals and other merchants of ideas is a further question. Ours is thus an enterprise that, although theoretical in character, is geared to the understanding of a reality that forms the subject matter of the empirical sci-ence of sociology, that is, the world of everyday life.

It should be evident, then, that our purpose is not to engage in philosophy. All the same, if the reality of everyday life is to be understood, account must be taken of its in-trinsic character before we can proceed with sociological analysis proper. Everyday life presents itself as a reality interpreted by men and subjectively meaningful to them as a co-herent world. As sociologists we take this reality as the object of our analyses. Within the frame of reference of sociology as an empirical science it is possible to take this reality as given, to take as data particular phenomena arising within it, without further inquiring about the foundations of this reality, which is a philosophical task. However, given the particular purpose of the present treatise, we cannot completely bypass the philosophical problem.

The world of everyday life is not only taken for granted as reality by the ordinary members of society in the subjectively meaningful conduct of their lives. It is a world that originates in their thoughts and actions, and is maintained as real by these. Before turning to our main task we must, therefore, attempt to clarify the foundations of knowledge in everyday life, to wit, the *objectivations* of subjective processes (and meanings) by which the *intersubjective* commonsense world is constructed.

For the purpose at hand, this is a preliminary task, and we can do no more than sketch the main features of what we believe to be an adequate solution to the philosophical prob-lem—adequate, let us hasten to add, only in the sense that it can serve as a starting point for sociological analysis. The considerations immediately following are, therefore, of the nature of philosophical prolegomena and, in themselves, presociological. The method we

Berger, P. and Luckmann, T. 1966. The reality of everyday life. In *The Social Construction of Reality: A Treatise in the Sociology of Knowledge*, pp. 19–28. Garden City, NY: Doubleday.

consider best suited to clarify the foundations of knowledge in everyday life is that of phenomenological analysis, a purely descriptive method and, as such, "empirical" but not "scientific"—as we understand the nature of the empirical sciences.

The phenomenological analysis of everyday life, or rather of the subjective experience of everyday life, refrains from any causal or genetic hypotheses, as well as from assertions about the ontological status of the phenomena analyzed. It is important to remember this. Commonsense contains innumerable pre- and quasi-scientific interpretations about everyday reality, which it takes for granted. If we are to describe the reality of commonsense we must refer to these interpretations, just as we must take account of its taken-for-granted character—but we do so within phenomenological brackets.

Consciousness is always intentional; it always intends or is directed toward objects. We can never apprehend some putative substratum of consciousness as such, only consciousness of something or other. This is so regardless of whether the object of consciousness is experienced as belonging to an external physical world or apprehended as an element of an inward subjective reality. Whether I (the first person singular, here as in the following illustrations, standing for ordinary self-consciousness in everyday life) am viewing the panorama of New York City or whether I become conscious of an inner anxiety, the processes of consciousness involved are intentional in both instances. The point need not be belabored that the consciousness of the Empire State Building differs from the awareness of anxiety. A detailed phenomenological analysis would uncover the various layers of experience, and the different structures of meaning involved in, say, being bitten by a dog, remembering having been bitten by a dog, having a phobia about all dogs, and so forth. What interests us here is the common intentional character of all consciousness.

Different objects present themselves to consciousness as constituents of different spheres of reality. I recognize the fellowmen I must deal with in the course of everyday life as pertaining to a reality quite different from the disembodied figures that appear in my dreams. The two sets of objects introduce quite different tensions into my consciousness and I am attentive to them in quite different ways. My consciousness, then, is capable of moving through different spheres of reality. Put differently, I am conscious of the world as consisting of multiple realities. As I move from one reality to another, I experience the transition as a kind of shock. This shock is to be understood as caused by the shift in attentiveness that the transition entails. Waking up from a dream illustrates this shift most simply.

Among the multiple realities there is one that presents itself as the reality par excellence. This is the reality of everyday life. Its privileged position entitles it to the designation of paramount reality. The tension of consciousness is highest in everyday life, that is, the latter imposes itself upon consciousness in the most massive, urgent and intense manner. It is impossible to ignore, difficult even to weaken in its imperative presence. Consequently, it forces me to be attentive to it in the fullest way. I experience everyday life in the state of being wide-awake. This wide-awake state of existing in and apprehending the reality of everyday life is taken by me to be normal and self-evident, that is, it constitutes my natural attitude.

I apprehend the reality of everyday life as an ordered reality. Its phenomena are prearranged in patterns that seem to be independent of my apprehension of them and that impose themselves upon the latter. The reality of everyday life appears already objectified, that is, constituted by an order of objects that have been designated as objects before my appearance on the scene. The language used in everyday life continuously provides me with the necessary objectifications and posits the order within which these make sense and within which everyday life has meaning for me. I live in a place that is geographically designated; I employ tools, from can openers to sports cars, which are designated in the technical vocabulary of my society; I live within a web of human relationships, from my chess club to the United States of America, which are also ordered by means of vocabulary. In this manner language marks the co-ordinates of my life in society and fills that life with meaningful objects.

The reality of everyday life is organized around the "here" of my body and the "now" of my present. This "here and now" is the focus of my attention to the reality of everyday life. What is "here and now" presented to me in everyday life is the *realissimum* of my consciousness. The reality of everyday life is not, however, exhausted by these immediate presences, but embraces phenomena that are not present "here and now." This means that I experience everyday life in terms of differing degrees of closeness and remoteness, both spatially and temporally. Closest to me is the zone of everyday life that is directly accessible to my bodily manipulation. This zone contains the world within my reach, the world in which I act so as to modify its reality, or the world in which I work. In this world of working my consciousness is dominated by the pragmatic motive, that is, my attention to this world is mainly determined by what I am doing, have done or plan to do in it. In this way it is ray world par excellence. I know, of course, that the reality of everyday life contains zones that are not accessible to me in this manner. But either I have no pragmatic interest in these zones or my interest in them is indirect insofar as they may be, potentially, manipulative zones for me. Typically, my interest in the far zones is less intense and certainly less urgent. I am intensely interested in the cluster of objects involved in my daily occupation—say, the world of the garage, if I am a mechanic. I am interested, though less directly, in what goes on in the testing laboratories of the automobile industry in Detroit— I am unlikely ever to be in one of these laboratories, but the work done there will eventually affect my everyday life. I may also be interested in what goes on at Cape Kennedy or in outer space, but this interest is a matter of private, "leisure-time" choice rather than an urgent necessity of my everyday life.

The reality of everyday life further presents itself to me as an intersubjective world, a world that I share with others. This intersubjectivity sharply differentiates everyday life from other realities of which I am conscious. I am alone in the world of my dreams, but I know that the world of everyday life is as real to others as it is to myself. Indeed, I cannot exist in everyday life without continually interacting and communicating with others. I know that my natural attitude to this world corresponds to the natural attitude of others, that they also comprehend the objectifications by which this world is ordered, that they also organize this world around the "here and now" of their being in it and have projects for working in it. I also know, of course, that the others have a perspective on this common world that is not identical with mine. My "here" is their "there." My "now" does not fully overlap with theirs. My projects differ from and may even conflict with theirs. All the same, I know that I live with them in a common world. Most importantly, I know that there is an ongoing correspondence between ray meanings and their meanings in this world, that we share a common sense about its reality. The natural attitude is the attitude of commonsense consciousness precisely because it refers to a world that is common to many men. Commonsense knowledge is the knowledge I share with others in the normal, self-evident routines of everyday life.

The reality of everyday life is taken for granted as reality. It does not require additional verification over and beyond its simple presence. It is simply there, as self-evident and compelling facticity. I know that it is real. While I am capable of engaging in doubt about its reality, I am obliged to suspend such doubt as I routinely exist in everyday life. This suspension of doubt is so firm that to abandon it, as I might want to do, say, in theoretical or religious contemplation, I have to make an extreme transition. The world of everyday life proclaims itself and, when I want to challenge the proclamation, I must engage in a deliberate, by no means easy effort. The transition from the natural attitude to the theoretical attitude of the philosopher or scientist illustrates this point. But not all aspects of this reality are equally unproblematic. Everyday life is divided into sectors that are apprehended routinely, and others that present me with problems of one kind or another. Suppose that I am an automobile mechanic who is highly knowledgeable about all American made cars. Everything that pertains to the latter is a routine, unproblematic facet of my everyday life. But one day someone appears in the garage and asks me to repair his Volkswagen. I am now compelled to enter the problematic world of foreign-made cars. I may do so reluctantly or with professional curiosity, but in either case I am now faced with problems that I have not yet routinized. At the same time, of course, I do not leave the reality of everyday life. Indeed, the latter becomes enriched as I begin to incorporate into it the knowledge and skills required for the repair of foreign-made cars. The reality of everyday life encompasses both kinds of sectors, as long as what appears as a problem does not pertain to a different reality altogether (say, the reality of theoretical physics, or of nightmares). As long as the routines of everyday life continue without interruption they are apprehended as unproblematic.

But even the unproblematic sector of everyday reality is so only until further notice, that is, until its continuity is interrupted by the appearance of a problem. When this happens, the reality of everyday life seeks to integrate the problematic sector into what is already unproblematic. Commonsense knowledge contains a variety of instructions as to how this is to be done. For instance, the others with whom I work are unproblematic to me as long as they perform their familiar, taken-for-granted routines—say, typing away at desks next to mine in my office. They become problematic if they interrupt these routines—say, huddling together in a corner and talking in whispers. As I inquire about the meaning of this unusual activity, there is a variety of possibilities that my commonsense knowledge is capable of reintegrating into the unproblematic routines of everyday life: they may be consulting on how to fix a broken typewriter, or one of them may have some urgent instructions from the boss, and so on. On the other hand, I may find that they are discussing a union directive to go on strike, something as yet outside my experience but still well within the range of problems with which my commonsense knowledge can deal. It will deal with it, though, as a problem, rather than simply reintegrating it into the unproblematic sector of everyday life. If, however, I come to the conclusion that my colleagues have gone collectively mad, the problem that presents itself is of yet another kind. I am now faced with a problem that transcends the boundaries of the reality of everyday life and points to an altogether different reality. Indeed, my conclusion that my colleagues have gone mad implies ipso facto that they have gone off into a world that is no longer the common world of everyday life.

Compared to the reality of everyday life, other realities appear as finite provinces of meaning, enclaves within the paramount reality marked by circumscribed meanings and modes of experience. The paramount reality envelops them on all sides, as it were, and consciousness always returns to the paramount reality as from an excursion. This is evident from the illustrations already given, as in the reality of dreams or that of theoretical thought. Similar "commutations" take place between the world of everyday life and the world of play, both the playing of children and, even more sharply, of adults. The theater provides an excellent illustration of such playing on the part of adults. The transition between realities is marked by the rising and falling of the curtain. As the curtain rises, the spectator is "transported to another world," with its own meanings and an order that may or may not have much to do with the order of everyday life. As the curtain falls, the spectator "returns to reality," that is, to the paramount reality of everyday life by comparison with which the reality presented on the stage now appears tenuous and ephemeral, however vivid the presentation may have been a few moments previously. Aesthetic and religious experience is rich in producing transitions of this kind, in as much as art and religion are endemic producers of finite provinces of meaning.

All finite provinces of meaning are characterized by a turning away of attention from the reality of everyday life. While there are, of course, shifts in attention within everyday life, the shift to a finite province of meaning is of a much more radical kind. A radical change takes place in the tension of consciousness. In the context of religious experience this has been aptly called "leaping." It is important to stress, however, that the reality of everyday life retains its paramount status even as such "leaps" take place. If nothing else, language makes sure of this. The common language available to me for the objectification of my experiences is grounded in everyday life and keeps pointing back to it even as I employ it to interpret experiences in finite provinces of meaning. Typically, therefore, I "distort" the reality of the latter as soon as I begin to use the common language in interpreting them, that is, I "translate" the non-everyday experiences back into the paramount reality of everyday life. This may be readily seen in terms of dreams, but is also typical of those trying to report about theoretical, aesthetic or religious worlds of meaning. The theoretical physicist tells us that his concept of space cannot be conveyed linguistically, just as the artist does with regard to the meaning of his creations and the mystic with regard to his encounters with the divine. Yet all these—dreamer, physicist, artist and mystic—also live in the reality of everyday life. Indeed, one of their important problems is to interpret the coexistence of this reality with the reality enclaves into which they have ventured.

The world of everyday life is structured both spatially and temporally. The spatial structure is quite peripheral to our present considerations. Suffice it to point out that it, too, has a social dimension by virtue of the fact that my manipulatory zone intersects with that of others. More important for our present purpose is the temporal structure of everyday life.

Temporality is an intrinsic property of consciousness. The stream of consciousness is always ordered temporally. It is possible to differentiate between different levels of this temporality, as it is intrasubjectively available. Every individual is conscious of an inner flow of time, which in turn is rounded on the physiological rhythm of the organism though it is not identical with these. It would greatly exceed the scope of these prolegomena to enter into a detailed analysis of these levels of intrasubjective temporality. As we have indicated, however, intersubjectivity in everyday life also has a temporal dimension. The world of everyday life has its own standard time, which is intersubjectively available. This standard time may be understood as the intersection between cosmic time and its socially established calendar, based on the temporal sequences of nature, and inner time, in its aforementioned differentiations. There can never be full simultaneity between these various levels of temporality, as the experience of waiting indicates most clearly. Both my organism and my society impose upon me, and upon my inner time, certain sequences of events that involve waiting. I may want to take part in a sports event, but I must wait for my bruised knee to heal. Or again, I must wait until certain papers are processed so that my qualification for the event may be officially established. It may readily be seen that the temporal structure of everyday life is exceedingly complex, because the different levels of empirically present temporality must be ongoingly correlated.

The temporal structure of everyday life confronts me as a facticity with which I must reckon, that is, with which I must try to synchronize my own projects. I encounter time in everyday reality as continuous and finite. All my existence in this world is continuously ordered by its time, is indeed enveloped by it. My own life is an episode in the externally factitious stream of time. It was there before I was born and it will be there after I die. The knowledge of my inevitable death makes this time finite *for me*. I have only a certain amount time available for the realization of my projects, and the knowledge of this affects my attitude to these projects. Also, since I do not want to die, this knowledge injects an underlying anxiety into my projects. Thus I cannot endlessly repeat my participation in sports events. I know that I am getting older. It may even be that this is the last occasion on which I have the chance to participate. My waiting will be anxious to the degree in which the finitude of time impinges upon the project.

The same temporal structure, as has already been indicated, is coercive. I cannot reverse at will the sequences imposed by it—"first things first" is an essential element of my knowledge of everyday life. Thus I cannot take a certain examination before I have passed through certain educational programs, I cannot practice my profession before I have taken this examination, and so on. Also, the same temporal structure provides the historicity that determines my situation in the world of everyday life. I was born on a certain date, entered school on another, started working as a professional on another, and so on. These dates, however, are all "located" within a much more comprehensive history, and this "location" decisively shapes my situation. Thus I was born in the year of the great bank crash in which my father lost his wealth, I entered school just before the revolution, I began to work just after the great war broke out, and so forth. The temporal structure of everyday life not only imposes prearranged sequences upon the "agenda" of any single day but also imposes itself upon my biography as a whole. Within the co-ordinates set by this temporal structure I apprehend both daily "agenda" and overall biography. Clock and calendar ensure that, indeed, I am a "man of my time." Only within this temporal structure does everyday life retain for me its accent of reality. Thus in cases where I may be "disoriented" for one reason or another (say, I have been in an automobile accident in which I was knocked unconscious), I feel an almost instinctive urge to "reorient" myself within the temporal structure of everyday life. I look at my watch and try to recall what day it is. By these acts alone I re-enter the reality of everyday life.

REVIEW QUESTIONS

1. What is the social construction of reality?

2. How can your social construction of reality influence your research?

3. What does it take to step back from your own reality in research? Can you do this completely? Must you?

Chapter 2: Combining Theory with Research Questions

Why do you think research is conducted? The main reason is that researchers hope their findings will contribute to the discipline and the various ways of knowing about life and the world. I have found that theory is one of the least understood terms for students who are learning about social science research. Regardless, it is very important for you to understand what theory is and how it is used in research. A theory is basically nothing more than a system of ideas that help explain various patterns in the world. Let's say it is almost midterms time and you believe that your teacher will put all the difficult questions at the end of the test and the easier questions at the beginning of the test. That is a theory. As a result, theories will guide you and give you clues about the direction in which to conduct research (Babbie, 1998).

Let me give you an example of how combining theories with research actually works. While I was in graduate school I was conducting research on transvestites (Wysocki, 1993). A transvestite is a person who wears the clothing of the opposite sex. I was investigating only males, who considered themselves to be heterosexual, but who wore women's clothing. At first I thought I would just describe what they were telling me about their lives: when they started cross-dressing, why they cross-dressed, and how they cross-dressed. That would have been just **descriptive**, and I believed it would not have added much to the literature on transvestism. There are many perspectives or theories that I could have drawn from to conduct this project. For instance, I could have used the medical model, which stated there was some genetic problem within the man's body to make him want to cross-dress. Or I could have used the deviance literature that stated that a man who wore the clothing of the opposite sex was deviant because what he was doing would not be considered normal by society's standards. However, since I considered myself a feminist sociologist, I wanted to investigate the social construction of sex, gender, and sexuality. This perspective basically states that we have all been taught how to portray ourselves based on what we have seen in the culture in which we live (Berger, 1966). So, the focus of my project changed by using this theory. Instead of using a descriptive focus I explored what aspects of femininity my respondents wanted to take on and what aspects of masculinity they wanted to get rid of (Wysocki, 1993).

LEVELS OF ANALYSIS AND THEORIES

There are many different ways to make sense of our social world and each way has resulted in different explanations. In 1970, T. S. Kuhn stated that scientists worked within paradigms. **Paradigms** are ways of viewing the world that dictate the type of scientific work that should be conducted and the kinds of theories that are acceptable. However, nothing stays the same, and over time, old paradigms are replaced by new ones (Kuhn, 1970).

As I stated earlier, **theories** involve constructing abstract interpretations that can be used to explain a wide variety of situations in the social world from various levels. Some theories involve a **macrolevel** analysis that looks at large-scale social systems, such as the government or economic system. Studies using this level of analysis could include wars, poverty, or unemployment. Other theories use a **microlevel** analysis, which studies the everyday behavior in situations of face-to-face interactions, such as how people decide who to marry or how children communicate on a playground. In between the macro and micro levels is the **mesolevel** analysis, which focuses on social groups and organizations, such as the classroom or an office. Let's say you have an interest in researching education. If you investigated education from the macrolevel, you could ask the question "How does College A differ from College B?" From the micro level, you could ask "How do women interact differently than men do in the classroom?," and from a mesolevel, you could ask, "How do computer science classes differ from sociology classes?"

While there are many different theories to use in your research, I am going to mention only the major ones. **Conflict theory** can be traced back to the writings of Karl Marx, who stated that power, ideology, and conflict are closely connected and that individuals are always in competition for resources or advantages. Those who hold the most power maintain their dominance over those without the power. If you wanted to study domestic violence, you could use the conflict theory to suggest that one person in the relationship has more power than the other does and, therefore, has more control over the situation that could lead to violence.

The **functionalist theory** was originally pioneered by Auguste Comte, who believed society is similar to an organism because it is made up of parts that contribute to keep society functioning as a whole. If everything in society has a function, then society maintains equilibrium because everyone and every social institution have a job or a specific role to play. Think about your own family and how each member probably has his or her own job to do. One person might be responsible for taking out the trash, another for cooking dinner, and another for paying the bills. Everyone in the family has a function, and therefore the home retains its equilibrium if everyone does his or her job.

Symbolic interactionist theory was influenced by the work of George Herbert Mead, who believed that language allows us to become self-conscious beings and that the key element in this process is the symbol. Social life actually depends on our ability to imagine ourselves in other social roles and our ability to communicate with others. One way to communicate is through the use of symbols and gestures. Having a common understanding of the symbols and gestures help us to make decisions about what is going on and how to respond in each situation. Have you recently told someone that you love him or her? Do you need to say this with words or are there symbols that mean the same thing? If you send a dozen long-stemmed roses to this person at work, would the roses be a symbol of your feelings?

I believe that **feminist theory** is an important theory to include here because the development of feminist theories has greatly influenced the way in which some researchers analyzed women's positions in society (Ollenburger & Moore, 1998). Beginning with the women's movement of the 1960s and 1970s, feminist theory explores the variables of sex, gender, race, and sexuality and focuses on inequality in all areas of life. In other words, feminist theory involves questions about *identity* and *differences* (Reinharz, 1992). Research on gender differences will let you know why men and women tend to work in different areas of a production plant and don't often work side by side (Bielby & Baron, 1986), why women, on average make less money than men who have the same amount of education (Bureau of Labor Statistics, 1998) and why the division of labor within the household is not equal (Berk, 1985). In my own work on various blood diseases, I focus on how women have been underdiagnosed and misdiagnosed when they show symptoms of a specific illness. The questions I ask are about the power differential between doctors and patients, and I explore whether or not women's complaints are minimized because they are women. Keep in mind that you don't have to be female or consider yourself a feminist to use a feminist perspective.

REFERENCES

Babbie, 2001. *The practice of social research.* 9th ed. Belmont, CA: Wadsworth/ Thomson Learning.

Berger, P. & Luckmann, T. 1966. The social construction of reality: A treatise in the sociology of knowledge. Garden City, NY: Doubleday.Berk, S. F. 1985. The gender factory: The apportionment of work in American households. New York: Plenum.

Bielby, W., & Baron, J. N. 1986. Men and women at work: Sex segregation and statistical discrimination. *American Journal of Sociology*, 91:759–799.

Bureau of Labor Statistics. 1998. Labor force statistics from the current population survey, Annual Average Tables from the January 1998 Issue of Employment and Earnings. {ONLINE] http://www.bls.gov/opub/mlr/1997/04/art2exc.htm#4a

Kuhn, T. 1970. *The structure of scientific revolutions.* Chicago: University of Chicago Press.

Ollenburger, J. C. & Moore, H. A. 1998. *A sociology of women* (2nd edition). Upper Saddle River, NJ: Prentice Hall.

Reinharz, S. 1992. *Feminist methods in social research.* New York: Oxford University Press.

Wysocki, D. K. 1993. Construction of masculinity: A look into the lives of heterosexual male transvestites. *Feminism and Psychology*, 3(2), 374–380.

INFOTRAC COLLEGE EDITION SUGGESTED READINGS AND DISCUSSION QUESTIONS

1. Use keyword searches for the terms " research" and "theory" on InfoTrac College Edition. Find an article of interest to you. Can you describe the theory that the author used in the research project? How was it used? What other theories might have been used? Would using a different theory change the results of the project?

2. Look up the articles by T. Harris & P. Hill, 1998, "'Waiting to Exhale' or 'breath(ing) again': A search for identity, empowerment, and love in the 1990s" *Women and language,*

21(2): 9 (Article A54370253) How has the theory in this article been used? What results do the authors find?

3. Look up articles in InfoTrac College Edition, such as "Dennis Rodman—'Barbie Doll Gone Horribly Wrong': Marginalized Masculinity, Cross-Dressing, and the Limitations of Commodity Culture" (Article A54776376) or "'The Nerd Within': Mass Media and the Negotiation of Identity Among Computer-Using Men" (Article A54776378). What kinds of research and theory are the authors using?

STREET CRIME, LABOR SURPLUS AND CRIMINAL PUNISHMENT, 1980–1990

Andrew L. Hoschstetler and Neal Sover

As stated in the introduction to this chapter, researchers may use various theories to study a particular research problem. In this article Hoschstetler and Sover used conflict theory to investigate street crime and labor surplus in 269 urban counties in the United States. In this longitudinal study, the researchers looked for a link between economic conditions and punishment and the direct effect of change in the size of the labor surplus on change in the use of punishment. Can you tell what level of analysis was used in this study?

There is enormous geographic and temporal variation in state use of punishment. In the United States, for example, there is well-documented regional and state-level variation in the use of imprisonment; in 1994, the incarceration rate (the number of imprisoned adults per 100,000 total population) was 462 for southern states but only 291 for the northeastern states (United States Bureau of Justice Statistics, 1996). Geographic variation is apparent also in use of the death penalty; whereas some states do not permit capital punishment, others routinely and regularly execute offenders. As for evidence of temporal variation in punishment, we need look no farther than recent history. In the years after 1973, America's training school, jail and prison populations climbed to historically unprecedented levels. The adult imprisoned population alone grew by more than 300 percent between 1975 and 1994 (United States Bureau of Justice Statistics, 1996). Explaining geographic and temporal variation in official use of imprisonment and other forms of punishment is a long-standing focal point of social problems theory and research. We continue this line of investigation by examining community-level determinants of change in the use of imprisonment by local courts in the United States during the 1980s.

Hoschstetler, A. & Sover, N. 1997. Street crime, labor surplus and criminal punishment, 1980–1990. *Social Problems*, 44(3): 358–368.

Background

In conflict-theoretical explanations, crime control is portrayed as a process unusually sensitive to the interests and machinations of dominant classes and elites. Grounded in neo-Marxism, analysts sketch criminal punishment as a strategy and mechanism employed by the state to control a class whose interests potentially are threatening to capitalist structures and elites. Viewed in this way, the use of punishment may fluctuate with levels of street crime, but it also varies with prevailing economic conditions. When the economy is strong and the labor surplus shrinks, punishment is relaxed; in times of economic stagnation or crisis, when the labor surplus grows larger, official use of punishment rises. It is during these times that the structures of criminal justice draw off increasing numbers of those now rendered superfluous for production. This means that:

> increased use of imprisonment is not a direct response to any rise in crime, but is an ideologically motivated response to the perceived threat of crime posed by the swelling population of economically marginalized persons. This position does not deny the possibility of increasing crime accompanying unemployment, but states instead that unemployment levels have an effect on the rate and severity of imprisonment *over and above* the changes in the volume and pattern of crime. (Box and Hale, 1982:22)

With roots in pioneering work by Rusche and Kirchheliner (1939), there are several complementary theoretical explanations for the link between surplus labor and punishment. They variously emphasize economic, political and ideological forces, and they impute a variety of motives to elites and to criminal justice managers (Chiricos and Delone, 1992). Our theoretical point of departure is the general proposition that the unemployed are a threat or source of concern for dominant groups which is alleviated or otherwise managed by increased punishment. It is their presumed declining stake in conformity and their mounting desperation that make the unemployed the primary target of intensified punishment initiatives. Behind these crack-downs is elite anxiety, perhaps over potentially increasing political consciousness (Adamson. 1984; Wallace, 1980), class conflict (Melossi, 1989), or rising levels of violent, expropriative street crime (Box and Hale, 1982). A swelling mass of the unemployed is "social dynamite" (Spitzer, 1975).

The structure of the American economy and the nature of American politics insure that both the shape and the dynamics of criminal justice reflect elite interests (Jacobs, 1979). This requires neither the assumption that they conspire in the process or that they orchestrate the actions of criminal justice managers. The aggregate objective consequences of their anxiety are one thing; institutional dynamics and the motives of criminal justice practitioners are another. Remarkably little is known, however, about mechanisms and processes by which elite concerns may be communicated to and acted upon by control managers and apprentices. This is an area in which Marxist theories of social control lack specificity and precision.

Increasing anxiety and resentment in the ranks of criminal justice may also contribute to harsher punishment during economic downturns and times of rising unemployment. Squeezed fiscally between increases in the cost of living and their marginal, stagnant salaries, functionaries find new merit in the notion that severe penalties are needed to counteract the heightened temptations of illicit activity caused by hard times. The widespread belief that unemployment causes crime and that severe punishment deters underlies an increasing proportion of their decisions. Day-to-day they do what they can to increase the odds that crime does not become an alternative to economic hardship. The end result of their countless individual decisions is increased severity of punishment. Thus, part of the aggregate-level escalation of punishment may be an unintended consequence of employees in control bureaucracies applying conventional assumptions to crime control. Evidence suggests that for individual defendants, judicial decisions to incarcerate vary significantly by employment status (Chiricos and Bales, 1991). Judges apparently view steady employment as an indicator of stability and unemployment as a sign of potential future trouble. Their actions may reassure elites even if this is not their intent. The relationship between labor surplus and penal sanctions requires assumptions about neither conspiracy nor specific direction.

The expanding crime-control apparatus that often accompanies the transformation and growth of punishment aids in the maintenance of stability and social order by providing jobs and a secure legitimate income for increasing numbers of the economically marginalized (Christie, 1994). The criminal justice system, therefore, plays a dual role in managing the disadvantaged, desperate, and potentially lawless; in addition to incapacitation, employment opportunities provided by the expansion of criminal justice function as a relief valve for social discontent.

When the economy is strong and unemployment is low, institutional growth in crime control may level off, use of punishment is relaxed, and inclusionary crime-control approaches gain support from elected officials and state managers (Cohen, 1985). This explanation for the changing use of punishment is consistent with the growth of rehabilitative ideologies and strategies in the United States during the years of post-World War II prosperity. It also helps explain why economic and structural transformations accompanying growth of the global economy, and the generalized anxiety they produce, has all but ended elected officials' public support for these "softer" crime-control approaches.

The preponderance of evidence from studies of the labor-surplus/punishment nexus supports conflict-theoretical explanations, even when fluctuation in street crime is controlled (Chiricos and Delone, 1992). Supportive evidence is provided, first, by nation-level studies both in Europe and in the United States which operationalize punishment as the rate of imprisonment (Box and Hale, 1982; 1985; Jankovic, 1977; Laffargue and Godefroy, 1989; Wallace, 1980). Not all investigators report a significant relationship between unemployment and imprisonment (Jacobs and Helms 1996), but a substantial majority do. Results from state-level studies of the unemployment/imprisonment nexus are mixed; studies that employ longitudinal methods generally find the strongest support for the hypothesized relationship, while cross-sectional studies report more contradictory findings (Chiricos and Delone, 1992).

Despite the generally confirmatory results of past research, there are reasons to question the labor-surplus/punishment relationship. To begin, methodological considerations suggest that nations and states may not be optimal units of analysis for investigating it. Since larger geographic units generally are more heterogeneous than smaller ones, national-level data are particularly likely to aggregate heterogeneity and mask substantial regional variation. This can confound and obscure empirical relationships of theoretical interest. In the United States, there is considerable intra-state variation in economic, demographic, crime and punishment variables. Analytically, state-level studies usually regress prison population variables on state demographic indicators despite the fact that inmates are not drawn randomly from its population, but largely from urbanized areas.

There is a theoretical reason as well for questioning the use of nations and states as units of analysis. Punishment policies generally are made at federal and state levels, but punishment is dispensed normally by *local* prosecutors and judges. Most serve local constituencies, and local political, structural and labor-market conditions likely constrain their decisions. Investigators are correct to use state-level data to examine variation in punishment policy (Link and Shover, 1986; Barlow, Barlow, and Johnson, 1996). Counties or SMSAs, however, may be a more appropriate unit of analysis for examining the relationship between labor surplus and punishment (Colvin, 1990; Jankovic, 1977; McCarthy, 1990). Consistent with findings from national- and many state-level investigations, the small number of county-level studies published thus far report a positive relationship between unemployment and the use of imprisonment (Chiricos and Delone, 1992).

Past county-level studies unfortunately are flawed by methodological shortcomings that limit confidence in theoretical understanding of the labor-surplus/punishment nexus. The theory linking historical change in punishment with change in the economy is a temporally dynamic one: as labor surplus increases criminal justice cracks down. Past county-level examinations of variation in use of imprisonment have employed cross-sectional analytic techniques that cannot assess these dynamic effects. Longitudinal techniques are required. Historically, problems of missing, inaccurate or inconsistently recorded information plagued county-level data. These shortcomings made investigators slow to use county-level data to examine justice issues. Complete and reliable county-level data became available in manageable format only recently. Despite an abundance of longitudinal national- and state-level studies of labor surplus and imprisonment, there are no dynamic spatial investigations at the county level.

The shortcomings of previous research diminish confidence in the underlying theoretical construction of the link between economic conditions and punishment. The present longitudinal study may help to rectify this. We test for a direct effect of *change* in the size of the labor surplus on *change* in the use of punishment while controlling for fluctuation in street crime and other variables. Thus, our methodology enables us to examine temporally dynamic causal relationships, and our use of counties as the units of analysis permits a test of the theoretical problem at the most appropriate aggregation.

Data and Methods

From correspondence with top-level criminal justice managers in the 50 states, we learned that 16 states could provide the requisite annual county-level prison commitment data. We began by selecting ten of these for inclusion in our state sample. We chose states from all regions of the United States, including only states with complete and apparently accurate data, and that would not require potentially time-consuming additional requirements to secure the needed data. The sample of states includes California, New Jersey, Ohio, Nebraska, Wisconsin, Illinois, Michigan, Mississippi, North Carolina and

TABLE 1 ■ COMPARISON OF SAMPLE AND AU COUNTIES WITH POPULATIONS 25,000 AND OVER

Variable	Sample	Population
Mean Population Size	134,266	120,868
Proportion White	.86	.88
Proportion Unemployed	.08	.08
Poverty Rate	.13	.14
Income per capita 1989	$ 12,689	$ 12,367

South Carolina. For each state, we then selected from the listing of counties published in the *Uniform Crime Reports* all counties within designated Standard Metropolitan Statistical Areas and all counties with a 1980 total population of more than 25,000 (United States Department of Justice, 1980). Because we are interested in how closely our resulting sample of 269 counties approximates characteristics of United States counties, we compared them to all 1,409 counties of similar size in the United States in 1980 (United States Bureau of the Census, 1994c). As Table 1 shows, we found that, save for population size (sample counties were somewhat larger than the population), the sample compares closely with the population.

Nevertheless, the fact that the relationship between our sample of 269 counties and populations of theoretical or policy significance is unknown mandates caution in generalizing from the findings. Data were collected for the years 1980 and 1990, principally from official state and federal records.

As most investigators have done, we use the official rate of unemployment as our measure of labor surplus. In doing so, we are not unmindful of the belief that it is an unsatisfactory measure of the true level of unemployment in a community. It does not, for example, include unemployed men and women who have ceased searching actively for a job. The limitations of our data, however, do not permit us to construct an alternative measure of the size of the labor surplus.

Since variation in state use of punishment generally is attributed to variation in street crime, we included in the analysis measures of both violent and nonviolent crimes known to the police. We also included as control variables socio-demographic characteristics that may contribute to the rate of prison commitments, chief among them the proportion of young adult males in the population (Cohen and Land, 1987; Inverarity and McCarthy, 1988). Since crime and imprisonment are experiences disproportionately characteristic of young males, counties with a high percentage of young men in their population generally have higher crime rates and, consequently, more imprisonment (Blumstein, 1983).

One of the most important changes in America's response to crime in the past 15 years is the dramatic increase of attention and resources devoted to drug-law enforcement. One indicator of this is a sharp increase in the proportion of the imprisoned population serving time for drug offenses (United States Bureau of Justice Statistics, 1996). In light of this development, it would be useful to include as controls county-level arrests and prison commitments for drug crimes. The necessary data are not available. Myers and Inverarity (1992) show, however, that increasing arrests from drug crimes do not mediate unemployment's relationship to or explain changing rates in state-level imprisonment.

Inclusion of crime rates in our analysis controls for the effect of age on imprisonment that is mediated by the crime rate. The effect of age on imprisonment should be minimal if the conventional assumption that the age of the population affects imprisonment via crime is true. But age structure also may influence imprisonment directly, particularly if, as seems likely, the population perceived as most dangerous by political-economic elites is young males with restricted access to legitimate labor markets (Box and Hale, 1982). Apart from any real threat from crime, large numbers of young males in a county may effect imprisonment by creating the perception of a threat from a population believed to be aggressive and difficult to control (Tittle and Curran, 1988). The effect of a county's age structure on imprisonment after controlling for crime is interpreted as a reflection of this age-threat process. We used age data both to control for the proportion of the population composed of males ages 20–34 and to test for this direct effect.

The use of imprisonment varies directly with the size of the non-white population (Carroll and Doubet, 1983; Joubert, Picou, and MacIntosh, 1981). Like the young and the unemployed, non-whites may be perceived as particularly threatening, restive and potentially criminal. The presence of non-whites is viewed by some criminal justice officials as an indicator of a crime problem and, therefore, increases the use of crime control and imprisonment. Although there is some evidence that blacks receive longer sentences than whites for similar offenses (e.g., Spohn, 1994), other studies suggest that the degree of discrimination against non-whites in sentencing and incarceration varies by social and economic context (Myers and Sabol, 1987; Myers and Talarico, 1986). For these reasons, we also controlled for the proportionate size of the non-white population.

Other measures of the economic health of a community may influence the use of imprisonment. Marxist theorists suggest that the poor are perceived to be a potential threat to social order. The effect of the impoverished working population on imprisonment is not reflected in unemployment rates. Increases in the proportionate size of the impoverished population may have an effect on change in imprisonment similar to unemployment. Consequently, poverty rates are included as a control variable, principally because they are a reasonable measure of an employed underclass. Poverty rates, however, represent only the percentage of a county's population who are officially poor and are not an indicator of the amount of wealth available to its families. Income is a better measure than poverty of the economic situation faced by them. A county's average personal income in 1980 dollars is included as a control variable to measure each county's economic health.

Given the methodological shortcomings of previous studies, we opted for statistical procedures that permit examination of changes in multiple cases at a few points in time. We used a panel design and analytic technique. Community values, traditions, cultures and institutional inertia all have an impact on both types and amounts of punishment employed against convicted offenders. Panel designs can account for both temporal and geographic variation. By observing the same counties at two points in time we insure that similar extraneous variables are in play in both time periods. We also can observe and analyze how change in some variables contributes to change in others and can even control for ongoing patterns of change common to all counties. A panel design permits us to investigate the effects of change in independent variables on change in imprisonment over the decade.

We used residual-change regression analysis to estimate changes in the level of variables in the panel from 1980 to 1990. This technique, which makes use of residual-change scores, has been employed to examine a variety of social problems (Bursik and Webb, 1982; Chamlin, 1992; Elliott and Voss, 1974). To derive a residual-change score, the level of a variable in 1990 is regressed on its level in 1980. The equation then is used to predict the level of each variable in 1990. Subtracting the predicted value from the observed value in 1990 yields a measure of residual change. Residual-change scores have two properties useful for this research. First, they provide a measure of change that is statistically independent of a variable's initial levels, removing a variable's initial level's effect on the subsequent level of that same variable. The result represents change that is not expected on the basis of the variable's initial level alone (Bohrnstedt, 1969). Residual-change regression permits an examination of how changes in the levels of independent variables affect change in imprisonment.

> Second, residual-change scores adjust for changes that other counties have undergone. They control the effects of trends common to all counties to determine change attributable to the variables of interest in a particular county. Since all 269 counties are used to estimate the regression equation which predicts the levels in 1990, the predicted values are automatically adjusted for change that other counties have undergone during the decade. Changes that occur across counties are controlled, leaving each county's unique change. We examine change by using two waves of data from 1980 and 1990 to determine change in socioeconomic variable's contribution to change in imprisonment This involves regressing the residual-change scores for imprisonment on the residual-change scores of the other variables. Changes in the independent variables, theoretically, should find expression in changes in imprisonment.

The presence of significant effects for crime in the absence of significance for unemployment will not support the hypothesis of an independent effect of unemployment on imprisonment.

Conclusions and Implications

Our findings can be summarized briefly. Change in violent street crime, in the proportionate size of the young male population, and in labor surplus contribute to change in the use of imprisonment while changing levels of property crime do not. These relationships persist even when street-crime rates and other presumed correlates of imprisonment are controlled. Our analysis, therefore, confirms findings from earlier investigations of the relationship between labor surplus and punishment. The criminal justice system grows increasingly punitive as labor surplus increases. The fact that our findings were achieved using both a unit of analysis more appropriate theoretically than measures employed by most investigators and a longitudinal design only strengthen confidence in them.

The observed relationship between violent street crime and punishment is consistent with results obtained by other investigators (e.g., Inverarity and McCarthy, 1988). That our findings differed for violent crime and property crime reinforces the importance of disaggregating crime rates in macro-level research. The relationship between the proportionate size of the young male population and punishment is not surprising. The fact that young males commit the majority of street crime means that in the aggregate they probably symbolize the threat of crime and disorder.

Although our principal objective has been a conflict interpretation of the relationship among street crime, labor surplus and punishment, the significance of our investigation is more than theoretical. At a time when public schools in many regions of the United States are under severe budgetary constraints, when major components of the nation's infrastructure have eroded, and millions of citizens cannot secure quality health care, expenditure of tax revenues for crime control has skyrocketed. It is only through a better understanding of the sources of these changes that we can predict their likely development or have any hope of controlling them. The findings of this study and others like it suggest an explanation for why past predictions about fluctuations in punishment that failed to include projected rates of unemployment or other economic measures have proven inaccurate.

References

Adamson, C. 1984. Toward a Marxian penology: Captive criminal populations as economic threats and resources. *Social Problems,* 31:435–458.

Barlow, D. E., Barlow, M. H., & Johnson, W. W. 1996. The political economy of criminal justice policy: A time-series analysis of economic conditions, crime and federal criminal justice legislation, 1948–1987. *Justice Quarterly*, 13:223–242.

Belsley, D. A., Kuh, E., & Welsh, R. E. 1980. *Regression diagnostics: Identifying influential data and sources of collinearity.* New York: Wiley.

Blumstein, A. 1983. Prisons: Population, capacity, and alternatives. In *Crime and Public Policy*, J. Q. Wilson (ed.), 229–250. San Francisco: ICS.

Bohrnstedt, G. W. 1969. Observations on the measurement of change. In *Sociological Methodology* 1969, E. F. Borgata & G. W. Bohrnstedt (eds.), 113–136. San Francisco: Jossey-Bass.

Box, S., & Hale, C. 1982. Economic crisis and the rising prisoner population in England and Wales. *Crime and Social Justice,* 17:20–35.

Box, S., & Hale, C. 1985. Unemployment, imprisonment and prison overcrowding. *Contemporary Crises,* 9:209–228.

Bursik, R. J., & Webb, J. 1982. Community change and patterns of delinquency. *American Journal of Sociology,* 88:24–42.

Carroll, L., & Doubet, M. B. 1983. U.S. social structure and imprisonment. *Criminology,* 21:449–456.

Chamlin, M. B. 1992. Intergroup threat and social control: Welfare expansion among states during the 1960s and 1970s. In *Social Threat and Social Control*, A. E. Liska (ed), 151–164. Albany: State University of New York Press.

Chiricos, T. G., & Bales, W. D. 1991 Unemployment and punishment: An empirical assessment. *Criminology* 29:701–724.

Chiricos, T. G., & Delone, M. A. 1992. Labor surplus and punishment: A review and assessment of theory and evidence. *Social Problems* 39:421–446.

Christie, N. 1994. *Crime control as industry: Toward GULAGS western style.* New York: Routledge.

Cohen, S. 1985. *Visions of social control.* Cambridge: Polity.

Cohen, L. E., & Land, K. L. 1987. Age structure and crime: Symmetry versus asymmetry and the projection of crime rates through the 1990s. *American Sociological Review* 52:170–183.

Colvin, M. 1990. Labor markets, industrial monopolization, welfare and imprisonment: Evidence from a cross section of U.S. counties. *Sociological Quarterly* 3 1:440–456.

Elliot, D. S., & Voss, H. L. 1974. *Delinquency and Dropout.* Lexington, Mass.: Heath.

Inter-university Consortium for Political and Social Research. 1991. *Uniform crime report: County level arrest and offenses data.* Ann Arbor: University of Michigan.

Inverarity, J., & McCarthy, D. 1988. Punishment and social structure revisited: Unemployment and imprisonment in the U.S., 1948–1984. *Sociological Quarterly* 29:263–279.

Jacobs, D. 1979. Inequality and police force strength: Conflict theory and coercive control in metropolitan areas. *American Sociological Review* 44:913–925.

Jacobs, D., & Helms, R. E. 1996. Toward a political model of incarceration: A time-series examination of multiple explanations for prison admission rates. *American Journal of Sociology* 102:323–357.

Jankovic, I. 1977. Labor market and imprisonment. *Crime and Social Justice* 8:17–31.

Joubert, P. E., Picou, J. S., & MacIntosh, A. 1981. U.S. social structure, crime, and imprisonment. *Criminology* 19:344–359.

Laffargue, B., & Godefroy. T. 1989. Economic cycles and punishment. *Contemporary Crises* 13:371–404.

Link, C. T., & Shover, N. 1986. The origins of criminal sentencing reforms. *Justice Quarterly* 3:329–341.

Liska, A. E., & Chamlin, M. B. 1984. Social structure and crime control among macrosocial units. *American Journal of Sociology,* 90:383–395.

McCarthy, B. 1990. A micro-level analysis of social structure and social control: Intrastate use of jail and prison confinement. *Justice Quarterly,* 7:325–340.

Melossi, D. 1989. An introduction: Fifty years later, punishment and social structure in comparative analysis. *Contemporary Crises,* 13:311–326.

Myers, G., & Inverarity, J. 1992. Strategies of disaggregation in imprisonment rate research. Presented at the annual meeting of the American Society of Criminology.

Myers, M. A., & Talarico, S. M. 1986. The social context of racial discrimination in sentencing. *Social Problems* 33:236–251.

Myers, S. L., Jr., & Sabol, W. J. 1987. Business cycles and racial disparities in punishment. *Contemporary Policy Issues,* 5:46–58.

Rusche, G., & Kirchheimer, O. 1939. *Punishment and social structure.* New York: Columbia University Press.

Spitzer, S. 1975. Toward a Marxian theory of deviance. *Social Problems,* 22:638–651.

Spohn, C. 1994. Crime and the social control of blacks: Offender/victim race and the sentencing of violent offenders. In *Inequality, crime, and social control,* G. S. Bridges & M. Myers (eds.), 249–268. Boulder, Colo.: Westview.

Tittle, C. R., & Curran, D. A. 1988. Contingencies for dispositional disparities in juvenile justice. *Social Forces,* 67:23–58.

U.S. Bureau of the Census. 1994a. *Revised estimates of county population characteristics 1980–1989.* Washington, DC: Estimates Division

U.S. Bureau of the Census. 1994b. *modified age, race and sex.* Washington, DC: Estimates Division.

U.S. Bureau of the Census. 1994c. *County and city data book: U.S.A. counties. (CD-ROM).* Washington, DC: U.S. Government Printing Office.

U.S. Bureau of Economic Analysis. 1994. *Regional Economic Information System 1969–1993.* (CD-ROM). Washington, DC: U.S. Government Printing Office.

U.S. Bureau of Justice Statistics. 1996. *Correctional populations in the United States 1994.* Washington, DC: U.S. Government Printing Office.

U.S. Bureau of Labor Statistics, 1992. *The consumer price index: Questions and answers.* Washington, DC: U.S. Government Printing Office.

U.S. Department of Justice, 1980. *Uniform crime reports for the United States.* Washington, DC: U.S. Government Printing Office.

Wallace, D. 1980. The political economy of incarceration trends in late U.S. capitalism. *Insurgent Sociologist,* 9:59–65.

REVIEW QUESTIONS

1. What are some of the links between surplus labor and punishment mentioned in this article?

2. Explain how the researchers used conflict theory in their project.

3. What questions might the researchers have asked if they had used feminist theory in their project, rather than conflict theory?

SCHOOL TRACKING AND STUDENT VIOLENCE

Lissa J Yogan

There has been much attention in the media recently regarding violence in schools, especially since the Columbine High School shootings in April 1999. As a result, it is important to find ways to curb this type of violence. Yogan used the theory of symbolic interactionism to explain the moral development children share with their teachers, how that moral development is affected by school practices, how these changes affect peer group interaction, how schools can positively influence and channel group formation, and ultimately reduce violence in schools.

During the late 1990s, parents and educators alike became increasingly worried about the safety of schools. Their concern was warranted. The U.S. Department of Education reports that while the overall incidence of school crime had not greatly changed in recent years, there had been an increase in some types of school crime. School crime became more violent. Since 1992, there had been more than 211 school deaths associated with violence (Wolf, 1998). A few of these killings made the national news. When the suspects and victims were identified as small-town, white, middle-class children, the nation became alarmed. Over the past two years, there have been numerous cries to form national, state, and local task forces to confront the growing problem of school violence. Many of these task forces began to examine school security systems, specifically the school's measures of crime prevention and control. Were there enough metal detectors? Were the entrances locked? Were there enough security guards in place? While these security measures might prevent some incidents of violence, they do nothing to help us understand why violent crime within schools has increased. In particular, they ignore the structure of the organization of schooling.

This article will focus on one aspect of school organizational structure: the effects that tracking (placing students in ability-based groups) has had on students' interactions with peers and adults. Looking at how and why students are tracked and how track placement affects their sense of self is one way of understanding the increase in school violence, and it can suggest organizational changes as a way to combat it. I will begin by reviewing several theories and concepts that underlie the process of self-development. Understanding how a person grows and develops and understanding how a school's structure may influence a person's self-development toward violent behavior can suggest organizational changes that will ultimately result in decreased use of violence.

Symbolic Interactionist Theory and Student-Teacher Interaction

Social interaction, or, specifically, the interaction of students with peers and adults, is the subject matter of symbolic interactionism, one of the main branches of sociological theo-

Yogan, L. J. 2000. School tracking and student violence. *Annals of the American Academy of Political & Social Science*, 567: 108–122

ry. Symbolic interactionism is based on the assumption that meaning and learning (education) are gained through interaction with others. How a person understands others, how others come to understand that person, and how the person comes to understand and identify himself or herself are part of the symbolic interaction process. It is through symbolic interaction that an individual develops a sense of self; who we are is partly a reflection of how others see us, as Charles Horton Cooley (1909) first pointed out. He called this idea the "looking glass self." In particular, we are shaped by our interactions with people who are significant to us. What is different for each of us is the group of people we consider to be significant; thus each of us undergoes a similar process to develop a unique self. Symbolic interactionism also delves into the role that perception and meaning play in these significant interactions.

We can use symbolic interactionism to understand the role of shared meaning in student-teacher interaction. Herbert Blumer (1969) states that symbolic interactionism rests on three simple premises. The first is that human beings act toward things on the basis of the meanings that the things have for them. The second premise is that the meaning of these things is derived from or arises out of the social interaction that one has with one's social counterparts. The third premise is that these meanings are handled and modified through an interpretive process used by the person in dealing with the things he or she encounters.

Using these three premises to look at teachers, it can be hypothesized that teachers will act toward students based on the meanings that students (as objects) have for them. This hypothesis was supported by the classic studies of Rosenthal and Jacobson (1968) and Rubovitz and Maehr (1971, 1975). In the Rosenthal and Jacobson study, the meaning that students had for teachers was controlled by the researchers. The researchers told the teachers that some of the students were likely to do well that year. In reality, the researchers randomly selected the students they labeled as likely to do well, yet the teachers acted toward the students based on the meanings that were given by the researchers (not by any actual measure of ability).

The second premise, that the meaning that students have for the teachers will be based on the social interaction that teachers have with their self-identified social counterparts, was also shown in the Rosenthal and Jacobson study. Teachers identified the researchers as their social counterparts and adopted their meanings rather than developing meanings independently.

The third premise, that the meanings given to students by the teacher's social counterparts will be modified through an interpretive process of the teacher, suggests that it is possible to change socially constructed meanings rather than simply adopt them. The changing of socially constructed meanings can be seen in the story of Jaime Escalante (Mathews, 1988). Escalante was the subject of the movie *Stand and Deliver* (1988). Escalante's social counterparts (other teachers) had decided that the Hispanic youths in their school would not be capable of learning, could not achieve at a college level, and would be doing well simply to graduate. He modified this interpretation and arrived at a new meaning. His new meaning of students was that these students could work college mathematical problems, could simultaneously manage school and home lives, and could succeed in high school. Escalante was able to modify the beliefs of his counterparts through the ideas he held about his abilities (self-evaluation) and through his beliefs about the barriers produced by racism and school ability groupings.

Understanding these three basic tenets of symbolic interaction is therefore helpful in formulating ideas about successful teacher-student interactions, but it does not completely address the process through which the three tenets are filtered. Two important questions that affect student-teacher interaction are (1) From where do groups of social counterparts (that is, teachers) derive their meanings of others? And (2) what are the interpretive processes that teachers use in modifying students' meanings?

George Herbert Mead (1934) provides one answer to the first question. He states that we each belong to a number of different socially functioning groups. Teachers and students may identify themselves as members of many different groups, including professional teachers' organizations, neighborhood communities, families, athletic organizations, and ethnic and religious groups. An individual identifies with a group or groups because he or she is able to understand the behaviors of members of these groups and integrate his or her own behavior with the behavior of the members. When individuals find it difficult to understand and integrate their behaviors with the behaviors of others, as sometimes happens in social interactions between students and teachers, it is likely that difficulty arises because the individuals are acting as members of two or more different social groups. In his description of social organization and the ideal of human society, Mead states, We often find the existence of castes in a community which make it impossible for persons to enter into the attitude of other people although they are actually affecting and are affected by these other people. The ideal of human society is one which does bring people so closely together in their interrelationships, so fully develops the necessary system of communication, that the individuals who exercise their own peculiar functions can take the attitude of those whom they affect. Remember that what is essential to a significant symbol is that the gesture which affects others should affect the individual himself in the same way. Human communication takes place through such significant symbols, and the problem is one of organizing a community which makes this possible.

This passage outlines two significant points that should be considered in teacher-student interactions. The first is that castes exist in communities and affect both members of the caste group and outsiders. Castes also exist in schools. (n1) There are several ways castes at school are generated and affected, not least through race, class, and gender stereotypes in the wider society. However, one way these social forces come together to produce school castes that are found to be "virtually irreversible" is through tracking (Lawrence, 1998, 52; see also Schafer, Olexa, and Polk, 1972). Tracking is the placement of students into groups based on perceived intellectual ability or readiness to learn. However, because schools are not pure caste societies, it is assumed that the shared meaning described in Mead's ideal human society can be approximated within a carefully structured classroom environment.

The creation of this special classroom environment is the second key point of Mead's passage for the present analysis. For the creation of such an environment, it is necessary that the teacher (one who initiates interaction for the purpose of education) understand how his or her significant symbols of communication affect students differently. In addition, the teacher must understand when and why students are using different symbols to communicate. Thus knowledge of a student's primary social reference group and how that group differs from other students' reference groups and the teacher's social reference group is necessary for socially congruent instruction. If the instruction is not socially congruent, students are not likely to understand their teacher, and they are less likely to engage in the learning process.

The point is that current interactions are complicated by past interactions. Just as the literature on HIV and AIDS warns that when one has sexual intercourse with someone, one is, in effect, making sexual contact with all the previous partners of that person, the theory on social interaction tells us that we bring aspects of our past interactions into our present ones. It is precisely because of this link between the past and the present that interactions become both the problem of and the solution to school violence.

Students who enter the classroom with a history of exposure to violence may carry that violence and the ways of thinking that rationalize violence into all their interactions. They may interpret some actions through this way of thinking. A teacher, who typically is not living in a violence-filled community, may not understand how students interpret his or her actions, may not understand how students resolve and make sense of their own interactions, and may draw on stereotypes as a reference for meaning. Unless we change the organizational structure of schools to break down castes and create a more heterogeneous grouping of people, students who do not share the teacher's background are not likely to be influenced by that teacher or the institution that the teacher represents. A lack of bonding with an important societal institution such as school can lead to deviant behavior and to more serious forms of rule violation involving violence.

Violence that results in death is an extreme form of deviance. Deviance or delinquency among youths has been studied for many years. Hirschi's social control theory (1969) says that delinquency occurs when youths fail to bond with conventional social institutions. Within society, there are several conventional institutions; one of these is the institution of education represented by schools and schoolteachers. Strong bonds with school, described by Hirschi as the individual's relationship with school or teachers, and the amount of time spent on school-related activities compared to the amount of time spent on non-school-related activities contribute to an individual's willingness to conform to societal conventions. When individuals are bonded to conventional institutions, they are less likely to act in deviant ways. Thus one of the keys to reducing violence within schools is to increase the bonds that students feel to the school or to conventional others within the school . However, one of the aspects of school organization that reduces bonding for certain groups is tracking.

Tracking

Increasing the bonds that students form to school through teachers is made more difficult by the process of tracking. "Tracking" is a word that is used to describe the ability groups established by the schools. Theoretically, these ability groups are supposed to enable more effective education because students with similar ability levels and readiness to learn will be taught together to their optimum level of academic performance. Teachers can concentrate on just one type of student instead of having to prepare lesson plans that account for more than one type, such as advanced, average, and remedial students.

In reality, however, tracking has not made education more effective. Instead, it has created and perpetuated many of society's problems. The institutional practice of tracking that is now common in most public schools has numerous effects on both teachers and students. It has been found to affect how students view themselves (self-identity), how they evaluate themselves (self-image), and how others view them (public identity) (Kelly and Pink, 1982, 55; Lawrence, 1998, 52). It has been criticized for the following reasons:

> More minority and lower income students are in the basic or low-ability tracks; placement in the track tends to be permanent, with little movement up or down in spite of students' learning and progress; and tracking has a labeling and stigmatizing effect so that teachers expect less of lower tracked students and frequently their expectations are correct. (Lawrence, 1998, 52)

Many of these effects can be related to self-development and social bonding. Tracking affects teachers' expectations of students' performance (Oakes, 1985; Kelly and Pink, 1982; Rosenthal and Jacobson, 1968). The concept of self-fulfilling prophecy tells us that if students are labeled as educationally inferior or superior, that is how they will perform. Thus tracking sends messages to students about inferiority and superiority.

Tracking also separates students on variables other than intellectual ability (Alexander, Cook, and McDill, 1978), including race, class, father's occupation, misconduct, and past academic record rather than IQ (Kelly and Grove, 1981). This means that students are denied the opportunity to interact in the classroom with a heterogeneous group of students. The odds are good that those in their classes will mirror their socioeconomic and minority or majority status.

Tracking also has produced qualitative and quantitative instructional differences (Gamoran, 1986; Karweit 1987). For those at the top, the belief is that their way is best, and their educational achievement provides all the evidence of success they need. For those at the bottom, school becomes yet another hurdle to achieving self-esteem and developing a positive sense of self. Studies have documented the harmful effects of tracking on the academic achievement of those students in the lower tracks (Oakes, 1985, 1990). Tracking has also created a structure in which students do not receive equal knowledge, skills, or credentials for success beyond high school. Those in the upper tracks usually receive an education that prepares them for college, while those in the bottom tracks receive an education that focuses on remedial skills, or what Willis (1993) described as "learning to labor."

In addition to the inequality in educational outcome associated with tracking, studies show that placement in tracks reflects a student's race and socioeconomic status. Low-income, African American, and Latino children are more frequently placed in low-level classes (regardless of achievement) than Euro-American children with higher family incomes (Oakes and Guiton, 1995; Welner and Oakes, 1996). Indeed, evidence suggests that, even controlling for IQ and previous ability, "blacks and low income students were still more likely to be found in the basic or low ability tracks" (Lawrence, 1998, 52; see also Schafer, Olexa, and Polk, 1972). Because tracking favors the students in the upper tracks over those in the lower tracks, it is easy to hypothesize that those in the lower tracks will be less likely to bond with the institution of school. It is still likely, however, that the students will bond with other students within their ability group, or track, especially those of similar racial, ethnic, gender, or class background. This is one of the problems of interaction: it is an ongoing process that can produce negative as well as positive outcomes, if organizational arrangements do not take account of its existence.

If students form bonds with other students who are similar to them, they are not as likely to diversify and expand their thinking as are students who bond with students who are dissimilar to them. Our knowledge grows as our range of experiences, both vicarious and real, grow. Each new experience or new way of thinking to which we are exposed may cause us to reevaluate that which we thought we knew (Perry, 1970). When we receive more supports than challenges, our thinking becomes stagnant. Thus students who are surrounded by students who share their social, ethnic, and class position in society (a support) are less likely to be challenged in their thinking. Stagnant thinking is not the goal of education.

One possible way to remedy this situation is for the students to form bonds with the teacher, who can then challenge their ways of thinking and help them grow. However, this option is complicated by reality. As discussed earlier, often the teacher is different from the student in age—sometimes by many years—as well as in other demographic characteristics. Not only are these differences magnified by tracking; they also may reflect differences in socioeconomic status and race. Even though the majority of students in many urban schools belong to a minority group, teachers continue to be predominantly white (U.S. Department of Education, 1993). Also, teachers belong to the middle class, but many students (particularly those in lower tracks) belong to the lower class. Thus it takes great effort and desire on the part of the student and the teacher to form a common bond. It is more likely that students will initially bond with other students. If we are to change thinking processes, students have to be given more opportunities to bond with other students who are both similar and dissimilar to them. The opinions of other students matter. How others see us affects our development of self. How others view us also affects our self-esteem.

Self-Esteem

Social interactions and the development of self are linked to self-esteem and the process of self-development described earlier. The concept of self-esteem is embedded in the theory of symbolic interaction. Self-esteem is also a conceptual component of the more inclusive process of self-conception. The process of self-conception is considered a key element in the relationship between individual behavior and the social organization of which the individual is a part. Linkages have been made between self-esteem and racial bias (Ashmore and Del Boca, 1976; Harding et al., 1969) and between self-esteem and teacher effectiveness (Edeburn and Landry, 1976). In both instances, the link between a person's self-evaluation and subsequent behavior can be seen.

At an individual level, needs for self-esteem and superior status are considered to be among the major causes and perpetuators of prejudice and racial discrimination (Allport, 1954; Ashmore and Del Boca, 1976; Harding et al., 1969; Tajfel and Turner, 1979). Self-esteem works through group identification to produce discriminatory behaviors in some individuals. All people desire positive evaluation by others and self. Tajfel and Turner (1979) have shown that people who have low self-esteem tend to seek positive evaluation by identifying a uniqueness (positive specialness) for their in-group over an identified out-group. In the United States, this often takes the form of (perceived) positive white in-group norms compared to (perceived) negative black out-group norms.

However, this identification can also take the reverse form. In the reverse form, minority students perceive or declare their culture and its norms as superior to those of their white, middle-class teacher. This need for positive distinctiveness leads to perceived inter-group competition and motivates prejudice and discriminatory behaviors. Within school, the need for positive distinctiveness may lead students and teachers in upper-level tracks to perceive the tracks as a form of competition and thus develop a prejudice against those in lower-level tracks. This phenomenon was demonstrated by Finley (1984), who noted that a competition existed between teachers for high-level or high-status students.

It has also been noted that a particular anti-achievement culture has developed among African American students, who are typically placed in lower tracks (Suskind, 1998; Fordham, 1988). The ideology within this culture says that to succeed academically is to become "white." Thus, within some groups that are typically relegated to the lower tracks, the need for positive distinctiveness leads to the formation of a culture that is the antithesis of the culture of the teacher, the educational process, and the school's perceived culture of academic success (Cohen, 1955).

Self-esteem has also been linked to achievement and performance. Research has shown a positive correlation between self-esteem and school achievement (Stevens, 1956; Fink, 1962; Williams and Cole, 1968; Simon and Simon, 1975). Additional studies have shown that teacher-student interaction is an important variable in the student's self-esteem and achievement. Edeburn and Landry (1976) state that teachers who themselves have a positive self-image affect their students more positively than do teachers who have a low or negative self-image. Davidson and Lang (1960) found that the more that children perceive their teachers' feelings toward themselves as positive, the better the academic achievement of the children. Thus positive teacher self-esteem is an important variable in reducing culturally induced prejudicial attitudes and is important in the successful educational interaction of teachers and students.

Unfortunately, tracking sends a message to those in the lower tracks that they are not as good as other students. Teachers all too often support this message as they talk down to students or dumb down the course requirements. Power (1993) found that track level does have a direct effect on self-esteem; as track level increases, so does self-esteem. Her analyses also indicate that a student's self-esteem is susceptible to the effects of track placement even years after the placement occurred. Students who were placed in the lower tracks in elementary school still showed decreased self-esteem in high school (31). This tells us that, although students age, they rarely are able to overcome the negative effects of tracking.

What has been described so far is theory and research evidence on self formation, an explanation of why some students become deviant, and the relationship of tracking to the development of self and to the development of bonds with schools or with individuals in schools. I would now like to discuss how these processes can lead to both the expression of violence and the elimination of violence by linking theory and research with the reality of life in today's society.

Schools, Society, and Violence

During the 1990s, many people pointed to the change in the family as the cause of violence. (n2) They suggested that the increase in one-parent households and two-income families had led to decreased attention to what our youths were doing. Of course, this change in family structure is linked to both political and economic changes in society. Through the implementation of no-fault divorce laws, the political system has made it easier for men and women to end marriages. The increased divorce rate has led to an increase in one-parent households. Our economic structure has increased opportunities for women to become employed outside the home, and downsizing and technological advances have made two incomes in a family more of a necessity than in the past. Thus the change in adult family members' ability to spend time with children reflects more than just a change in the institution of the family. It reflects much broader changes in society.

From their beginnings, schools have mirrored society. The school model still commonly used is one that is based on the structure of factories. Students enter at a set time (similar to punching a time clock); they move down the assembly line of reading, writing, and arithmetic; and they emerge at graduation as a finished product. Through tracking, schools reflect the economic and racial segregation of society. School districts are tied to place of residence, and school funds are commonly tied to property taxes. Both districts and their property taxes reflect the extreme residential segregation common in the United States. What is intriguing is why schools mirror society when they do not have to do so.

One of the American school's early tasks was to socialize immigrants. In other words, early in the history of public education, schools were seen as the institution most able to change individuals. Schools could socialize and make those deemed inferior (immigrants) into model citizens who would understand and support the norms and values (such as democracy and equality for all) of their new culture. Somewhere along the way, schools quit socializing into model citizens those deemed inferior and instead instituted processes that maintained the inferior student's entering status. Today, when students graduate, their master status is still likely to be their race or socioeconomic status. In the past, an immigrant's ethnicity or socioeconomic status became less important if he or she were educated. In large part, society's acceptance of an immigrant was due to the fact that the immigrant had been socialized through heterogeneous interaction. That interaction took place in schools where there were no tracks. There was simply a heterogeneous group of students who interacted with and learned about each other over the course of several years. Both immigrant and native born were changed by the experience. Values and norms merged, and, at the end, both immigrant and native born had roughly the same status in society.

Remember that symbolic interactionists tell us that who we are is determined by our social interactions with significant others. If I have a family and friends who are moral, law-abiding, happy people who tell me consistently good things about myself, I am probably a person who is moral, law abiding, and happy. But if I have family, friends, or a society that tells me I am worthless, that breaking some laws is acceptable, and that others' lives are not worth much, then I am likely to become a person that is angry, disobedient, and potentially dangerous. What happens if I am isolated? I get the message that society does not want to be with me, and I might interpret that in such a way as to become jealous of or angry with society. Insofar as tracking contributes to this separation and isolation, it also contributes to the general level of school violence, although evidence of a direct relationship between tracking and delinquency remains unclear (Lawrence, 1998).

Schools are the one institution that have in the past proved themselves successful at transforming individuals' place in society. They did this through carefully structured interactions between students and teachers. Today, instead of mirroring society's faults, schools should use the opportunity and time given to them to model a more positive society. They can and should help create a society in which students from all different educational, racial, and economic backgrounds interact. Tracking does not do this. Currently tracking reinforces social class and racial segregation patterns. Moreover, it does not just separate; it tells one group that it is better than another. One of the most common ways that peer groups and friendships are formed is through classroom formation and shared experiences. It is critical to the development of self and to cognitive growth that individuals are exposed to diverse ways of thinking. Good teachers can make this happen.

Clearly, there is also a strong need for leadership within schools and, specifically, within classrooms. In recent years, the teaching profession has not attracted the nation's best and brightest. This is a serious problem. Teachers may be one of the few adults whom children have in their lives on any consistent basis. The economic demand on parents, particularly mothers, has decreased the amount of time they have to spend with their children. Thus the responsibility of teachers to be role models and moral guides is increased. Teachers need to take time to talk about what is right and wrong. They need to help teach citizenship, civility, respect, and compassion for others. They need to offer thoughtful critiques of society and the media and thought-provoking questions about how to handle difficult situations without resorting to violence. As a society, we cannot afford for teachers to be moral relativists. Too many children do not have enough adults willing or present to offer solid moral teaching and guidance. If students are taught problem-solving skills by watching action films or by other teens who see multiple reasons why it is acceptable to use violence against someone else, they are more likely to resort to violence when they face a problem. Students today need more than heterogeneous groupings within their schools. They need strong teachers who know how to connect with them and how to simultaneously build their self-esteem and challenge their ways of thinking and problem solving.

Notes

(n1) Castes might also operate in subgroups at schools, such as jocks, preppies, skaters, thespians, gangstas, goths, and so on.

(n2) In a nonscientific survey of Internet users, a CNN (1999) poll reported that parents were seen as the leading cause of school violence by 29 percent of the 59,698 respondents, followed by access to guns and the media.

References

Alexander, Karl L., Martha Cook, & Edward L. McDill. 1978. Curriculum tracking and educational stratification: some further evidence. *American Sociological Review,* 43:47–66.

Allport, Gordon W. 1954. *The nature of prejudice.* Reading, MA: Addison-Wesley.

Ashmore, Richard D., & Frances K. Del Boca. 1976. Psychological approaches to understanding intergroup conflicts. In *Towards the elimination of racism,* ed. Phyllis A. Katz. New York: Pergamon.

Blumer, Herbert. 1969. *Symbolic interactionism: Perspective and method*. Berkeley: University of California Press.

CNN. 1999. CNN Interactive Quickvote. Available http://www.cnn.com/POLL/results/661.html.

Cohen, Albert. K. 1955. *Delinquent boys: The culture of the gang*. New York: Free Press.

Cooley, Charles Horton. 1909. *Social organization*. New York: Scribner.

Davidson, Helen H., & Gerhard Lang. 1960. Children's perceptions of their teachers' feelings toward them related to self-perception, school achievement, and behavior. *Journal of Experiential Education*, 29:107–118.

Edeburn, Carl E., & Richard G. Landry. 1976. Teacher self-concept and student self-concept in grades three, four, and five. *Journal of Educational Research*, 69:372–375.

Fink, Martin B. 1962. Self-concept as it relates to academic underachievement. *California Journal of Education Research*, 13:57–62.

Finley, Merrilee K. 1984. Teachers and tracking in a comprehensive high school. *Sociology of Education* ,57:233–243.

Fordham, Signithia. 1988. Racelessness as a factor in Black students' school success: pragmatic strategy or pyrrhic victory? *Harvard Educational Review*, 58:54–84.

Gamoran, Adam. 1986. Instructional and institutional effects of ability grouping. *Sociology of Education*, 59:185–198.

Harding, John, Harold Prochansky, Bernard Kutner, & Isidor Chein. 1969. Prejudice and ethnic relations. In *Handbook of social psychology*, ed. Lindzay Gardner & Elliot Aronson-, 2nd ed., Vol. 5. Reading, MA: Addison-Wesley.

Hirschi, Travis. 1969. *Causes of delinquency*. Berkeley: University of California Press.

Karweit, Nancy. 1987. Diversity, equity, and classroom processes. In *The social organization of schools*, ed. Maureen T. Hallinan. New York: Plenum.

Kelly, Delos H., & Winthrop D. Grove. 1981. Teachers' nominations and the production of academic "misfits." *Education*, 101:246–263.

Kelly, Delos H., & William T. Pink. 1982. School crime and individual responsibility: The perpetuation of a myth? *Urban Review*, 14(1):47–63.

Lareau, Annette. 1989. *Home advantage: Social class and parental intervention in elementary education*. Washington, DC: Falmer.

Lawrence, Richard. 1998. *School crime and juvenile justice*. New York: Oxford University Press.

Lee, Valerie E., & Julia B. Smith. 1995. Effects of high school restructuring and size on early gains in achievement and engagement for early secondary school students. *Sociology of Education*, 68:241–270.

Mathews, Jay. 1988. *Escalante: The best teacher in America*. New York: Henry Holt.

Mead, George Herbert. 1934. *Mind, self, and society: From the standpoint of a social behaviorist*. Chicago: University of Chicago Press.

Oakes, Jeannie. 1985. *Keeping track: How schools structure inequality*. New Haven, CT: Yale University Press.

Oakes, Jeannie 1990. *Multiplying inequalities: The effects of race, social class, and tracking on opportunities to learn math and science*. Santa Monica, CA: RAND.

Oakes, Jeannie, & Gretchen Guiton. 1995. Matchmaking: The dynamics of high school tracking decision. *American Educational Research Journal,* 32(1):3–33.

Perry, William, Jr. 1970. *Intellectual and ethical development in the college years*. New York: Holt, Rinehart & Winston.

Power, Ann Marie R. 1993. *The effects of tracking on high school students' self-esteem*. Master's thesis, University of Notre Dame.

Ray, Karen. 1995. *Grant High School case report*. Los Angeles: University of California at Los Angeles, Center for Research for Democratic School Communities.

Rosenthal, Robert & Lenore Jacobson. 1968. *Pygmalion in the classroom: Teacher expectation and pupils' intellectual development*. New York: Holt, Rinehart & Winston.

Rubovitz, Pamela C., & Martin L. Maehr. 1971. Pygmalion analyzed: Toward an explanation of the Rosenthal-Jacobson findings. *Journal of Personality and Social Psychology,* 19:197–203.

Rubovitz, Pamela C., & Martin L. Maehr .1975. Teacher expectations: A special problem for Black children with White teachers? In *Culture, child, and school: Sociocultural influences on learning*, ed. Martin L. Maehr & William M. Stallings. Monterey, CA: Brooks/Cole.

Schafer, Walter, Carol Olexa, & Kenneth Polk. 1972. Programmed for social class: Tracking in high school. In *Schools and delinquency*, ed. Kenneth Polk & Walter Schafer. Englewood Cliffs, NJ: Prentice Hall.

Simon, William E., & Marilyn G. Simon. 1975. Self-esteem, intelligence, and standardized academic achievement. *Psychology in the Schools,* 12:97–100.

Stand and Deliver. 1988. *An American Playhouse* Theatrical Film, Menendez/Musca & Olmos Production. Burbank, CA: Warner Brothers.

Stevens, Peter H. 1956. *An investigation of the relationship between certain aspects of self-concept and student's academic achievement*. Ph.D. diss., New York University, 1956. Abstract in Dissertation Abstracts 16:2531–2532.

Suskind, Ron. 1998. *A hope in the unseen: An American odyssey from the inner city to the Ivy League*. New York: Broadway Books.

Tajfel, Henri, and John C. Turner. 1979. An integrative theory of intergroup conflict. In *The social psychology of intergroup relations*, eds. William G. Austin & Stephen Worchel. Monterey, CA: Brooks/Cole.

U.S. Department of Education. National Center for Education Statistics. 1993. *Digest of education statistics*. Washington, DC: Government Printing Office.

Van Galen, Jane. 1987. Maintaining control: The structuring of parent involvement. *In schooling in social context: Qualitative studies*, ed. G. W. Noblit & W. T. Pink. Norwood, NJ: Ablex.

Wells, Amy Stuart & Jeannie Oakes. 1998. Tracking, detracking, at the politics of educational reform: A sociological perspective. In *Sociology of education: Emerging perspectives*, ed. Carlos Alberto Torres & Theodore R. Mitchell. Albany: State University of New York Press.

Welner, Kevin G., & Jeannie Oakes. 1996. (Li)ability grouping: The new susceptibility of school tracking systems to legal challenges. *Harvard Educational Review,* 66(3):451–470.

Williams, Robert L., & Spurgeon Cole. 1968. Self-concept and school adjustment. *Personnel and Guidance Journal,* 46:478–481.

Willis, Paul E. 1993. *Learning to labour: How working class kids get working class jobs.* Aldershot, United Kingdom: Ashgate.

Wolf, Stephen M. 1998. Curbing school violence: Our youth, and our schools, need support before an incident occurs—Not after. *Attache (U.S. Airways)* Sept. 9.

REVIEW QUESTIONS

1. How did Yogan use the theory of symbolic interactionism in this paper? What would have been different if the author had used another theory?

2. What does the author mean when she states that "teachers will act toward students based on the meanings that students (as objects) have for them?"

3. Can you come up with your own questions and thoughts about a study you might consider on school violence? What theory would you use and why?

STUDYING POSTMODERN FAMILIES: A FEMINIST ANALYSIS OF ETHICAL TENSIONS IN WORK AND FAMILY RESEARCH

Lori A. McGraw, Anisa M. Zvonkovic, and Alexis J. Walker

McGraw, Zvonkovic, and Walker used feminist theory to study the families of fishermen. The work and family contexts of commercial fishing families provided the researchers with an opportunity to explore the diverse ways that couples with children adapted to the comings and goings of the husbands who tended to be gone from home for long periods of time. Consequently, the wives of the commercial fishermen tended both to run their households and maintained heavy involvement in the business aspects of their husbands' occupations. Furthermore, the researchers dealt with the ethical tensions they encountered in their multi-method research project.

The complexity of ethical concerns inherent in family research is often minimized within conventional, positivist approaches that emphasize objectivity and value-free inquiry. Consistent with positivism, family researchers tend to downplay or ignore the relationship between themselves and participants and to decontextualize their research findings from the surrounding social environments (Leslie & Sollie, 1994). A primary assumption of conventional social science is that truth can be found through the separation of the researcher and the researched. Feminists believe, however, that science is a social activity embedded in a sociocultural context and shaped by personal concerns and commitments (Nielsen, 1990; Thompson, 1992). Feminists argue that there is no such thing as a disinterested stance to knowledge construction. Through dialogue and reflexivity, researchers aim to create a broader knowledge base (Baber & Allen, 1992; Neilsen, 1990), a base that is emergent from people in relationship with one another (Lather, 1988; 1991). Reflexivity is a process whereby researchers place themselves and their practices under scrutiny, acknowledging the ethical dilemmas that permeate the research process and impinge on the creation of knowledge.

Our concern is with the ethical tensions we encountered in a multi-method research project investigating the work and family processes of Northwest fishing families. We were drawn to these concerns for reasons both practical (recruitment and retention problems) and political (differing agendas between us and our participants). Although our study was carefully designed to meet fundamental criteria for good (positivist) empirical research, combined with a feminist goal of giving wives in our study an opportunity to tell their own stories, we met considerable resistance from both potential and committed participants. We came to recognize that our goal of understanding family processes within a particular work and family context was not shared by some of our participants, who seemed to focus instead on changing policies to increase fishermen's "rights" to fish.

McGraw, L., Zvonkovic, A. M., & Walker, A. J. 2000. Studying postmodern families: A feminist analysis of ethical tensions in work and family research. *Journal of Marriage & the Family,* 62(1), 68–78

In response, we engaged in a reflexive process among ourselves and with our research participants to expand our understandings of the tensions we encountered. We designed and carried out a qualitative study to learn our participants' views on the research process and to glean insights on how to conduct more ethical research. Below, we set the stage for our qualitative study by describing fishing families and our initial project. Then, we offer a rationale by reviewing the literature on ethical issues in research.

Initial Phases: Treading Turbulent Waters

The work and family contexts of commercial fishing families provide an opportunity to explore the diverse ways that couples with children adapt to the comings and goings of the husbands. Fishermen tend to be gone from home for long periods of time, depending on such factors as where they fish and the type of fish they catch. Consequently, wives of commercial fishermen tend both to run their households and to maintain heavy involvement in the business aspects of their husbands' occupations. Many fishing wives—the way the women in our study identified themselves—also engage in wage-paying work. A primary aspect of our study was to understand the ebb and flow of fishing family life, a life characterized by separations and reunions.

Although we had support from Oregon's Sea Grant Program and Fishing Family Coordinators (fishing wives hired by Oregon's Sea Grant Cooperative Extension Program to lead fishing wives' organizations), commitment to participate in our project was low. Only 22 couples agreed to complete telephone interviews. Furthermore, despite several strategies to enhance and maintain couples' participation, only 7 of these 22 couples completed the project. We also used the survey method to obtain a larger sample of fishing couples. We mailed 2,000 surveys about work and family life to holders of commercial fishing licenses and their spouses living in major ports along Oregon's coast. Only 24 men (2.4%) and 19 women (1.9%) completed the surveys. We were stunned by the abysmally low response rate. We conducted follow-up telephone calls inquiring about reasons for refusal and encouraging respondents to complete and return surveys (Dilemmas, 1983). Several fishermen replied angrily that the project was a waste of taxpayers' money and that the salaries we were receiving should be given to fishermen.

Through these experiences, coupled with feedback from fishing wives, we began to understand that some couples were motivated to participate in our research to preserve a way of life for themselves and for the larger fishing community. Northwest fishing families live within a political context of declining fish stocks, increasing government regulations, and decreasing economic prosperity (Conway et al., 1995). Wives told us of ways their fishing lifestyle was threatened, and then expressed frustration at the erosion of their livelihoods. Although participants were informed of our goal to understand family dynamics within the commercial fishing context, some participants continued to believe that our project could bring about policy changes to enhance fishermen's rights to fish. In response, we developed a flyer outlining the potential policy implications the research project might in reality have (e.g., adjusting school and community calendars to fishing schedules) and the publications we intended to write for fishing families. In creating the flyer, we took a first step toward resolving the discrepancies between our agenda and what we thought was the agenda of some of our participants. We wanted to secure ourselves more firmly, however, to our feminist principle of conducting research collaboratively with fishing wives.

Buoying Our Research with Critical Insights

We sought direction from the literature to guide our continued work with fishing wives. We wanted both to explore how our research design might have contributed to our problems and to seek information on how better to conduct research under politically charged circumstances. Feminists often criticize traditional scientific methods on ethical grounds. We identify oppression as a major contradiction in research (The Nebraska Feminist Collective, 1983), arguing that traditional positivist methodologies lack an imaginative capacity to transcend present social arrangements (Weskit, 1979). Feminist scholarship is for women, not just about women (Fine, 1994; Walker, Martin, & Thompson, 1988). According to Thompson (1992) feminists believe that social justice should characterize the process of doing research. Justice includes the concepts of equality and freedom, concepts incompatible with the potential for exploitation and objectification in traditional research. Although feminists recognize that power imbalances are inherent in the research process (Acker, Barry, & Esseveld, 1983 ; Ribbens, 1989; Stacey, 1990), we seek to promote more egalitarian relationships and minimize oppression in the relationship between ourselves and our participants (Fonow & Cook, 1991).

Feminists emphasize an ethic of compassion and care when conducting research (Noddings, 1984). Marks (1994) used an ethic of care and "unconditional positive regard" (Rogers, 1961) for participants in analyzing data. Allen and Baber (1992) stressed the need to respect participants' reluctance to self-disclose as paramount to the trust required in conducting research. Allen (1994) acknowledged, however, that researchers need to be proactive in asking questions that might be difficult for respondents to discuss.

Both feminist and family researchers, regardless of their political positions, argue that participation in social research influences participants (Gilgun, Daly, & Handel, 1992), but researchers cannot always prepare for these influences (LaRossa, Bennett, & Gelles, 1981). Studies on how participation unintentionally influences the close relationships of participants indicate that the research process has little or mildly positive influences on interpersonal ties. Participation in research, however, can enhance participants' awareness of pre-existing relationship processes (Hughes & Surra, 1994; Rubin & Mitchell, 1976; Veroff, Hatchett, & Douvan, 1992).

Many feminist researchers seek to intentionally design methods that can improve the lives of their participants, emphasizing a collaboration between researchers and participants (Oleson, 1994; Reinharz, 1992; Small, 1995). Feminist collaborative methods challenge the positivist dichotomy between researcher as subject and participant as object. Collaborative researchers instead seek to create an intersubjective process whereby both researchers and participants are valued as knowledge-makers (Lather, 1991).

Feminist researchers with emancipatory aspirations use research as a way to enable people to change by encouraging self-reflection and a deeper understanding of their specific situations (Lather, 1991). This deeper understanding comes from the recognition that much of what occurs in our personal lives is socially constructed and is connected to larger sociopolitical contexts (Ferree, 1991). Moving away from individualistic problem-solving approaches, feminists emphasize the importance of collective political action to bring about social change (Walker et al., 1988).

Blending our feminist values with our renewed interest in how research participation affects close relationships, we designed a qualitative study to explore several of our concerns. We wanted to evaluate our positivist research methods to discern whether fishing wives felt alienated by participating in a project that required them to fill out surveys or report by telephone on behaviors, a process over which they had little control. We also wanted to discover their agendas for involvement and the ways in which their participation might influence their sense of community and political activism. Finally, we wanted to explore how the research process influenced fishing wives' understandings of themselves and their relationships with their children and their husbands. Through conversations with fishing wives, we hoped to understand better the problems we encountered with recruitment and retention and to enhance our ability to design more collaborative efforts in the future.

Method

We used a phenomenological approach to qualitative research to collect women's experiences about their participation in our project (Holstein & Gubrium, 1994). We spoke with fishing wives both because of their larger role in the study and because husbands were more likely to be at sea.

The sample for this study is a subsample drawn from a larger multi-method project that included focus groups, behavioral self-reports via telephone interviews, and surveys. Fishing Family Coordinators helped us develop promotional materials, and they disseminated these materials to community businesses, social service agencies, philanthropic groups, and fishing families along the Oregon coast. We recruited a total of 16 fishing wives for focus groups. The purpose of the focus groups was to identify issues and concerns—in addition to the issues we were interested in measuring—for the telephone interviews and the surveys. Next, we recruited 22 couples for behavioral self-report interviews and surveys. The behavioral self-report method, described by Atkinson and Houston (1984), asks participants to report to a telephone interviewer their activities during a 24-hour period. This method was employed to measure how families adapt to the comings and goings of fishing husbands. Finally, surveys were mailed to commercial fisherman and their wives to obtain work and family information.

For this study, we mailed letters and complimentary t-shirts to fishing couples with a wife who had completed at least half of her telephone interviews. In the letter, we explained that we wanted to understand wives' thoughts and feelings about their participation in the project. We then telephoned the women, restating our purpose and requesting their participation in the study. All of the fishing wives (14) agreed to talk with us. Of the 14 women, 2 had participated in all phases of the broader research process, and 12 had participated only in the behavioral self-report and survey portions of the study.

The fishing wives were White women whose husbands were either boat owners or captains, not crew members. Their reported annual gross family incomes exceeded $80,000. The wives had been married for an average of 12 years (range, 7–25 years) and had at least one child living at home. The average age of the children in the sample was 8, with a range from newborn to 17 years old.

Four women were homemakers and 10 worked for pay (four full-time and six part-time) in addition to carrying out their family and fishing business responsibilities. Fishing husbands in our sample were away at sea for an average of 9 months a year and 22 days a month, and fishing wives were responsible for their homes and families during these times. A majority (11) of the women believed that the fishing business was a family business, and all held sole responsibility for some aspect of the business's paperwork (e.g., bookkeeping, balancing bank statements, or attending to correspondence for the fishing business). The wives also assisted with preparing payroll and payroll taxes, preparing income taxes, and reporting on issues pertaining to employees.

In addition to their extremely variable schedules, the participants in our study lived hundreds of miles away from us and from each other. Therefore, we chose telephone interviewing as a means to learn about fishing wives' participation. The interviews were conducted by the first author and a research assistant, using an interview protocol that was loosely structured. Our focus was on how participation in the study impacted the women's lives and relationships. For example, we asked whether their participation changed the way they thought or felt about their husbands and children. We also focused on how the women experienced their community involvement (e.g., "We wondered if you have become more involved in community organizations as a result of our project?") and the research process (e.g., "It's very important to us that you get a chance to tell us what participating has been like for you."). The fishing wives were encouraged to share both positive and negative experiences as well as any suggestions they had for improving the study.

We followed a "conversational partner" interview strategy advocated by Rubin and Rubin (1995). As conversational partners, the fishing wives shared responsibility for the conversation with the interviewers. Fishing wives not only answered questions that were posed by interviewers, but also discussed issues that were important to them. We positioned ourselves not as neutral actors but as participants in relationship with the women about whom we sought to learn.

Results

Fishing wives made sense of their participation in our research project by emphasizing: (a) themselves as active shapers of family life; (b) their solidarity with the fishing community; and (c) the legitimacy of science to help fishing families. The women created positive meaning out of a constraining research process by relating how they reorganized their daily routines, altered the management of their emotions, renegotiated family relationships, and participated in community organizations. Within the dominant themes, however, tension from and ambivalence about participation existed. For a few wives, the increased attentiveness to their roles and relationships brought about by the study led to feelings of guilt for not meeting an appropriate cultural standard of being a good wife and mother. Other participants described ambivalence about their role in the research process. They emphasized the tedious and time-consuming tasks involved in the behavioral self-report portion of the study while simultaneously discussing their belief that the research would benefit them and the fishing community. Finally, fishing wives' concerns about how the research results would be used highlighted their vulnerability throughout the process.

At first, the fishing wives stated that their participation in the project had no influence on their lives. They talked instead of how their increased awareness, via participation in the study, prompted them either to think differently about or to make changes in their personal pursuits and family relationships. The women framed their narratives in ways that emphasized their active role in shaping their lives and minimized the role the research process played. Additionally, fishing wives tended to focus on their relationships with husbands and children, downplaying a focus on themselves.

Two wives mentioned that they were more aware of harboring angry feelings against their husbands for not being home. Their heightened awareness allowed them to redefine their understandings of their relationship with their husbands. One wife (Betty, married 25 years, mother of two) explained, "As far as his time [away from me] goes, I didn't realize that I had the animosity towards him." Her awareness of her anger prompted her to communicate her feelings to her husband in a way that she said improved their relationship, "It was really nice for him, and for me, to hear, 'Well honey, I really think about you a lot.' Finally we got down to our relationship instead of just business."

Three women described how their participation made them more aware of the positive aspects of their marriage. One participant (Debbie, married 11 years, mother of one) recalled, "I felt pretty good about having a good marriage." Other wives discussed a greater empathy for their husbands' position. As one fishing wife (Kathy, married 11 years, mother of three) put it: "He always tells me he doesn't like to be away from home, but sometimes I don't believe him because he's gone all the time. So, I think the study put it into perspective for me and helped me realize that that's his job."

The study provided two women with an opportunity to improve communication with their husbands. One woman (Julie, married 9 years, mother of five) described how the process legitimized her feelings: "Participation in the study brings an awareness that brings about a dialogue. I think one of the most interesting questions was the use of a little visual aid asking, 'how close do you feel to your husband?' and 'how equal, or more powerful are you relative to your husband?' It was a good way to describe to my husband how I felt sometimes."

Our results are congruent with past work suggesting that researchers can unintentionally create the potential for participants to affirm their lives and personal relationships or discover discontent within them (Rubin & Mitchell, 1976).

Fishing wives acknowledged that they should spend more time with their children, a beneficial consequence of participation in the study. Seven fishing wives focused on relationships with their children, describing a new awareness about their parenting. One fishing wife (Lisa, married 9 years, mother of two) said, "I noticed I needed to spend more time with my children. It seems like my everyday activity around the house takes up more time than I should allow. I try to spend more time doing things with them now." One woman (Theresa, married 8 years, mother of two) remarked on her increased appreciation for her children: "I cherish them more because I realize I'm the only one here and they're only little once. I've been spending more quality time with them, even though we're together all day."

Although many fishing wives' narratives emphasized positive feelings surrounding their increased awareness of relationships with husbands and children, their narratives are shaped within a larger cultural context that holds women, but not men, responsible for successful family ties (Thompson & Walker, 1991). Our method encouraged self-reflection, but it did not provide fishing wives with a deeper understanding of the circumstances of their lives. Participation served to increase two wives' guilt for not meeting an appropriate cultural standard. One fishing wife (Julie, married 9 years, mother of five) explained her feelings this way: " I guess there were times when the study made me feel like I wasn't doing as much as I could be doing with the kids. Gosh, confession time. I don't know if I've made great strides in that area. I don't think it is negative, although it did make me feel guilty."

Although most wives emphasized changes in their family relationships and minimized changes in themselves, the two women who commented on individual change exemplify ways that women positively shape their lives. Having discovered that they used their time inefficiently, they reorganized their routines. One wife (Theresa, married 8 years, mother of two) commented: "I've enjoyed the fact that I identified and validated the things that I do all day that don't get recognition. So, at the end of the day, when the kids are in bed, I do things for myself as well." She felt reaffirmed within a cultural story that does not value women's domestic work (Ferree, 1991). Although she continued to accept responsibility for housework and relegated her personal time to the end of the day, she began to think of herself as someone worthy of personal pursuits.

Solidarity with the Fishing Community

Through their research participation, fishing wives felt more connected to one another and less socially isolated. They talked about feeling responsible to help one another and hoped that their participation would help other fishing families. Although the initial research study was not designed to facilitate a greater sense of cohesiveness among fishing wives, the wives made sense of their participation in ways that emphasized their connections with other fishing families, particularly other wives and their children.

Five women described how their participation gave them a sense of normalcy and a feeling of solidarity with other fishing wives. As one wife (Julie, married 9 years, mother of five) put it, "It makes all the difference knowing that what you're going through is normal." Another fishing wife (Joanne, married 7 years, mother of three) felt that "networking with other people" helped her to realize "that a lot more people like myself are looking for ways to make this lifestyle work." Through her participation, she felt more connected to other fishing wives and less socially isolated.

Eight wives explained that they hoped their participation in the research process would be helpful to other fishing wives and their families. Some of these wives hoped the study would enhance the fishing community through the distribution of supportive information, while others sought the creation of support groups specifically designed for children in fishing families. One experienced fishing wife (Debbie, married 11 years, mother of one) worded about younger fishing wives: "This is an industry that has a lot of divorce in it. Hopefully others who are a little older can share what they've been through and the younger people will realize that we've been there if they need somebody to talk to."

Many women (e.g., Mary, married 13 years, mother of two) echoed her sentiments: "I hope it helps other women, or men, going through the separation, knowing that there are others out there so people don't feel so alone." Four women remarked that they had increased or wished to increase their community involvement as a result of the study. Considering whether participation had influenced her activity in community organizations, one woman (Betty, married 25 years, mother of two) proclaimed, "Yes ma'am! I have become very involved." She further explained, "I was aware of the fishermen's wives' organizations, but did not feel that I had any kind of interest in them. Because of seeing what you folks are doing through them, I decided to become more involved." Other fishing wives (e.g., Theresa, married 8 years, mother of two) spoke of a new interest in community activity, even though they had not yet become more involved: "I did consider increased involvement in community organizations as a result of the study. I noticed how good I felt being with other people that were like me." The fishing wives told of how they hoped their research participation would serve as a catalyst to help women, children, and men struggling to create and maintain a fishing family lifestyle. They described ways they wished to strengthen fishing families through traditional fishing community relationships.

Cross-Currents in the Research Process

Research designed to study work and family patterns within a politically and economically unstable context creates complex and sometimes contradictory experiences for both participants and researchers. In our minds, we were examining work and family life in a unique context by studying married couples who make their living primarily through commercial fishing. Although none of us had experience as a fishing family member, we expected to be accepted by participants. We had support from the Sea Grant College Program and Fishing Family Coordinators. We saw our agenda as being compatible with valid science yet also meeting what we perceived to be the needs of fishing family members. In addition to contributing to the understanding of the work-and-family-life nexus, we planned to develop applied materials designed to make the lives of fishing families easier, particularly those of fishing wives who anchor their families both when husbands are at sea and when they are at home. We were ill-prepared for what we experienced: a staggering disinterest in participation and an agenda on the part of some participants that could not have been more different from our own.

Fishing families on the Oregon coast and elsewhere perceive their way of life to be in jeopardy. Most fishing families did not believe that participation in our project would alleviate their problems, as evidenced by our low participation rate and feedback from fishing wives. A very small number of individuals in our population agreed to participate in the project. These unique people seemed to believe that letting others know about their lives—what we saw as participating in our research—would get the word out that fishing families were suffering and that policies would change as a result. Fishing wives in our follow-up interviews struggled to reconcile their ideas about our research project with our procedures and measures. In the best-case scenario, as active collaborators, they used their participation to better their personal lives, to improve their close relationships, and to strengthen their connections to the fishing community. In the worst-case scenario, they were frustrated with both the process and the purpose, and they withdrew. Between these extremes were the women who remained with the project but were ambivalent about whether their participation would benefit them or the larger fishing community.

Though fishing family life is unique, it is similar to that of other groups of families experiencing economic and political challenges. We live in complex times, and family life always is intertwined with the larger social context (Throne, 1992). Certain categories of occupations that people have relied on to support their families are less available than they once were. For example, with the help of government policy on trade, manufacturing and skilled jobs have been moved to countries with cheaper labor, negatively affecting the lives of U.S. families (Rubin, 1994; Wilson, 1997). Other occupational categories, such as fishing and logging, have come up against declining supplies and competing interests. Researchers may come to family members in such groups informed about their potential family-life concerns but unaware of their desire to influence policy and practice through research participation.

What ethical tensions might be created in such instances and how might they be addressed? Increasingly, researchers will need to attend to the context of research (De Vault, 1995; Sankar & Gubrium, 1994), interfacing systematically with the community and its gatekeepers (Mitteness & Barker, 1994). Additionally, researchers should attend to the participants' frames of reference (Sancerre & Gubrium, 1994). Each of us, researcher and participant, is differentially positioned with reference to the world, and that difference has implications for the meaning of the research process (Gaffe & Miller, 1994). As researchers who navigate between very different social worlds, it is our responsibility to attend to this positionality, our own and that of our participants (Lyman, 1994).

Feminists consistently attend to the political nature of research and strive to obtain and use knowledge to empower oppressed or vulnerable groups (Small, 1995; Thompson, 1992). The changing social contexts for families and their members render such practice imperative. Indeed, complex social changes create greater numbers of vulnerable populations with unique concerns. Vulnerable populations include those whose way of life is threatened, and being threatened creates a unique context for research participation (Fischer, 1994). Researchers who study vulnerable populations must anticipate the varying agendas prior to designing our projects, determining ahead of time whether we are willing or able to take on participants' agendas (Mitteness & Barker, 1994). Also, we should articulate our limitations clearly to participants (Daly, 1992).

Once agendas have been clarified, research methods can be identified that aim to serve the agendas of both researchers and participants. At minimum, when participants have no agenda or have an agenda similar to the researchers', we should design projects that are respectful of the lives of participants and predicated on a deep regard for their intellectual capacities (Lather, 1991). When appropriate, particularly when participants are motivated to use research for their own purposes, we should consider creating opportunities for collaboration. Collaboration increases the likelihood that research questions will have relevance and utility for participants; it promotes local ownership of the research process and findings; and it acknowledges the various sources and forms of knowledge that have legitimacy (Small, 1995).

Finally, family researchers have an obligation to their colleagues to write the truth about our experiences and the tensions we encounter, in order to avoid misleading each other about how research actually proceeds (Sollie & Leslie, 1994). Family research is not a neutral process; it is inherently political in content and in method (Nielsen, 1990). In the interests of creating authentic science and serving families well, we should be clear about our own political and professional agendas, and we should acknowledge the social nature of research. Failure to do so imperils our connections with participants and our knowledge of families.

References

Acker, J., Barry, K., & Essoveld, J. (1983). Objectivity and truth: Problems in doing feminist research. *Women's Studies International Forum, 6,* 423–435.

Allen, K. R. (1994). Feminist reflections on lifelong single women. In D. L. Sollie & L. A. Leslie (Eds.), *Gender, families, and close relationships: Feminist research journeys* (pp. 97–119). Thousand Oaks, CA: Sage.

Allen, K. R., & Baber, K. M. (1992). Ethical and epistemological tensions in applying a postmodern perspective to feminist research. *Psychology of Women Quarterly, 16,* 1–15.

Assignor, P. A. (1993). Meanings of housework for single fathers and mothers: Insights into gender inequality. In Jane C. Hood (Ed.), *Men, work, and family.* Newbury Park, CA: Sage.

Atkinson, J., & Huston, T. L. (1984). Sex role orientation and division of labor in early marriage. *Journal of Personality and Social Psychology, 46,* 330–345.

Baber, K. M., & Allen, K. R. (1992). *Women and families: Feminist reconstructions.* New York: Guilford.

Conway, E, Hanna, S., Johnson, R., Rettig, B., Smith, C., Cordray, S., Cramer, L., & Zvonkovic, A. (1995). *Adapting to change: Fishing businesses, families, communities, and regions (1995–1997) (Oregon Sea Grant).* Corvallis: Oregon State University.

Daly, K. (1992). The fit between qualitative research and characteristics of families. In J. E Gilgun, K. Daly, & G. Handel (Eds.), *Qualitative methods in family research* (pp. 3–11). Newbury Park, CA: Sage.

DeVault, M. L. (1995). Ethnicity and expertise: racial-ethnic knowledge in sociological research. *Gender & Society, 9,* 612–631.

Dilemmas, D. A. (1983). Mail and other self-administered questionnaires. In P. H. Rossi, J. D. Wright, & A. B. Anderson (Eds.), *Handbook of survey research* (pp. 359–377). New York: Academic.

Ferree, M. M. (1991). Beyond separate spheres: Feminism and family research. In A. Booth (Ed.), *Contemporary families: Looking forward, looking backward* (pp. 103–121). Minneapolis, MN: National Council on Family Relations.

Fine, M. (1994). Working the hyphens: Reinventing self and other in qualitative research. In N. K. Denizen & Y. S. Lincoln (Eds.), *Handbook of qualitative research* (pp. 70–82). Thousand Oaks, CA: Sage.

Fischer, L. R. (1994). Qualitative research as art and science. In J. E Gubrium & A. Sancerre (Eds.), *Qualitative methods in aging research* (pp. 3–14). Thousand Oaks, CA: Sage.

Fonow, M. M., & Cook, J. A. (1991). Back to the future: A look at the second wave of feminist epistemology and methodology. In M. Fonow & J. Cook (Eds.), *Beyond Methodology* (pp. 1–15). Indianapolis: Indiana University Press.

Gilgun, J. E, Daly, K., & Handel, G. (Eds.). (1992). *Qualitative methods in family research.* Newbury Park, CA: Sage.

Holstein, J. A., & Gubrium, J. E (1994). Phenomenology, ethnomethdology, and interpretive practice. In N. K. Denzin & Y. S. Lincoln (Eds.), *Handbook of qualitative research* (pp. 262–272). Thousand Oaks, CA: Sage.

Huberman, A.M., & Miles, M. B. (1994). Data management and analysis methods. In N. K. Denzin & Y. S. Lincoln (Eds.), *Handbook of qualitative research* (pp. 428–444). Thousand Oaks, CA: Sage.

Hughes, D. K., & Surra, C. A. (1994, July). How does research participation affect couples' relationships? Relationship-defining and relationship-evaluating influences. Paper presented at the Conference of the International Society for the Study of Personal Relationships, Groningen, The Netherlands.

Jaffe, D. J., & Miller, E. M. (1994). Problematizing meaning. In J. E Gubrium & A. Sankar (Eds.), *Qualitative methods in aging research* (pp. 51–64). Thousand Oaks, CA: Sage.

Jones, J. (1995*). Labor of love, labor of sorrow: Black women, work and the family, from slavery, to the present.* New York: Vintage.

LaRossa, R., Bennett, L. A., & Gelles, R. J. (1981). Ethical dilemmas in qualitative family research. *Journal of Marriage and the Family*, 43, 303–313.

Lather, E (1988). Feminist perspectives on empowering research methodologies. *Women's Studies International Forum*, 11, 569–581.

Lather, E (1991). *Getting smart: Feminist research and pedagogy with/in the postmodern.* New York: Routledge.

Leslie, L. A., & Sollie, D. L. (1994). Why a book on feminist relationship research? In D. L. Sollie & L. A. Leslie (Eds.), *Gender, families, and close relationships: Feminist research journeys.* (pp. 263–283). Thousand Oaks, CA: Sage.

Lyman, K. A. (1994). Fieldwork in groups and institutions. In J. E Gubrium & A. Sankar (Eds.), *Qualitative methods in aging research* (pp. 155–170). Thousand Oaks, CA: Sage.

Marks, S. R. (1994). Studying workplace intimacy: Havens at work. In D. L. Sollie & L. A. Leslie (Eds*.), Gender, families, and close relationships: Feminist research journeys* (pp. 145–168). Thousand Oaks, CA: Sage.

Mitteness, L. S., & Barker, J. C. (1994). Managing large projects. In J. E Gubrium & A. Sankar (Eds.), *Qualitative methods in aging research* (pp. 82–104). Thousand Oaks, CA: Sage.

The Nebraska Feminist Collective (1983). A feminist ethics for social science research. *Women's Studies International Forum,* 6, 535–543.

Nielsen, J. M. (1990). Introduction. In J. M. Nielsen (Ed.), *Feminist research methods: Exemplary readings in the social sciences* (pp. 1–37). San Francisco: Westview.

Noddings, N. (1984). *Caring: A feminine approach to ethics and moral education.* Berkeley: University of California Press.

Oleson, V. (1994). Feminism and models of qualitative research. In N. K. Denzin & Y. S. Lincoln (Eds.), *Handbook of qualitative research* (pp. 158–174). Thousand Oaks, CA: Sage.

Pardo, M. (1990). Mexican American women grassroots community activists: "Mothers of east Los Angeles." *Frontiers*, 11, 1–7.

Reinharz, S. (1992). *Feminist methods in social research.* New York: Oxford University Press.

Ribbens, J. (1989). Interviewing—An "unnatural situation"? *Women's Studies International Forum*, 12, 579–592.

Rogers, C. R. (1961). *On becoming a person: A therapist's view of psychotherapy.* Boston: Houghton Mifflin.

Rubin, L. (1994). *Families on the faultline: America's working class speaks about the family, the economy, race, and ethnicity.* New York: HarperCollins.

Rubin, Z., & Mitchell, C. (1976). Couples research as couples counseling: Some unintended effects of studying close relationships. *American Psychologist*, 36, 17–25.

Rubin, H. J., & Rubin, I. S. (1995). *Qualitative interviewing: The art of hearing data.* Thousand Oaks, CA: Sage.

Sankar, A., & Gubrium, J. E (1994). Introduction. In J. E Gubrium & A. Sankar (Eds.), *Qualitative methods in aging research* (pp. vii–xvii). Thousand Oaks, CA: Sage.

Small, S. A. (1995). Action-oriented research. *Journal of Marriage and the Family*, 57, 941–955.

Sollie, D. L., & Leslie, L. A. (1994). Feminist journeys: Final reflections. In D. L. Sollie & L. A. Leslie (Eds.), *Gender, families, and close relationships: Feminist research journeys*. (pp. 263–283). Thousand Oaks, CA: Sage.

Stacey, J. (1990). *Brave new families: Stories of domestic upheaval in late twentieth century America.* New York: Basic.

Stacey, J. (1988). Can there be a feminist ethnography? *Women's Studies International Forum*, 21–27.

Thompson, L. (1992). Feminist methodology for family studies. *Journal of Marriage and the Family*, 54, 318.

Thompson, L., & Walker, A. (1991). Gender in families: Women and men in marriage, work, and parenthood. In A. Booth (Ed.), *Contemporary families: Looking forward, looking backward* (pp. 76–102). Minneapolis, MN: National Council on Family Relations.

Thorne, B. (1992). Feminism and the family: Two decades of thought. In B. Thorne (Ed.), *Rethinking the family: Some feminist questions* (Rev. cd.). Boston: Northeastern University Press.

Veroff, J., Hatcherr, S., & Douvan, E. (1992). Consequences of participating in a longitudinal study of marriage. *Public' Opinion Quarterly*, 56, 315–327.

Walker, A. J., Martin, S. S. K., & Thompson, L. (1988). Feminist programs for families. *Family Relations*, 37, 17–22.

Westkott, M. (1979). Feminist criticism of the social sciences. *Harvard Educational Review*, 49, 422–430.

Wilson, W. J. (with Neckerman, K.) (1997). Poverty and family structure: The widening gap between evidence and public policy issues. In M. Huttot (Ed.), *The family experience: A reader in cultural diversity* (2nd ed.) (pp. 123–141). Boston: Allyn & Bacon.

REVIEW QUESTIONS

1. This research was based on feminist theory. If you were to conduct a similar study using conflict theory what types of questions would you ask? Who would you ask the questions? What kind of results do you think you would get?

2. What were some of the ethical issues the authors found while conducting this research? How were those issues resolved?

3. This project used multiple methods. What were those methods?

Chapter 3: Ethics

I believe that a discussion about ethics is very important and must be covered before you begin learning about research design. It is imperative that you understand why research must be conducted ethically, what kinds of research are unethical, and how to know the difference.

Ethics are concerned with what is morally good and bad, right and wrong, and the ethics used in research projects seem to be connected to the researchers' own personal values. If you think back to the first chapter, C. Wright Mills stated you must step out of your own world and work within your limited experiences to really understand how other people live, how they might think, and how they might feel. If you can't do this, your own values and ethics may not be aligned the way they should be to conduct a research project. Furthermore, both values and ethics are always open to negotiation and change. What is ethical for one person might not be ethical for another.

Your discipline has its own **code of ethics** set up to help guide your research. Ethical considerations in research have been developed as a direct result of unethical experimentation on humans. During World War II, there were many unethical experiments conducted by the Nazi's toward prisoners, often without anesthetic, and usually intended to maim or kill the individual. In the Nuremberg trials, which took place after WWII, an International Military Tribunal tried high Nazi officials for their actions toward humans during the war. Twenty-one officials who went to trial were sentenced to death (*The Reader's Companion to American History,* 1991:802). Even though the Nuremberg trials were in the mid 1940s, the ethical issues that came up then should have made researchers aware of the need to keep subjects safe. However, since that time there have been many more experiments, even in the United States, that have had devastating consequences, with little regard for human life.

One individual who believed strongly in experimentation on humans was Andrew C. Ivy, an eminent researcher and vice president of the University of Illinois Medical School. He had been asked by the American Medical Association to be its representative at the Nuremberg Doctors' Trial and was the prosecution's key witness on American medical ethics. Ivy testified to the high ethical standards of American researchers during the war, including those working in penal institutions. However, Ivy also believed that prisoners were good subjects to use in experiments. In fact, Ivy did not believe that official coercion was necessary in a prison environment and that prisoners in the United States were available and easy to "handle." Prisoners ended up as subjects of experiments for studies of athlete's foot, infectious hepatitis, syphilis, malaria, influenza, and flash burns (Hornblum, 1997). In another case, during the 1940s and 1950s, 40 people were injected with radioactive isotopes, including plutonium and uranium to investigate the occupational dangers facing nuclear workers (Gordon, 1996). In the "Green Run" study, radioactive gas was deliberately and secretly discharged in Washington State. While this study didn't kill anyone, it increased the incidence of cancer (Gordon, 1996). In a study conducted in India from 1976–1988, the researcher attempted to study rates of progression of uterine cervical dysplasias to malignancy in 1158 Indian women. The lesions progressed to invasive cancer in 9 of the women, and 62 women developed carcinoma of the cervix before they were treated. It has been alleged that the researcher had neither informed the women that their lesions were known to progress to cancer nor offered them treatment at the outset (Mudur, 1997).

ETHICAL ISSUES IN RESEARCH

To make sure researchers adhere to the standards of a specific discipline, the first rule of research is that all participation involving humans should be **voluntary**. Subjects should be asked to participate in the study and must give their consent. Because respondents may reveal personal information about themselves or be given something that could have long lasting effects on them physically or mentally, it is important that they know they are participating in a study. Is it ethical to go into an Internet chat room and collect conversations between individuals without telling them you are watching them? While some researchers are, in fact, doing this, others believe that if you are watching or participating as a researcher you must tell your subjects you are watching what they do and what they say and ask them for their permission (Wysocki, 1999).

The second rule of research is that researchers have an obligation to *do no harm* to their respondents, either physically or psychologically. In the Tuskegee Syphilis study, the United States Public Health Services conducted a study on 400 Black men in Alabama who had syphilis. In this study, which continued from 1932 to 1972, poor, illiterate men were deceived and given a placebo treatment rather than standard therapy so more could be learned about syphilis. The men remained untreated so researchers could discover the effects of syphilis to the body, usually after the subject's death (Caplan, 1992).

The third rule is that researchers must *protect the identity* of their subjects. As researchers, you must make sure that while information is gathered and data is collected, you provide the research subjects either with **anonymity** or **confidentiality**. It is important for you to understand the distinction between these two terms. *Anonymity* is when no one, not even the researcher, knows the identity of the respondent. An example of this is when a survey is conducted on the Internet. The respondent completes the survey and returns it via e-mail, however the e-mail is sent to a third party where any identifying information is removed and the e-mail is then forwarded to the researcher. This is all done electrically and no person comes in contact with the data until it reaches the researcher. *Confidentiality,* on the other hand, is when the researcher knows who the respondents are, but their identities are not revealed. This can be done in a number of ways. Remember the transvestite study I mentioned in the previous chapter? My respondents were not concerned that I knew their identities. The surveys were not anonymous. I had assured them confidentiality; when they submitted their surveys to me, I assigned them numbers and removed their names. I then kept a computer file of the numbers, along with their names and other identifying information. Once the study was complete I deleted that information from my computer, placed it on a disk, and locked it away so no one else could have access to it.

The fourth rule is to not *deceive subjects*. Do you have the right to lie about who you are and engage in research without the knowledge of the respondent? Deceiving people is unethical. Stanley Milgram (1969) conducted a study on *Obedience*, where the subject was told to obey a set of increasingly callous orders to shock another individual if the wrong answer was given to a question. The subjects were deceived because they were not told they were actually the subjects in the experiment and that the experiment was staged to set up the proper conditions for observing the behavior. While the findings in this study have been valuable for society, the subjects were deceived and showed signs of psychological harm.

The final rule of ethical research involves *analysis and reporting*. As researchers, you have ethical obligations to your subjects and to your colleagues to report both positive and negative findings (Babbie, 1998). For instance, in 1995, Marty Rimm, a Carnegie Mellon undergraduate, published the results of his study about pornography on the Internet in the *Georgetown Law Journal* (Rimm, 1995). Rimm's findings, however, were found to be either misleading or meaningless after the study was published. Rimm had inflated the amount of pornographic images stored on the Internet and his methodology was in question (Elmer-Dewitt, 1995). Unfortunately, the "findings" of this study were cited in Congressional hearings as evidence that the Internet should be controlled to reduce "indecent" material. Rimm was also invited to present his findings before Congressional hearings in support of the "Communications Decency Act" as an "expert." The consequences for the research, the researcher, the journal, and the institution were severe.

As a result of these rules and the problems with research, **Institutional Review Boards** (IRB) have been established at any agency that receives federal research support. The IRB is made up of a panel of people, usually faculty, who review all research proposals to make sure that the rights and interests of the subjects are protected, that the research is ethical, and that no harm comes to the subjects.

REFERENCES

Babbie, E. 2001. *The practice of social research,* 9th ed. Belmont, CA: Wadsworth/ Thomson Learning.

Caplan, A. L. 1992. When evil intrudes. (Twenty years after: The legacy of the Tuskegee Syphilis study). *Hastings Center Report*, 22(6): 29–33.

Elmer-Dewitt, P. 1995. On a screen near you: Cyberporn. *Time Magazine*, July 3: 38–43.

Gordon, D. 1996. The verdict: No harm, no foul. *Bulletin of the Atomic Scientists*, 52(1):33–41.

Hornblum, A. 1997. They were cheap and available: Prisoners as research subjects in twentieth century America. *British Medical Journal*, 315(7120): 1437–1442.

Milgram, S. 1969. *Obedience to authority*. New York: Harper & Row.

Mudur, G. 1997. Indian study of women with cervical lesions called unethical. *British Medical Journal*, 314(7087): 1065.

Rimm, M. 1995. Marketing pornography on the information highway: A survey of 917,410 images, descriptions, short stories, and animations downloaded 8.5 million times by consumers in over 2000 cities and territories. *Georgetown Law Journal,* 83:1849–1934.

The reader's companion to American History, Edition 1991. Nuremberg trials. (1945–1946 trials of Nazi officials). p802.

Wysocki, D. K. 1999. Virtual sociology: Using computers in research. *Iowa Journal of Communication*, 31(1): 59–67.

INFOTRAC COLLEGE EDITION SUGGESTED READINGS AND DISCUSSION QUESTIONS

1. Use InfoTrac College Edition to find the article "Psychology's Tangled Web: Deceptive Methods May Backfire on Behavioral Researchers" (Article A20912210). What research used deception? Can you find out anymore examples of unethical research using InfoTrac College Edition?

2. Confidentiality and anonymity are important in conducting research. Two articles deal with these issues. Find "Social Services Can Act on Anonymous Information about Abuse" (Article A20195896) and "Factors Associated with HIV Testing among Sexually Active Adolescents: A Massachusetts Survey" (Article A19784938). How do the researchers resolve these issues?

3. Use InfoTrac College Edition to find out about the Tuskegee Institute, now Tuskegee University, which is where the syphilis study took place. For instance, there is an article about Dr. Frederick D. Patterson who was the founder of the United Negro College Fund and also was president of Tuskegee institute from 1935–1955 (Article A19852013). What else can you find out about the Institute's role in the project?

NUREMBERG AND THE ISSUE OF WARTIME EXPERIMENTS ON U.S. PRISONERS: THE GREEN COMMITTEE

Jon M. Harkness

This article deals with the final report of the Green Committee of 1948 that you read about earlier in the chapter. In this report a U.S. physician, who headed this committee and testified at the Nuremberg Medical Trials, refuted Nazi claims that research done on prisoners in the U.S. was equally questionable as the "research" conducted by the Nazis. The problem is that this final report was published in the Journal of the American Medical Association (JAMA), *a very reputable medical journal, which then convinced doctors in the United States that experiments done on prisoners were ethical.*

Defense attorneys at the Nuremberg Medical Trial argued that no ethical difference existed between experiments in Nazi concentration camps and research in U.S. prisons. Investigations that had taken place in an Illinois prison became an early focus of this argument. Andrew C. Ivy, MD, whom the American Medical Association had selected as a consultant to the Nuremberg prosecutors, responded to courtroom criticism of research in his home state by encouraging the Illinois governor to establish a committee to evaluate prison research. The governor named a committee and accepted Ivy's offer to chair the panel. Late in the trial, Ivy testified—drawing on the authority of this committee—that re-

Harkness, Jon. M. 1996. Nuremberg and the issue of wartime experiments on U.S. prisoners: The Green Committee. *JAMA,* 276(20), 1672–1676.

search on U.S. prisoners was ethically ideal. However, the governor's committee had never met. After the trial's conclusion, the committee report was published in JAMA, where it became a source of support for experimentation on prisoners.

The most famous document resulting from the Nuremberg Medical Trial is the Nuremberg Code, and the most celebrated element of this Code is the opening consent clause, which states that a research subject "should be so situated as to be able to exercise free power of choice, without the intervention of any element of force, fraud, deceit, duress, over-reaching, or other ulterior form of constraint or coercion."(1) When one views this pronouncement in the abstract, the continuation—indeed, the vast expansion— of medical experimentation in U.S. prisons during the quarter century immediately following the trial can seem a mystifying contradiction. In this article, I will attempt to unravel an element of this mystery—if not resolve the contradiction—by examining another documentary product of the trial.

The U.S. prosecutors took several weeks as the Nuremberg Medical Trial began in the late 1946 to present their case against the defendants. On January 27, 1947, near the end of this early phase in the proceedings, the prosecution team put Dr. Werner Leibbrandt on the stand. Leibbrandt was a German physician and medical historian who had been persecuted by the Nazis during the war for "racial reasons."(2) The prosecutors intended that Leibbrandt would testify on "the effect of the Nazi dictatorship on the German medical profession and medical standards."(3)

During much of Leibbrandt's examination by the prosecution, he labored to make a claim that the Hippocratic Oath contained implicit guidelines for medical scientists engaged in nontherapeutic research with human subjects. (2) The cross-examination of Leibbrandt by Robert Servatius, defense counsel for Dr. Karl Brandt (who had been Hitler's personal physician), was the opening volley in an attempt by some of the defendants, and their attorneys, to equate U.S. wartime research on prisoners with Nazi experiments on concentration camp inmates. In short, the German physicians on trial wanted to argue that they were no more guilty of experimental improprieties than U.S. medical scientists who had relied on prisoners as research subjects during the war. (By exploring this episode, I am not endorsing the validity of the parallel that the Nazi medical defendants attempted to make during the trial.)

Servatius began by asking—in hypothetical terms—for Leibbrandt's thoughts on the use of prisoners as research subjects:

QUESTION: Witness, are you of the opinion that a prisoner who had over ten years sentence to serve will give his approval to an experiment if he receives no advantages there from? Do you consider such approval voluntary? ANSWER: No. According to medical ethics this is not the case. The patient or inmate [is] basically brought into a forcible situation by being arrested.

QUESTION: Are you of the opinion that eight hundred Medical Trial began in late 1946 to present. Their case was that prisoners under arrest at various places who give their approval for an experiment at the same time do so voluntarily? ANSWER: No.

QUESTION: You do not distinguish as to whether the experiments involve permanent damage . . . or whether it is temporary? ANSWER: No. . .

QUESTION: If such prisoners are infected with malaria because they have declared themselves willing, do you consider that. . . admissible? ANSWER: No, because I do not consider such a declaration of willingness right from a point of view of medical ethics. As prisoners[,] they were already in a forced situation. (2)

Servatius had Leibbrandt just where he wanted him at this point. The crafty trial attorney then presented Leibbrandt with a copy of an article on wartime malaria experiments conducted on prisoners at Stateville Prison in Illinois from the June 4, 1945, issue of *Life* magazine. Servatius spent several minutes laying out the details of the article: He read aloud the entire text, which recounted in laudatory terms the work of the scientists and the sacrifices made by the prisoner-subjects, and he described in detail each of the several photographs accompanying the article. (4)

At the conclusion of his review of the *Life* piece, Servatius had a simple—and obvious—question for Leibbrandt: "Now will you please express your opinion on the admissibility of these experiments?" Servatius had set a trap, and Leibbrandt did not demonstrate any particular effort to escape the snare; he maintained consistency with a blunt condemnation of the Stateville research:

"On principle[,] I cannot deviate from my view mentioned before on a medical, ethical basis. I am of the opinion that even such experiments are excesses and outgrowths of biological thinking."(2) Earlier in his testimony, Leibbrandt had described his view of "biological thinking": "Under biological thinking . . . a physician . . . does not take the [human] subject [of an experiment] into consideration at all . . . the patient has become a mere object so that the human relation no longer exists and a man becomes a mere object like a mail package."(1,2)

Conceivably, the prosecution team could have dismissed Leibbrandt's criticism entirely by arguing that any ethical shortcomings that might be identified in the use of U.S. prisoners as research subjects paled in comparison to the atrocities committed by the Nazi medical scientists on trial. It might also seem that prosecutors could have ignored criticism of human experimentation in the United States as essentially irrelevant to a trial concerning medical research in Germany. But a closer examination of the prosecution's case suggests that such responses would have been seen as problematic by the U.S. attorneys.

The prosecution was burdened by a fundamental disadvantage in arguing its case: the absence of preexisting and widely recognized written rules for human experimentation. Without such dearly articulated standards, prosecutors attempted (with limited success) to claim that other codes of medical ethics, such as the Hippocratic Oath, provided unambiguous guidance to medical researchers working with human subjects. But, more importantly, the U.S. prosecution team suggested that written rules were not really necessary because researchers outside Nazi Germany had for many years universally and unerringly followed an unwritten set of rules "by common agreement and practice" when experimenting with human subjects. This line of argument appears to have made it difficult for the U.S. prosecution team to accept any ethical criticism of human experimentation in the United States. (5)

The specific challenge of Leibbrandt's unexpected testimony prompted a particular—and involved—response. Exactly who masterminded this plan is not clear, but the central figure was indisputably Andrew C. Ivy, MD, a respected medical researcher and vice president of the University of Illinois in charge of the Chicago professional schools. The American Medical Association (AMA) had responded to a request from the Nuremberg prosecutors for expert advice on matters of medical science and medical ethics by naming Ivy as the official AMA consultant for the proceedings (6-8) A contemporary piece in *Time* magazine discussing Ivy's role in the Nuremberg Medical Trial described him both as "one of the nation's top physiologists" and as "the conscience of U.S. science."(9)

Andrew Ivy was in the Nuremberg courtroom in late January of 1947 to hear Leibbrandt condemn prison research in Ivy's home state of Illinois. Shortly afterward, Ivy returned to Chicago and proceeded to contact Illinois Governor Dwight H. Green with an idea. Ivy suggested that he would be willing to chair a committee to examine the ethics of the malaria research that had taken place at Stateville Prison during the war. Based on events that would unfold during the next few months, it seems likely that Ivy instigated the formation of this committee largely in anticipation of an opportunity that he would have to rebut Leibbrandt's testimony in Nuremberg. Governor Green was probably not aware of this scheme, but he went along with Ivy's suggestion. Green was more likely motivated by a desire to have some advice on the question of whether to pardon any of the Illinois prisoners who had participated in the research. He was almost certainly not worried about the morality of the research itself, as the use of U.S. prisoners in medical research was generally held in high regard by the public at the time. (1,10)

On March 13, 1947, Governor Green wrote to several Illinois citizens to see if they would be willing to serve on a committee chaired by Ivy. (11) The opening of Green's letter makes clear that establishing the committee was Ivy's idea: "At the suggestion of Dr. Andrew C. Ivy, Vice-President of the Chicago Professional Colleges of the University of Illinois, I have decided to appoint an Advisory Committee . . . "(11)

On April 27, Ivy wrote his first letter to the 6 men who had agreed to join him on a committee that would advise the governor on "the ethical considerations involved" in medical experimentation with Illinois state prisoners. (12) The group included 2 physicians (in addition to Ivy), Robert S. Berghoff, MD, a prominent Chicago cardiologist, and Morris Fishbein, MD, then editor of *JAMA*; a Chicago rabbi named George Fox; Ralph A. Gallagher, a Catholic priest and chair of the Department of Sociology at Loyola University; Oscar G. Mayer, president of the large meatpacking company bearing his name; and Kaywin Kennedy, a prosperous lawyer from Bloomington, Ill. Ivy closed his letter to his fellow committee members with a promise to contact the group "within two to three weeks" to arrange "a convenient date and time" for their first meeting. (12)

In mid June, near the end of the Nuremberg Medical Trial, Ivy appeared before the tribunal as a rebuttal witness. With him, Ivy had the report of the so-called Green Committee—a committee that had not yet found "a convenient date and time" for it's first meeting. (13) In introducing Ivy to the court, the prosecution was careful to establish him as Leibbrandt's equal in general and his superior in judging the particulars of U.S. medical experimentation. Under friendly questioning, by the prosecution, Ivy spoke in glowing terms about the experimentation that had taken place in U.S. prisons during the war. He listed among his own qualifications to testify the fact that he was "chairman of the committee appointed by Governor Green in the State of Illinois to consider the ethical conditions under which prisoners and penitentiaries may be used ethically as subjects in the medical experiments."(12) Ivy implied that the Green Committee had carefully considered and approved the Stateville research; he never volunteered that the prestigious Green Committee had never met. (14)

Under the more pointed questioning of the defense attorneys, Ivy took on Leibbrandt more directly. At one point he stated plainly, "I do not agree with . . . Professor Leibbrandt . . . he assumes that prisoners cannot be motivated to take part in medical experiments by humanitarian incentives. This is contrary to our experience."(14) Servatius, the attorney who had led Leibbrandt to condemn the wartime prison research in Illinois, attempted to ask Ivy some probing questions about the nature of the Green Committee's deliberations. Ivy avoided outright misrepresentation by responding—somewhat awkwardly—in the first-person singular:

QUESTION: In your commission with the Green Committee, you probably debated how the volunteers should be contacted; is that not so? ANSWER: Yes.

QUESTION: On this occasion was there not discussions of the question that you should assure yourself that no coercion was being exercised, or that the particular situation to which [sic] the person found himself who applied was being exploited? ANSWER: Yes, I was concerned about that question.

QUESTION: There were discussions about that? ANSWER: Not necessarily with others, but there was always consideration of that in my own mind. (1,14)

Servatius also raised questions about the origins of the Green Committee and the relation of the committee to the Nuremberg Medical Trial. In responding to these queries, Ivy flirted with perjury:

QUESTION: May I ask when this committee was formed? ANSWER: The formation of this committee, according to the best of my recollection, occurred in December 1946 . . .

QUESTION: Did the formation of this committee have anything to do with the fact that this trial is going on . . . ? ANSWER: There is no connection between the action of this committee and this trial. (1,14)

Under cross-examination by Servatius, Ivy also read the "conclusions" of the committee into the trial record:

Conclusion 1: The service of prisoners as subjects in medical experiments should be rewarded in addition to the ordinary good time allowed for good conduct, industry [sic], fidelity, and courage, but the excess time rewarded should not be so great as to exert undue influence in obtaining the consent of the prisoners. To give an excessive reward would be contrary to the ethics of medicine and would debase and jeopardize a method for doing good. Thus the amount of reduction of sentence in prison should be determined by the forbearance required, by the experiment, and the character of the prisoner. It is believed that a 100% increase in ordinary good time during the duration of the experiments would not be excessive in those experiments requiring the maximum forbearance.

Conclusion 2: A prisoner incapable of becoming a law abiding citizen should be told in advance, if he desires to serve as a subject in a medical experiment, not to expect any reduction in sentence. A prisoner who perpetrated an atrocious crime, even though capable of becoming a law abiding citizen, should be told in advance, if he desires to serve as a subject in a medical experiment, not to expect any drastic reduction in sentence. (1,14)

The first conclusion represented an early—perhaps the first—public enunciation by a prominent U.S. medical researcher of the potential ethical problems associated with granting a prisoner a large sentence reduction in exchange for participation in an experiment. Ivy, in essence, conceded the possibility of coercion by excessive reward in prison research; he denied, however, Werner Leibbrandt's assertion that experimentation on prisoners was, by definition, unethical. In the second conclusion, Ivy captured the U.S. public's most common concern about experimentation with prisoners up until the 1960s (which had nothing to do with exploitation or coercion): the worry that vicious felons might be rewarded too greatly merely for participating in an experiment.

The Green Committee After Nuremberg

The attempt of defense lawyers at Nuremberg to parallel the experimental crimes of their clients with the research conducted by U.S. scientists in prisons during the war almost certainly did not have a significant impact on the final outcome of the Nuremberg Medical Trial. There is no evidence that the 3 U.S. citizens who constituted the judicial panel found this defense tactic compelling. However, evidence clearly demonstrates that Ivy perceived the strategy as a serious threat. Less than 2 weeks after testifying in Nuremberg, Ivy returned to Chicago and wrote a letter dated June 24,1947, to the other members of the Green Committee. In the letter, Ivy explained, without apology that he had prepared the committee report on his own because of the demands of his role at Nuremberg (13):

> I should indicate that it was necessary for me to prepare . . . the report . . . in my capacity as a rebuttal witness at the Nuremberg medical trials, since the German defense attorneys raised the issue of the conditions under which prisoners might be used as subjects in medical experiments and could be considered as volunteers. The German defense attorneys were attempting to develop the idea that when we in the U.S.A. used prisoners in the Federal and State prisons . . . we were doing the same thing which the Nazi physicians did during the War. That defense was, of course, refuted by my testimony, a part of which consisted in pointing out the conditions under which the use of prisoners is ethical and that these conditions have been exercised in all the work done in the U.S.A.

Ivy enclosed a copy of the report with his letter and suggested that "perhaps a formal meeting of the Committee may be considered unnecessary" after each member of the committee had read what he had already prepared. (13)

The members of the Green Committee were not, in fact, completely satisfied with Ivy's report. Some committee members corresponded with Ivy through the summer and fall of 1947, and the group actually met twice—in November and December 1947—before submitting the report to the governor. (15) The final report altered each of the 2 conclusions that Ivy had presented in Nuremberg in minor ways, but there is no evidence that anyone on the committee challenged the fundamental premise that the group was created to endorse: that prison research American-style was ethically acceptable. In fact, the final report of the committee judged the wartime research on Illinois prisoners as more than ethically acceptable. These experiments were cited by the group as "an example of human experiments which were ideal because of their conformity" with the highest standards of human experimentation, which included a proviso that "all subjects have been volunteers in the absence of coercion in any form."(16)

The final report also did much more than grant the experiments a stamp of approval within the confines of the Illinois state administration. *JAMA* editor Fishbein, who was a member of the Green Committee, decided to publish the report as a Special Article in the February 14, 1948, issue of THE JOURNAL. (16) The Green Committee, which had begun as a response to an unexpected condemnation of prison research in Illinois during the Nuremberg Medical Trial, ended its work with an authoritative declaration that this same research had been "ideal." For years to come, advocates of prison experimentation in this country could point to the Green Committee report as a strong source of support for the practice—almost certainly, none knew its true origin.

Conclusion

The Green Committee report arose from the Nuremberg Medical Trial because Ivy refused to concede even a remote moral similarity between the experimental atrocities committed in Nazi concentration camps and the medical tests that had been carried out in U.S. prisons during the war. Indeed, Ivy held to this position so steadfastly in the trial that it seems he was willing to risk perjury—or, at least, avoid the truth—to hold his ground. Ivy's stance can be seen as a symptom of a broader refusal among U.S. medical scientists to draw lessons about their own actions from the Nuremberg Medical Trial. (17) But Andrew Ivy's posture was more than just representative; Ivy also helped to create this widespread attitude. His thoughts and deeds during the trial, especially as eventually reflected in the Green Committee report that appeared in *JAMA,* contributed to a widespread failure among U.S. medical scientists to grapple with the difficult ethical questions about their own work that the Nuremberg Medical Trial might have raised. In effect, as Ivy assured the judges in Nuremberg that there was nothing ethically suspect about experimentation with prisoners in the United States, he sent the same message to his U.S. colleagues.

References

1. Trials of War Criminals Before the Nuremberg Military Tribunal. Vol. 2: Military Tribunal, Case 1, *United States v Karl Brandt,* et al, October 1946–April 1949. Washington, D.C.: U.S. Government Printing Office; 1950. For more complete references to the material in this article, see Harkness, J. M., *Research Behind Bars: A History of Nontherapeutic Research on American Priso*ners. Madison: University of Wisconsin—Madison; 1996:137–152. Thesis.

2. Leibbrandt testimony. In *Complete Transcripts of the Nuremberg Medical Trial, National Archives* Microfilm, M587 (microfilm reel 3), January 27,1947, pp. 1961–2028.

3. Taylor, T. *Final Report to the Secretary of the Army on the Nuremberg War Crimes Trials.* Washington, D.C.: U.S. Government Printing Office; 1949:89.

4. Prison Malaria: Convicts Expose Themselves to Disease So Doctors Can Study It. *Life.* June 4, 1945: 43–44, 46.

5. Ivy, A. C. Report on War Crimes of a Medical Nature Committed in Germany and Elsewhere on German Nationals and the Nationals of Occupied Countries by the Nazi Regime During World War II. 1946. (A copy of this unpublished report can be found at the National Library of Medicine and in the Archive of the American Medical Association.)

6. Dragstedt, C. A. Andrew Conway Ivy. *Q Bull Northwestern Univ Med School.* Summer 1944:139–140.

7. Grossman, M. I. Andrew Conway Ivy (1893–1978). *Physiologist.* April 1978:11–12.

8. Bill, D. B. A. C. Ivy-reminiscences. *Physiologist.* October 1979:21–22.

9. Citizen doctor. *Time.* January 13, 1947:47.

10. Annas, G. J, and Grodin, M. A. *The Nazi Doctors and the Nuremberg Code: Human Rights in Human Experimentation.* New York: Oxford University Press; 1992:204.

11. Letter from Governor Dwight H. Green to Morris Fishbein, March 13, 1947. Archives of the University of Chicago Library, Morris Fishbein Papers, Box 98:2.

12. Letter from Andrew C. Ivy to Rev Ralph A. Gallagher, S J; Rev. Ralph Wakefield; Dr. G. George Fox; Dr. Morris Fishbein; Mr. Kaywin Kennedy; Dr. Robert S. Berghoff; and Mr. Oscar G. Mayer, April 21, 1947. Archives of the University of Chicago Library, Morris Fishbein Papers, Box 98:2.

13. Letter from Andrew C. Ivy to Dr. Robert S. Berghoff, Dr. Morris Fishbein, Rabbi George Fox, Father Ralph Gallagher, Mr. Kaywin Kennedy, and Mr. Oscar Mayer, June 24, 1947. Archives of the University of Chicago Library, Morns Fishbein Papers, Box 98:2.

14. Ivy testimony. In *Complete Transcripts of the Nuremberg Medical Trial*, National Archives Microfilm, M887 (microfilm reels 9 and 10), June 12–16, 1947, pp. 9029–9324.

15. Archives of the University of Chicago Library, *Morris Fishbein Papers*, Box 98:2.

16. Ethics Governing the Service of Prisoners as Subjects in medical Experiments: Report of a Committee Appointed by Governor Dwight H. Green of Illinois. *JAMA.* 1948; 136:457–458.

17. Advisory Committee on Human Radiation Experiments. *Final Report of the Advisory Committee on Human Radiation Experiments.* Washington, D.C.: U.S. Government Printing Office; 1995:137–154.

REVIEW QUESTIONS

1. Why did the AMA use Ivy to represent the U.S. on medical experimentation during the Nuremberg Medical Trials?

2. What does Ivy say about using prisoners for medical experimentation? How does he justify this?

3. Do you think it is important to read about something that took place so long ago?

PROBLEMS OF ETHICS IN RESEARCH

Stanley Milgram

Stanley Milgram carried out his study on obedience at Yale University from 1960–1963. In reaction to the "systematic slaughter on command" of so many people during World War II, Milgram wanted to determine why individuals would actually obey authority even when they knew what they were being asked to do was wrong. This experiment involved a "teacher," who was the real focus of the experiment, instructed to shock the "learner" when a wrong answer was given. The point of the experiment was to see how far a person would go when ordered to inflict pain on the "learner."

The purpose of the inquiry described here was to study obedience and disobedience to authority under conditions that permitted careful scrutiny of the phenomenon. A person was told by an experimenter to obey a set of increasingly callous orders, and our interest was to see when he would stop obeying. An element of theatrical staging was needed to set the proper conditions for observing the behavior, and technical illusions were freely employed (such as the fact that the victim only appeared to be shocked). Beyond this, most of what occurred in the laboratory was what had been discovered, rather than what had been planned.

For some critics, however, the chief horror of the experiment was not that the subjects obeyed but that the experiment was carried out at all. Among professional psychologists a certain polarization occurred. The experiment was both highly praised and harshly criticized. In 1964, Dr. Diana Baumrind attacked the experiments in the *American Psychologist,* in which I later published this reply:

> In a recent issue of *American Psychologist, a* critic raised a number of questions concerning the obedience report. She expressed concern for the welfare of subjects who served in the experiment, and wondered whether adequate measures were taken to protect the participants.
>
> At the outset, the critic confuses the unanticipated outcome of an experiment with its basic procedure. She writes, for example, as if the production of stress in our subjects was an intended and deliberate effect of the experimental manipulation. There are many laboratory procedures specifically designed to create stress (Lazarus, 1964), but the obedience paradigm was not one of them. The extreme tension induced in some subjects was unexpected. Before conducting the experiment, the procedures were discussed with many colleagues, and none anticipated the reactions that subsequently took place. Foreknowledge of results can never be the invariable accompaniment of an experimental probe. Understanding grows because we examine situations in which the end is unknown. An investigator unwilling to accept this degree of risk must give up the idea of scientific inquiry.

Milgram, S. 1969. *Obedience to Authority.* Harper & Row: New York.

Moreover, there was every reason to expect, prior to actual experimentation, that subjects would refuse to follow the experimenter's instructions beyond the point where the victim protested; many colleagues and psychiatrists were questioned on this point, and they virtually all felt this would be the case. Indeed, to initiate an experiment in which the critical measure hangs on disobedience, one must start with a belief in certain spontaneous resources in men that enable them to overcome pressure from authority.

It is true that after a reasonable number of subjects had been exposed to the procedures, it became evident that some would go to the end of the shock board, and some would experience stress. That point, it seems to me, is the first legitimate juncture at which one could even start to wonder whether or not to abandon the study. But momentary excitement is not the same as harm. As the experiment progressed there was no indication of injurious effects in the subjects; and as the subjects themselves strongly endorsed the experiment, the judgment I made was to continue the investigation.

Is not the criticism based as much on the unanticipated findings as on the method? The findings were that some subjects performed in what appeared to be a shockingly immoral way. If, instead, every one of the subjects had broken off at "slight shock," or at the first sign of the learner's discomfort, the results would have been pleasant, and reassuring, and who would protest?

A very important aspect of the procedure occurred at the end of the experimental session. A careful postexperimental treatment was administered to all subjects. The exact content of the dehoax varied from condition to condition and with increasing experience on our part. At the very least, all subjects were told that the victim had not received dangerous electric shocks. Each subject had a friendly reconciliation with the unharmed victim, and an extended discussion with the experimenter. The experiment was explained to the defiant subjects in a way that supported their decision to disobey the experimenter. Obedient subjects were assured of the fact that their behavior was entirely normal and that their feelings of conflict or tension were shared by other participants. Subjects were told that they would receive a comprehensive report at the conclusion of the experimental series. In some instances, additional detailed and lengthy discussions of the experiments were also carried out with individual subjects.

When the experimental series was complete, subjects received a written report which presented details of the experimental procedure and results. Again, their own part in the experiments was treated in a dignified way and their behavior in the experiment respected. All subjects received a follow-up questionnaire regarding their participation in the research, which again allowed expression of thoughts and feelings about their behavior.

The replies to the questionnaire confirmed my impression that participants felt positively toward the experiment. In its quantitative aspect (see Table 8), 84% of the subjects stated they were glad to have been in the experiment; 15% indicated neutral feelings; and 1.3% indicated negative feelings. To be sure, such findings are to be interpreted cautiously, but they cannot be disregarded.

TABLE 8. EXCERPT FROM QUESTIONNAIRE USED IN A FOLLOW-UP STUDY OF THE OBEDIENCE RESEARCH

Now that *I* have read the report, and all things considered . . .	Defiant (%)	Obedient (%)	All (%)
1 I am very glad to have been in the experiment	40.0	47.8	43.5
2 I am glad to have been in the experiment	43.8	35.7	40.2
3 I am neither sorry nor glad to have been in the experiment	15.3	14.8	15.1
4 I am sorry to have been in the experiment	0.8	0.7	0.8
5 I am very sorry to have been in the experiment	0.0	1.0	0.5

Note: Ninety-two percent of the subjects returned the questionnaire. The characteristics of the non-respondents were checked against the respondents. They differed from the respondents only with regard to age; younger people were over-represented in the non-responding group.

Further, four-fifths of the subjects felt that more experiments of this sort should be carried out, and 74% indicated that they had learned something of personal importance as a result of being in the study.

The debriefing and assessment procedures were carried out as a matter of course, and were not stimulated by any observation of special risk in the experimental procedure. In my judgment, at no point were subjects exposed to danger and at no point did they run the risk of injurious effects resulting from participation. If it had been otherwise, the experiment would have been terminated at once.

The critic states that, after he has performed in the experiment, the subject cannot justify his behavior and must bear the full brunt of his actions. By and large it does not work this way. The same mechanisms that allow the subject to perform the act, to obey rather than to defy the experimenter, transcend the moment of performance and continue to justify his behavior for him. The same viewpoint the subject takes while performing the actions is the viewpoint from which he later sees his behavior, that is, the perspective of "carrying out the task assigned by the person in authority."

Because the idea of shocking the victim is repugnant, there is a tendency among those who hear of the design to say "people will not do it." When the results are made known, this attitude is expressed as "if they do it they will not be able to live with themselves afterward." These two forms of denying the experimental findings are equally inappropriate misreading of the facts of human social behavior. Many subjects do, indeed, obey to the end, and there is no indication of injurious effects.

The absence of injury is a minimal condition of experimentation; there can be, however, an important positive side to participation. The critic suggests that subjects derived no benefit from being in the obedience study, but this is false. By their statements and actions, subjects indicated that they had learned a good deal, and many felt gratified to have taken part in scientific research they considered to be of significance. A year after his participation one subject wrote: "This experiment has strengthened my belief that man should avoid harm to his fellow man even at the risk of violating authority."

Another stated: "To me, the experiment pointed up . . . the extent to which each individual should have or discover firm ground on which to base his decisions, no matter how trivial they appear to be. I think people should think more deeply about themselves and their relation to their world and to other people. If this experiment serves to jar people out of complacency, it will have served its end."

These statements are illustrative of a broad array of appreciative and insightful comments by those who participated.

The 5-page report sent to each subject on the completion of the experimental series was specifically designed to enhance the value of his experience. It laid out the broad conception of the experimental program as well as the logic of its design. It described the results of a dozen of the experiments, discussed the causes of tension, and attempted to indicate the possible significance of the experiment. Subjects responded enthusiastically; many indicated a desire to be in further experimental research. This report was sent to all subjects several years ago. The care with which it was prepared does not support the critic's assertion that the experimenter was indifferent to the value subjects derived from their participation.

The critic fears that participants will be alienated from psychological experiments because of the intensity of experience associated with laboratory procedures. My own observation is that subjects more commonly respond with distaste to the "empty" laboratory hour, in which cardboard procedures are employed, and the only possible feeling upon emerging from the laboratory is that one has wasted time in a patently trivial and useless exercise.

The subjects in the obedience experiment, on the whole, felt quite differently about their participation. They viewed the experience as an opportunity to learn something of importance about themselves, and more generally, about the conditions of human action.

A year after the experimental program was completed, I initiated an additional follow-up study. In this connection an impartial medical examiner, experienced in outpatient treatment, interviewed 40 experimental subjects. The examining psychiatrist focused on those subjects he felt would be most likely to have suffered consequences from participation. His aim was to identify possible injurious effects resulting from the experiment. He concluded that, "although extreme stress had been experienced by several subjects, none was found by this interviewer to show signs of having been harmed by his experience . . .. Each subject seemed to handle his task (in the experiment) in a manner consistent with well-established patterns of behavior. No evidence was found of any traumatic reactions." Such evidence ought to be weighed before judging the experiment.

At root, the critic believes that it is not proper to test obedience in this situation, because she construes it as one in which there is no reasonable alternative to obedience. In adopting this view, she has lost sight of this fact: A substantial proportion of subjects do disobey. By their example, disobedience is shown to be a genuine possibility, one that is in no sense ruled out by the general structure of the experimental situation.

The critic is uncomfortable with the high level of obedience obtained in the first experiment. In the condition she focused on, 65% of the subjects obeyed to the end. However, her sentiment does not take into account that within the general framework of the psychological experiment obedience varied enormously from one condition to the next. In some variations, 90% of the subjects disobeyed. It seems to be not only the fact of an experiment, but the particular structure of elements within the experimental situation that accounts for rates of obedience and disobedience. And these elements were varied systematically in the program of research.

A concern with human dignity is based on a respect for a man's potential to act morally. The critic feels that the experimenter *made* the subject shock the victim. This conception is alien to my view. The experimenter tells the subject to do something. But between the command and the outcome there is a paramount force, the acting person who may obey or disobey. I started with the belief that every person who came to the laboratory was free to accept or to reject the dictates of authority. This view sustains a conception of human dignity insofar as it sees in each man a capacity for choosing his own behavior. And as it turned out, many subjects did, indeed, choose to reject the experimenter's commands, providing a powerful affirmation of human ideals.

The experiment is also criticized on the grounds that "it could easily effect an alteration in the subject's . . . ability to trust adult authorities in the future." . . . However, the experimenter is not just any authority: He is an authority who tells the subject to act harshly and inhumanely against another man. I would consider it of the highest value if participation in the experiment could, indeed, inculcate a skepticism of this kind of authority. Here, perhaps, a difference in philosophy emerges most clearly. The critic views the subject as a passive creature, completely controlled by the experimenter. I started from a different viewpoint. A person who comes to the laboratory is an active, choosing adult, capable of accepting or rejecting the prescriptions for action addressed to him. The critic sees the effect of the experiment as undermining the subject's trust of authority. I see it as a potentially valuable experience insofar as it makes people aware of the problem of indiscriminate submission to authority.

Yet another criticism occurred in Dannie Abse's play, *The Dogs of Pavlov,* which appeared in London in 1971 and which uses the obedience experiment as its central dramatic theme. At the play's climax, Kurt, a major character in the play, repudiates the experimenter for treating him as a guinea pig. In his introduction to the play, Abse especially condemns the illusions employed in the experiment, terming the setup "bullshit," "fraudulent," "cheat." At the same time, he apparently admires the dramatic quality of the experiment. And he allowed my rejoinder to appear in the foreword to his book. I wrote to him:

> I do feel you are excessively harsh in your language when condemning my use of illusion in the experiment. As a dramatist, you surely understand that illusion may serve a revelatory function, and indeed, the very possibility of theater is founded on the benign use of contrivance.
>
> One could, viewing a theatrical performance, claim that the playwright has cheated, tricked, and defrauded the audience, for he presents as old men individuals who are, when the greasepaint is removed, quite young; men presented as physicians who in reality are merely actors knowing nothing about medicine,

etc., etc. But this assertion of "bullshit," "cheat," "fraud" would be silly, would it not, for it does not take into account how those exposed to the theater's illusions feel about them. The fact is that the audience accepts the necessity of illusion for the sake of entertainment, intellectual enrichment, and all of the other benefits of the theatrical experience. And it is their acceptance of these procedures that gives you warrant for the contrivances you rely upon.

So I will not say that you cheated, tricked, and defrauded your audience. But, I would hold the same claim for the experiment. Misinformation is employed in the experiment; illusion is used when necessary in order to set the stage for the revelation of certain difficult-to-get-at truths; and these procedures are justified for one reason only: they are, in the end, accepted and endorsed by those who are exposed to them . . .

When the experiment was explained to subjects they responded to it positively, and most felt it was an hour well spent. If it had been otherwise, if subjects ended the hour with bitter recriminatory feelings, the experiment could not have proceeded.

This judgment is based, first, on the numerous conversations I have had with subjects immediately after their participation in the experiment. Such conversations can reveal a good deal, but what they showed most was how readily the experience is assimilated to the normal frame of things. Moreover, subjects were friendly rather than hostile, curious rather than denunciatory, and in no sense demeaned by the experience. This was my general impression, and it was later supported by formal procedures undertaken to assess the subjects' reaction to the experiment. The central moral justification for allowing a procedure of the sort used in my experiment is that it is judged acceptable by those who have taken part in it. Moreover, it was the salience of this fact throughout that constituted the chief moral warrant for the continuation of the experiments.

This fact is crucial to any appraisal of the experiment from an ethical standpoint.

Imagine an experiment in which a person's little finger was routinely snipped off in the course of a laboratory hour. Not only is such an experiment reprehensible, but within hours the study would be brought to a halt as outraged participants pressed their complaints on the university administration, and legal measures were invoked to restrain the experimenter. When a person has been abused, he knows it, and will quite properly react against the source of such mistreatment.

Criticism of the experiment that does not take account of the tolerant reaction of the participants is hollow. This applies particularly to criticism centering on the use of technical illusions (or "deception," as the critics prefer to say) that fails to relate this detail to the central fact that subjects find the device acceptable. Again, the participant, rather than the external critic, must be the ultimate source of judgment.

While some persons construe the experimenter to be acting in terms of deceit, manipulation, and chicanery, it is, as you should certainly appreciate, also possible to see him as a dramatist who creates scenes of revelatory power, and who brings participants into them. So perhaps we are not so far apart in the kind of work we do. I do grant there is an important difference in that those exposed to your theatrical illusions expect to confront them, while my subjects are not forewarned. However, whether it is unethical to pursue truths through the use of my form of dramaturgical device cannot be answered in the abstract. It depends entirely on the response of those who have been exposed to such procedures.

One further point: the obedient subject does not blame himself for shocking the victim, because the act does not originate in the self. It originates in authority, and the worst the obedient subject says of himself is that he must learn to resist authority more effectively in the future.

That the experiment has stimulated this thought in some subjects is, to my mind, a satisfying consequence of the inquiry. An illustrative case is provided by the experience of a young man who took part in a Princeton replication of the obedience experiment, conducted in 1964. He was fully obedient. On October 27, 1970, he wrote to me:

"Participation in the 'shock experiment' . . . has had a great impact on my life. When I was a subject in 1964, though I believed that I was hurting someone, I was totally unaware of why I was doing so. Few people ever realize when they are acting according to their own beliefs and when they are meekly submitting to authority. . . . To permit myself to be drafted with the understanding that I am submitting to authority's demand to do something very wrong would make me frightened of myself. . . . I am fully prepared to go to jail if I am not granted Conscientious Objector status. Indeed, it is the only course I could take to be faithful to what I believe. My only hope is that members of my board act equally according to their conscience. .

He inquired whether any other participants had reacted similarly, and whether, in my opinion, participation in the study could have this effect.

I replied:

"The experiment does, of course, deal with the dilemma individuals face when they are confronted with conflicting demands of authority and conscience, and I am glad that your participation in the study has brought you to a deeper personal consideration of these issues. Several participants have informed me that their own sensitivity to the problem of submission to authority was increased as a result of their experience in the study. If the experiment has heightened your awareness of the problem of indiscriminate submission to authority, it will have performed an important function. If you believe strongly that it is wrong to kill others in the service of your country, then you ought certainly to press vigorously for CO status, and I am deeply hopeful that your sincerity in this matter will be recognized."

A few months later he wrote again. He indicated, first, that the draft board was not very impressed with the effect of his participation in the experiment, but he was granted CO status nonetheless. He writes:

The experience of the interview doesn't lessen my strong belief of the great impact of the experiment on my life. You have discovered one of the most important

causes of all the trouble in this world. . . . I am grateful to have been able to provide you with a part of the information necessary for that discovery. I am delighted to have acted, by refusing to serve in the Armed Forces, in a manner which
people must act if these problems are to be solved. With sincere thanks for your
contribution to my life . . .

In a world in which action is often clouded with ambiguity, I nonetheless feel con-
strained to give greater heed to this man, who actually participated in the study, than to a
distant critic. For disembodied moralizing is not the issue, but only the human response of
those who have participated in the experiment. And that response not only endorses the
procedures employed, but overwhelmingly calls for deeper inquiry to illuminate the issues
of obedience and disobedience.

References

Lazarus, R. 1964. A laboratory approach to the dynamics of psychological stress.
American Psychologist, 19: 400–411.

REVIEW QUESTIONS

1. Do you believe that the benefits outweighed the risks in this study?

2. Do you agree with Milgram that this study was not harmful to the subjects?

3. Why wouldn't this study be considered ethical today?

THE ETHICS OF CONDUCTING SOCIAL-SCIENCE RESEARCH ON THE INTERNET

James C. Hamilton

---

*The Internet and the World Wide Web have advanced our ability to gain information at an
amazing rate. Each year, more and more individuals have either their own personal computers or access to computers in their schools, libraries, or places of work. With technological advances comes the possibility for researchers to connect with people who might
otherwise be difficult to reach either because of the proximity to the researcher or the desire of the individual to remain anonymous. While more and more researchers are using
the Internet to gather data, change doesn't happen without the possibility of problems that
are addressed in this article by Hamilton.*

James C. Hamilton. 1999. The ethics of conducting social-science research on the Internet *Chronicle of Higher Education,* Dec. 3, 1999 46 (15) p. B6(2)

Over the past four or five years, the amount of social-science research conducted on the Internet has increased exponentially. More than 100 World Wide Web sites now invite visitors to participate in a wide variety of scientific research, or in activities that resemble scientific research, including personality tests, intelligence tests, and opinion surveys.

One example of a site that was developed to carry out legitimate research is maintained by psychologists at the University of Washington and Yale University, who are using the Internet to study complex thought processes (http://www.depts.washington.edu/iat/). Other sites bear a superficial resemblance to those used for legitimate research, but are designed solely for entertainment purposes. For instance, visitors to the Free Internet Love Test site (http://www.lovetest.com) can provide information—including astrological signs—about themselves and their partners, and receive feedback about their compatibility.

The growth of research on the Internet has outpaced the efforts of researchers—and advocates for the ethical treatment of research participants—to understand the implications of this new methodology and to develop guidelines for its responsible use. The Internet clearly is a very powerful research tool, and its benefits—such as the ability to reach large numbers of people, at very low cost—are alluring. But like all powerful tools, it can be destructive if it is not used properly, or if it falls into the wrong hands.

An Internet search that I conducted suggests that on-line researchers are not consistently employing the safeguards that are used to protect participants in traditional research. For example, in studies not conducted on line, participants must read and sign a statement that describes the research and explains their rights. Although on-line researchers could easily convey the same type of information on a Web page, many on-line research sites dispense with that important safeguard.

Complicated studies often require that researchers give participants additional information, beyond the informed-consent statement. In practice, many studies are so complex that it is impossible to give participants a full explanation of the research before they participate, without running the risk of skewing the results. As an example, participants who are told that a study concerns how the race of a defendant influences jurors' decisions are likely to alter their responses to appear unprejudiced. Therefore, many researchers give participants a post-experimental debriefing—that is, they provide a full explanation of the research only after the participants have completed the experiment. On-line researchers could design their Web sites to send participants to a debriefing page after they are finished, but many do not.

What's more, even if researchers include a debriefing page, they cannot make participants read it. That problem highlights some of the ethical issues raised by the fact that researchers have so little control over the nature of participants' experiences in on-line research.

In face-to-face studies, researchers can see if participants have an adverse reaction to the study and can take steps to assist them—perhaps by terminating their participation and debriefing them with extra care. In on-line studies, it is not possible for researchers to safeguard the emotional well-being of participants in the same way. Many researchers have opted to address that limitation by providing disclaimers, which state that people should not participate if they feel that they cannot handle the emotional impact of the procedure or of any feedback they might receive.

Although that might seem to be a sensible way to deal with the problem, current ethical guidelines prohibit the use of such disclaimers. Federal agencies that support research—as well as scientists' professional organizations—assert that researchers must protect the rights of their participants, and that they cannot simply ask people to sign away those rights.

Another ethical risk posed by on-line research has to do with the confidentiality of data collected over the Internet. In general, most Internet users enjoy complete anonymity. Unless someone provides personal information voluntarily, there is almost no practical way to determine the identity of a visitor to a given Web site. Although it is possible to identify the Internet address from which a particular message was sent, that address rarely belongs to a single identifiable individual. Even at academic institutions in which professors' computers are connected directly to the Internet, a machine might well use a different address each time the professor turns it on.

The anonymity that is common on line makes it possible for individuals to submit data on multiple occasions—either accidentally or intentionally—with virtually no chance of being detected. Because such multiple responses on a wide scale can invalidate a study, researchers may ask participants for identifying information, such as e-mail addresses. Or a researcher might use something called a cookie to identify the computer from which each participant submitted his or her response. However, both of those methods compromise the researcher's ability to guarantee the confidentiality of the data.

Even worse, computer hackers can easily intercept participants' responses to online studies. If they also intercept identifying information, the results for the participants could be disastrous—particularly if the study deals with sensitive issues, such as criminal or sexual behavior.

Usually institutional review boards—which work to insure that all research involving human subjects complies with applicable legal and ethical standards—save researchers from any breaches of confidentiality and other ethical lapses. However, some on-line research is being conducted without the required approval of an IRB Recently, a doctoral student at a major U.S. university confided to me that neither he nor his dissertation chairman had thought to secure IRB approval for his on-line dissertation research.

Even when IRB's are consulted about on-line research, they may be ill-equipped to evaluate the studies. Based on my correspondence with members of IRB's around the country. I estimate that roughly half of the members have received proposals for on-line research, while only a few of the members have reported that their IRB had developed guidelines for evaluating ethical risks and safeguards in such research.

Careful evaluation of proposals for online research requires considerable expertise in the area of Internet hardware and software. To properly evaluate those proposals, IRB members need to know who will run the Web site: the researcher, from his or her own computer; the staff of a university's computer center; or a third party. If the researcher does not have complete control of the computer serving the site, the IRB must know the identities of everyone who will have access to the data, and how confidentiality will be maintained.

Beyond those general issues, IRB members need to deal with specific technical questions. These include whether data are collected only when the participant hits the "submit" button, or before the participant decides that he or she is finished; whether the participant is automatically referred to a debriefing page if he or she quits in the middle of the study; and whether participants can delete their data after they learn the purpose of the study. It takes considerable technical savvy to know enough to ask such questions, let alone to evaluate the answers.

As technology becomes increasingly sophisticated, more experimenters will be able to have on-line research sites, but the danger is that fewer will have adequate knowledge of how their sites work, in order to insure the well-being of the participants. As a result, IRB's will also have to begin evaluating the technical credentials of on-line researchers, to insure that they—or their technological consultants—have sufficient expertise to implement the appropriate technical safeguards.

Perhaps the greatest threat to on-line research is the danger to its credibility posed by data-collection sites established primarily for commercial or entertainment purposes. Those Web sites far outnumber academic-research sites, and in many cases, it is not easy to sort out which is which.

Although many commercial data-collection sites are forthcoming about who is sponsoring the research and how the data will be used, several such sites attempt to make money by deceiving participants. For example, several commercial sites appear to offer free personality or intelligence testing—but after completing the tests, participants are informed that they need to pay for a full report of their performance. Other commercial sites promise more-elaborate feedback to visitors who provide identifying information for the sponsor's database. Sites that employ such deceptive tactics may make the public suspicious of all data-collection sites, including those that serve legitimate scientific purposes.

Data-collection sites that are designed primarily for entertainment (such as the Pooh-Piglet Psychometric Personality Profiler, at http://www.ggw.org/donor-ware/pooh/, where you can discover whether you are more like Pooh, Piglet, Tigger, or Eeyore) might have an equally damaging effect on the public's attitude toward on-line scientific research. Most of the entertainment sites are operated by private individuals for their own amusement, and are designed to provide feedback to visitors, not data for the site's owner. It is likely that visitors might fill out the forms several times, with different data, to see what kinds of feedback they get—about whether they're introverted or extroverted, say, or what kind of person they should marry.

Such sites may lead Web surfers to believe that it is important to respond accurately or honestly to on-line tests, questionnaires. Or surveys—or even to respond only once. Were participants in on-line scientific experiments to take the same approach, the data they provided would be of no use.

Rather than trying to enforce higher standards on such sites, academic researchers should put their efforts into doing a better job of identifying the scholarly nature of their sites. Few researchers make use of design elements that would help reassure potential participants about the legitimacy of their research. Those elements include the prominent display of the name and logo of the researcher's university, information allowing participants to contact the researcher, and links to other sites with information about the researcher's credentials, such as the Web page of his or her department and the site of the IRB that approved the study.

We need guidelines to help researchers and members of IRB's alike insure that on-line research is both scientifically and ethically sound. Professional and governmental organizations that advocate support for science, such as the American Association for the Advancement of Science and the National Science Foundation, as well as groups that promote research in the social sciences, such as the American Psychological Society, should work together to establish such guidelines.

At a minimum, the guidelines should require all on-line researchers to provide information that would permit participants to contact the researcher, a means for obtaining participants' fully informed consent, full disclosure of any risks to their confidentiality, a post-experimental debriefing page, and a way for the participants to learn about the results of the study. The guidelines also should include up-to-date information on the technologies used to conduct on-line research and a set of criteria for evaluating the technical aspects of proposed on-line studies.

Ideally, the guidelines would standardize on-line research in a way that would help Internet users to distinguish academic-research sites from other kinds. It would also be useful for IRB's to maintain a list—on line, of course—of on-line studies that they have approved.

Once the guidelines have been put into practice, we will need to educate the public about them, and about making well-informed decisions on participating in online research. The organizations that created the guidelines could set up a Web site for the public that would explain the risks and benefits of on-line research, and make potential participants aware of ways to distinguish legitimate, scientific-research sites from commercial or entertainment sites. Researchers could provide a link from their sites to that public-education site.

On-line research holds much promise for many academic disciplines. However, we will not serve the interests of science if we do not make sure that such research is conducted ethically. We must not forget our responsibilities to our participants, even when we meet them only in cyberspace.

REVIEW QUESTIONS

1. Find a survey on the Internet. Can you tell if the survey is from an academic institution? Has it been approved by an IRB?

2. Can research on the Internet be anonymous? Does it need to be?

3. Do you think observing behaviors in a chat room should have IRB approval before the observations begin?

■

Chapter 4: Research Design

Before you actually begin learning about specific research designs, it is important to have an understanding about some of the terms that you will hear throughout your research methods class. There are numerous reasons to conduct research. In fact, there are almost as many reasons as there are researchers. Furthermore, research studies may have multiple purposes; however, the most common reasons for conducting research are to explore, describe, and explain the phenomenon that is being studied (Babbie, 1998).

THE REASONS FOR RESEARCH

Exploratory research may be the first stage of a research project that could give the researcher new knowledge about a phenomenon in order to design a more in-depth secondary study. For instance, an exploratory study was conducted to study the experiences of 40 HIV-positive mothers. The study was specifically set up to explore the social service agencies designed to help the women, to learn how the women coped with the infection, particularly as it related to parenting, and to determine their concerns, preferences, and plans for the future care of their children. The researchers explored the lives of the women who talked about their problems at the individual and family level, the organizations and providers level, and the policy and community level. Then the researchers were able to make recommendations for providers and design new studies to see which recommendation were most helpful (Marcenko & Samost, 1999).

Descriptive research allows the researcher to develop ideas about a topic and then describe the phenomenon in question. Descriptive research usually begins with a well-defined topic, then the research is conducted to describe the topic accurately. For instance, Nnorom, Esu-Williams, and Tilley-Gyado (1996) studied HIV, tuberculosis, and syphilis in Nigeria. Their objectives were to determine the distribution by age group, of tuberculosis (TB), syphilis, and HIV in Nigeria and to establish any association between these diseases. The researchers also wanted to estimate the male to female ratio of HIV and syphilis infections in Nigeria and to estimate the urban to rural ratio of HIV and syphilis infections in Nigeria. The researchers accomplished this task by using the results generated from the 1993/94 national HIV/Syphilis sentinel serosurvey that was carried out in seventeen of the thirty states in Nigeria. The results from this descriptive study allowed recommendations to be made about where to focus HIV/STD interventions and where more diagnostic, prophylactic, and therapeutic interventions should be encouraged.

The third purpose of research is to provide an **explanation** of some phenomenon. After you have explored a topic and have a fairly good description of it, you might begin to wonder about it. You might want to know why it happens the way it does. Does it always happen that way, or if something else were around would it happen in a different way? For example, the researchers just described studied the distribution of TB, syphilis, and HIV in Nigeria. Now they might want to explain why some areas have higher incidences of these diseases than other areas do. Could it be the lack of health care in some areas? Could it be the lack of education? Would putting more education in some of the areas with the highest infection rates ultimately lower the rates of infection?

Units of Analysis

Another aspect of research that can be somewhat confusing is that of **units of analysis**. Units of analysis refer to the type of unit researchers use when measuring variables. The most common units of analysis are the individual, the group, the organization, the social category, the social artifact, the social institution, and the society.

If there is a classroom of 30 students who have been asked in a survey to rate 300 teachers in a university, the individual who is doing the rating is the unit of analysis. If another study compares the amounts of money spent at two different hospitals, then an organization (the hospital) would be the unit of analysis. If you were rating bumper stickers to see how many were political and how many were social, then a social artifact (bumper stickers) would be the unit of analysis. And if you asked to compare the gross national project in the United States with that of Germany, what would your unit of analysis be?

The Time Dimension

Time plays an important role in research because it helps describe changes or differences in behaviors within a framework of different ages or stages across the life span. You might want to know if marriage is the same now as it was 50 years ago. Maybe you found a study about how individuals picked their mates during the 1920s. Can you use that study to see if there is a change in the way individuals currently pick their mates?

The **longitudinal method** allows you to assess the change in behavior of one group of subjects at more than one point in time. Let's say you wanted to test a group of 10-year-olds, who live with parents who smoke, in 1980 to see if they smoked. Then you wanted to test them again in 1982, 1984, 1986, and so on until they were 21-years-old. This would be considered longitudinal because you are examining the changes in smoking habits in these children over an extended period of time. The advantage of this type of study is that it allows for changes over a long period of time; however, the main disadvantage to this type of study is that it is expensive because you must keep track of the subjects for the duration of the study. Furthermore, the dropout rate for this type of study may be high because people move, they don't leave forwarding addresses, or they change their minds about participating in the study.

The **cross-sectional method**, however, examines several groups of people at one point in time. So, if you wanted to conduct the same study about smoking habits that we just mentioned, you might conduct the study in 1990 on 10-year-olds, 12-year-olds, 14-years-olds, and all the way up to 21-year-olds. If all your subjects grew up in households where smoking was going on, you might be able to tell when the children made a decision to smoke or not smoke themselves. The major advantages of this type of study are that it is inexpensive, it involves a short time span, and there is a lower drop out rate. The disadvantages, however, are that it reveals nothing about the continuity of the phenomenon on a person-by-person case, the subjects may be the same chronological age, but may be of different maturational ages, and it gives no ideas which direction of change that a group might take.

REFERENCES

Babbie, E. 2001. *The practice of social research,* 9th edition. Belmont, CA: Wadsworth/ Thomson Learning.

Marcenko, M. O., & Samost, L. 1999. Living with HIV/AIDS: The voices of HIV-positive mothers. *Social Work,* 44(1): 36.

Nnorom, J. A., Esu-Williams, E. ; Tilley-Gyado, A. 1996. HIV, Tuberculosis and Syphilis in Nigeria: a descriptive study. *AIDS Weekly Plus*, Sept 23: 28

INFOTRAC COLLEGE EDITION SUGGESTED READINGS AND DISCUSSION QUESTIONS

1. Use InfoTrac College Edition to locate any articles that interest you. If you are interested in domestic violence you could refer to the article called "Drinking and Marital Aggression in Newlyweds: An Event-Based Analysis of Drinking and the Occurrence of Husband Marital Aggression" (Article A55017665), or if you are interested in nutrition you could refer to the article "2-Year Tracking of Children's Fruit and Vegetable Intake (Article A20944900). After locating an article, see if you can figure out the independent and dependent variables. What about the units of analysis?

2. Locate a longitudinal study such as "A longitudinal Study of Hong Kong Adolescents' and Parents' Perceptions of Family Functioning and Well-Being" (Article A53449277) on InfoTracCollege Edition. What was the hypothesis? Can you see that there would be any consequences of having the study go over a long period of time? How would you design the study without it being longitudinal? Now look for a cross-sectional study called "Cross-Validation of the Temptation Coping Questionnaire: Adolescent Coping with Temptations to Use Alcohol and Illicit Drugs (*)" (Article A55639802). Can you talk about the differences between the two types of research designs?

PUBLIC ASSISTANCE RECEIPT AMONG IMMIGRANTS AND NATIVES: HOW THE UNIT OF ANALYSIS AFFECTS RESEARCH FINDINGS

Jennifer Van Hook, Jennifer E. Glick, and Frank D. Bean

In this article Van Hook, Glick, and Bean studied the differences in rates of public assistance between immigrant and native households. Using the 1990 and 1991 panels of the Survey of Income and Program Participation, the researchers found the differences were only significant at the level of larger units of analysis. Therefore, the way the researcher defined the unit of analysis could have played a major role in the results of the study and the lives of people.

Why choose one unit of analysis or presentation over another? In analyzing data or presenting results on welfare usage, a researcher might select individuals or a unit that involves the collection of individuals in some more aggregate form, such as families or households. Most studies that compare immigrants' and natives' welfare use rely on such aggregate-level units. In these studies, if one or more individuals within the unit receive public assistance income, the entire unit is classified as a welfare-receiving unit. There are several reasons for selecting such aggregates as the unit of analysis and presentation. First, household and resident family members often share resources and amenities (Greenhalgh, 1982; Lloyd, 1995) and are often grouped together for determining eligibility for welfare. Second, for administrative purposes, public officials may require statistics that use aggregate-level units such as families because these units better approximate eligibility units. Third, researchers and advocates of the poor may find statistics that use aggregate units particularly meaningful for assessing the determinants of public assistance receipt. This is because welfare use arguably derives from the characteristics of the units of eligibility (i.e., the circumstances of the family and the ability of potential earners in the family to support their dependents), not necessarily from the characteristics of each of the individuals, particularly the children.

Four kinds of aggregate-level units that have been or can be used for presenting statistics on welfare receipt are the household, family household, family, and minimal household unit. The household has been the most frequently used unit for analyzing and presenting data on immigrants' welfare receipt. Research on household recipiency clearly shows that receipt among immigrant households has increased over the last two decades (Bean et al., 1997; Borjas, 1994; Borjas & Trejo, 1991;Trejo, 1992). By 1980, immigrants' recipiency had surpassed natives', a trend that has continued during the 1980–1990 decade. A disadvantage of comparisons involving all households is that some contain unrelated individuals who may not share resources or participate in decisions relating to long-term resource consumption or production (Greenhalgh, 1982; Kuznets,

Van Hook, J., Glick, J. E., & Bean, F. D. 1999. Public assistance receipt among immigrants and natives: How the unit of analysis affects research findings. *Demography*, 36(1): 111–120.

1978). One solution is to present results for family households, or households containing individuals related through blood, marriage, or adoption (Kuznets, 1978). The presentation of results for family households typically excludes single-person households and households containing unrelated individuals (Blau, 1984; Jensen, 1988; Tienda & Jensen, 1986). Compared with studies based on households, studies based on family households report similar patterns but smaller immigrant-native differences (Jensen, 1988; Tienda & Jensen, 1986).

The presentation of results at the household or even the family household level, however, may misrepresent the level of recipiency, both because multiple sources of recipiency can exist within the same household or family household and because unrelated individuals are excluded. For example, most analyses simply examine whether any member of a household receives welfare without considering the number of welfare grants going to the household. A single-recipient household may contain one recipient or several, depending upon the complexity of the household. Further, samples restricted to family households could omit some types of welfare receipt. Because samples restricted to family households do not include single individuals (who may be eligible for SSI but not AFDC), they may be more likely to detect recipiency of AFDC than of SSI.

The family (or subfamily) has been considered an appropriate unit of analysis and presentation because families, rather than individuals or households, are used to determine eligibility for AFDC (Simon, 1984). Families are defined as co-residential units containing the family head, spouse (if present), and dependent children. Multiple-family units may reside within the same household. Welfare eligibility is based on the resources of one family regardless of the potential recipients' access to the resources of co-residential or nonresidential extended family members. Therefore, it may be more accurate to consider the characteristics of spouses, partners, and dependent children than to consider those of the entire household or family household when examining welfare use. As with samples of family households, however, samples of families do not include single or unrelated individuals and therefore exclude many SSI recipients.

An alternative is to use the minimal household unit. The minimal household unit, often relied on in research on extended family households, refers to the smallest identifiable unit within a household that has the potential to reside independently of others (Biddlecom, 1994; Ermisch & Overton, 1985; Glick, Bean, & Van Hook, 1997). Families as well as single individuals are counted as separate units. Presenting results for minimal household units offers the advantage of using families (i.e., they approximate the unit used to determine eligibility) while including data for single, unrelated individuals.

As the preceding discussion implies, the goal among many researchers studying immigrants' welfare receipt has been to focus on units that approximate co-residential groups that share resources or that are considered as a single unit when applying for welfare (e.g., Bean et al., 1997). This goal, however, may not be appropriate for addressing some kinds of research questions. For instance, researchers attempting to compare the per capita costs of welfare recipiency between immigrants and natives might be best served by presenting results for samples of individuals. Because welfare grants to families and couples increase with the number of dependents (U.S. House of Representatives, 1994), researchers presenting results for households or families in order to compare the "welfare burden" of two groups may reach erroneous conclusions to the degree that household or family size and recipient density differ appreciably between the two groups. Further, in analyses of the fiscal implications of immigration, the National Research Council recommends relying on individuals (Smith & Edmonston, 1997) because aggregate-level units are temporally unstable. Researchers using longitudinal analyses of welfare use may have difficulty tracking families or households over time when they break apart and re-form (Citro & Michael, 1995; Lloyd, 1995).

More important for present purposes, not all persons grouped together in aggregate-level units are identical with respect to welfare receipt and other important social indicators such as nativity status. In many cases, a welfare-receiving household is counted as one household no matter how many recipients it contains, and immigrant households are counted as receiving welfare even if no immigrant household members received welfare (i.e., if U.S.-born household members received welfare). Such heterogeneity within households is no small issue. Although most immigrants live in households headed by immigrants and most natives live in households headed by natives (over 95% in both cases), 25% of adults and 80% of children living in households headed by immigrants are U.S.-born citizens (estimated from the 1990 U.S. Public Use Micro-data Sample). The extent to which unit nativity composition is problematic largely depends on how researchers treat U.S.-born children living in immigrant households. If researchers adopt the household (or other aggregate units) as the unit of analysis and define its nativity based on the nativity of the householder (e.g., Borjas, 1994) or the nativity of the householder or the householder's spouse (e.g., Bean et al., 1997), they assume, intentionally or not, that native-born children are immigrants. Because nativity-related eligibility criteria for AFDC and other public assistance for children are based on children's place of birth, not the nativity of parents, and because immigrant parents are not eligible for AFDC benefits in their first five years of residence in the United States, some immigrant households can be classified as households receiving welfare only because of the presence of a native-born child.

Data and Measures

To examine the extent to which comparisons of immigrant and native recipiency are affected by the unit of presentation, we use data from the 1990 and 1991 panels of the Survey of Income and Program Participation (SIPP). One major reason for using the SIPP, as opposed to the CPS or U.S. census data, to study the consequences of presenting results for individual-, family-, and/or household-level units is that it is the only large data source that contains detail regarding which children and other dependents are covered by public assistance payments. We combine the 1990 and 1991 panels to obtain enough cases to allow the calculation of reliable estimates for immigrants by type of assistance received.

The unit of analysis is the individual because welfare recipiency is determined from SIPP data for each person. For the presentation of results, we construct samples of individuals, family members (individuals residing with relatives), minimal household units, families, households, and family households. We group individuals into units according to their living arrangements and familial relationships as of January 1990 or 1991 (depending on the year of the SIPP panel). Minimal household units are co-residential family units and single individuals. Thus, the primary family unit (containing the householder; spouse; and any single, dependent children under age 25, additional family units in the household (married couples with or without dependent children, single parents with a child or children), and single adults aged 25 or older are all counted as separate units.

TABLE 1 ■ Unweighed Numbers of Cases in Each Sample, By Nativity

Sample	Immigrants	Natives
Households	3,268	26,643
Minimal Household Units	4,017	31,624
Individuals	6,463	71,138
Family Households	2,680	18,608
Families	2,670	18,067
Family Members	5,509	59,841

Source:Survey of Income and Program Participation, 1990 and 1991 panels.

Each single adult, including unmarried parents living in the homes of their adult children, is classified as a separate unit. Families are defined as minimal household units that contain two or more related individuals. The household sample contains all households as defined by the U.S. Census Bureau. Family households are the subset of households that contain two or more individuals related to the household head. Finally, family members are individuals who reside with relatives. The family, family household, and family member samples differ from the others in that the units in the family samples are composed of family members, not the full set of persons interviewed in the SIPP as are the units in the individual, minimal household unit, and household samples. Hereafter, we refer to the samples of family members, families, and family households as the family samples.

Immigrants are broadly defined as foreign-born persons living in the United States, and natives are defined as U.S.-born persons. Individuals born abroad of American parents and those born in U.S. Outlying Areas (e.g., Puerto Rico) are counted as native born. Unfortunately, the SIPP does not collect country-of-birth information for children under age 15. For most of these children, we use mother's, and in some cases, father's, place of birth as a proxy: If the child's natural mother is foreign born and immigrated after the child was born, then the child is classified as foreign born; otherwise, the child is classified as U.S. born. We are unable to match 12% of the children with their natural mothers. For this group, we use the natural father's or a guardian's nativity as a proxy. Using these procedures, we classify 98% of children as either foreign born or U.S. born. The remaining 2% of children are classified as having the same nativity as the head of their family unit. The weighted percentage of children classified as foreign born following these procedures is 3.3%, a figure that is larger than the percentage calculated from 1990 U.S. census data (2.7%; the two estimates are significantly different at $p < .05$). Units in which the head or the spouse of the head is foreign born are classified as immigrant, and the remaining units are defined as native. Units in which the head or spouse was born in an outlying area or is a foreign-born post-secondary student are excluded from the sample, and persons living in such units are excluded from the individual-level samples. (FN5) Hence, even though persons born in U.S. Outlying Areas are initially classified as native born, most are eventually excluded from the samples of individuals. The number of cases in each of the samples are presented separately by nativity in Table 1.

The SIPP collects monthly data on who in each household receives various types of cash public assistance benefits and which dependents, if any, are covered by the welfare payments. We define recipients as those who report receiving, or are reported as having received, at least one type of public assistance income during the month of January 1990 or 1991 (depending on year of the SIPP panel). The types of public assistance that we count as welfare are the three primary cash assistance programs: AFDC, SSI, and General Assistance. Recipient units are defined as those in which at least one member is a recipient. We differentiate between recipients of the two major types of cash assistance, AFDC and SSI, because the two programs serve different populations and involve different types of policy responses. (FN6) We define AFDC and SSI recipients and recipient units in the same way as described previously for recipiency of any type of public assistance. For example, AFDC recipients are those who are reported as having received or as having been covered by AFDC in January and AFDC recipient units are those containing at least one AFDC recipient.

Results

Rates of public assistance receipt among immigrants and natives are presented in Table 2 for households, minimal household units, individuals, family households, and families. In the case of the individual-level statistics presented in Table 2, we treat children as immigrant or native based on their estimated place of birth, not the birthplace of their parents or household head. As shown in the top panel of the table, use of any type of public assistance among immigrants exceeds that among natives when larger units of aggregation are used. In both the household-based comparisons (i.e., households, minimal household units, and individuals) and the family-based comparisons (i.e., family households, families, and family members), the level of welfare receipt for immigrants is significantly higher than that for natives only in the cases of the most aggregated units (household or family households). (FN7) Welfare receipt is not significantly higher among immigrants than among natives in the cases of the smaller units. Thus, research comparing welfare receipt of immigrants and natives can reach divergent conclusions based solely on the use of different units of analysis or presentation.

Does this finding hold up when we examine different types of welfare receipt? When all sources of welfare are separated into cash assistance received from AFDC, from SSI, or from other sources (not examined here), the patterns observed for "any type of public assistance" are generally replicated, especially in the case of SSI: The use of larger-sized units makes immigrants' receipt appear higher relative to natives' than does the use of smaller-sized units. When nativity differences are examined, the differences involving AFDC are not statistically significant for any of the units, although in each of the three aggregate units involving families, AFDC receipt of natives exceeds that of immigrants. In the case of SSI, however, immigrants' receipt exceeds natives' receipt, irrespective of the unit examined. Thus, as we have argued elsewhere (Bean et al. 1997), the findings of research based on immigrant-native comparisons of welfare receipt also depend on the type of welfare receipt examined.

We cannot determine why immigrant-native comparisons are affected by using different units of presentation from simple examinations of units. For the sake of brevity, we focus only on how assessments of immigrant levels of receipt vary depending on whether

TABLE 2 ■ PUBLIC ASSISTANCE RECIPIENCY AMONG IMMIGRANTS AND NATIVES, BY UNIT OF PRESENTATION AND PUBLIC ASSISTANCE PROGRAM, JANUARY 1990/1992

	Percentage Who Received Public Assistance Benefits			
	Immigrants	Natives	Immigrants-Natives	Standard Error of the Difference
Any Type of Public Assistance				
Households	8.30	6.62	1.68*	.536
Minimal Household Units	6.85	6.19	.66	.439
Individuals	6.52	5.75	.77	.527
Family Households	8.56	7.02	1.54*	.610
Families	6.86	6.41	.45	.553
Family Members	6.60	5.85	.75	.575
AFDC				
Households	3.38	3.06	.32	.353
Minimal household units	2.79	2.70	.09	.287
Individuals	3.42	3.75	−.33	.391
Family Households	4.15	4.31	−.16	.440
Families	4.29	4.67	−.38	.447
Family Members	4.03	4.44	−.41	.459
SSI				
Households	4.78	3.48	1.30*	.413
Minimal household units	3.88	3.23	0.65*	.334
Individuals	2.79	1.66	1.13*	.348
Family Households	4.42	2.83	1.59*	.443
Families	2.61	1.74	0.86*	.343
Family Members	2.30	1.12	1.18*	.342

Source: Survey of Income and Program Participation, 1990 and 1991 panels

* Difference is statistically significant ($p < .05$).

household-level versus individual-level units are used. To estimate the magnitude of the contribution of nativity differences in household size, in the average number of recipients per receiving unit, and in household nativity composition to household-level differences in welfare receipt, we decompose the differences following the procedure outlined by Das Gupta (1993). Although the overall nativity differences in AFDC receipt are not statistically significant, some of the separate components might be. Hence, we repeat the decomposition analyses for each of the three welfare measures: overall welfare, AFDC, and SSI receipt. Because age is important in different ways for AFDC and SSI receipt, we examine children and adults separately.

The difference in overall welfare recipiency between immigrants and natives measured at the household level is 1.68 percentage points, a gap that is statistically significant. Much of the difference in welfare is due to (a) differences in rates measured at the individual level, (b) differences in household size, (c) differences in recipient clustering, (d) differences in household nativity composition, and (e) differences in recipient nativity composition. Because households contain both adults and children, each of the components (except the individual-rate component) is further broken down into a part due to adults and a part due to children. The numbers in the far right-hand column of the table can be interpreted as the amount and direction of the immigrant-minus-native difference if immigrants and natives were identical on each of the other variables examined. The other factors also contribute to the immigrant-native difference, some operating to increase it and others to reduce it. For example, the higher recipient clustering within immigrant households reduces the household differential by nearly three fourths of a percentage point (0.70), indicating that the household-level differences would be even larger if welfare receipt were not more concentrated within immigrant households. Similarly, if the lower homogeneity of households (i.e., lower proportions of immigrants in immigrant households than of natives in native households) were the only factor at work, the direction of the difference between immigrants and natives would be reversed.

Summary and Discussion

The results show that immigrant-native comparisons of welfare recipiency depend on the unit chosen for the analysis and presentation of data. When welfare receipt is evaluated at the level of larger units, such as households or families, immigrants exceed natives in the extent to which they receive welfare. In the cases of smaller units, however, there are no differences between immigrants and natives in overall welfare receipt. However, immigrants exceed natives in SSI but not AFDC receipt, irrespective of the unit of analysis or presentation used. The findings also indicate that if immigrants and natives had identical living arrangements, immigrants' receipt would not significantly exceed natives' receipt in the case of AFDC, but it would exceed natives' receipt more in the case of SSI. The nativity difference in AFDC receipt would even reverse direction (although the difference would not be statistically significant) if immigrants and natives had identical living arrangements. Aggregate-level comparisons of welfare receipt by nativity thus tend to overstate use of AFDC but to understate use of SSI among immigrants in comparison with natives. However, nativity differences are also affected by group differences in children's nativity. When native-born children in households headed by immigrants are treated as foreign born, AFDC receipt of immigrant households is statistically significantly lower than that of native households.

Broadly speaking, the work presented here illustrates a set of problems that can occur in many research situations. Group comparisons of rates can be sensitive to the choice of unit of analysis or presentation, and discrepancies in results between studies using different units of analysis or presentation can arise from group differences in living arrangements.

Moreover, multivariate analyses do not adjust for the confounding influences of group differences in characteristic clustering or aggregate unit size. For instance, one may use a sample of households to estimate models that control for household size and composition and that adjust the independent variable to take into account multiple recipients per receiving household. Estimates of the group differentials produced by such models, however, fail to replicate the standardized differentials estimated by the method used in this paper (e.g., see Das Gupta, 1993). The reason is that, unlike the standardized differentials we estimate based on Eq. (2), multivariate models do not hold the individual-level rate constant. Rather than treat only the aggregate unit size as a measure of the dispersion of a population of persons and characteristics across households, multivariate models treat covariates, such as household size, as determinants of the probability that one or more individuals in a household display a given characteristic. The predicted prevalence rates differ from those observed because different aggregate unit sizes have different levels of association with the rates, not because a fixed number of persons and recipients are redistributed across households. Hence, rather than rely only on multivariate modeling to fix the problems associated with using a particular unit of analysis, researchers should be selective about their choices of the units of analysis and presentation.

References

Bean, F. D., J. V. W. Van Hook, & J. E. Glick. 1997. Country-of-origin, type of public assistance and patterns of welfare recipiency among U.S. immigrants and natives. *Social Science Quarterly,* 78:432–451.

Biddlecom, A.E. 1994. *Immigration and co-residence in the United States since 1960.* Paper presented at the annual meeting of the Population Association of America, Miami.

Blau, F. 1984. The use of transfer payments by immigrants. *Industrial and Labor Relations Review,* 37(2):222–239.

Borjas, G. J. 1994. The economics of immigration. *Journal of Economic Literature,* 32:1667–1717.

Borjas, G. J. & S. J. Trejo. 1991. Immigrant participation in the welfare system. *Industrial and labor Relations Review,* 44(2):195–211.

Citro, C. F. & R. T. Michael, eds. 1995. *Measuring poverty: A new approach.* Washington, DC: National Academy Press.

Das Gupta, P. 1993. *Standardization and decomposition of rates: A User's Manual.* U.S. Bureau of the Census, Current Population Reports, Series P23-186. Washington, DC: U.S. Government Printing Office.

Ermisch, J. F., & E. Overton. 1985. Minimal household units: A new approach to the analysis of household formation. *Population Studies,* 39:33–54.

Fix, M. and J.S. Passel. 1994. Perspective on immigration: A series of three op-ed articles. *Los Angeles Times*, August 1–3.

Glick, J.E., F.D. Bean, & J.V.W. Van Hook. 1997. Immigration and changing patterns of extended household/family structure in the United States: 1970–1990. *Journal of Marriage and the Family,* 59:177–191.

Goldscheider, F.K., & L.J. Waite. 1991. *New families, no families? The transformation of the American home.* Berkeley/Los Angeles: University of California Press.

Greenhalgh, S. 1982. Income units: The ethnographic alternative to standardization. *Population and Development Review,* 8(Supplement):70–91.

Jensen, L. 1988. Patterns of immigration and public assistance utilization, 1970–1980. *International Migration Review,* 22(1):51–83.

King, M., & S.H. Preston. 1990. Who lives with whom? Individual versus household measures. *Journal of Family History,* 15(2):117–132.

Kuznets, S. 1978. Size and age structure of family households: Exploratory comparisons. *Population and Development Review,* 4(2):187–223.

Levitan, S. A. 1985. *Programs in aid of the poor* (5th ed.). Baltimore: Johns Hopkins University Press.

Lloyd, C. B. 1995. Household structure and poverty: What are the connections? Population Council, Social Science Research, Research Division Working Papers, No. 74.

Ruggles, P. 1990. *Drawing the line: Alternative poverty measures and their implications for public policy.* Washington DC: Urban Institute Press.

Simon, J. 1984. Immigrants, taxes, and welfare in the United States. *Population and Development Review,* 10(1):55–69.

Smith, J. P., & B. Edmonston, eds. 1997. *The New Americans: Economic, demographic, and fiscal effects of immigration.* Washington, DC: National Academy Press.

Tienda, M., & L. Jensen. 1986. Immigration and public assistance participation: Dispelling the myth of dependency. *Social Science Research,* 15:372–400.

Trejo, S. J. 1992. Immigrant welfare recipiency: Recent trends and future implications. *Contemporary Policy Issues,* 10(2):44–53.

U.S. Bureau of the Census. 1993. *Survey of income and program participation (SIPP) 1990 waves 1-8 longitudinal microdata file technical documentation.* Washington, DC: U.S. Bureau of the Census.

U.S. Commission on Immigration Reform. 1994. *U.S. immigration policy: Restoring credibility, report to Congress.* Washington, DC: U.S. Commission on Immigration Reform.

U.S. Commission on Immigration Reform. 1997. *Becoming an American: Immigration and immigrant policy, report to Congress.* Washington, DC: U.S. Commission on Immigration Reform.

U.S. House of Representatives, Committee on Ways and Means. 1994. *1994 Green Book: Background material and data on programs within the jurisdiction of the Committee on Ways and Means.* Washington, DC: U.S. Government Printing Office.

REVIEW QUESTIONS

1. What units of analysis were used for this study?

2. What were the differences in the results based on the units of analysis used?

3. Is there another unit of analysis the researchers could have used? What would it have been? Do you think it would have shown different results?

GENDER ROLE ATTITUDES OF AMERICAN MOTHERS AND DAUGHTERS OVER TIME

Judy Rollins Bohannon and Priscilla White Blanton

Using the theory of symbolic interactionism that we learned about in Chapter 2, Bohannon & Blanton suggested that parents are the primary socializing agents for their children. Therefore, they believed that mothers and daughters would have similar ideas about marriage, children, and careers. Using 40 of the mothers and daughters who had participated in a similar study almost 20 years earlier, the researchers compared the three variables over time in this longitudinal study.

Symbolic interaction theorists assume that people are born asocial into a world of meanings that are translated to each child through interactions with significant and generalized others who are the primary socializing agents for each new generation (Mead, 1934). Symbolic interaction theorists in the United States have long proposed that parents are the most influential socializing agents for their children (Cooley, 1902; Sullivan, 1947; Turner, 1962). Empirical evidence has provided support for this theoretical premise (Barak, Feldman, & Noy, 1991; Huston & Carpenter, 1985; Katz & Boswell, 1986).

Another concept related to symbolic interaction is emergence, which is derived from Blumer's (1969) emphasis on the dynamic and processual character of self and society. Emergence refers to the belief that the self is constantly in development. This belief is in contrast to Hickman and Kuhn's (1956) description of the self as a structure of stable attitudes, determined early in life. On the basis of these concepts, it seems reasonable to look at mothers in the United States as primary socializing agents for the formation of their daughters' attitudes. It also seems reasonable to assume that both the mothers' and the daughters' attitudes may change over time.

Research on the intergenerational transmission of attitudes has indicated that parents' attitudes in general, and mothers' attitudes in particular, are significant predictors of the attitudes of their daughters (Acock & Bengston, 1978; Arditti, Godwin, & Scanzoni, 1991; Dalton, 1980; Jennings & Niemi, 1982; Smith, 1983). In his self-in-relation model, Surry (1985) maintained that the self is organized and developed within the context of significant relationships. For women, these significant relationships seem to be with their mothers. Rollins and White (1982) investigated the influence that American mothers have on the attitudes of their 10–14-year-old daughters on topics such as marriage, children, and careers. The basic premise of their study suggested that mothers are the primary significant others in the formation of their daughters' attitudes. They considered mothers and daughters in three different intact family environments: (a) traditional (in which the mother had not worked outside the home since the birth of her daughter); (b) dual-work environment (in which mothers were employed in jobs that require no formal training during the past 5 years); and (c) dual-career environment (in which mothers were employed in

Rollins Bohannon, J. & White Blanton, P. 1999. Gender role attitudes of American mothers and daughters over time. *Journal of Social Psychology*, 139(2), 173–180.

high status, nontraditional jobs during the past 5 years). Indeed, the results of the study indicated that mothers' attitudes and the attitudes of their young daughters are significantly related, although the attitudes differ across the groups. The dual-career mother-daughter dyads had the least traditional attitudes regarding marriage, children, and careers.

Longitudinal studies regarding gender role attitudes are few; those that have been conducted have focused primarily on mothers and adolescent daughters (McDonald, 1980; Thornton, Alwin, & Camburn, 1983). Our follow-up study of the Rollins and White (1982) research focused on the original sample of mothers and daughters and examined mother-daughter attitudes toward marriage, children, and careers approximately 15 years after the original study.

Daughters ranged in age from 25 to 29 years. Researchers have done little research with participants from this stage of adulthood, and we found no evidence of any longitudinal designs that examined the relationships of attitudes between adult daughters and their mothers. On the basis of the theoretical premises of symbolic interaction, we expected to find that mothers and daughters from Rollins and White's original study would still have similar attitudes toward children, marriage, and careers. As a result of emergence, we expected that not only would daughters' attitudes have changed because of maturation and interaction, but mothers' attitudes also would have changed because of interactions they have had with others, including their young adult daughters.

The purposes of our study were (a) to ascertain if, approximately 15 years later, young adult daughters in the United States still had attitudes about marriage, children, and careers that were similar to their mothers' attitudes and (b) to examine mothers' and daughters' attitudes over time. We hypothesized that mothers in the United States might still be significant socializers for their daughters.

Method

The original sample was drawn from the southern United States. The mothers' education levels ranged from attended high school to received graduate degree. At the time of the original study, the daughters were in middle school. Currently, the daughters' education levels ranged from graduated from high school to attended graduate school.

The mothers from the original study received letters asking them to supply the names and addresses of their daughters who participated in that study. Of the original sample of 75 mothers (25 traditional mothers, 25 dual-work mothers, and 25 dual-career mothers), 48 mothers responded. This represented a response rate of 64% and was considered very good because of the time that had elapsed between the original study and our follow-up research.

The 48 daughters were sent letters explaining the replication of the original study. A total of 40 daughters responded, all agreeing to participate. The mothers of those 40 young women were again sent letters telling them that their daughters were participating in the second study. All 40 mothers responded, and the final sample included the 40 mother-daughter dyads. This sample represented 83% of the possible dyads for which the mothers provided their daughters' addresses (53% of the original group). The mean ages of the mothers and daughters in the follow-up study were 56.8 and 27.4, respectively.

All of the mothers and daughters were sent a demographic questionnaire, a subscale of the Attitude Towards Women Scale (ATW; Spence, Helmreich, & Stapp, 1973), and a

TABLE 1 ■ MEAN SCORES ON MEASURES OF MOTHERS' AND DAUGHTERS' GENDER ROLE ATTITUDES AT TIME 1 AND TIME 2

	Time 1		Time 2	
Attitude	Mothers	Daughters	Mothers	Daughters
Children	10.95	11.40	9.90	9.25
Marriage	11.60	11.775	9.20	8.975
Career	25.55	23.87	20.70	19.85

subscale of the Sex-Role Orientation Scale (SRO; Brogan & Kutner, 1976). These subscales were the same ones used to collect the original data. We used the same 16 items selected from the short version of the ATW and 10 items selected from the SRO. Both subscales are 4-point, Likert-type scales. As in the earlier study, both the ATW and the SRO were modified to include in the subscales only those items that measured attitudes toward marriage, children, and careers. For both scales, the scores for each item pertaining to a particular variable were summed to obtain the respondents' attitudinal scores. The reliability coefficients for the combined scales were .83 for mothers and .82 for daughters.

The numerical range for attitudes toward marriage and children was 6 to 24, and the range for attitudes toward career was 14 to 64. Lower scores indicated more nontraditional attitudes.

The data from the 40 mothers and daughters were analyzed without regard to the original groups because of the smaller sample sizes at Time 2. It was not necessary to compare these same groups again because the purpose of our study was to see if mothers and daughters still held similar attitudes about children, marriage, and careers. Mother's occupation was not a variable.

Results

Univariate tests for the effect of each gender role variable showed that mothers and daughters did not differ significantly on any of the three variables (Table 2). However, the attitudes of both groups had changed significantly over time. The scales for the variables were arranged so that lower scores represented less traditional attitudes. Therefore, the mean scores for both mothers and daughters indicated that over the 15 years that had elapsed, their attitudes had become less traditional (Table 1).

Discussion

In the original study, the mothers and their daughters (ages 10–14) had similar attitudes about children, marriage, and careers. The hypothesis that mothers are primary socializing agents for their daughters was supported, a finding that is consistent with symbolic interaction theory. Findings from our follow-up study suggest that mothers' and daughters' attitudes about these three variables are still similar, even though the daughters are young

TABLE 2 ■ UNIVARIATE TESTS FOR MOTHERS' AND DAUGHTERS' ATTITUDES ABOUT CHILDREN, MARRIAGE, AND CAREERS OVER TIME

Source	Variable	[M.sup.2]	F	Sig.
RELAT	Children	0.400	0.050	.824
	Marriage	2.500	0.003	.956
	Career	63.756	2.741	.106
TIME	Children	102.400	13.814	.001(*)
	Marriage	270.400	45.047	.000(*)
	Career	787.656	58.390	.000(*)
RELAT x TIME	Children	12.100	2.630	.113
	Marriage	1.600	0.355	.555
	Career	6.806	0.406	.502

Note: All degrees of freedom were 1, Sig. = significance; RELAT = differences overall between mothers and daughters.

* $p < .05$.

adults. Arditti and colleagues (1991) found that even when daughters grow up, their gender role attitudes still appear to be significantly similar to those of their mothers. Our findings continue to support at least a bi-directional influence of mothers and daughters as significant others regarding attitude formation.

However, mothers' and daughters' attitudes changed over time, although they changed in a similar pattern for both groups. Additionally, the scores indicated a more nontraditional view of children, marriage, and careers than the researchers had found 15 years earlier. This finding seems to be consistent with societal norms in the United States that appear to have embraced a more liberal interpretation of appropriate role behaviors for women over the past two decades.

Thornton and colleagues (1983) tested mothers at different intervals for 18 years and found that gender role attitudes were predictable over 3-year time periods, although predictability decreased systematically over the 18 years. They attributed this change to changes in societal attitudes over time, rather than to the transition to a later stage in life. The lack of consistency in attitudes over time supports their results.

This finding also supports the usefulness of the concept of emergence not only for daughters, who are more often expected to change as they mature and have many new social interactions, but also for mothers as they grow older and have different social interactions. From our follow-up study, it appears that attitudes are processual in nature, and predicting attitudes from one time to another may prove inaccurate.

Our findings also appear to support the self-in-relation theory (Surry, 1985), which maintains that the self is organized and develops within the context of significant relationships. The studies that found that daughters maintain their connectedness with their mothers (Calloni & Handal, 1992) and have a continuous engagement with them

(Rosenzweig, 1991) have validity when we believe that connectedness and engagement are bi-directional.

The limitations of this follow-up study include the smaller sample size, even though over half of the original respondents were located after 15 years. The generalizability is limited because of the sample size and the nonrandom design of the study.

The issue of the direction of socialization needs to be addressed. More longitudinal studies need to be conducted to determine who is the significant other regarding the formation of the gender role attitudes of adult daughters and their mothers. A key question is whether mothers remain the primary source of daughters' gender role attitudes or whether daughters become one of the primary socializing agents for their mothers as both the mothers and the daughters age.

References

Acock, A. C., & Bengston, V. L. (1978). On the relative influence of mothers and fathers: A covariance analysis of political and religious socialization. *Journal of Marriage and the Family*, 40, 519–530.

Arditti, J. A., Godwin, D. B., & Scanzoni, J. (1991). Perceptions of parenting behavior and young women's gender role traits and preferences. *Sex Roles*, 25(3/4), 195–211.

Barak, A., Feldman, S., & Noy, A. (1991). Traditionality of children's interests as related to their parents' gender stereotypes and traditionality of occupations. *Sex Roles*, 24, 511–524.

Blumer, H. (1969). *Symbolic interactionism: Perspective and method*. Englewood Cliffs, NJ: Prentice-Hall.

Brogan, D., & Kutner, N. G. (1976). Measuring sex-role orientation: A normative approach. *Journal of Marriage and the Family*, 2, 31–39.

Calloni, J. C., & Handal, P. J. (1992). Differential parental attachment: Empirical support for the self-in-relation model. *Perceptual and Motor Skills*, 75, 904–906.

Cooley, C. H. (1902). *Human nature and the social order*. New York: Scribner.

Dalton, R. J. (1980). Reassessing parental socialization: Indicator unreliability versus generational transfer. *American Political Science Review*, 74, 421–431.

Hickman, C. A., & Kuhn, M. H. (1956). *Individuals, groups, and economic behavior*. New York: Dryden.

Huston, A. C., & Carpenter, C. J. (1985). Gender-related differences in social interaction: The influence of adults. In L. C. Wilkinson & C. B. Marret (Eds.), *Gender influence in classroom interaction* (pp. 149–163). New York: Academic Press.

Jennings, M. K., & Niemi, R. (1982). *Generations and politics: A panel study of young adults and their parents*. Princeton, NJ: Princeton University Press,

Katz, P, A., & Boswell, S. (1986). Flexibility and traditionality in children's gender roles. *Genetic, Social, and General Psychology Monographs*, 112, 105–147.

McDonald, G. W. (1980). Parental power and adolescents' parental identification: A reexamination. *Journal of Marriage and the Family*, 42, 289–296.

Mead, G. H. (1934). *Mind, self and society*. Chicago: University of Chicago Press.

Rollins, J., & White, P. N. (1982).The relationship between mothers' and daughters' sex-role attitudes and self-concepts in three types of family environment. *Sex Roles*, 8, 1141–1155.

Rosenzweig, L. W. (1991). "The anchor of my life": Middle-class American mothers and college-educated daughters 1880–1920. *Journal of Social History*, 25, 5–25.

Smith, T. E. (1983). Parental influence: A review of the evidence of influence and theoretical model of the parental influence process. In A. C. Kerckhoff (Ed.), *Research in sociology of education and socialization* (Vol. 4, pp.13–45). Greenwich, CT: JAI.

Spence, J., Helmreich, R., & Stapp, J. (1973). Attitudes toward women scale. *Bulletin of the Psychonomics Society*, 2, 219–220.

Sullivan, H, S. (1947). *Conceptions of modern psychiatry*. Washington, DC: William A. White Psychiatric Foundation.

Surrey, J. L. (1985). *Self-in-relation: A theory of women's development*. Work in progress, Stone Center for Developmental Services and Studies, Wellesley College.

Thornton, A., Alwin, D. F., & Camburn, D. (1983). Causes and consequences of sex role attitudes and attitude change. *American Sociological Review*; 48, 211–227.

Turner, R. H. (1962). Role-taking process versus conformity. In A. Rose (Ed.), *Human behavior and social processes: An interactionist approach*. Boston: Houghton Mifflin.

REVIEW QUESTIONS

1. State some of the benefits of making this study longitudinal? What does it do to the 1982 findings?

2. How many of the original participants were the researchers able to find? Do you think they found enough?

3. Explain the three variables the researcher used for this project.

CONSEQUENCES OF PARTICIPATING IN A LONGITUDINAL STUDY OF MARRIAGE

Joseph Veroff, Shirley Hatchett, and Elizabeth Douvan

In this study, Veroff, Hatchett, and Douvan suggest there might be some consequences to conducting longitudinal studies. Using the data from a 4-year study of black and white newlyweds, couples were randomly selected to be in either a large study group or a smaller control group. The subjects in the larger study groups received more frequent and intense interviewing over the duration of the study. Notice how more interaction over a longer period of time could affect that outcome of the study.

There are some issues that researchers who use survey methodology would like to repress. Perhaps the most disturbing of these is the possibility that the methods they use may actually cause a short- or long-term change in the very phenomenon they are trying to measure—in other words, that certain survey research designs, particularly longitudinal ones, may comprise an unintentional intervention that changes attitudes or behavior or both, Here we present research from an experimental manipulation in a 4-year longitudinal study of marital adjustment and stability among black and white urban newlyweds that suggests that such effects may occur.

We incorporated this experimental design in response to a concern raised by human subjects review boards at both the University of Michigan and the National Institute of Mental Health. Both groups wondered whether long-term, in-depth inquiry into the bases of affection, conflict, difficulties and problems in a marriage, perceptions of each other, attitudes toward gender roles, general levels of well-being in the marriage, and the like could raise concerns in a married couple about each other that would not have been considered had we not asked about them.

In research directly relevant to the question, Wilson et al. (1984) found that having undergraduates explain their dating relationships (i.e., telling them to "list all the reasons you can think of why your relationship . . . is going the way it is' ') had a disruptive effect on attitude-behavior consistency—that is, the relationship between feelings toward their partners and whether the couple is dating several months later, as compared to a control group. Wilson, Kraft, and Dunn (1989) have reanalyzed the data and have found that the disruptive effect occurs only for couples who had been dating a short amount of time. Various explanations are offered. The ones given greatest credence focus on the assumption that people in longer relationships probably have more consistent schemas about the relationship and hence are less likely to generate new material about the relationship in the interview that would disrupt the connection between present attitude and future behavior. This should be less true for the shorter relationships. The implication of these results for our study is that interviewing newlyweds who had known each other a long time might be less disruptive of their ongoing relationship than interviewing newlyweds who have been

Veroff, J., Hatchett, S., & Douvan, E. 1992. Consequences of participating in a longitudinal study of marriage. *Public Opinion Quarterly,* 56: 325–327.

in shorter relationships. One might have similar expectations with regard to whether or not the couples lived together before marriage. We might assume that cohabitation would give the couples broader experiences to develop schemas that are more resistant than those of couples who did not live together.

Wilson et al. (1989) are doing parallel research on other attitude objects besides dating partners—particularly political figures. In that context, they find that there is a bi-directional attitude change when subjects are asked to generate explanations for their attitudes. Some become more positive over time; some more negative. Following Wilson's lead, we would expect an increased variance on measures of marital well-being over time for couples we intensively interviewed at more points than for a control group interviewed less intensively and for a shorter period of time.

Thus, there is some evidence to suggest that the kind of effect that concerned the human subjects board might result from our 4-year prospective study of newlyweds in first marriages. Little is known about attitudinal or behavioral change resulting from data collection. However, we generated two general hypotheses about what types of effects we might find when we examine marital adjustment and well-being among randomly sampled couples in our main study and control groups. First, following Wilson et al.'s (1989) lead, we explored whether there was greater variance in marital quality measures in the second year among the study group compared to the control group. Second, we felt that the general effect of more frequent and intensive interviews would be positive by the fourth year, with the main study group having better marital adjustment and stability than the control group. We felt that both of these effects would be smaller for couples who had considered themselves a couple for a longer period of time, Wilson, Kraft, and Dunn's (1989) research suggested.

Method

Two samples—a main study group and a control group—were each randomly selected from a sampling frame of eligible couples applying for marriage licenses in Wayne County, MI, during a 3-month period (April–June 1986). To be eligible, the marriage had to be the first for both, and the wife had to be 35 or younger. In the first and third years of the study, both spouses in the main study group were first interviewed using standard structured questionnaires containing both open and fixed response questions. These face-to-face interviews averaged 80 minutes. Later, on another day, they were interviewed together using two innovative techniques. They were first asked to construct a joint narrative, to "tell the story" of their relationship, and then they participated in a revealed differences task (explained further below). These interviews were audiotaped and averaged 30 minutes. In years 2 and 4, spouses were interviewed separately by telephone for an average of 15 minutes, again using structured questionnaires.[1] Race of interviewer and respondent were matched for the face-to-face interviews.

In comparison, the control group was interviewed minimally over the 4-year period. In order to get baseline data for the control group, wives received a short structured interview averaging 7 minutes in the first year. In years 2 and 4, the control couples were contacted by phone using the same method as for the main study group. However, in year 2, the controls were asked only a subset of the questions (all closed-ended) with the inter-

TABLE 1 ■ RESPONSE RATES AND BASES OF ATTRITION FOR STUDY AND CONTROL
RESPONDENTS (BY YEAR)

	Number of Respondents in Eligible Sample[a]	Responded %	Refused %	Not Located or Interviewed
Year 1:				
Study	1,148	65	22	13
Control	172[b]	69	9	22
Year 2:				
Study	746	92	3	4
Control	114	92	0	7
Year 3:				
Study	681	85	8	7
Control[c]	—	—	—	—
Year 4:				
Study	559	90	5	5
Control	102	86	7	7

[a] In year 1, this was the original listed sample minus all those respondents who turned out not to be married or not living in Wayne County; in years 2–4 this represented the number of people who were interviewed in the prior year and were still married.

[b] Only the wives in the couples listed were interviewed; the response rate, noninterviews, and refusals are based on the wives only.

[c] The control sample not interviewed in year 3.

views averaging 5 minutes, compared to the 15 minutes for the main study. Between waves, study group couples were sent an anniversary card with an enclosed postcard to be returned if they had moved or changed phone numbers. No contact was made with the control group between waves.

In the first year of the study, 373 main study couples—199 black and 174 white—were interviewed in their homes 3–7 months after they were married. The overall response rate for the study was 66 percent,[2] which is high given that the cooperation of both spouses was needed for inclusion in the study. Fifty-nine wives in the control group, 36 percent of them black, were interviewed during the same period in the first year. Table 1 presents, for the study group and the control group separately, the eligible sample of respondents[3] for that year; response rate (the number interviewed/the number of eligible respondents); percent refusals; and percent not interviewed, which could be for a variety of reasons (sickness, impossible to locate, moved too far away for interviewing). There were no significant differences in response rates in black and white study samples, but the black control sample responded at a significantly lower rate than the white control sample. Within race, the response rates for study and control samples are comparable.

The topics in the structured questionnaires in years 1 and 3 for the main study included the following: the quality and density of couples' networks; the way they interact with each other, with considerable focus on how they handle conflicts; their feelings about their relationship, including irritations, sexual tensions, and ways they care for each other; how they assign household chores and their attitudes toward these arrangements; their perceptions of themselves and each other, and their ideals for themselves and each other; their general well-being and specific marital well-being; and much more. The questionnaires in years 2 and 4 contained mostly closed format questions, which represented replications of items included in main marital well-being measures, significant life events, and selected other topics.

As noted earlier, the couple interview included two novel procedures. In the narrative, the couple told an open-ended story of their relationship using only a storyboard with topical markers cuing coverage of their first meeting, their courtship, the wedding, life after the wedding, and hopes for the future. This was a difficult task for some couples, who gave less involved or merely descriptive stories. However, most couples became involved in the storytelling task, which for them presented a chance to pull together many strands of their relationship. Some spouses were surprised to hear each other's version of their experience as a couple. In the second procedure, husbands and wives separately rated the importance of a number of marital ideals (e.g., "If you're fighting, cool off before you say too much") and then had to resolve their differences. This procedure often elicited large differences in attitudes toward marriage. We were interested in the way the couples resolved their differences, but the couples were clearly interested in how they differed on important marital issues and ideals.

Results

We evaluated our general hypotheses using two approaches. First, we examined the variance on overall attitudinal indicators of marital well-being for the study and control group to see if, like Wilson et al. (1989), we found bi-directional changes between the first and second year. Next, we looked at the effects of being in the main study or the control group on marital stability and on several indicators of marital adjustment or well-being.

The first approach yielded some evidence supporting Wilson et al.'s (1989) findings that explaining art attitude can enhance that attitude in some people but disrupt it in others and hence induce an increased variance in that attitude. Whereas there were no study group-control group differences in the variances on a measure of marital satisfaction in the first year, by the second year the variance on that measure was significantly higher in three of the four gender x race groups. And again by year 4 there were no significant study group-control group differences in variance. These results thus gave us some indirect evidence that our main study methodology may have had disruptive effects on the marital well-being of some respondents. Although it was plausible to think that the amount of time a couple lived together as a couple would be a moderating factor in affecting this pattern (the variance effect should be minimal for long-term couples and clearest for couples who had not lived together before marriage), an analysis testing this hypothesis using a question asked of the couples about their cohabitation history yielded no significant findings.

Our second approach yielded nonsignificant results with regard to marital stability over the 4 years but did yield some provocative results using attitudinal assessments of marital experience in the fourth year. When we compared the separation and divorce rates of couples at the end of the study, we found that the main study couples appeared to have fared worse than the control couples. We found that 9 percent of the original control sample and 15 percent of the original study sample were known to be divorced or separated at the end of the study. This difference proved to be nonsignificant in a logit analysis of the divorced/separated versus married status of couples at year 4, which included two other variables known to be significantly related to both the couple's study status and fourth-year marital status: race (black couples were more likely to become divorced and were proportionally more represented in the study sample); and wives' initial feelings about the ease of talking with their husbands (lower in the divorced couples and higher in the control sample). Even if we included those respondents who are nonascertained on marital status as part of the divorced/separated group,[4] the predictive power of study status is not significant, although the trend becomes stronger. Testing a model that includes race as a factor interacting with study status also yields no significant results, nor does a model that includes how long a couple lived together before marriage as an interacting factor. Thus, the initial study status difference in marital stability washes out with proper controls.

A different picture emerges when we compare the attitudes that study versus control status couples express about their marital quality the fourth year. Many of couples not interviewed at the end of the study were those who were nonrespondents or who were not followed because they separated or divorced over the first 3 years. Admittedly, this would leave us with couples who are on the whole better off. However, there still could be differences in the marital quality of study and control group couples that could speak to our overall hypothesized effect.

How to measure marital quality in the fourth year? We had many options, since the control sample was given more attitudinal questions in the fourth year than they were given in previous panels. Crohan and Veroff (1989) distinguished four factors for the overall perceptions and feelings about marriage measured in our study. These reflect (1) the couple's general happiness; (2) the sense of competence each spouse feels in the spouse role; (3) perceptions of equity in the relationship; and (4) the sense of control each spouse feels to make things right in the relationship. The following presents one prototypic item for each dimension of marital well-being:

Marital happiness (five items). "Taking things altogether, how would you describe your marriage."? Would you say your marriage is very happy, a little happier than average or not too happy?"

Marital competence (two items). "Since you have been married, how often have you felt you were not as good a (wife/husband) as you would like to be—often, sometimes, rarely or never?"

Marital equity (two items). "All in all, considering how much each of you put into your marriage, who would you say gets more out of being married—you, your (wife/husband) or both of you equally?"

Marital control (two items). "Every (wife/husband) experiences times when things between (herself/himself) and (her husband/his wife) are not going as well as (she/he) would like. When such times come up for you, how often do you feel that you can do or say something to make things better—most of the time, sometimes or hardly ever?"

To evaluate our hypothesis of better marital quality as the result of being involved in the study group versus the control group, we used these four measures of overall marital quality and two measures tapping specific aspects of the relationship—the sexual aspect and an index of marital tension.

These two indices were two of five factors emerging from a factor analysis of all specific marital qualities not assessed in the Crohan and Veroff (1989) indices. These were the only two significantly correlated with the central measure of marital happiness and, hence, relevant to assessing well-being. Prototypic items for each of these scales are listed below.

Negative aspects of sexual life (three items). "How often in the past month did you feel upset about the way the two of you were getting along in the sexual part of your relationship—often, sometimes, rarely, or never?"

Marital tension (four items). "During the past month, how often did you feel irritated or resentful about things your (wife/husband) did or didn't do—often, sometimes, rarely or never?"

When certain aspects of marital quality or well-being were assessed, the study group marriages appear to have fared better than those of the control group. For marital equity, we found a significant main effect for study status and a significant interaction effect of gender, race, and study status. Study group couples perceived more equity in their marriages at the end of the study than did control couples. The significant interaction comes from the fact that the main effect was particularly true for black wives. Also, wives and husbands in the study group felt more competent in their spousal roles than those in the control. The other results suggest that marital tensions are higher in control couples and that black study group wives are less likely than black control wives to perceive their sex life as negative. All in all, these results suggest that better-adjusted marriages may have developed among study couples as a result of the more frequent and more involved interviewing.

Summary and Discussion

Apart from trying to assess whether our marriage study design had negative or positive effects on the marriages we were monitoring, we were also attempting to address a more general question of whether longitudinal survey studies of social phenomenon can inadvertently effect short- or long-term changes in the natural course of things.

Our evidence suggests that being part of an intensive, longitudinal study focused on feelings one has about his or her marriage, and perceptions of the feelings of one's spouse, may result in both attitudinal and behavioral changes among newlywed couples. Similar to Wilson et al. (1989), we found some significant results that suggest negative effects on the natural life course of the marriages of our respondents. Although we realize the negative effect (the greater variance in marital satisfaction expressed by the study group compared to the control group) is merely suggestive, we think it is important to consider. We also found clear evidence of positive effects of being in the study. The marriages of study group couples after 4 years seem more adjusted. Perhaps the study group interviewing experience caused couples to focus on a number of issues earlier in their marriage than they would have done naturally. We had no control over spouses talking after the interviewers left. And it may be that the marriages of couples that remained intact to the end of the study were better off as a consequence of their having reflected on these issues. While Wilson's research suggested that those who had been in relationships for shorter time periods were more susceptible to either positive or negative changes, we found no such evidence. Using how long the couple lived together before marriage as an indicator of length of intimate association, we found no significant results or even marginal trends for relationship length as a moderator on the effects of study status on increased variance in satisfaction, stability, or fourth year marital quality.

Whether results of this study would generalize to less extensive and intensive surveys of marriage or other interpersonal relationships is an open question. Nevertheless, the results should alert survey researchers, who have become increasingly interested in asking respondents complex questions about significant people, that the topics they probe may linger as issues in their respondents lives.

This study may also alert researchers to parallel effects that may occur when surveys inquire in depth about any topic that has not been well considered prior to the survey. Wilson and his colleagues have evidence that asking people about their reasons for supporting certain political figures can disrupt their original attitudes. Although their work has been primarily with undergraduate students, similar results could be found in the general population. Their research strongly suggests that political voting preferences, not just voting behavior, may be affected by a survey interviewer asking respondents why they have a particular view. More than a quarter of our marriage study was composed of similar open-ended questions. Although the results presented here are tentative, researchers should consider the possibility that their studies, especially if they use in-depth interviews about personal matters, may unintentionally trigger new perspectives in respondents and subsequently change their lives. We are too tempted to see respondents as passive beings dutifully conforming to their role in the survey interview. They may be more reactive than we think.

Notes

[1] Because the telephone interviewing staff was almost all white, an experiment was conducted in the second year to detect race of interviewer effects among blacks interviewed over the phone. The black sample was randomly split into two groups, one done by white telephone interviewers and the other by black field interviewers using their home telephones. No race of interviewer effects were found.

[2] This couple response rate is larger than one would expect if an 80 percent response rate was obtained for each spouse separately. The joint probability of getting the couple given this individual rate would be .64 or 64 percent.

[3] In the first year, this figure excluded those who, in the original listing obtained from the county clerk office, did not get married or whose address at time of interviewing was not in Wayne county; in subsequent years it excluded those from whom there was no interview in the prior year or having been interviewed in the prior year said they were separated or divorced Or that their spouse had died.

[4] There would be reason to believe that there were numerous unhappy, if not divorced and separated, couples among those who were not interviewed because we could not contact them or they refused to be interviewed. Evidence for this assertion comes from an analysis of whether an index of expressed marital happiness in a preceding year differentiates those who were and were not interviewed in the subsequent year. For years 2–4, consistent results, most of them significant at the .05 level: compared to those who were interviewed, those not interviewed reported being less happy in the preceding year when they were interviewed.

References

Anderson, Barbara A., Brian D. Silver, and Paul R. Abramson. 1988. The effects of the race of the interviewer on measures of electoral participation by Blacks in SRC national election studies. *Public Opinion Quarterly,* 52:53–83.

Clausen, Aage. 1968. Response validity: Vote report. *Public Opinion Quarterly,* 41:56–6,1.

Crohan, Susan E., & Joseph, Veroff. 1989. Dimensions of marital well-being among White and Black Newlyweds. *Journal of Marriage and the Family,* 51:373–384.

Kraut, Robert E., & John B. McConahey. 1973. How Being Interviewed Affects Voting: An Experiment. *Public Opinion Quarterly,* 37:381–398.

Traugott, Michael W., & John P. Katosh. 1979. Response validity in surveys of voting behavior. *Public Opinion Quarterly,* 43:359–377.

Yalch, Richard F. 1976. Pre-election interview effects on voter turnout. *Public Opinion Quarterly,* 40:331–336.

Roloado. 1984. Effects of analyzing reasons on attitude-behavior consistency. *Journal of Personality and Social Psychology,* 47:5–16.

Wilson, Timothy D., Dana S. Ductn, Jane A. Bybee, Diane B. Hyrnan, & John A. Roloado. 1984. Effects of Analyzing Reasons on Attitude-Behavior Consistency. *Journal of Personality and Social Psychology,* 47:5-16

Wilson, Timothy D., Dana S. Dunn, Delores Kraft, & Douglas J. Lisle. 1989. Introspection, attitude change and attitude-behavior consistency: The disruptive effects of explaining why we feel the way we do" In *Advances in Experimental Social Psychology,* ed. L. Berkowitz, 22:287–343. Orlando, FL: Academic Press.

Wilson, Timothy D., Dolores Kraft, & Dana S. Dunn. 1989. The disruptive effects of explaining attitudes: The moderating effect of knowledge about the attitude object." *Journal of Experimental Social Psychology,* 25:379–400.

REVIEW QUESTIONS

1. What did the researchers find that was problematic with this longitudinal study?

2. What was the difference between the control group and the research group? How did that difference affect the outcome of the project?

3. Would it have been better to do a cross-sectional design? Why or why not?

Chapter 5: Conceptualization and Operationalization

QUALITATIVE VERSUS QUANTITATIVE RESEARCH

Regardless of how you collect your data, it will be in the form of *raw data*. This means that the data has not been processed in anyway at all. It is really pretty impossible to do much with raw data. Suppose you have a class and you have some basic information about class members such as this:

Student #	Name	Feelings about the Class	GPA	Final Grade
1	Sam	Hate It	2. 5	54
2	Lucy	Bored by it	3. 8	87
3	Wilbur	Love the class	4. 0	100
4	Fran	Hate it	4. 0	98
5	Craig	Bored	2. 9	76

The table has raw data. You really don't know what any of it means and you must find out. In **quantitative research**, the raw data that has been gathered must be converted into some type of numerical equivalents before you can do some type of analysis and statistical testing. These numerical equivalents are necessary to describe the data and to explain whether or not the data supports your hypothesis, which we will be discussing a little later. For instance, in the above table you can convert the GPAs of all of the students to find the class GPA average. In **qualitative research**, on the other hand, the data is collected from notes, observations, and interviews, and it usually is not summarized by numbers or analyzed with statistics. In this chapter we will be focusing on how you begin to define a concept so you can gather the raw data you will need for your project.

Suppose you heard a news report that said, "Students who believe in God and go to a place of worship have higher GPAs." Would you be curious about it and want to know if it is true? What kind of question could you ask? You would first need to come up with a **hypothesis**, which is a tentative statement about the empirical relation that involves a relationship between two or more **variables**. The variable is a characteristic or property that can vary by taking on different values. The **independent variable** is the variable hypothesized to cause, or lead to, a variation in the dependent variable. The **dependent variable**, on the other hand is the variable whose variation is hypothesized to depend on or be influenced by the independent variable.

Forming a research question involves defining the **concept** or the mental image that summarizes a set of similar observations, feelings, or ideas. How will you know exactly how to design your research project unless you understand exactly what you are going to measure? Since research questions tend to revolve around concepts and variables, which are often not easy to distinguish between, they must be carefully defined so others will understand precisely what you mean and what you are measuring.

Let's say that your hypothesis is as follows: "The more religious a person is, the better his or her success in college will be. " In this case your dependent variable would be success, which you believe would be influenced by your independent variable, which is religiosity. I find it easier for students to visualize this with an arrow.

(Independent Variable)   (Dependent Variable)

Religiosity   Success

The term religiosity is very abstract. What do you think it really means? You first need to conceptualize religiosity. **Conceptualization** means that you will identify and define the concept so you can study it. So, you can conceptualize religiosity as someone who goes to a house of prayer at least one time a week, says prayers every night before going to bed, follows the ten commandments exactly, and believes in a higher power. With those ideas in mind, you now have a working agreement about what the term religiosity means. Now that you have conceptualized religiosity, you are able to indicate the presence or absence of the concept by specifying one or more indicators. An **indicator** is what you choose to be the reflection of the variable you are studying. So, praying every night would be an indicator of how religious a person is. But maybe you and your classmates don't have the same ideas about religiosity. Therefore, you might want to group this concept into "feelings of religiosity" and "actions of religiosity. " These groups would be called **dimensions**. As a result, it is possible to divide the concept of religiosity according to different sets of dimensions.

Now that you have your variable figured out, you have to decide how you are going to **operationalize** it for your particular study. To operationalize your variable, you must say exactly how you will be measuring the variable. To find out how religious a person really is, you might ask the following questions:

1. How many times have you been to a place of worship in the last month?

2. Do you believe in a praying every night before you go to bed?

So, you have gone from abstractly thinking about a term that you want to research to figuring out exactly what you want to know about the term, and how you will measure it to find out if your hypothesis is correct.

Another aspect that is very important to the research process is to find out how **valid** your measurements are. To measure the **validity** of a question, you must be sure that what you are using to operationalize your variable is actually measuring the variable you have stated you were studying. You want to make sure the measurement you use is measuring the entire variable, not just part of the variable. Let's say you want to study success in your research methods class. If you use only the question "what grade did you get in research methods?," does that really tell you how successful a student is?. What other questions would you need to ask to measure this? I believe there are a number of ways to measure a student's success and that grades are only part of it. What other indicators can be used to measure a person's success in a class?

CONSTRUCTING QUESTIONS

You might think it is easy to ask people questions. In fact, you probably ask questions all the time. However, when you are writing questions for a research project there are things that you must take into consideration. For instance, you wouldn't want to ask the question "Are you religious?" Why wouldn't you? What types of answers would you receive? Would everyone's responses really answer the question you want to ask?

There are many kinds of questions. Some questions are **open-ended,** where the respondents are asked to provide their own answers to the question. Other questions are **close-ended,** where the respondents are asked to select an answer from a list of possible answers. Some questions are very good, and others are not useful. It is important that you know the difference. Questions should also be relevant to your hypothesis and variables. If the question has nothing to do with either, then it shouldn't be in your **questionnaire**. Questions should be clear and asked in a straightforward manner, such as "What grade did you receive on your last methods test?"

What about this question: "Do you know how to design a questionnaire, and what grade did you receive on your methods test?" This question is **double-barreled** because it has an *and* in it. Therefore, the question actually becomes two questions, making it difficult for the respondents to know what they are answering. How would you answer this question?: "Do you never not want chocolate for dinner?" This question would be considered a **double negative** and would also be difficult for your respondents to answer. Finally, you need to consider the **social desirability** of your question. If you ask the question, "Do you beat your animals?," do you think anyone would actually answer the question?

INFOTRAC COLLEGE EDITION SUGGESTED READINGS AND DISCUSSION QUESTIONS

1. Using the variable "social class,", find articles such as "Stratification, class and health: Class relations and health inequalities in high modernity" (Article A55084105) or "The social networks and resources of African American eighth graders: Evidence from the National Education Longitudinal study of 1988" (Article A54657537). Can you tell how these articles operationalize the variable? Can you locate other articles in the InfoTrac College Edition database that use social class?

2. Everyone falls in love with someone. Look up the word "love" on InfoTrac College Edition. Your search should result in giving you a few options. Look up various articles on love such as "Three-dimensional love" (Article A18668472), "T'ang Chun-i's philosophy of love" (Article A20653028), and "Urban African American adolescent parents: Their perceptions of sex, love, intimacy, pregnancy, and parenting" (Article A53870299). How is love operationalized in each of these articles? Is there a difference?

CONCEPTUALIZATION OF TERRORISM

Jack P. Gibbs

As you have learned, conceptualizing a variable is not always easy to do. There are many different ways to conceptualize the same term. Therefore, it is important to state how you are using the concept in the project you are conducting. In this article, Gibbs discusses the issues and problems that surround the conceptualization of terrorism. While most definitions are based on purely personal opinions, Gibbs goes beyond a definition of terrorism by emphasizing the definition's bearing on five major conceptual questions, each of which introduces a major issue and/or problem.

Definitions of terrorism are controversial for reasons other than conceptual issues and problems. Because labeling actions as "terrorism" promotes condemnation of the actors, a definition may reflect ideological or political bias (for lengthy elaboration, see Rubenstein, 1987). Given such considerations, all of which discourage attempts to define terrorism, it is not surprising that Laqueur (1977, p. *5)* argued that

> A comprehensive definition of terrorism does not exist nor will it be found in the foreseeable future. To argue that terrorism cannot be studied without such a definition is manifestly absurd.

Even granting what Laqueur implies—that terrorism is somehow out there awaiting definition—it is no less "manifestly absurd" to pretend to study terrorism without at least some kind of definition of it., Leaving the definition implicit is the road to obscurantism.

Even if sociologists should overcome their ostensible reluctance to study terrorism (for a rare exception, see Lee, 1983), they are unlikely to contribute to its conceptualization. The situation has been described succinctly by Tallman (1984, p. 1121): "Efforts to explicate key concepts in sociology have been met with stifling indifference by members of our discipline. "

There are at least two reasons why sociologists commonly appear indifferent to conceptualizations. First, Weber and Parsons gave the work a bad name in the eyes of those sociologists who insist (rightly) on a distinction between substantive theory and conceptual analysis. Second, conclusive resolutions of conceptual issues are improbable because the *ultimate* justification of any definition is an impressive theory that incorporates the definition. Nonetheless, it is crippling to assume that productive research and impressive theories are possible without confronting conceptual issues and problems. The argument is not just that theorizing without definitions is sterile, nor merely recognition that theory construction and conceptualization should go hand in hand. Additionally, one can assess definitions without descending to purely personal opinion, even when not guided by a theory.

Systematic tests of a theory require definitions of at least *some* of the theory's constituent terms; but test findings, even those based on the same units of comparison, will diverge if each definition's empirical applicability is negligible, meaning if independent

---

* Gibbs, J. P. Conceptualization of terrorism. *American Sociological Review*, 54 (3), 329–340. Used only 329–334.

observers disagree when applying the definition to identify events or things. To illustrate, contemplate a question about any definition of terrorism: How much do independent observers agree in judging whether or not President Kennedy's assassination was terrorism in light of the definition? As subsequent illustrations show, simple definitions may promote agreement in answers to the Kennedy question and yet be objectionable for theoretical reasons; but the immediate point is that an empirically applicable definition does not require a theory. By contrast, given evidence that a definition promises negligible empirical applicability, no theory can justify that definition.

Still another "atheoretical" criterion is the definition's consistency with convention. That criterion cannot be decisive, because it would preclude novel definitions; but it is important when the field's professionals must rely on outsiders" for data and, hence, presume appreciable congruence between their definitions and those of the outsiders. That consideration is particularly relevant here, because in analyzing terrorism social scientists often rely on reports of government officials, journalists, and historians.

Conceptual issues and problems haunt virtually all major terms in the social and behavioral sciences, and any definition is ambiguous if it does not answer questions bearing on those issues and problems. There are at least five such questions about terrorism. First, is terrorism *necessarily* illegal (a crime)? Second, is terrorism *necessarily* undertaken to realize some particular type of goal and, if so, what is it? Third, how does terrorism *necessarily* differ from conventional military operations in a war, a civil war, or so-called guerrilla warfare? Fourth, is it *necessarily* the case that only opponents of the government engage in terrorism? Fifth, is terrorism *necessarily* a distinctive strategy in the use of violence and, if so, what is that strategy?

The questions are answered in light of a subsequent definition of terrorism, but more that a definition is needed. The pursuit of a theory about terrorism will be furthered by describing and thinking about terrorism and all other sociological phenomena in terms of one particular notion, thereby promoting the recognition of logical and empirical associations. The most appropriate notion is identified subsequently as "control," but a defense of that identification requires a definition of terrorism (*not* of "terror").

A Definition of Terrorism

Terrorism is illegal violence or threatened violence directed against human or nonhuman objects, provided that it:

(1) was undertaken or ordered with a view to altering or maintaining at least one putative norm in at least one particular territorial unit or population;

(2) had secretive, furtive, and/or clandestine features that were expected by the participants to conceal their personal identity and/or their future location;

(3) was not undertaken or ordered to further the permanent defense of some area

(4) was not conventional warfare and because of their concealed personal identity, concealment of their future location, their threats, and/or their spatial mobility, the participants perceived themselves as less vulnerable to conventional military action; *and*

(5) was perceived by the participants as contributing to the normative goal previously described (*supra*) by inculcating fear of violence in persons (perhaps an indefinite category of them) other than the immediate target of the actual or threatened violence and/or by publicizing some cause.

Clarification, Issues, and Problems

In keeping with a social science tradition, most definitions of terrorism are set forth in a fairly brief sentence (see, e.g., surveys by Oots, 1986, pp. *5–8,* and Schmid & Jongman, 1988, pp. 32–38). Such definitions do not tax the reader's intellect or patience, but it is inconsistent to grant that human behavior is complex and then demand simple definitions of behavioral types.

The illegality of terrorism. Rubenstein's definition (1987, p. 31) is noteworthy if only because it makes no reference to crime or illegality: "I use the term 'terrorism' . . . to denote *acts of small-group violence for which arguable claims of mass representation can be made.* " However, even granting that terrorism is an illegal action, there are two contending conceptions of crime, one emphasizing the *reactions* of officials as the criterion and the other emphasizing normative considerations (e.g., statutory law). Because of space limitations, it is not feasible to go much beyond recognizing the two contending conceptions. It must suffice to point out that an action may be illegal or criminal (in light of statutes and/or reactions by state officials) because of (1) where it was planned; (2) where it commenced; and/or (3) where it continued, especially in connection with crossing a political boundary. Such distinctions are relevant even when contemplating the incidence of terrorism.

One likely reaction: But why is terrorism *necessarily* a crime? The question suggests that *classes* of events or things exist independently of definitions. Thus, it may appear that "stones" and "humans" denote ontologically *given* classes, but in the context of gravitational theory stones and humans are *not* different. However, to insist that all definitions are *nominal* is not to imply that conventional usage should be ignored; and, again, the point takes on special significance when defining terrorism. The initial (unnumbered) part of the present definition is consistent with most other definitions and also with this claim: most journalists, officials, and historians who label an action as "terrorism" evidently regard the action as illegal or criminal. However, it is not denied that two populations may differ sharply as to whether or not a particular action was a crime. As a *necessary* condition for an action to be terrorism, only the statutes and/or reactions of officials in the political unit where the action was planned or took place (in whole or in part) need identify the action as criminal or illegal.

Violence and terrorism. Something like the phrase "violence or threatened violence" appears in most definitions of terrorism (see Schmid and Jongman, 1988, p. *5).* As in those definitions, the phrase's key terms are here left as primitives; and whether they must be defined to realize sufficient empirical applicability can be determined only by actual attempts to apply the definition.

Despite consensus about violence as a *necessary* feature of terrorism, there is a related issue. Writers often suggest that only humans can be targets of violence, but many journalists, officials, and historians have identified instances of destruction or damage of nonhuman objects (e.g., buildings, domesticated animals, crops) as terrorism. Moreover, terrorists pursue their ultimate goal through inculcation of fear and humans do fear damage or destruction of particular nonhuman objects.

The ultimate god of terrorists. The present definition indicates that terrorists *necessarily* have a goal. Even though it is difficult to think of a human action that is not goal oriented, the consideration is controversial for two reasons. One reason is the allegation that terrorists are irrational or mentally ill (see, e.g., Livingston, 1978, pp. 224–239; and Livingstone's commentary, 1982, p. 31 on Parry), which raises doubts as to whether terrorists have identifiable goals. The second reasons why part I of the definition is controversial: many sociologists, especially Durkheimians, do not emphasize the purposive quality of human behavior, perhaps because they view the emphasis as reductionism. In any case, a defensible definition of virtually any term in sociology's vocabulary requires recognition of the relevance of internal behavior (e.g., perception, beliefs, purpose). Thus, without part I of the present definition, the distinction between terrorism and the *typical* robbery becomes obscure. The typical robber does not threaten violence to maintain or alter a putative norm; he or she is concerned only with behavioral control in a particular situation.

A defensible definition of a norm is not presumed (see Gibbs, 1981, pp. 9–18, for a litany of difficulties). Rather, it is necessary only that at least one of the participants (those who undertake the violent action or order it) view the action as contributing to the maintenance or alteration of some law, policy, arrangement, practice, institution, or shared belief.

Part 1 of the definition is unconventional only in that goals of terrorists are *not* necessarily political. Many definitions create the impression that all terrorism is political (for a contrary view, see Wilkinson, 1986, p. 51), but the very term "political terrorism" suggests at least two types. The concern of social scientists with terrorism typologies is premature (see. e.g., the commentary by Oots [1986, pp. 11, 301 on Mickolus's notions of international, transnational, domestic, and interstate terrorism). No terrorism typology amounts to a *generic* definition (see the survey in Schmid & Jongman, 1988, pp. *39–59),* and without the latter the former is bound to be unsatisfactory.

Military operations and terrorism. To repeat a previous question: How does terrorism *necessarily* differ, if at all, from conventional military operations in a war, civil war, or so-called guerrilla warfare? The question cannot be answered readily because there are no clearly accepted definitions of conventional military operation, war, civil *war,* and guerrilla warfare. "Guerrilla" is especially troublesome because journalists are prone to use the word without defining it but such as to suggest that it is synonymous with terrorism (a usage emphatically rejected by Laqueur, 1987, and Wilkinson, 1986).

Conventional military operations differ from terrorism along the lines indicated by parts 2, 3, and 4 of the definition. However, the definition does not preclude the possibility of a transition from terrorism to civil war. One tragic instance was the Easter Rising in Ireland (1916), when rather than perpetuate the terrorism tradition, a small group of Irish seized and attempted a permanent defense of government buildings in Dublin, vainly hoping that the populace would join them in open warfare. Today, it is terrorism rather than civil war that haunts Northern Ireland, and the term "guerrilla warfare" has no descriptive utility in that context

Terrorism as a special strategy. One feature of terrorism makes it a distinctive (though not unique) strategy in violence. That feature is described in part 5 of the definition.

Part 5 is controversial primarily because it would exclude action such as this threat: "Senator, if you vote for that bill, it will be your death warrant. " Why would such a threat not be terrorism? A more theoretically significant answer is given subsequently. Here it must suffice to point out that scores of writers have emphasized "third-party" or "general" intimidation as an essential feature of terrorism; and journalists, officials, or historians only rarely identify "dyadic intimidation" (X acts violently toward Y but *not* to control 2's behavior) as terrorism.

"State terrorism" as a special issue. Zinam's definition (1978, pp. 244–45) illustrates one of many reasons why definitions of terrorism are so disputable: "[Terrorism is] the use

or threat of violence by individuals or organized groups to evoke fear and submission to obtain some economic, political, sociopsychological, ideological, or other objective. " Because the definition would extend to the imposition of legal punishments by government officials to prevent crimes through *general* deterrence, in virtually all jurisdictions (see Morris, 1966, p. 631) some aspects of criminal justice would qualify as terrorism; and Zinam's definition provides no basis for denying that it would be "state terrorism. " Even granting that a state agent or employee acts for the state only when acting at the direction or with the consent of a superordinate, there is still no ostensible difference between the use or threat of violence in law enforcement and Zinam's terrorism.

Had Zinam defined terrorism as being *necessarily* illegal or criminal, then many instances of violence by a state agent or employee at the direction or with the consent of a superordinate would not be terrorism. However, think of the numerous killings in Nazi Germany (Ernst Roehm, the Storm Troop head being a well-known victim) during the Night of the Long Knives (June 30, 1934). Hitler ordered the slaughter, and *at rite time* the killings were illegal in light of German statues; but Hitler publicly acknowledged responsibility, and the only concealment was that perceived as necessary to surprise the victims. Surely there is a significant difference between such open, blatant use of coercion by a state official (dictator or not) and the situation where regime opponents are assassinated but officials disavow responsibility and the murders are so secretive that official complicity is difficult to prove. The "rule of terror" of Shaka, the famous Zulu chief, is also relevant. Shaka frequently ordered the execution of tribal members on a seemingly whimsical basis, but the orders were glaringly public (see Walter, 1969). Shaka's regime illustrates another point: in some social units there may be no obvious "law" other than the will of a despot, in which case there is no basis to describe the despot's violence as illegal. The general point: because various aspects of government may be *public* violence, to label all of those aspects "terrorism" is to deny that terrorism has any secretive, furtive, or clandestine features.

Given the conceptual issues and problems that haunt the notion of state terrorism, it is hardly surprising that some writers attribute great significance to the notion, while others (e.g., Laqueur, 1987, pp. *145–146)* seem to reject it. The notion is not rejected here, and the following definition does not make it an extremely rare phenomenon. State terrorism occurs when and only when a government official (or agent or employee) engages in terrorism, as previously defined, at the direction or with the consent of a superordinate, but one who does *not* publicly acknowledge such direction or consent.

The foregoing notwithstanding, for theoretical reasons it may prove desirable to limit the proposed definition of terrorism *(supra)* to *nonstate* terrorism and to seek a quite different definition of *state* terrorism. Even so, it will not do to presume that all violence by state agents is terrorism. The immediate reason is that the presumption blurs the distinction between terrorism and various kinds or aspects of law enforcement. Moreover, it is grossly unrealistic to assume that all instances of genocide or persecution along racial, ethnic, religious, or class lines by state agents (including the military) are terrorism regardless of the means, goals, or circumstances. Nor is it defensible to speak of particular regimes (e.g., Stalin's, Hitler's, Pol Pot's) as though all of the related violence must have been state terrorism. For that matter, granted that the regimes were monstrous bloodbaths, it does not follow that the state agents in question made no effort whatever to conceal any of their activities and/or their identity. Readers who reject the argument should confer with American journalists who attempted to cover Stalin's Soviet Union, Hitler's Germany, or Pol Pot's

Cambodia. Similarly, it is pointless to deny that secretive, clandestine, or furtive actions have been characteristic of "death squads" (many allegedly "state") in numerous Latin American countries over recent decades. It is commonly very difficult to prove that such groups murder with the knowledge and/or consent of state officials; but the difficulty is one justification for identifying the murders as terrorism, even though the state-nonstate distinction may be debatable in particular instances.

Difficulties in Empirical Application

One likely objection to the present definition of terrorism is its complexity; but, again, demands for simplicity are inconsistent with human behavior's complexity. Nonetheless, application of the definition does call for kinds of information that may not be readily available. Reconsider a previous question: Was President Kennedy's assassination terrorism? The present definition does not permit an unequivocal answer, largely because there are doubts about the goals of the assassination and whether or not it was intimidation. If terrorism were defined as simply "the illegal use or threat of violence," an affirmative answer to the Kennedy question could be given; but the definition would also admit *(inter alia)* all robberies and many child abuses. Similarly, the phrase "for political purposes" would justify an affirmative answer to the Kennedy question; but the implication would be a tacit denial of *apolitical* terrorism, and divergent interpretations of "political" are legion. Finally, although a definition that specifically includes "murder of a state official" would maximize confidence in an affirmative answer to the Kennedy question, there must be doubts about the feasibility of such an "enumerative" definition of terrorism. And what would one make of the murder of a sheriff by his or her spouse?

The general point is that a *simple* definition of terrorism tends to delimit a class of events so broad as to defy valid generalizations about it (reconsider mixing presidential assassinations, robberies, and child abuses) or so vague that its empirical applicability is negligible. In the latter connection, the Kennedy illustration indicates the need to grant this methodological principle: the congruence dimension (but not the feasibility dimension) of a definition's empirical applicability is enhanced when independent observers agree that the definition cannot be applied in a particular instance because requisite information is not available. If that principle is not granted, sociologists will try to make do with simple definitions and whatever data are readily available.

Presumptive and possible terrorism. Comparative research on terrorism commonly is based on the use of the term "terrorism" by journalists or officials. Hence, insofar as the use of data on *presumptive* terrorism can be justified, a definition's utility is enhanced by its correspondence with the use of the term "terrorism" by journalists and officials. Although only potentially demonstrable, my claim is that the present definition corresponds more with such use of the term than does any simpler definition, such as: terrorism is illegal violence.

Even when terrorism research is based on *descriptions* of violent events, as in newspaper stories, there may be cases that can be designated as *possible* terrorism even though the information is not complete; and a definition's empirical applicability can be assessed in terms of agreement among independent observers in such designations. In that connection, the present definition points to the kind of information needed for truly defensible research on terrorism, which is not the case when investigators try to make do with a much simpler definition, or no definition at all.

References

Durkheim, Émile. 1949. *The division of labor in society*. New York: Free Press.

Gibbs, Jack P. 1981. *Norms, deviance, and social control*. New York: Elsevier.

Harris, Marvin. 1979. *Cultural materialism*. New York: Random House.

Laqueur, Walter. 1977. *Terrorism*. London: Weidenfeld and Nicolson.

Laqueur, Walter, 1987. *The age of terrorism*. London: Weidenfeld and Nicolson.

Lee, Alfred M. 1983. *Terrorism in Northern Ireland*. Bayside, NY: General Hall.

Livingston, Marius H., ed, 1978. *International terrorism in the contemporary world*. Westport, CT: Greenwood.

Livingstone, Neil C. 1982. *The war against terrorism*. Lexington, MA: Heath.

Morris. Norval. 1966. Impediments of Penal Reform. *University of Chicago Law Review*, 33:627–656.

Noakes, Jeremy. 1986. The origins, structure and function of Nazi terror. Pp. 67–87 in *Terrorism, ideology, and revolution*, edited by Noel O'Sullivan. Brighton, England: Harvester.

Oots, Kent L. 1986. *A political organization approach to transnational terrorism*. Westport, CT: Greenwood.

Parsons, Talcott. 1951. *The social system*. New York: Free Press.

Rubenstein, Richard E. 1987. *Alchemists of revolution*. London: I. B. Tauris.

Schmid, Alex P., and Albert J. Jongman. 1988. *Political terrorism*. Rev. ed. Amsterdam: North-Holland.

Skocpol, Theda. 1979. *States and social revolution*. London: Cambridge University Press.

Tallman, Irving. 1984. Book review. *Social Forces* 62:1121—1122.

Walter, Eugene V. 1969. *Terror and resistance*. New York: Oxford University Press.

Weber, Max. 1978. *Economy and society*. 2 vols., continuous pagination. Berkeley: University of California Press.

Wilkinson, Paul. 1986. *Terrorism and the liberal state*. 2nd ed. New York: New York University Press

Zinam, Oleg. 1978. Terrorism and violence in light of a theory of discontent and frustration. Pp. 240–268 in *International terrorism in the contemporary world,* edited by Marius H. Livingston. Westport, CT: Greenwood.

Review Questions

1. What are some of the problems and issues around personal definitions of terrorism?

2. How did Gibbs end up conceptualizing terrorism?

3. What type of research can be done based on the new definitions of terrorism?

A Systematic Qualitative Evaluation of Levels of Differentiation in Families with Children at Risk

Yeudit Avnir and Ron Shor

In this article the researchers wanted to increase their understanding of the dynamics within the parent-child relationship in families whose children were at risk because their parents' child-rearing practices were dysfunctional. Once again it is important to define the concept, and these researchers address the issue of using the concept of differentiation and go into detail about how they operationalized this variable.

Different theoretical frameworks have been implemented in the development of research and assessment strategies of situations of children at risk. A review of these frameworks reveals two major deficits. The first is that there is lack of sufficient attention to the nature of the dynamics within the focal system (i.e., the parent-child system) in cases of child maltreatment. The second related deficit is that these models most often do not provide specific and concrete guidelines about how to analyze daily events in parent-child relationships. Such events can serve as a basis for assessing problems in parent-child relationships and for assessing change in parenting approach as a result of therapeutic work. The ecological model, for example, when applied to the area of child maltreatment illuminates the importance of including multidimensional factors in assessing situations of risk of abuse and neglect of children (e.g., Browne, 1988; Thomlison, 1997), but it does not focus on or provide specific guidelines for assessing the dynamics of parent-child relationships. Other theories, such as attachment and psychodynamic theories, do relate to the focal system of parent-child relationships, but they focus mainly on specific aspects that may lead to child maltreatment such as deficits in empathy or in the connectedness between a parent and a child (e.g., Fashenbach, 1989; Steele, 1980; Tuohy, 1987). Such specific perspectives do not provide a sufficient base as to what to observe and how to analyze the problems in the complex and diverse daily dynamics of the parent-child relationship in situations of children at risk.

In this paper, application of the concept of differentiation to the context of families with children at risk will be presented as a central concept for analyzing the difficulties of parents in relating to their children. In addition, a systemic qualitative framework for assessing parents' levels of differentiation and for assessing changes in their approach towards their children will be presented. This framework was implemented in research that evaluated the level of differentiation of parents who participated in a short-term therapeu-

Avnir, Y & Shor, R. 1998. A systematic qualitative evaluation of levels of differentiation in families with children at risk. *Families in Society: The Journal of Contemporary Human Services* 79(5): 504–514.

tic group program for families with children at risk, under the auspices of the Social Welfare Department of Jerusalem. The main objective of the program was to improve the parents' relationships with their children, thus reducing the risk for child maltreatment.

Differentiation is a concept that was included in Bowen's family systems theory (Bowen, 1978) and describes individuals in terms of interactive relationship patterns (Aylmer, 1986). According to Bowen, a family that has a balanced relationship between separateness and connectedness is a family with a high level of differentiation (Kerr & Bowen, 1988). The concepts of separateness and connectedness have been used also by other theoreticians and researchers of family relationships (e.g., Minuchin, 1974; Olson, Sprenkle & Russel, 1979), although each of their perspectives is somewhat different, both in terminology and conception. Differentiation is reflected primarily in the family system's interactional patterns for maintaining interpersonal distance, and thus, in the system's tolerance for both individuality and intimacy, and it exists on a continuum from high to low levels of differentiation (Kerr & Bowen, 1988). Within families that have a low level of differentiation, the boundaries are regulated in extreme ways: enmeshment patterns in which an insufficient separateness or faulty boundaries prevent autonomy and individuality, or disengagement patterns in which rigid boundaries between family members allow autonomy at the expense of intimacy, support, and responsiveness (Minuchin, 1974). Hoffman (1975) describes these poorly differentiated patterns as either "too richly cross-joined" or "too poorly cross-joined. " Poorly differentiated patterns are reflected in family members' preoccupation with self and absence of empathy, regard, and respect for the uniqueness and individuality of others. Behaviors often reflect assumptions that other members are either not capable of functioning in accordance with their developmental levels, or are capable of functioning well beyond their developmental levels (Anderson & Sabatelli, 1990).

A central quality of a relationship that has a high degree of differentiation is a relationship in which there is a dialogue. Dialogue relates to the ability of two people to relate to each other in an open manner and to exchange ideas around subjects that are important to them while respecting the unique self of each of them (Friedman, 1992). Bowen uses the term "person to person" to describe such relationships (Bowen, 1978). Boszormenyi-Nagy & Krasner (1987) note that "genuine dialogue" is thought to be the necessary context for mature individuation to occur. A genuine dialogue, with its emphasis on fairness, trust, and ongoing relatedness offers both the potential for self-delineation (the definition of self in relation to significant others) and self-validation (affirming one's self worth through caring for others). Both disengagement and enmeshment characterize lack of differentiation by the fact that there is no constructive dialogue enabling the uniqueness of the family member to be actualized.

The concept of differentiation, when applied to parenting, describes an age-appropriate balance of separateness and connectedness for children. Differentiated relationships between parents and children can be defined as those in which the parent is able to differentiate between the emotional world of the parent and that of the child, to allow the child to develop autonomy, to be sensitive to the child's needs, and to develop a dialogue including communication of confirmation and respect. Parent-child interactions in well-differentiated families allow children to experience and express their individuality while remaining intimately connected to the parent (Sabatelli & Mazor, 1985). The parent is able to build a relationship with a child in which processes such as the extent of dependence, decision making regarding family matters and areas of interests will indicate a balance in the family relationships between cohesiveness and uniqueness. In poorly differentiated enmeshed systems, parental intrusiveness and a blurring of personal boundaries work against individual autonomy and individuality that may in time interfere with the child's development. Parental control and authority are often stressed in response to the child's effort to act autonomously. In the disengaged pattern the lack of involvement and care may lead to neglect of children (Anderson & Sabatelli 1992; Minuchin, 1974).

Practice experience indicates that among parents who participated in the therapeutic groups for parents with children at risk in Jerusalem, a dialogue with their children has often been missing, and a low level of differentiation was observed. In such families, the child is often perceived by his/her parents in a mechanical way. Parents approach their children as though they can activate them according to the their wishes and plans without taking into consideration the child's self and his/her right to actualize his/her uniqueness. The child's "failure" to fulfill the parents' wishes could lead to maltreatment.

Studies also indicate a relationship between low level of differentiation and the risk of child maltreatment. Abusive mothers have been shown in studies to have difficulty interacting with their children in developmentally appropriate ways (Crittenden & Bonvillian, 1984, Bousha & Twentyman, 1984). These mothers were described as having difficulties to interact reciprocally with their children and to pace their interactions to their children's needs. They appeared to be responding to their own internal needs, rather than being able to accurately perceive and respond to the child's cues. Dore and Fagan (1993) found that neglecting mothers also have difficulty interacting with their children in a developmentally appropriate way. The neglecting mothers in their sample were less developmentally appropriate than non-maltreating mothers in play interactions with their children. For example, they tended to either overwhelm their children with quick responses or were too slow in responding to them, and they frequently used many more controls and directions than were developmentally appropriate. Support for the relationships between low level of differentiation and child maltreatment could be drawn also from studies in which depressed affect and internalizing behaviors of adolescents have been linked to parents' controlling behavior and failure to grant sufficient autonomy to their children (Allen, Hauser, Eickholt, Bell, & O'Connor, 1994; Fauber, Forehand, Thomas, & Weirson, 1990; Gjerde and Block, 1991).

A Framework for Research and Assessment of Levels of Differentiation

A common research methodology used to assess the dynamics of parent-child relationships relies on the responses of family members to questionnaires. However, problems in accurate reporting have been noted with maltreating parents (Reid, Kavanagh, & Baldwin, 1987). Self-report methods often reflect more the wish of the parents for relationships than the actual way that they approach the relationships. In a western society that emphasizes ideals of tolerance, openness, and pluralism between parents and children, there is a chance that parents will provide desirable responses that may stand in sharp contradiction to what actually occurs within a family. To overcome this limitation, a qualitative method was developed and applied in research used to evaluate changes in the parenting approach of participants in a short-term therapeutic group program (the group consisted of three couples and four single mothers). This method relied on content analysis of the descriptions by the parents themselves of their relationships with their children. The descriptions were documented during the therapeutic process and in nonstructured interviews before and after the group therapy. The utilization of this method was based on the assumption that as much as the person describes his/her relationship with another in an open manner, it is possible to receive a closer look at the unique quality of the relationship.

Operationalization of Differentiation

The first stage in the development of the systemic qualitative evaluation of parents' differentiation (SQEPD, Avnir, 1997) was the operationalization of the dimensions contained in differentiation in parent-child relationships, in a way enabling analysis of daily events between parents and children. This served as the basis for the content analysis of the parents' descriptions.

The operationalization of the dimensions of differentiation attempted to capture specific patterns of the relationship between parents and children. A parent helps a child develop into an adult each day and each hour, while doing activities that have significance and importance in shaping the internal and external world of the child. The main dimensions of differentiation developed for the analysis of the daily dynamics in a parent-child relationship were based on Bowen's theory as well as on other theoreticians and researchers of family relationships (e.g., Karpel, 1976; L'abate, 1976; Olson, Sprenkle & Russel, 1979). They are as follows:

1. *Continual need for familiarity with the uniqueness of the child.* This relates to the continual need to learn about and be familiar with the child's world. In an undifferentiated approach with an enmeshment pattern, because of the over-involvement between family members, the parent may perceive his/her familiarity with the child's world as a given and, may, for example, interpret the child's wishes according to his/her own wishes, fears, and beliefs. In the disengaged pattern in an undifferentiated approach, the parent may be disconnected from the child's world and may, for example, ignore the cues and expressions of the child.

2. *Adjusting pace.* This relates to the need to consider the pace of the child and to adjust the parent's pace to that of the child. An example of an undifferentiated enmeshed pattern could be conducting the family's activities according to the parent's pace, and an example of an undifferentiated disengaged pattern could be that there is a lack of connection between the parents' and the child's activities.

3. *Privacy.* This relates to the parents' respect for the child's need for privacy in the emotional, cognitive, and behavioral areas. In an undifferentiated enmeshed pattern, the parent can intrude into each aspect of the child's life, while in the undifferentiated disengaged pattern, there is almost no opportunity to share feelings, thoughts, and activities between parents and children.

4. *Accepting differences.* This relates to the parent's recognition of the child's right to be different from what the parent wishes and expects, and that the parent perceives the child as different from the other siblings in the family. An example of an undifferentiated enmeshed approach could be for the parent to demand that the child will fit a

set standard and to demand sameness among all of his/her children without considering the uniqueness of each child. In the undifferentiated disengaged approach, there could be a distance that does not allow the parent to recognize the child's differences from other children.

5. *Autonomy of choice.* This relates to the parents' enabling the child to make choices according to his age level. In the enmeshed form of lack of differentiation, the parent could make decisions regarding the child's life without considering the child's choices and needs. In the disengaged form of lack of differentiation, the parent could be totally uninvolved in the child's decisions.

6. *Enabling relationships with others.* This relates to the parent enabling the child to develop relationships with other members of the family and with people outside the family. In an undifferentiated enmeshed form of relationship, the parent may demand exclusiveness in his/her relationship with the child or he/she may include the child in coalitions that are aimed to serve the parent's fights with others. The undifferentiated disengaged form could be manifested by lack of involvement or support by the parent for the child as he/she explores the possibilities for the development of relationships with others.

7. *Personal power.* This relates to the extent and kind of power that the parent perceives that he/she and the child have. A supportive approach of a parent in a child's development of his/her unique characteristics requires a belief by the parent that the child has internal sources of personal power allowing him/her to function independently in the world. An impasse to such a supportive approach could be not only lack of belief by the parent in the child's personal power, but also lack of belief by the parent in his/her own personal power to function independently without the children. The undifferentiated enmeshed dynamic could be manifested when a parent perceives that he/she has total power and the child is totally powerless. In such situations there is no opportunity for expression of the child's individuality. The opposite situation which could be present in this dynamic could be when the parent feels powerless and dependent on his/her children. In the undifferentiated disengaged dynamic, because of the distance from the child, there could be situations in which the parent feels total power without recognizing the resources of the power of the child.

8. *A mediating factor.* This relates to the fact that dialogue could be a mediating factor in each of the above dimensions. It could demonstrate the parent's willingness to get to know the child and give expression to his/her individuality. When differentiation exists through dialogue, there is a balance between the needs of the parent (parents' self') and those of the child (child's self). Both the undifferentiated enmeshed dynamic and the undifferentiated disengaged dynamic could be characterized as lacking a functional dialogue between a parent and a child. In the undifferentiated enmeshed dynamic, the self of the parent and self of the child could be experienced as one system and, therefore, the parent may not feel the need for a dialogue. The flow of information in this case could be unidirectional in the form of lecturing about the parent's thoughts or giving instructions without any opportunity for the child to express his/her thoughts. In the undifferentiated disengagement dynamic, the self of the parent and the self of the child could be experienced as two foreign selves. There could be situations in which there are almost no conversations between a parent and a child.

Evaluation of Levels of Differentiation

The systemic qualitative evaluation of parents' differentiation (SQEPD) for content analysis of parents' descriptions of their relationship with their children was developed. This framework enabled determination of the level of differentiation in the analyzed descriptions and the relating of this level to the relevant dimensions of differentiation. The parents' descriptions were taped and transcribed both in the interviews conducted before and after the therapeutic program and also during the therapeutic sessions (content analysis was done only for the interviews). Since the contents of the descriptions of each family were analyzed separately, the analysis of each family was defined as a case study. The unit of analysis was stories in which the parents described their relationships with their children (the word "story" relates to descriptions of thoughts or events that focus on one subject of the parent-child relationship; 299 stories were analyzed). The level of differentiation was analyzed in each story according to the following components: (a) the subject of the story, (b) participants in the story, (c) general characteristic of the story, (d) the parent's perception of the activity of the other, (e) the meaning of the activity of the other for the teller, (f) the emotional experience of the parent, (g) the focus of the difficulty/achievement according to the parent, (h) the parent's feeling of power, (i) the parent's way of coping with the presented situation.

For each of the dimensions a detailed guide for categorizing and evaluating the content of the parents' descriptions was developed. To illustrate the application of this systemic framework, content analysis on one story from each of the interviews conducted with one mother is presented. The aim of the analysis of these examples is to demonstrate how the systemic framework can be used when examining case studies to determine the levels of differentiation in a parent's relationship with his/her child and to assess change in the parent's approach.

The stories in the following examples relate to the descriptions by Sara, a mother of two daughters, who participated in the group with her husband Uri. The couple's two daughters are Daniela, who is four-and-a-half years old, and Liora, who is three years old. The couple was referred to the social welfare department as a result of a report from a hospital of an incident of physical violence by the mother toward Daniela. In the first story from the first interview conducted prior to the treatment, the interviewer began by asking the mother about her view of her relationship with her daughter Daniela.

The mother: "Daniela, because of her smartness, her sharpness, her smartness [sic] and her understanding, is probably independent. She is independent as a result of this and strong. Therefore it is very difficult for me with her in many things. I have difficulties around decisions. It is difficult for me even to cooperate with her to do something, even regarding a small example: a game. She decides and she wants and she is first. And even if I did not explain the game to her, she does not let me get close to her, not even to show her the game. And of course in every thing she always thinks that l am wrong. Every thing is a burden for me. Everything is difficult for me because of her smartness, and when I talk with her and explain things to her, she even tries to respond and tell me what she is thinking about. And it is very difficult for me to tell her what to do during the day, she does not like it and does not want it because of her smartness and her desire to be independent."

Analysis of the mother's level of differentiation in this story according to the SQEPD follows:

- The subject of the story: How the mother views her relationship with Daniela.
- Participants in the story: The mother and Daniela.
- General characteristic of the story: Negative experiences.
- Activity of the other from the parent's perception: Daniela is smart, sharp, independent, and strong.
- The meaning of the activity of the other for the teller: Negative, it is difficult for the parent.
- Emotional experience of the parent: Anger.
- The focus of the difficulty/achievement: Difficulty with the child.
- The parent's feeling of power: Powerlessness.
- Ways of coping: An attempt to coerce the mother's desires; there is no dialogue.
- Conclusion: Undifferentiated enmeshment with a focus on the powerlessness of the parent (the personal power dimension).

The mother's response indicated that the girl's desire for autonomy and independent activities was experienced by the mother as negative and made her angry. The word "smartness" was repeated several times. Each time, smartness and independence were experienced as negative characteristics that created difficulties. The girl, for example, did not allow her mother to explain the game, and this was perceived as a competition about who knows what and who does not know. There was no indication of pride about the girl's capabilities, only feelings of frustration and anger. The mother was not able to develop a dialogue with the girl. It made her angry that the girl expressed her thoughts when the mother wanted to explain things. She felt that in this way the girl devalued her. On the other hand, she at the same time devalued the legitimacy of the desire of the girl for independence. In this story, there is no direct report of violence but of a dynamic that could lead to frustrated reactions by the mother and, in fact during the interview, there were other descriptions in which Sara talked about outbursts, swearing and beating of the girl.

The second interview, which was conducted after the group therapy, reflected a more differentiated approach by the mother towards Daniela. There was better recognition of the personal power of the girl and better adjustment to the girl's pace. In addition, the mother focused to a greater degree on her other daughter with an attempt to understand her. The following description demonstrates the change:

The mother: "Before, I acted as if I am the mother, and I can decide, and this it. The rules were very strong and difficult. Today, when I see and understand, and receive explanations from you and from other persons about what a child is, and that she is, in fact, a person with her own feelings, decisions, mind and ability for expression, and can even correct me. Today, I see that she is this person, I accept and understand it in the best way, so I am changing. I am listening to the child. For example, at 9:30 she called me from her room since she was probably afraid to come out since she knows that I don't permit her. It made me feel very good. I saw what kind of a girl she is. She said that she cannot fall asleep. I thought, I did not know what to say, and then I gave her something to read. You know what you could do, draw or write or do what ever you want in your room. Since this is the way that I had been given explanations, I see it as the right way. You can not force a person to fall asleep. So, like myself when I can not fail asleep, I know no matter what, I will not fall asleep. Therefore I gave her freedom. " [Sara described that she allowed the girl to be in the living room a little bit since the girl could not fall asleep after reading books.] "Then she was totally satisfied. It was excellent for her, and she went to sleep. Then I was satisfied, and she was satisfied. So if I can do this, if I can activate my mind and thoughts at the same time, then the results are good. So today I understand that she has feelings and wants. And she went to sleep with happiness, she said 'good night father, good night mother. ' So I felt very good; all of us benefited from this. "

Analysis of the mother's level of differentiation in this story according to the systemic framework follows:

- The subject of the story: Difficulties of the girl to fall asleep.
- Participants in the story: The mother and Daniela.
- General characteristic of the story: Positive experiences.
- Activity of the other from the parent's perception: The daughter has desires.
- The meaning of the activity of the other for the teller: Positive for the girl and for the mother.
- Emotional experience of the parent: Positive
- The focus of the difficulty/achievement: Achievement of the parent in relating to the child.
- The parent's feeling of power: Satisfying.
- Ways of coping: Learning from messages, enabling activity according to the pace of the girl, there is no anger.
- Conclusion: Differentiation with the focus on the continual need for familiarity dimension.

The mother's response in the beginning of the story was one of recognition of the individuality of the child and the need to be attuned to her; throughout the story she described actual implementation of this perception. This story demonstrated recognition by Sara that it is not possible to coerce her daughter to sleep. Through a process of exploration and learning from the girl's cues, she succeeded in finding an adaptive solution. This process also indicated a situation in which the power was not perceived as being totally within the daughter or within the mother. As Sara said "all of us benefited from it. "

A Framework for Assessing Change and for Comparison

To receive a more complete picture of the level of differentiation expressed in the interviews and to provide a base for comparison among the interviews, a framework for summarizing the analyses of the stories in each interview was developed. The identification of the overall pattern in each interview could provide a base not only for comparison of the level of differentiation at two points of time in one family (assessing change), but also for comparing the level of differentiation among different families.

A framework was developed to show the conclusions that were received from the analyses of all the stories in each interview. , There are four categories for the levels of differentiation along the different dimensions which are differentiation, dilemmas, undifferentiated enmeshed patterns, and undifferentiated disengaged patterns. The last two categories included two components—the child's self and the parent's self—that relate to the balance between the focus on the child's self or the parent's self. (In differentiation, a balance exists between these two factors, and there is no significant emphasis on either the child's self or parent's self.)

The category of dilemmas was added during the content analysis after questions were raised about whether sections of the case studies could be characterized by one unified pattern (differentiation or lack of differentiation) and about whether the move from lack of differentiation to differentiation was total. Initial analysis of the stories indicated that responses were usually not pure. There were stories that expressed differentiation, enmeshment or disengagement. However, it became clear that an intermediate category was needed that would relate to dilemmas around the attempts to reach differentiation. Dilemmas and attempts to reach differentiation (such as a parent's awareness of a specific need of his/her child but not knowing how to respond) were marked on the borders between differentiation and undifferentiation.

The analysis of the first interview (in which Sara felt that her own self was devalued) was defined in the level of differentiation category as lack of differentiation enmeshment with a focus on the parent's self and in the dimension of differentiation category as personal power. The analysis of the second interview (in which Sara coped with the difficulty of Daniela's falling asleep) was defined in the level of differentiation category as differentiation and in the dimension of differentiation category as continual need for familiarity.

A summary of the data was used to compare the general patterns of the levels of differentiation in each interview. Since the number of analyzed stories in each interview was not equal and since there was a need to create a basis for comparing the two interviews, the percentage of the number of the analyzed stories in each level of differentiation was calculated. In the presented case study of Sara, for example, a summary of the levels of differentiation of the two interviews shows that 26% (n = 6) of the stories in the second interview, as opposed to 5% (n = 1) of the stories in the first interview, were classified as differentiation. The first interview clearly reflects a dominant pattern of lack of differentiation. In the second interview, it was possible to see an increase in the indications of differentiation that implies a change toward a more functional parenting approach.

Conclusions

Two main factors were found to be essential in developing and applying the concept of differentiation of self into a relevant assessment and research instrument in families with children at risk. The first is the way in which this relatively abstract concept was operationalized, and the second is the nature of the qualitative method that was developed for content analyses of the case studies.

The multidimensional operationalization of the concept of differentiation provided a concrete and specific framework for examining the ongoing daily events and problems in parent-child relationships on one hand and captured the complex issues in parent-child dynamics on the other. In addition, it provided a base to examine common patterns among families with children at risk (such as difficulties in developing a dialogue), as well as the unique problems of each family. The focus of the dimensions of differentiation on daily aspects of parents' relationship with their children removes the emphasis of the therapeutic work from issues to which the parents may have difficulties changing (e.g., the history of the parents) to the parents' daily struggles in their relationship with their children. Coping with these struggles could be perceived as feasible and desirable for the parents.

The SQEPD was found to be an effective way to study sensitive issues among at-risk families within the context of social welfare services. In studying problems such as parents' malfunctioning relationship with their children, parents may have a tendency not to reveal patterns that are generally considered to be inappropriate in responding to direct and structured questions (e.g., self-report questionnaires). However, by analyzing the content of the parents' free descriptions before and after the therapeutic process, and by conducting the interviews as an integral part of the participation in the therapeutic program, the risk for responses reflecting social desirability was reduced. In addition, the potential for insight into parents' views and family processes was increased. A limitation of this method is that it could be affected by the practitioner-researcher's subjective interpretation of the analyzed situations. However, the SQEPD assisted in reducing the subjectivity of the analyses.

By use of the SQEPD, it was possible to evaluate the level of differentiation in a manner that did not interfere with the treatment. The focus was the subjective world of the parents and the issues that concerned them. This evaluation could serve as a helpful tool for social workers in the family and child welfare field in assessing the problems in a parent-child relationship. It could also provide a tool to assess therapeutic progress and a data base for setting new therapeutic objectives (for example, analyses of the case studies indicated a need to work with the parents on ways to develop a dialogue with their children and to become familiar with their children's unique characteristics). This method of analysis could provide an accessible nonintrusive instrument for practitioners and researchers in evaluating practices with families and children at risk.

References

Allen, J. P., Hauser, S. T., Eickholt, C., Bell, K. L., & O'Connor, T. G. (1994). Autonomy and relatedness in family interactions as predictors of expressions of negative adolescent affect. *Journal of Research on Adolescence*, 4(4), 535–552.

Anderson, S. A, & Sabatelli R. (1990). Differentiating differentiation and individuation: Conceptual and operation challenges. *The American Journal Family Therapy*, 18(1), 32–50.

Anderson, S. A., & Sabatelli, R. M. (1992). The differentiation in the family system scale (DIFS). *The American Journal of Family Therapy*, 20(1), 77–89.

Avnir, Y. (1997). *Perception of the child as a differentiated person: A criterion for the evaluation of change in a group-work program for improvement of parents-children relations in children-at-risk families*. Unpublished master's thesis, The Hebrew University of Jerusalem, Israel.

Aylmer, R. C. (1986). Bowen family systems marital therapy. In N. S. Jacobson, & A. S. Gurman (Eds.), *Clinical handbook of marital therapy* (pp. 107–148).

Bousha, D. M., & Twentyman, C. T. (1984). Mother-child interactional style in abuse, neglect, and control groups: Naturalistic observations in the home. *Journal of Abnormal Psychology*, 93(1), 106–114.

Bowen, M. (1978). *Family therapy in clinical practice*. New York: Aronson.

Bozormenyi-Nagy, I., & Krasner, B. (1987). *Between give and take: An introduction to contextual therapy*. New York: Brunner Mazel.

Browne, D. H. (1988). High risk infants and child maltreatment: Conceptual and research model for determining factors predictive of child maltreatment. *Early Child Development and Care*, 31, 43–53.

Crittenden, P. M., & Bonvillian, J. D. (1984). The relationship between maternal risk status and maternal sensitivity. *American Journal of Orthopsychiatry*, 54(2), 250–262.

Dore, M. M., & Fagan, J. (1993). Mother-child play interactions in neglecting and non-neglecting mothers. *Early child development and care*, 87, 59–68.

Fashenbach, N. D. (1989). Empathy and physical abuse. In D. C. Cicchetti (Ed.), *Child Maltreatment*. Cambridge: Cambridge University Press.

Fauber, R., Forehand, R., Thomas, A. M., & Wierson, M. (1990). A mediational model of the impact of marital conflict on adolescent adjustment in intact and divorced families: The role of disrupted parenting. *Child Development*, 61, 1112–1123.

Friedman, M. (1992). *Dialogue and the human image*. London: Sage.

Gjerde, P. E, & Block, J. (1991). Preadolescent antecedents of depressive symptomatology at age 18: A prospective study. *Journal of Youth and Adolescence*, 20, 217–223.

Hoffman, L. (1975). Enmeshment and too richly cross-joined system. *Family Process*, 14, 457–468.

Karpel, M. (1976). Individuation: From fusion to dialogue. *Family Process*, 15, 65–82.

Kerr, M. E., & Bowen, M. (1988). *Family Evaluation: An approach based on Bowen theory*. New York: . . Norton.

L'abate. (1976). *Understanding and helping the individual in the family*. New York: Grune & Straton.

Minuchin, S. (1974). *Families and family therapy*. Cambridge, MA: Harvard University Press.

Olson, D. H., Sprenkle, D. H, & Russel, C. S. (1979). Circumplex model of marital and family systems: Cohesion and adaptability dimensions, family types, and clinical applications. *Family Process,* 18(1), 3–27.

Reid, J. B., Kavanagh, K., & Baldwin, D. V. (1987). Abusive parents' perceptions of child problem behaviors: An example of parental bias. *Journal of Abnormal Child Psychology*, 15, 457–466.

Sabatelli, R. M., & Mazor, A. (1985). Differentiation, individuation, and identity formation: The integration of family system and individual developmental perspective. *Adolescence*, 20(79), 619–633.

Steele, B. (1980). Psychodynamic factors in child abuse. In C. H. Kempe & E. Melfer (Eds.), *The battered child* (pp. 49–86). Chicago: University of Chicago Press.

Thomlison, B. (1997). Risk and protective factors in child maltreatment. In M. W. Fraser (Ed.), *Risk and resilience in childhood: An ecological perspective.* Washington, DC: NASW Press.

Tuohy (1987). Psychoanalytic perspective on child abuse. *Child and Adolescent Social Work,* 4(1), 25–40.

REVIEW QUESTIONS

1. How did these researchers operationalize the concept differentiation?

2. What dimensions of differentiation did they use?

3. Can you think of another way they could have operationalized the concept of differentiation?

DYNAMIC DIMENSIONS OF FAMILY STRUCTURE IN LOW-INCOME AFRICAN AMERICAN FAMILIES: EMERGENT THEMES IN QUALITATIVE RESEARCH

Robin L. Jarrett and Linda M. Burton

There are numerous ways to conceptualize family structure. Usually in studies about African American low-income families, there is a contrast between those that are one-parent, female-headed households and those that are two-parent intact family units. This article shows how the way in which a variable is operationalized can make a huge difference in both the research and the findings.

In the past two decades, dramatic increases in the number of economically disadvantaged households headed by females have renewed scholarly interest in the relationship between persistent poverty and family structure (McLanahan & Sandefur, 1994; Ross & Sawhill, 1975; Wilson, 1987). According to Wu and Martinson (1993, p. 213), "the most common measure of family structure [used in quantitative survey-based studies of family structure] is a dichotomous snapshot contrasting intact families and non-intact families. "In these studies intact families are often defined as those in which both biological parents are present in the household. Non-intact families are principally characterized as single female-headed households (see also Cooksey, 1990; Michael & Tuma, 1985).

Jarrett, R. L., & Burton, L. M. 1999. dynamic dimensions of family structure in low income African American families: Emergent themes in qualitative research. *Journal of Comparative Family Studies,* 30(2), 177–184.

While research that defines family structure according to level of intactness and household composition has provided insights on broad demographic changes occurring in families, it has yet to identify and explore additional dimensions of family structure that are salient in the lives of economically disadvantaged families. We argue, as have Wu and Martinson (1993), that family structure may be an "omnibus variable" comprised of multiple latent dynamic dimensions beyond household composition and level of intactness. These latent dynamic dimensions represent the mechanisms that produce family structure effects. The exploration of such mechanisms may tell us more precisely what aspects of family structure are influencing the outcome of interest.

A number of social scientists have suggested that qualitative research, namely ethnographic studies, are particularly appropriate for exploring dynamic dimensions of family structure (Axinn, Frick, & Thornton, 1991; Burton, 1995a; Jarrett, 1990, 1994, 1995, in press; Rank, 1992). Ethnographic research, given its focus on intense, continuous, and often microscopic observations of families in a specific environment or culture, provides rich and informative insights on the fluid aspects of family structure as they are experienced in day-to-day family life. Such insights are rarely captured in demographic and survey research which rely heavily on data collected from structured questionnaires administered to respondents at discrete points in time (Ross & Sawhill, 1975).

The purpose of this paper is to describe the dynamic dimensions of family structure that we identified and observed in two recent qualitative community-based studies of African American family life. The dynamic dimensions include: extended family networks; the socioeconomic structure of extended family networks; the pace of change in family structure; and the age structure of family members. We propose that these dimensions move beyond prevailing conceptualizations of family structure and provide important conceptual starting points for survey researchers to develop comprehensive assessments of the relationship between family structure and outcomes in economically disadvantaged African American families. The dimensions of the family structure are:

- *Extended Family Networks*: The family members who are related by blood, marriage, and adoption (fictive and legal) and who share domestic and familial care-giving obligations.

- *Socioeconomic Structure of Extended Family Networks*: The economic and social assets of family members who comprise the extended family network.

- *Pace of Change in Family Structure*: The frequency of modifications in family composition through birth, death, and marriage.

- *Age Structure of Family Members*: The age distance between generations within a family.

Data Collection and Methods

The dynamic dimensions of family structure reported here were derived from two independently conducted qualitative studies (see Burton, 1992, 1995b; Burton, Obeidallah, & Allison, in press; Jarrett, 1992, 1993, 1994 for detailed discussions of methods and substantive findings). Study 1 was conducted in 10 communities in a large Midwestern city. The communities are almost exclusively African American and have a disproportionate number of low-income households. The data presented were collected between January 1988 and July

1989. The purpose of the study was to explore the social, economic, and family strategies that poor single mothers used to cope with poverty.

Study 2 was conducted in 18 communities in a northeastern city. The communities are predominantly African American and have high proportions of low-income households. The data presented were collected over a period of three years beginning July 1989. The purpose of the study was to examine the relationship among socioeconomic context, intergenerational family structure, and role transitions in African American families with pregnant teenagers.

Data for study 1 were collected from 82 African American women who ranged in age from 20 to 29 and a smaller sub-sample of the families of nine of these women. The women who participated in the research were identified through neighborhood Head Start programs. The participants had personal characteristics that placed them at risk for persistent poverty: They had never been married, lived in impoverished or economically transitional inner-city neighborhoods, received Aid to Families with Dependent Children (AFDC), and most began their childbearing careers during adolescence.

Data for Study 2 were collected from 48 multi-generation African American families. The families who participated in the study were identified through social service agencies, local churches, and community informants. These families were selected because they represented the modal multigenerational family structure for African American kin in their neighborhoods. For all of the families interviewed, the household head either received welfare or was classified as working-poor based on the official poverty line.

Data gathering for both studies included taped interviews with participants, participant observation in community and family events, and interviews with community leaders and social service agency personnel. In both studies a team of research assistants collected qualitative data on the families using these strategies. The data generated using these strategies were transcribed and then analyzed using the grounded theory approach (Glaser & Strauss, 1967). The grounded theory approach is a style of analyzing qualitative data using a specific coding scheme to generate a profile of conceptual themes and relationships among variables that emerge in the data (Strauss, 1987). Several themes emerged in the qualitative data concerning dynamic dimensions of family structure. These themes were compared across the two studies for consistency.

Although the studies were conducted by two researchers in two different communities and involved distinct sampling frames, findings from both studies, with respect to family structure and dynamics, were remarkably consistent. Moreover, there was minimal variation in the characteristics of both samples (i.e., family SES, family and household composition, neighborhood SES). Excerpts from both studies that are representative of the modal themes which emerged in both data sets will be used to illustrate the dynamic dimensions of family structure among economically disadvantaged African Americans.

Results

Four dimensions of family structure inductively emerged from the studies that are important for understanding impoverished African American families: (1) extended family networks, (2) the socioeconomic structure of extended family networks, (3) the pace of change in family structure, and (4) the age structure of family members. We explore each dimension below, noting the variability within each dimension and how they enhance or constrain families in their ability to cope with poverty.

Extended family networks. The first dimension of family structure is extended family networks. The identification of family members who are related by blood, marriage, and adoption and who share domestic and familial care-giving obligations is a critical factor in how single mothers manage domestic tasks. Two patterns, female heads lacking ties to other households and female heads with ties to other households, were identified.

In female-headed households lacking assistance from extended kin, women have a more difficult time maintaining domestic and childcare tasks. In similar households with support from extended kin, women can satisfactorily manage despite the constraints of poverty. Theses examples expand on the household and level of intactness conceptualizations of family structure. They identify the importance of extraresidential kin for female heads-of-household and highlight their impact on domestic and childcare responsibilities. The identification of extended kinship ties further highlights a more general conceptual point. Family intactness measures often confound the distinction between family and household. Family refers to a set of social relationships, while household refers to residence or living arrangements (Dickerson, 1995). Key family members who are in frequent interaction with one another, fulfilling childcare and domestic tasks, do not always live coresidentially. Thus, some single mothers and children may live independently but are interactionally attached to other households.

The socioeconomic structure of extended family networks. The second dimension of family structure is the socioeconomic structure of extended family networks. Related to the first dimension of extended family structure, the economic and social assets of family members who comprise the extended family network create distinct "resource pools" and influence prospects for individual social mobility. Two types of resource pools, homogeneous and heterogeneous, were identified. Homogeneous resource pools are created by economic sharing between extended kin with a limited range of economic assets. All or most of its members are poor. Heterogeneous resource pools are created by economic sharing between extended kin with a wider range of economic statuses. Some members are poor while others are economically secure.

In homogeneous resource pools all participating family members have access to the same limited assets. Poor family members can assist one another with basic survival needs, but their support does not alter the life chances of individual family members. In heterogeneous resource pools, poorer family members with ties to better-off kin have access to a wider range of assets. Economically secure family members can assist poorer family members with mobility enhancing activities, such as access to better schools, mentoring relationships, and job networks, and their economic support can change the life chances of individual family members.

The pace of change in family structure. The third dimension of family structure that emerged in our research is the pace of change in family structure. The frequency of modifications in family composition has implications for how families monitor or supervise their children and adolescents. Two patterns of change, consistent and episodic, were identified. The former represents a pattern in which changes in family structure are frequent and simultaneous. The latter represents a pattern in which changes in family structure are infrequent and singular.

Consistent change depletes family energies, making it difficult to perform basic child and youth monitoring tasks. Episodic change allows families to satisfactorily manage transitions, making it possible to fulfil essential supervision responsibilities.

The age structure of family members. The fourth, and final, dimension is the age structure of kin. The age distance between generations within a family influences how families define role relations and authority patterns. Two age structures, age-condensed and age-extended, were identified. The former represents a pattern in which the age distance between generations is narrow, ranging from 13–17 years. The latter represents a pattern in which the age distance between generations is broad, ranging from 18 or more years.

In age-condensed families, the narrow span between generations reflects inconsistency between chronological age, developmental Stage, and family role. These inconsistencies can promote age-inappropriate behaviors between parents and their children. In age-extended families, the broader span between generations reflects consistency between chronological age, developmental stage, and family role. Normatively appropriate age spans between generations encourage age-appropriate behaviors.

While poor African American families may be similarly defined as non-intact, there may be differences in age patterns within these family structures. The generational structure of family members highlights the importance of exploring the precise age-intervals between family members and their impact on parent-child role and authority relations.

Discussion

The purpose of this report was to describe the dynamic dimensions of family structure that emerged in our two recent qualitative studies of impoverished African American families. Four dimensions of family structure were identified: extended family networks; the socioeconomic structure of extended family networks; the pace of change in family structure; and the age structure of family members.

The discussion also identified variability within each of the four dimensions and related variability in family functioning. Although we illustrated each dimension using two examples, it is important to note that African American family dynamics vary along a continuum and encompass a broader range of behaviors than those discussed here. Further, the specific family functioning behaviors associated with each dimension may also vary. For example, the limited parental authority pattern found in some age-condensed families may be absent if there are other supportive adults in the extended family network (Martin & Martin, 1978; Stack, 1974). More generally, this example suggests the need to understand how the interaction between dynamic dimensions of family structure influences overall family functioning.

Our findings parallel those in past qualitative studies. Previous studies provide similar descriptions of extended family networks (Aschenbrenner, 1975; Martin & Martin, 1978); socioeconomic structures within extended family networks (Zollar, 1985); patterns of change in family structures (Stack, 1974; Valentine, 1978; see also Burton, 1990; 1995b); and age structures within families (Ladner, 1971; Stack, 1974; Tatje, 1974; see also Bengtson, Rosenthai, & Burton, 1990; Burton, 1996; Burton, Obeidallah, & Allison, in press). The similarity of our descriptive findings with previous studies suggests the presence of identifiable family structure patterns among low-income African American families.

Our qualitative analyses, however, expand on past qualitative studies in a critical way. While previous research implicitly describes dynamic dimensions of family structure, our analyses explicitly conceptualize these processes. This analytic work highlights the conceptual and theoretical richness of qualitative research and facilitates further systematic exploration of family structure dimensions.

More generally, the comparisons between past and recent qualitative studies and the comparative collaboration between our two, separately conducted studies emphasize the importance of synthesizing individual qualitative studies. Such efforts provide baseline information for subsequent qualitative studies and encourage the building of a cumulative knowledge base on family structure.

The observations from our study suggest direction for future research concerning family structure among poor African American families. First, qualitative researchers will need to continue to explore the dynamic dimensions of family structure. With recent field data, researchers can expand on the dimensions we presented or identify new ones.

Second, future research will need to consider the value of the conceptual groundwork laid by innovative studies of African American family structure for understanding other families. While our fieldwork and discussion focused on changes in African America family structure, similar changes in European American family structures are also being recognized (Crosbie-Burnett & Lewis, 1993).

Finally, future research concerned with broader conceptualizations of family structure among poor African American families will need to consider the utility of multi-method approaches. Exemplary studies can demonstrate how qualitative and quantitative methods used together can promote more accurate and dynamic understandings of family life (see for example Axinn et. al., 1991; Rank, 1992).

References

Ascenbrenner, J. 1975. *Lifelines: Black families in Chicago*. New York: Holt, Rinehart & Winston.

Axinn, W. G., Fricke, E. T. & Thornton, A. 1991. The microdemographic community-study approach: Improving survey data by integrating the ethnographic method. *Sociological Methods,* 20:187–217.

Bengtson, V. L., Rosenthai, C., & Burton, L. M. 1990. Families and aging. Pp. 263–287 in Binstock, R. & George, L. (eds.), *Handbook of aging and the social sciences*. New York: Academic Press.

Burton, L. M. 1990. Teenage childbearing as an alternative life-course strategy in multigeneration Black Families. *Human Nature,* 1:123–143.

Burton, L. M. 1992. Black grandparents rearing children of drug-addicted parents: Stressors, outcomes, and social service needs. *Gerontologist,* 32:744–751.

Burton, L. M. 1995a. *Family structure and nonmarital fertility: Perspectives from ethnographic research. Report to Congress on out-of-wedlock childbearing* (pp. 147–165). Department of Health and Human Services. Pub. No. (PHS) 951257.

Burton, L. M. 1995b. Intergenerational patterns of providing care in African American families with teenage childbearers: Emergent patterns in an ethnographic study.

Pp. 79–96 in Schaie, K. W., Bengtson, V. L. & Burton, L. M. (eds.), *Intergenerational issues in aging.* New York: Springer.

Burton, L. M. 1996. Age norms, the timing of family role transitions, and intergenerational care-giving among Aging African American women. *Gerontologist* 36:199–208.

Burton, L. M., Obeidallah, D., & Allison, K... Ethnographic perspectives on social context and adolescent development among inner-city African-American Teens. In Jessor, R., Colby, A. & Shweder, R. (eds.), *Essays on ethnography and human development.* Chicago: University of Chicago Press.

Cooksey, E. C. 1990. Factors in the resolution of adolescent premarital pregnancies. *Demography,* 27:207–218.

Crosbie-Burnett, M., & Lewis, E. A. 1993. Use of African-American family structures and functioning to address the challenges of European-American postdivorce families. *Family Relations,* 42:243–248.

Dickerson, B. J. 1995. Centering studies of African American single mothers and their families. Pp. 1–20 in Dickerson, B. J. (ed.), *African American single mothers: understanding their lives and families.* Thousand Oaks, California: Sage.

Glaser, B., & Strauss, A. 1967 *The discovery of grounded theory.* Chicago: Aldine.

Jarrett, R. L. 1990. *A comparative examination of socialization patterns among low-income African Americans, Chicanos, Puerto Ricans, and Whites: A review of the ethnographic literature.* New York: Social Science Research Council.

Jarrett, R. L. 1992. A family case study: An examination of the underclass debate. Pp. 172–197 in Gilgun, J. Handel, G. & Daley, K. (eds.), *Qualitative methods in family research.* Newbury Park, CA: Sage.

Jarrett, R. L. 1993. Focus group interviewing with low-income minority populations. " Pp. 184–201 in Morgan, D. (ed.), *Conducting successful focus groups.* Newbury Park, CA: Sage.

Jarrett, R. L.1994. Living poor: Family life among single parent, African-American women. *Social Problems,* 41:30–49.

Jarrett, R. L. 1995. Growing up poor: The family experiences of socially mobile youth in low-income African-American neighborhoods. *Journal of Adolescent Research,* 10:111–135.

Jarrett, R. L. In Press. Mothers and grandmothers in poverty: An adaptational perspective. *Journal of Comparative Family Studies.*

Ladner, J. A . 1971. *Tomorrow's tomorrow: The Black woman.* New York: Anchor.

Martin, E., & Martin, J. 1978. *The Black extended family.* Chicago: University of Chicago Press.

McLanahan, S., & Sandefur, G. 1994. *Growing up with a single parent: What hurts, what helps.* Cambridge, MA: Harvard University Press.

Michael, R. T., & Tuma, N. B. 1985. Entry into marriage and parenthood by young men and women: The influence of family background. *Demography,* 22:515–544.

Rank, M. R. 1992. The blending of qualitative and quantitative methods in understanding childbearing among welfare recipients. Pp. 281–300 in Gilgun, J., Daley, K. & Handel, G. (eds.), *Qualitative methods in family research*. Newbury Park, CA: Sage.

Ross, H. L., & Sawhill, I. V. 1975. *Time of transition: the growth of families headed by women*. Washington, DC: Urban Institute.

Stack, C. B. 1974. *All our kin: Strategies for survival in a Black community*. New York: Harper & Row.

Stack, C. B. & Burton, L. M. 1993. Kinscripts. *Journal of Comparative Family Studies,* 24:157–170.

Strauss, B. 1987. *Qualitative analysis for social scientists*. Cambridge, MA: Cambridge University Press.

Tatje, T. A. 1974. *Mother-daughter dyadic dominance in Black American kinship*. Evanston, IL.: Northwestern University, Department of Anthropology. Unpublished Dissertation.

Valentine, B. L. 1978. *Hustling and other hard work: Life styles of the ghetto*. New York: Free Press.

Wilson, W. J. 1987. *The truly disadvantaged: The inner city, the underclass, and public policy*. Chicago: University of Chicago Press.

Wu, L. L., & Martinson, B. 1993. Family structure and the risk of a premarital birth. *American Sociological Review,* 58:210–232.

Zollar, A. C. 1985. *A member of the family: Strategies for Black family continuity.* Chicago: Nelson-Hall.

REVIEW QUESTIONS

1. Explain the various dimensions used in the study.

2. The researchers used data from two qualitative studies. What were they?

3. How was the data gathered for the studies?

Chapter 6: Indexes and Scales

In the last chapter you learned some of the basic foundations for **quantitative** research. Quantitative research is when there is a numerical representation and manipulation of the variables for the purpose of describing and explaining the topic being studied. In this chapter you will learn how to create reliable **measurement** techniques, where you can transform your concepts into variables. You already know that virtually any social phenomenon you can think about can be studied. However, the key to designing a research project is to make sure that you can accurately measure your variables, either directly or indirectly.

A Few More Things to Think About

Before we begin, a few terms and concepts need to be explained. Not all variables are **mutually exclusive**, where they fit neatly into attributes of the variable. For instance, suppose you wanted to know the marital status of your respondents. The **variable** "marital status" would have the attributes of married, divorced, single, and widowed. Now, if you wanted to ask a question about the variable "religion," you might not want to list all the possibilities. Instead, you may have an **exhaustive attributes** list where you list only the most common religions such as Jewish, Catholic, and Methodist. You can also add "other" to the list and allow your respondents to fill in their own religions.

What happens, however, if the variable you are measuring isn't as easy to measure as the two previous examples? Let me give you an example. Many of my students are very concerned with their grades. In fact, some don't want to take a research methods course, and even avoid taking it until their senior year, because they don't want it to hurt their grade point average (GPA). Well, I always ask them how they define "success" in a class. How do you define it? Is it based only on your GPA? For some, it might be. However, I would **operationalize** the abstract concept of "success" in other ways, as well. In fact, I would operationalize "success" as a student who understands the definitions in taught in class and knows how to put those concepts to use in his or her own research project. So, what kinds of response would I get if I asked my students, "Are you successful in this research methods class?" Unless I have operationalized success for them, their definitions might be different from each other's and my definition. So, based on my definition of success, I might ask them a few questions such as, "What was your last test grade in the class?," "Define an independent variable and a dependent variable," "Design an experiment and state the hypothesis and the variables that you would use." If students can do all of these things, then they fit into my definition of the concept of "success." But there is more to think about than just asking a few questions.

SCALES AND INDEXES

Scales and **indexes** are often interchanged and therefore can be confusing. Both give researchers information about the variables they are studying and make it possible to assess the quality of the measurement. Scales and indexes tend to increase **reliability** and **validity**, while they condense and simplify the data that is collected. An *index* is a combination of items into a single numerical score. This score is obtained when various parts of the construct are each measured and then combined into one measure. For example, *U.S. News and World Report* evaluates Ph.D. programs in 5 major disciplines almost every year. They rank the programs using objective measures such as the entering students' test scores, faculty/student ratio, and reputation ratings from both inside and outside of academia. Various people also judge the overall academic quality of the programs on a scale of 1 (marginal) to 5 (distinguished). Once all the indicators are measured, researchers re-scale the final score to rank each of the programs (Garrett, Morse, & Flanigan, 1999). If you visit the *U.S. News and World Report* Web site (http://www.usnews.com/usnews/edu/beyond/gradrank/gbsocio.htm) you will see that in 1998 the top ten Ph.D. programs in Sociology were as follows:

University of Wisconsin—Madison	4.8
University of California—Berkeley	4.7
University of Chicago	4.7
University of Michigan—Ann Arbor	4.5
University of North Carolina—Chapel Hill	4.5
University of California—Los Angeles	4.3
Harvard University (MA)	4.2
Stanford University (CA)	4.2
Princeton University (NJ)	4.1
Northwestern University (IL)	4.0

Scales refer to a special type of measurement, where the numbers are assigned to positions that indicate varying degrees of the variable being considered. In other words, scales can measure the intensity or pattern of a response along a continuum and are often used when the researcher wants to measure the respondents' feelings about something. For instance, in a study to assess the associations between quality of life and attitudes toward sexual activities in adolescence, *The Comprehensive Quality of Life Scale* was used. This scale measured students' objective and subjective quality of life in seven areas: material well-being (possessions), health, productivity, intimacy, safety, place in the community, and emotional well-being. Subjective quality of life was assessed on two dimensions: satisfaction (responses were made on a 7-point scale ranging from delighted to terrible) and importance (responses were made on a 5-point Likert scale ranging from could not be more important to not at all important).

The **Likert Scale** is one of the most common scales, and one you have probably even seen. This scale was developed in the 1930s by Rensis Likert and asks the respondent to indicate whether they agree or disagree with a statement. For example, you may have completed a student evaluation where you rate your professor at the end of a semester. The evaluations at my school look like this:

Overall how would you rate the teaching in this course?

A = Superior

B = Above Average

C = Average

D = Below Average

E = Unsatisfactory

The **Bogardus Social Distance Scale** measures the social distance separating groups from one another. The scale was developed in the 1920s by Emory Bogardus who wanted to measure the willingness of members from one ethnic group to associate with members of another ethnic group. Other groups can include religious, political, or deviant groups. This scale assumes that a person who refuses contact or is uncomfortable around a person from the group in question will answer negatively as the items move closer. For instance, you might ask the question, "Do you like getting to know people from other cultures?" The individual you asked might say "no." However, using the Bogardus social distance scale, you could use the following series of questions:

Please state yes or no to the following statements about how comfortable you would be having a person from (another country):

_____ As a student enrolled in your college

_____ As a student in your class

_____ As a student sitting next to you in class

_____ As a student living in the same dorm as you do

_____ As your roommate

If you find your respondents begin answering no as the questions become closer in proximity, then you might see that the respondents are uncomfortable with people from other countries as they get closer to them.

REFERENCES

McCabe, M. P. & Cummins, R. A. 1998. Sexuality and quality of life among young people. *Adolescence,* 33 (132) :761(1)

Garrett, G., Morse, R. J., & Flanigan, S. M. 1999. How we rank graduate schools. *U.S. News and World Report*, [ONLINE]
http://www.usnews.com/usnews/edu/beyond/gradrank/gbrank.htm

INFOTRAC COLLEGE EDITION SUGGESTED READINGS AND DISCUSSION QUESTIONS

1. Type the words "Survey Design" into InfoTrac College Edition. You should come up with several articles. Read through some of them and see if you can locate how they talk about their survey instrument. How was their survey distributed? Did they do follow-up mailings? What were the results?

2. Make a spreadsheet with the following headings: (1) Subjects, (2) Age range of sub-
    jects, (3) Distribution method used, (4) Subject of study, (5) Response rate

    After locating the following articles and filling in the information under the appropriate
    heading for each article, can you make any statement about what subjects and which
    methods results in the highest response rate?

    Prenatal consultation: Role and Perspective of the Pediatric Surgeon (Article
    A55880839)

    Sexuality of the Spina Bifida Male: Anonymous Questionnaires of Function and
    Knowledge (Article A55880909)

    No exit? The effect of health status on dissatisfaction and disenrollment from health
    plans (Article A54895732)

    Alcohol Use and Psychosocial Well-Being among Older Adults (Article A54700619)

    Soft drink consumption among US children and adolescents: nutritional conse-
    quences (Article A54455080)

3. Find five more articles on your own by typing Response rate into InfoTrac College
    Edition.

Environmental Waste: Recycling Attitudes and Correlates

Knud S. Larsen

*In this article, a Likert-type scale was developed and used to measure attitudes toward re-
cycling among 452 male and female undergraduates. The instrument had high correlations and satisfactory reliability. There was a predictable relationship between attitudes
toward recycling and attitudes toward environmental issues, rights issues, and political
participation.*

Solutions to the increasingly serious problem of environmental waste in the United States
are at least partially dependent on attitudes about recycling. In their comprehensive review
of the literature, Van Liere and Dunlap (1980) concluded that positive attitudes and behaviors regarding recycling are most prevalent among people who are young, politically liberal, and from large households. These findings have also been supported by the studies of
Samdahl and Robertson (1989) and by that of Howenstein (1993), although Howenstein
concluded that there is considerable recycling potential in almost all demographic groups,
provided there is sufficient motivation.

Larsen, K. S. 1995. Environmental waste: Recycling attitudes and correlates. *Journal of Social Psychology,* 135(1): 83–89

That environmental awareness and a sense that the environment is personally relevant lead to an increased incidence of recycling has been documented in a number of studies. Baldassare and Katz (1992) noted that perceived environmental threat is highest among younger respondents, women, liberals, and Democrats, but that those most likely to recycle perceive environmental waste as a serious threat to their personal health and well-being. The relationship between recycling and environmental awareness and personal relevance has also been demonstrated by Lansana (1992). Oskamp, Harrington, Edwards, and Sherwood (1991) found that demographic variables did not predict participation in recycling programs but that knowledge about environmental conservation did. Owning a house and intrinsic motives to recycle were also related to recycling behavior (Oskamp et al., 1991; Lansana, 1992).

Simmons and Widmar (1990) found that recyclers were more likely than nonrecyclers to believe in environmental conservation and to feel personally responsible for the condition of the environment but that such positive attitudes may not result in recycling if knowledge about recycling is lacking. Likewise, Vining and Ebreo (1992, 1994) found that recyclers' behavior was motivated more by concern about the environment than by financial incentives or other rewards. Thus, environmental awareness and a sense of personal responsibility for the environment are critical to a successful recycling program.

Positive attitudes about recycling may also be related to other environmentally relevant attitudes, such as negative attitudes toward transporting nuclear waste on the nation's highways (Larsen, 1994a) or positive attitudes toward protecting the depleted salmon runs in the Pacific Northwest (Larsen, 1994b). People who have positive attitudes toward recycling tend to be politically liberal. Thus positive attitudes toward recycling may be correlated with the protection of prisoners' rights and positive attitudes toward birth control.

Because the aforementioned studies (which yielded relationships between environmental awareness, attitudes, and recycling behavior) were based on survey questions, it was not possible to evaluate reliability and validity. In addition, whereas previous research indicates only tendencies and individual differences, researchers need to explore deviations from central tendencies and to assess group differences more adequately. With these goals in mind, I developed a Likert-type scale to measure attitudes toward recycling environmental waste.

Method

A total of 452 undergraduates (195 men, 257 women) at Oregon State University participated in the five phases of the study. The participants' mean age was 21.22 years. The scales I used in the five phases of the present study were of the Likert type and were administered with the usual instructions.

Phase 1: Item analyses. The item pool consisted of 81 statements, 40 keyed in a positive direction and 41 in a negative direction. The statements were edited independently by a five-person research team, using Edwards's (1957), a priori criteria for unidimensional statements. The item pool was administered to 49 male and 51 female undergraduates (mean age = 20.80). Item analysis yielded 20 items (10 positive, 10 negative).

Attitudes Toward Recycling (ATR) Scale and Part-Whole Correlations

Part-Whole Items	Statement correlation + / −
1. I only generate a small amount of waste, so I don't believe I am responsible for clean up.	.81 −
2. I would recycle magazines.	.76 +
3. We should not clean up all waste disposal sites.	.75 −
4. Enough is being done to clean up the environment.	.75 −
5. The world's oceans are not in need of cleaning up by people.	.74 −
6. Recycling is too much of a hassle to bother with.	.73 −
7. People should share the responsibility of cleaning up the environment.	.72 +
8. I would recycle plastics.	.72 +
9. I would take an active role in recycling.	.71 +
10. I see no reason to recycle.	.70 −
11. I would take advantage of recycling programs available to me.	.70 +
12. I think all packaging, no matter what the cost, should be recyclable.	.70 +
13. I would recycle even if pick up services for recycling were not available.	.69 +
14. Some people exaggerate the true amount of pollution in the world.	.69 −
15. Non-recycled waste created in the past is not an issue worth addressing.	.68 −
16. I would use water saving devices in my home.	.68 +
17. If I were asked to volunteer for a clean up group, I would.	.67 +
18. I would use phosphate free laundry detergent.	.67 +
19. I would not vote in favor of a measure to ban styrofoam packaging.	.67 −
20. I see no purpose in sorting garbage.	.67 −

Phase 2: Reliability and construct validity—attitudes toward the transportation of nuclear waste and pro-environmental paradigms. A survey consisting of (a) the 20-item Attitudes Toward Recycling (ATR) Scale, (b) the 12-item Pro-Environment Scale (Dunlap & Van Liere, 1978), and (c) 30 items pertaining to attitudes toward the transportation of nuclear waste (Larsen, 1994b) was administered to 50 male and 50 female undergraduates (mean age = 21.50).

Phase 3: Attitudes toward recycling and the preservation of river salmon. Two separate surveys were conducted. In the first survey a 20-item scale about attitudes toward declining salmon runs (Larsen, 1994b) was administered with the ATR Scale. The survey was administered to 39 male and 41 female undergraduates (mean age = 20.95).

In a separate study the ATR Scale and the SR scale were included in a survey along with a 21-item scale that measured attitudes toward political participation (Milbrath, 1968; Johnson, 1981). The respondents were 45 male and 65 female undergraduates (mean age = 19.30).

Phase 4: Attitudes toward recycling and prisoners' rights. This survey included the ATR Scale and a 20-item scale that measured prisoners' rights (Larsen, 1994b). The respondents were 18 male and 62 female undergraduates (mean age = 20.75).

Phase 5: Attitudes toward recycling and birth control. The ATR Scale was combined with Wilke's (1967) 22-item Birth Control Scale. The respondents were 43 male and 35 female undergraduates (mean age = 23.41).

Discussion

The results indicated that the ATR Scale had satisfactory internal homogeneity and moderate construct validity coefficients, findings that support the use of this scale in environmental research aimed at understanding attitudes toward recycling. The 20 items selected from the item pool had moderate to high part-whole correlations and an impressive corrected Spearman-Brown coefficient.

The ATR Scale was significantly correlated with scales measuring other environmental issues, supporting the notion of a coherent basis for environmental attitudes. People who favored recycling were also opposed to the transportation of nuclear waste on the nation's highways. Other environmental issues correlated with positive attitudes toward recycling were general pro-environmental attitudes, a desire to protect depleted salmon runs in the Pacific Northwest, and positive attitudes toward birth control.

Almost all the items in the ATR might be useful in other Western countries, but comparative testing is needed. In addition, some of the findings, such as those regarding the salmon runs, are more salient in the Pacific Northwest. Whether the present findings and the ATR Scale might also be useful elsewhere in the world must also be determined.

Finally, the relationship between positive attitudes toward recycling, political participation, and prisoners' rights suggest that there is a connectedness between positive environmental attitudes, personal responsibility, and broader social concern.

References

Baldassare, M., & Katz, C. (1992). The personal threat of environmental problems as predictor of environmental practices. *Environment and Behavior,* 24(5), 602–616.

Dunlap, R. E., & Van Liere, K. D. (1978). The "new environmental paradigm." *Journal of Environmental Education,* 9(4), 10–19.

Edwards, A. L. (1957). *Techniques of attitude scale construction.* New York: Appleton-Century-Crofts.

Howenstein, E. (1993). Market segmentation for recycling. *Environment and Behavior,* 25, 86–102.

Johnson, E. S. (1981). Research methods in criminology and criminal justice. Englewood Cliffs: NJ: Prentice-Hall.

Lansana, F. M. (1992). Distinguishing potential recyclers from nonrecyclers: A basis for developing recycling strategies. *Journal of Environmental Education,* 23(2), 16–23.

Larsen, K. S. (1994a). Attitudes about the transportation of nuclear waste: The development of a Likert scale. *Journal of Social Psychology,* 134, 27–34.

Larsen, K. S. (1994b). *Unpublished environmental scales.* Corvallis: Oregon State University.

Milbrath, L. (1963). The nature of political beliefs and the relationship of the individual to government. *American Behavioral Scientist,* 12, 28–34.

Oskamp, S., Harrington, M. J., Edwards, T. C., & Sherwood, D. I. (1991). Factors influencing household recycling behavior. *Environment and Behavior,* 23(24), 494–519.

Samdahl, D. M., & Robertson, R. (1989). Social determinants of environmental concern: Specification and test of the model. *Environment and Behavior,* 21, 57–81.

Simmons, D., & Widmar, R. (1990). Motivations and barriers to recycling: Toward a strategy for public education. *Journal of Environmental Education,* 22(1), 13–18.

Van Liere, K. D., & Dunlap, R. E. (1980). Environmental concern: A review of hypotheses, explanations, and empirical evidence. *Public Opinion Quarterly,* 44, 181–197.

Vining, J., & Ebreo, A. (1992). Predicting recycling behavior from global and specific environmental attitudes and changes in recycling opportunities. *Journal of Applied Social Psychology,* 20, 1580–1607.

Vining, J., & Ebreo, A. (1994). What makes a recycler? A comparison of recyclers and nonrecyclers. *Environment and Behavior,* 22(1), 55–73.

Wilke, W. H. (1967). Birth Control Scale. In M. E. Shaw & J. M. Wright (eds.), *Scales for the measurement of attitudes* (pp. 136–137). New York: McGraw-Hill.

REVIEW QUESTIONS

1. What is a likert scale? Why was it used in this study?

2. What is the Attitudes Toward Recycling (ATR) Scale? What does it measure?

3. What was the relationship between positive attitudes toward recycling?

IMPLICIT THEORIES OF INTELLIGENCE AND SELF-PERCEPTIONS OF ACADEMICALLY TALENTED ADOLESCENTS AND CHILDREN

Karen E. Ablard and Carol J. Mills

With a number of different scales available for use, in this study, Ablard and Mills used a 6-point Likert scale and asked third- through eleventh-grade academically talented students to rate their beliefs on the stability of intelligence. Thee students also rated themselves on similar scales for how "smart" and "hardworking" they thought they were and how much they "liked hard tasks." What the researchers found was surprising. Some of the students, even though they were talented, were actually at risk for underachievement because they believed they had low ability and that intelligence is stable.

Ablard, K. E. & Mills, C. J. 1996. Implicit theories of intelligence and self-perceptions of academically talented adolescents and children. *Journal of Youth and Adolescence*, 25 (2): 137–149.

Personal or implicit theories of intelligence are unrelated to actual ability as assessed by measures of intelligence, but have a definite impact on cognition and behavior in academic situations (Dweck and Bempechat, 1983). According to Dweck and colleagues (e.g., Dweck and Elliott, 1983), children tend to emphasize one of two implicit theories of intelligence that can be distinguished by differing beliefs in the relative stability of intelligence and the role of effort. One view is that intelligence is changeable, or incremental in nature as a result of effort. Persons with such a view believe intelligence consists of a dynamic, ever-expanding repertoire of skills and knowledge that is increased through one's efforts (Dweck and Bempechat, 1983). The contrasting implicit theory is that intelligence is a stable trait or entity judged by performance on an academic task. Persons adhering to this theory focus on the "fixedness" or inherent nature of intelligence.

The importance of implicit views of intelligence is their link to effort and preference for challenge. For example, children with an incremental view of intelligence tend to increase their effort as task difficulty increases with the primary intent to understand the task and ultimately to increase knowledge (Heyman and Dweck, 1992). On the other hand, children with an entity view are more concerned with the success of their performance (especially as viewed by others) than what they might learn (Heyman and Dweck, 1992). They often avoid challenging tasks that involve a high degree of risk for poor performance and subsequent evaluations of incompetence (Dweck and Leggett, 1988). While incremental theorists focus on the acquisition of competence, entity theorists focus on the confirmation of competence.

If students with an entity view of intelligence typically do not exert effort on challenging tasks and even avoid such tasks, they should almost certainly fall short of their academic potential. Although not reaching one's potential and the avoidance of challenging tasks are serious issues for all students, they are of particular concern for academically talented students who have the aptitude to perform at a high level in rigorous academic environments. And, indeed, maladaptive motivational responses leading to underachievement can be found in very bright children (Bandura and Dweck, 1985, discussed in Heyman and Dweck, 1992; Licht and Dweck, 1984). In fact, it has been reported that some of the most "motivationally vulnerable" students are those who have had the most success in grade school, especially bright girls (Licht and Shapiro, 1982, reported in Heyman and Dweck, 1992), and highly able students with entity views and inaccurately low perceptions of their ability. Additionally, research has revealed differences among academically talented students in the type and difficulty level of school courses chosen over a period of years, differences not accounted for solely by intelligence (Kolitch and Brody, 1992; Swiatek and Benbow, 1991).

The underachievement of gifted students in typical school environments is often attributed to curriculum that is not sufficiently challenging (Rimm and Lovance, 1992; Sisk, 1988). But perhaps lack of challenge encourages an entity view, because hard work is not necessary, and even when effort is exerted it is not rewarded by higher grades. The role of implicit theories of intelligence has not been sufficiently studied as an important factor in underachievement of the gifted. Moreover, many academically talented students are involved in programs that are specifically designed to challenge them. In such situations, are students with the view that intelligence is stable more "at risk" for underachievement than equally able students with a view that intelligence is unstable, especially when the stability view is accompanied by underestimations of their ability? Although underachievement is of great concern for all students, it is particularly troubling when observed in students with exceptional ability.

Because of the potential effects on academic achievement, awareness of academically talented students' implicit views of intelligence, as well as their self-perceptions of their ability, effort, and preference for challenge, could be beneficial to educators. Although little research has focused on implicit views of highly able students, there has been some speculation that brighter students have views that promote the attainment and maintenance of academic goals that help them to be more successful in the academic environment than less able students (Dweck, 1986). This would suggest that highly able students believe intelligence is unstable and there is some evidence that supports this supposition. In a study of gifted and nongifted students, the gifted students were more likely than the other students to view intelligence as unstable (Alexander, 1985). Is a view that intelligence is unstable, therefore, more likely to facilitate achievement in highly able students? And what about those students with high ability who believe intelligence is stable? Are their views maladaptive, placing them at particular risk for underachievement?

Related issues in this area have been not adequately researched (especially in highly able populations) such as age- and gender-related differences in implicit views of intelligence. And the little research there is has yielded inconsistent findings. For example, adults have been found to believe intelligence is more stable than elementary school students (Ablard and Baker, 1989), although studies have not found a difference between older and younger elementary school students (e.g., Bempechat et al., 1991). For gender differences, of high ability junior high students, girls reported an entity view relative to boys (Leggett, 1985, discussed in Dweck, 1986). However, for high school students, boys (gifted and nongifted students combined) reported an entity view relative to girls (Schommer and Dunnell, 1994). Clearly, differences in view of intelligence across age and gender are not yet understood.

The purpose of the present study, therefore, was to begin to explore how academically talented students view intelligence and if there were age- and gender-related differences. Because the most distinguishing feature of entity and incremental theories is stability, perceived stability of intelligence was our primary focus. Academically talented students have been identified by teachers, parents, and peers as being "intelligent"; therefore their views of the stability of intelligence should be highly salient and potent factors affecting their achievement-related behavior. We also examined how self-perceptions (of effort, preference for challenge, and ability) were related to these general perceptions of intelligence. By restricting the range of ability in the group to the top one-half of 1% of the population in terms of verbal and/or quantitative reasoning ability (although the group is by no means completely homogeneous in terms of ability), it was possible also to examine age- and gender-related differences without the additional variable of ability levels. Specific goals of the study were to examine the following in a group of academically talented students: (a) perceived stability of intelligence; (b) school-level and gender differences in views of intelligence; (c) the relationship between students' views of intelligence and their self-perceptions of effort, preference for challenge, and ability; and (d) the number and type of students with particular combinations of intelligence views and self-perceptions that may place them at risk for future underachievement.

In the past, implicit theories have typically been assessed as if they are dichotomous. For example, Dweck and colleagues (Bandura and Dweck, 1985, described in Dweck and Leggett, 1988; Bempechat et al., 1991; Dweck and Bempechat, 1983) have assessed views as either entity or incremental; and Alexander (1985) assessed views that intelligence changes or does not change. Treatment of views as dichotomous limits statistical power. In the present study, instead of assessing views of intelligence as dichotomous, students were asked to rate their beliefs on a continuum that allowed for a greater range of stability views and the possibility of borderline views. Because research has shown that theories of intelligence are unrelated to actual ability, it was expected that the distribution of students' views of the stability of intelligence would approximate a normal distribution.

Methods

Participants were 153 academically talented students (60% boys) who ranged from the 3rd through the 11th grade and who attended advanced-level courses offered by the Center for Talented Youth at Johns Hopkins University. This group of students consisted of a random sample of students at course sites in Maryland and Pennsylvania. The gender composition of the sample reflects other academically talented samples of students enrolled in special courses. To qualify for courses, students had to score at the 97th percentile or above for their respective grade levels on standardized achievement or aptitude tests.

They also had to score at the 70th percentile or higher when compared to norms for students from two to five grade levels above their own (depending on the age of the student) on above-level quantitative and verbal reasoning tests. Tests designed for older students (i.e., "above level") are utilized to prevent ceiling effects and to make finer distinctions among students' abilities. Based on these scores, students in the study can be considered to be at least in the top one-half of the 99th percentile for their grade level for quantitative and/or verbal reasoning.

During the first week of summer courses, students were asked to complete a questionnaire that requested students to describe the stability of intelligence on a 6-point scale from "stays the same" (1) to "changes a lot" (6). A score of 1 was categorized as an extreme stability view, a score of 2 as a moderate stability view, a score of 3 or 4 as borderline views, a score of 5 as a moderate instability view, and a score of 6 as an extreme instability view. Students were also asked to describe themselves in terms of their effort expended on academic tasks, preference for challenging tasks, and ability. For effort, students rated themselves from "not hardworking" (1) to "very hardworking" (6); for preference for challenge from "not like hard tasks" (1) to "like hard tasks a lot" (6); and for ability from "not smart" (1) to "very smart" (6). Only those students who completed all questions were included in data analyses.

Results

The distribution of students' responses reflected a continuum of perceived stability of intelligence. The distribution of responses is best described as a bell-shaped curve with slightly more frequent responses toward an instability view (–.10 skewness). Almost one-half of all students (48%) indicated borderline responses, a response corresponding to scores of 3 or 4. If students' responses were forced into an extreme view as done in most studies (split between scores of 3 and 4), slightly more than one-half (55%) would be classified as having an instability view. It should be noted, however, that 30% of these students had borderline views.

School level was determined by grade level ranges: elementary (3rd–5th grades), middle (6th–8th grades), and high school (9th–11th grades). Examination of percentages by school level demonstrated that 37% of high school students, 34 percent of middle school students, but only 14% of elementary school students had a stability view (i.e., scores of 1 or 2). A similar but reverse pattern was found for an instability view (i.e., scores of 5 or 6); there was a substantially lower percentage of high school students (16%) with this view than middle school (34%) or elementary school students (28%). Interestingly, the youngest group of students (in elementary school) had the largest percentage (59%) of borderline views. The distributions for males and females were similar.

Because beliefs about intelligence have been found to be related to effort and preference for challenge, as well as perceptions of ability, Pearson correlations were conducted to examine these relationships. There were no significant relationships between view of intelligence and any of the self-perceptions (ability r = -.04, effort r = .10, and preference for challenge r = .06).

Potential gender differences in self-perceptions were examined by t-tests. For ability and preference for challenge, there were no gender differences. Females perceived themselves (ability M = 4.56, SD = .78; challenge M = 3.89, SD = 1.19) in the same way that males perceived themselves (ability M = 4.82, SD = .93; challenge M = 3.78, SD = 1.42). For effort, however, females (M = 4.44, SD = 1.11) rated themselves as being harder workers than males (M = 4.03, SD = 1.33), t(151) = 1.96, p = .05.

It was of further interest to determine the percentage of students who might be at risk for underachievement based on their combination of intelligence views and self-perceptions. Based on self-perceptions alone, those academically talented students with low self-ratings for ability, effort, or preference for challenge could be potentially at risk. Surprisingly, there was a small percentage of students who indicated low perceptions (scores of 1 or 2) for effort and preference for challenge. Using Fisher's z test, no significant gender differences for these self-ratings were found, although slightly more males than females indicated low ratings for challenge and effort. Last, none of the students gave low self-ratings for ability (scores of 1 or 2), although a sizeable group of students did indicate perceived moderate ability (a score of 3 or 4), certainly an underestimation for these talented students. A slightly but not significantly higher percentage of females than males underestimated their ability.

Of particular interest was the identification of students who believed intelligence is stable who also indicated low ability for themselves, a group with the highest potential for underachievement. Of the students who indicated moderate or extreme stability views (i.e., score of 1 or 2), approximately one-third (13 students) also indicated relatively low perceptions of ability. Of these 13 students, there were equivalent percentages of females (n = 7) and males (n = 6). Furthermore, most of these 13 students were in high school (n = 7), rather than in middle school (n = 5) or elementary school (n = 1). Because of the small group sizes, these differences should be interpreted with caution.

Discussion

In most research, implicit theories of intelligence have been examined as a dichotomous variable (Bandura & Dweck, 1985, described in Dweck and Leggett, 1988; Bempechat et al., 1991; Dweck & Bempechat, 1983). The present results showed that when perceived stability of intelligence is assessed as a potentially continuous variable, perceptions vary widely from extreme stability to extreme instability views and approximate a normal distribution. In this study, academically talented students exhibited wide variation in their beliefs about the stability of intelligence, with one-half of the group reporting borderline views. A dichotomous classification would have distorted the range and differences in views that many students possessed. Future research in implicit views of intelligence may want to consider the usefulness of assessing views of intelligence in this way.

In support of prior research (Ablard & Baker, 1989), the present study found that older students' views, like adults' views, were more representative of a stability view. One suggested explanation for developmental differences is that as students get older they obtain more experience with society's increasing emphasis on performance relative to other students, especially for students identified as gifted, and therefore they adopt a view that intelligence is stable (Bempechat et al., 1991). Even though there were overall school level group differences, there were wide variations within school level. There were stability theorists in elementary school and instability theorists in high school. This variation most likely is due to wide differences in students' individual academic experiences over time, as well as their unique perceptions of these experiences. Individual differences among students in terms of cognitive and personality characteristics are additional factors that should be considered.

No gender differences were found for perceived stability of intelligence, in contrast to findings of other studies (Leggett, 1985, discussed in Dweck, 1986; Schommer & Dunnell, 1994). Females did perceive themselves, however, as harder workers than males, a perception difference that may have been associated with a greater percentage of females having instability views than found in other student samples. It is possible that academically talented females have different self-perceptions and related implicit theories than less talented females. When the percentage of females with perceptions associated with underachievement is considered (low ability, low effort, and low preference for challenge), there was not a greater inclination for females than males to be in these groups, as has been previously suggested by research (Dweck, 1986).

An interesting result of the present study was that perceived stability of intelligence was not related to self-perceptions of effort and preference for challenge, as would be predicted by prior research (Dweck & Bempechat, 1983; Dweck & Leggett, 1988). It is possible that self-perceptions of academically talented students are more homogeneous than self-perceptions of other samples of students, thus ameliorating the relationship between these self-perceptions and views of intelligence. Furthermore, these students are more likely to experience boredom in school because of their high academic abilities (Rimm & Lovance, 1992; Sisk, 1988), and thus may not typically exert effort and may welcome challenge whatever their view of intelligence. In addition, few of them are likely to have experienced significant academic "failure" to this point. For them, failure may not even be what other students consider as failure; instead, mediocrity may define failure for academically talented students.

A principal reason for the lack of significant relationships in the present study may be inherent to the nature of the assessment. In contrast to prior research by Dweck and colleagues (discussed in Dweck & Leggett, 1988), but similar to other research (Alexand

1985; Bempechat et al., 1991), we did not assess students' beliefs regarding the possible role of effort in intelligence. By definition, entity theorists believe intelligence can change because of effort, a belief that yields effort when challenged (Dweck, 1986; Dweck & Bempechat, 1983). Future research should consider assessing students' perceptions of the role that effort, as well as a variety of other factors (e.g., task characteristics, interest of the topic, etc.), play in the instability of intelligence. Perhaps effort can enhance intelligence but it is not the sole factor.

Like other studies, we based views on a one-item assessment, a procedure that may have inadequately measured the full range and complexity of implicit views of intelligence. Prior researchers have asked students (a) "Can intelligence change?" (Alexander, 1985), or (b) "Kids say you can get smarter, but other kids say you're a certain amount smart. Which belief do you agree with?" (Bempechat et al., 1991). The answers to each of these questions, as well as the answer to the question posed in the present study, all provide important information. However, each answer is only a small piece of a more global conception of intelligence. Future research efforts should focus on developing a more comprehensive assessment of implicit views of intelligence. These efforts should consider some of the important issues raised in this paper: (a) implicit views appear to encompass more than perceptions of the stability of intelligence and (b) implicit views are more continuous than previously considered.

Research on implicit views of intelligence should and will continue, because these views can greatly affect achievement behaviors. Because effort is needed when learning novel and complex material, an incremental view has been shown to be most adaptable when students are presented with these types of material (Licht & Dweck, 1984). The most adaptable view across situations may be a borderline view because it should be flexible and easily modified to match the learning environment. In fact, the present study found that of the two extreme groups and a borderline group, the largest group of gifted students was in the borderline group, believing intelligence was moderately stable/unstable. Such a finding gives support to Dweck's (1986) suggestion that brighter children have more adaptive views of intelligence than other students. Longitudinal studies that examine the effect of intelligence views across academic situations and in conjunction with influences from others (e.g., teachers and parents) will provide the information necessary to determine the adaptability of views of intelligence.

In summary, implicit theories of intelligence are important for understanding differences in classroom performance and perhaps for predicting long-term achievement differences among academically talented students. More research, however, is still needed to (a) a more comprehensive assessment of implicit views of intelligence, (b) examine heories of intelligence and self-perceptions are related to actual academic achievement behaviors, (c) investigate how these relationships may es, and (d) describe how they may change over time.

er, L. (1989, April). Why Johnny or Janie can read: Children's and attributions. Paper presented at the biennial meeting of the Society Child Development.

Alexander, P. (1985). Gifted and nongifted students' perceptions of intelligence. *Gifted Child Quarterly,* 29: 137–143.

Bempechat, J., London, P., and Dweck, C. S. (1991). Children's conceptions of ability in major domains: An interview and experimental study. *Child Study Journal,* 21: 11–35.

Dweck, C. S. (1986). Motivational processes affecting learning. *American Psychologist,* 41: 1040–1048.

Dweck, C. S., & Bempechat, J. (1983). Children's theories of intelligence: Consequences for learning. In Paris, S., Olson, G., & Stevenson, H. (Eds.), *Learning and Motivation in the Classroom*.Hillsdale, NJ: Erlbaum.

Dweck, C. S., & Elliott, E. S. (1983). Achievement motivation. In Mussen, P. H. (gen. ed.) and Hetherington, E. M. (ed.), *Handbook of Child Psychology: Vol. IV, Social and Personality Development*. New York: Wiley.

Dweck, C. S., & Leggett, E. L. (1988). A social-cognitive approach to motivation and personality. *Psychological Review,* 95: 256–273.

Heyman, G. D., & Dweck, C. S. (1992). Achievement goals and intrinsic motivation: Their relation and their role in adaptive motivation. *Motivation and Emotion,* 16: 231–247.

Kolitch, E. R., & Brody, L. E. (1992). Mathematics acceleration of highly talented students: An evaluation. *Gifted Child Quarterly,* 36: 78–85.

Licht, B. G., & Dweck, C. S. (1984). Determinants of academic achievement: The interaction of children's achievement orientations with skill area. *Developmental Psychology,* 20: 628–636.

Rimm, S. B., & Lovance, K. J. (1992). How acceleration may prevent underachievement syndrome. *Gifted Child Today,* 79: 9–14.

Schommer, M., & Dunnell, P. A. (1994). A comparison of epistemological beliefs between gifted and non-gifted high school students. *Roeper Review,* 16: 207–210.

Sisk, D. A. (1988). The bored and disinterested gifted child: Going through school lockstep. *Journal of Educ Gifted,* 11: 5–17.

Swiatek, M. A., & Benbow, C. P. (1991). A ten-year longitudinal follow-up of participants in a fast-paced mathematics course. *Journal for Research in Mathematics Education,* 22: 138–150.

REVIEW QUESTIONS

1. What type of scale was used for this project? Why did the researchers use this scale?

2. What did the researcher feel was wrong with using a scale that just asked students to agree or disagree with certain statements about their talents?

3. Was there a difference in self-perceptions between males and females? What was it? Explain in detail.

THE REVERSE SOCIAL DISTANCE SCALE

Motoko Y. Lee, Stephen G. Sapp, and Melvin C. Ray

These researchers created a "reverse" Social Distance Scale by modifying Bogardus's Social Distance Scale to measure minority groups' perceptions of the social distance established by the majority group between itself and minority groups.

The social distance between a minority group and the majority group—the most powerful group, but not necessarily the largest—has been postulated by the present authors to be based on the minority group's reaction to its perceived rejection or acceptance by the majority group, rather than on the majority group's reaction to the minority group. Thus, Bogardus's Social Distance Scale (1925), which was created from the perspective of the majority group, cannot be used to explain the nature of this type of social distance. To assess a minority group's perceptions of the distance established by the majority group between itself and the minority group (rather than the distance a minority group has established between itself and the majority group), researchers need a different type of measure.

The literature contains no mention of such a scale, and although numerous accounts of minority perceptions of prejudice appear in the writings of W. E. B. Du Bois (Weinberg, 1992) and others (e.g., Cleaver, 1967; Finkenstaedt, 1994; Grier, 1968; Silberman, 1964; & West, 1993), such accounts tend to be qualitative. A review of the following studies provides additional evidence of the need for a "reverse" Social Distance Scale.

Netting (1991) reported that Chinese immigrants in Canada tended to reject Whites and other groups instead of seeking acceptance from them. "Anglos would accept Poles, the only white minority represented in the study, and Chinese. However, Chinese would not accept Anglos" (p. 101). If the goal is understanding a minority viewpoint, then it is more important to assess the distance perceived by the Chinese immigrants as having been created by the White Canadians than it is to assess the actual social distance between the two groups, because the former perspective is that of the minority group. Left unanswered by Netting's study was the question of whether the Chinese and the Polish immigrants' perceptions of acceptance by the Anglos were the same or similar.

Muir and Muir (1988) used Bogardus's Social Distance Scale in their study of White and Black middle-school children from the Deep South. These researchers found that, by ⁀⁀ly teens, most of the White children had adopted an adult pattern of relating to ⁀⁀ of civil acceptance and social rejection, whereas a majority of Black chil- ⁀⁀cially as well as publicly. The Black middle-school students were ⁀⁀ of the White middle-school students than the White students were ⁀⁀ he Black children's perception of the extent of their social accept- ⁀⁀ren—a factor that would have provided more information about the ⁀⁀tance of the White children—was not examined.

S., & Ray, M. 1996. The reverse social distance scale. *Journal of Social*): 17–25.

McAllister and Moore (1991) used Bogardus's Social Distance Scale in Australia to measure majority and minority groups' perceptions of social distance from each other. McAllister and Moore attempted to explain the variation in the groups' perceptions without considering the conditional nature of the social distance established by the minority groups between themselves and the majority group. The factors that were considered by McAllister and Moore accounted for very little of the variation in social distance that was created by the two immigrant minority groups—far less than the amount of variation that was accounted for in relation to the Australian majority group ($[R.sup.2] = .02$ for the combined European immigrant group and $.01$ for the Southeast Asian group vs. $.11$ for the Australians, 1991, p. 100).

Tuch (1988, p. 184) tried to account for the variation in social distance among Blacks and Whites toward each others' groups, using several socioeconomic predictors. As in McAllister and Moore's study, the variables that were selected explained considerably less about the Blacks' social distance from the Whites (7%) than about the Whites' social distance from the Blacks (27%).

Wilson (1986) observed that studies addressing the correlates of Blacks' racial distance preferences have been few, and their results, inconsistent. In addition, Wilson observed that social variables predicted the social distance preferred by Blacks much more poorly than they predicted the social distance preferred by Whites.

The common finding in these studies—that the selected variables explained Blacks' preference for social distance toward Whites more poorly than they explained Whites' preference for social distance toward Blacks—suggests that important explanatory variables that would account for the social distance preferences of minority groups toward the majority group were lacking in this research. To explain the minority variation in social distance, researchers need a measure of the minority's perception of the social distance established by the majority group between itself and the minority group, because this perception is assumed to be the basis upon which minorities will establish their preferred social distance from the majority group. Even Bogardus (1959, p. 77), in his study of factors that would determine the distance between nations, called people of other nations' friendliness and open-heartedness the "nearness factors."

Method

Our objectives in the present study were to assess the feasibility of a "reverse" Social Distance Scale, to determine whether such a scale would differentiate among different minority groups, and to revise the scale, if necessary, based on participants' responses. We mailed a questionnaire to approximately 1,000 minority students (U.S. citizens and permanent residents) at a state university in the spring of 1993. We received 108 completed and usable questionnaires. The present results, although not generalizable, were satisfactory in light of our objectives.

The extremely low return rate for the questionnaire was probably a reflection of indifference to or avoidance of the topic of rejection/acceptance by the majority group. Responding to our Reverse Social Distance Scale may have been difficult for certain minorities. Several students, all of whom were Black, returned the questionnaire without having answered the Reverse Social Distance Scale question. These students wrote c

ments such as, "Do not ask these questions. I am an American" or "This type of question perpetuates the division between whites and blacks." If, as we suspect, this type of reaction was common among those who did not return their questionnaires, then the nonparticipants' perceptions about rejection/acception by the majority group may have differed from those of the participants. This possibility was not explored in the present study but should be investigated.

We created the Reverse Social Distance Scale by modifying the items on Bogardus's Racial Distance Scale (Miller, 1991, p. 382). The proposed scale items (distance criteria) were as similar as possible to those on Bogardus's scale, but we did make some modifications so that the items would appear realistic to college students. In contrast to Bogardus's scale, which assesses respondents' willingness to accept members of other groups in various roles (e.g., as a fellow citizen, as a neighbor), the Reverse Social Distance Scale assesses respondents' perceptions of how other groups accept them in these roles.

Items that were likely to have been experienced by college students were phrased "Do they mind . . . ?", and the other items as "Would they . . . ?" The items and the instructions for the Reverse Social Distance Scale were as follows:

Considering typical Caucasian Americans you have known, not any specific person nor the worst or the best, circle Y or N to express your opinion.

Y N 5. Do they mind your being a citizen in this country?

Y N 4. Do they mind your living in the same neighborhood?

Y N 3. Would they mind your living next to them?

Y N 2. Would they mind your becoming a close friend to them?

Y N 1. Would they mind your becoming their kin by marriage?

We did not include Bogardus's Social Distance Scale in the present study because we wanted to avoid any contamination that might result from the use of Bogardus's scale and the Reverse Social Distance Scale on the same questionnaire. We did include the Twenty Statements Test (TST; Kuhn & McPartland, 1954), however; the respondents were asked to write 20 responses (at most) to the question "Who am I?"

Results

The aggregated data for the three groups are reported in Table 1. The category entitled other minorities included diverse groups, such as Japanese Americans, Chinese Ameri-
Native Americans, and other Americans, whose ancestors had immigrated from
as India, Sri Lanka, Vietnam, and Laos. These groups were combined into
them was large enough to be considered individually in the analysis.
that there was a significant difference among the three means.
tudents' mean score was significantly higher than those of the
ting that, on average, the African American students perceived the
the Caucasian Americans to be greater than the other two groups
ups did not differ significantly from each other. The reason we con-
significance was to determine the magnitude of the differences in the
e generalizations about the results.

TABLE 1: ANALYSIS OF VARIANCE RESULTS

Group	N	M	SD
African Americans	48	3.65	1.74
Hispanic Americans	25	1.60	1.12
Other minorities	35	1.80c	1.80

Between groups: F(2, 105) = 23.8, p = .001

Note. Means with different subscripts differ significantly at .05.

c This category included Japanese Americans, Chinese Americans, Native Americans, and Americans whose ancestors had come from India, Sri Lanka, Vietnam, and Laos.

Although the scale's coefficient was high enough to be acceptable, we examined a few cases in which the responses seemed contradictory and used the respondents' comments to revise the instructions for the scale and the wording of some items. The original version of the instructions contained the adjective "typical" (Bogardus used "stereotypic"), but 1 respondent criticized this term as stereotyping. Because the purpose of the scale is to assess perceptions of the distance associated with the collective majority group, or the generalized other of that group, not perceptions of the distance associated with specific individuals in that group, we recommend that future researchers use the word "most," instead of "typical" or "stereotypic," in the instructions to the scale.

There were also some contradictions with regard to the responses for the citizenship item. A few persons perceived that Caucasian Americans minded having them as fellow citizens even though the Caucasian Americans did not mind them living in the same neighborhood. These participants may have equated the concept of citizenship with rights and duties and, therefore, have viewed it as encompassing more than living in the same community. Although the citizenship item was included in Bogardus's scale, future researchers would do better to replace this item with one that pertains to a simpler concept, such as living in the same community.

We examined TST responses for the students whose scores were at either end of our scale: strong acceptance (1) or strong rejection (6). Eleven of the 48 African American students received a score of 6; of these 11 students, 6 used "African" or "Black" as their first identifier, 1 used this type of label as his or her 19th identifier, and 4 did not use a racial identifier. Six African American students received a score of 1; of these 6 students, 3 used a racial identifier in their first response to the TST, and the other 3 did not use a racial identifier at all.

None of the 25 Hispanic students received a score of 6, but 17 received a score of 1. Of these 17 students, 4 used an ethnic identifier in their 2nd, 5th, 6th, or 15th response, and the remaining 13 did not use an ethnic identifier.

Of the 35 (predominantly Asian) students in the Other Minorities group, only 1 received a score of 6. This participant used a racial identifier in his or her fourth response. Eighteen of the students in the Other Minorities group scored 1; of these students, 10 did not use a racial/ethnic identifier, 6 used a racial/ethnic identifier in their first response, 1 used a racial/ethnic identifier in his or her second response, and 1 used a racial/ethnic identifier in his or her ninth response.

Discussion

The Reverse Social Distance Scale assesses minority groups' perceptions of the social distance established by the majority group between itself and minority groups. The scale differentiated between the African American students and the other two minority groups, Hispanics and Other Minorities, in the present study, but not between the latter two groups.

Researchers (McAllister & Moore, 1991, pp. 96–97) have discussed several alternatives that might account for social distance, including social learning theory (Allport, 1954), theory focusing on social experience of education (Harding, Proshansky, Kutner, & Chein, 1969), economic competition theory (Baker, 1978), contact theory (Tajfel, 1982), and the theory of authoritarian personality (Adorno, Frenkel-Brunswik, Levinson, & Sanford, 1950). However, these theories seem to be more applicable to majority group prejudice toward minority groups than to minority group prejudice toward the majority group.

Researchers have tended to ignore the influence of minority group perceptions regarding their acceptance or rejection by the majority group on the degree of social distance minority groups establish between themselves and the majority group. As Walsh (1990) indicated, researchers (e.g., Griffitt & Veitch, 1974; Van den Berghe, 1981) have recognized the role of the majority group's acceptance or rejection of minority groups on the social distance between the majority and minorities; nevertheless, Bogardus's Social Distance Scale has continued to be researchers' (e.g., Walsh's) major tool.

We assumed that minority groups in multiethnic or multiracial societies do not isolate themselves by choice, but prefer to be accepted by the majority group and to have equal access to resources and rewards. We also assumed that minority group members perceive a social distance that has been established by the majority group, between their own-group and the majority group, even though minority groups' perception of this distance may differ from that of the majority group. The social distance minority groups perceive as having been established by the majority group influences the degree of social distance the minority group will establish between itself and the majority group; therefore, we expected the relationship between the Reverse Social Distance Scale and Bogardus's Social Distance Scale to be positive. We did not explore this relationship, however, because we did not include Bogardus's Social Distance Scale in the present study, to avoid any contamination of the results.

Tajfel and Turner (1986) suggested that self-identification with one's own-group is dependent upon one's evaluation of the comparisons between one's own-group and out-groups, regarding the attributes and characteristics that are valued by one's own-group. These researchers posited that members of a group whose social identity is not satisfactory will either try to improve their group's identity or leave their present group to join a group whose identify is more positive. Thus, the member of a minority group's perceived rejection or acceptance by the majority group is likely to affect the way this individual feels about the social identity of his or her own-group.

In line with Tajfel and Turner's reasoning, we examined the responses of the highest and lowest scorers on the Reverse Social Distance Scale. Six of the 11 respondents who received a score of 6 (strongest perceived rejection) used a racial/ethnic identifier in their 1st response to the TST. These participants (the first category described by Tajfel and Turner, 1986) would be likely to distance themselves from the majority and to try to establish their own separate identities. The participants who used a racial identifier in their 19th TST response and the 4 participants who did not use a racial identifier at all would be likely to try to establish their own separate self-identity or to find another group to identify with (Tajfel and Turner's second category).

The 41 respondents who received a score of 1 (strongest perceived acceptance) would be unlikely to distance themselves from the majority. Four respondents used a racial/ethnic identifier in their 5th, 6th, 9th, or 15th response on the TST, and 26 did not use a racial/ethnic identifier at all. The 14 respondents who used a racial/ethnic identifier in their 1st or 2nd response to the TST might distance themselves from the majority group to the extent that they would prefer to limit intimate relationships (i.e., mate, kin) to members of their own-groups.

The relationship between the participants' scores on the Reverse Social Distance Scale and their choices of self-identifiers provided some insight about the possible effect of minority groups' perceptions of the social distance established by the majority group on minority group members' self-concept. More research is needed, however, to explore the consequences of minority groups' perceptions of social distance for the degree of social distance minority groups establish between themselves and the majority group, as well the consequences of these perceptions for minority groups' self-concept.

References

Adorno, T. W., Frenkel-Brunswik, E., Levinson, D. J., & Sanford, R. N. (1950). *The authoritarian personality*. New York: Harper.

Allport, G. W. (1954). *The nature of prejudice*. Reading, MA: Addison-Wesley.

Babbie, E. (1989). *The practice of social research* (5th ed.). Belmont, CA: Wadsworth.

Baker, D. (1978). Race and power: Comparative approaches to the analysis of race relations. *Ethnic and Racial Studies*, 1, 316–335.

Bogardus, E. S. (1925). Measuring social distance. *Journal of Applied Sociology*, 9, 299–308.

Bogardus, E. S. (1959). *Social distance*. Yellow Spring, OH: Artichild.

Cleaver, E. (1967). *Soul on ice*. New York: McGraw-Hill.

Finkenstaedt, R. L. H. (1994). *Face-to-face: Blacks in America, White perceptions and Black realities*. New York: William Morrow.

Grier, W. H. (1968). *Black rage*. New York: Basic Books.

Griffitt, W., & Veitch, R. (1974). Preacquaintance attitude similarity and attraction revisited: Ten days in a fallout shelter. *Sociometry*, 37, 163–178.

Harding, J., Proshansky, H., Kutner, B., & Chein, I. (1969). Prejudice and ethnic relations. In G. Lindzey & E. Aronson (Eds.) *Handbook of social psychology*, (2nd ed., Vol. 5, pp. 1–76). Reading, MA: Addison-Wesley.

Kuhn, M. H., & McPartland, T. S. (1954). An empirical investigation of self-attitudes. *American Sociological Review*, 19, 68–76.

McAllister, I., & Moore, R. (1991). Social distance among Australian ethnic groups. *Sociology and Social Research,* 75, 95–100.

Miller, D. C. (1991). *Handbook of research design and social measurement* (5th ed.). Newbury Park, CA: Sage.

Muir, D. E., & Muir, L. W. (1988). Social distance between Deep-South middle-school Whites and Blacks. *Sociology and Social Research*, 72, 177–180.

Netting, N. S. (1991). Chinese aloofness from other groups: Social distance data from a city in British Columbia. *Sociology and Social Research*, 75, 101–103.

Silberman, C. E. (1964). *Crisis in Black and White*. New York: Random House.

Tajfel, H. (1982). *Social identity and intergroup relations*. Cambridge: Cambridge University Press.

Tajfel, H., & Turner, J. C. (1986). The social identify theory of intergroup behavior. In S. Worchel & W. G. Austin (Eds.), *Psychology of intergroup relations* (pp. 7–24). Chicago, IL: Nelson-Hall.

Tuch, S. A. (1988). Race differences in the antecedents of social distance attitudes. *Sociology and Social Research*, 72, 181–184.

Van den Berghe, P. (1981). *The ethnic phenomenon*. New York: Elsevier.

Walsh, A. (1990). Becoming an American and liking it as functions of social distance and severity of initiation. *Sociological Inquiry*, 60, 177–189.

Weinberg, M., (Ed.). (1992). *The words of W. E. B. Du Bois: A quotation sourcebook*. Westport, CT: Greenwood.

West, C. (1993). *Race matters*. Boston: Beacon.

Wilson, T. C. (1986). The asymmetry of racial distance between Blacks and Whites. *Sociology and Social Research*, 70, 161–163.

REVIEW QUESTIONS

1. Explain why the "reverse" Social Distance Scale was created?

2. What were the findings from this project?

3. What is the difference between the social distance of minorities and that of majorities? Explain them.

Chapter 7: Sampling

As you have previously learned, one of the goals of research is to describe or identify specific characteristics about a specific group or population. This isn't too difficult if the group you are studying is small, such as a group of 10 or 12 children in a daycare setting. In this case, all you would need to do is observe or interview all of the children. However, this process of figuring out who to study becomes more difficult if the group is larger. Let's say you want to find out about the quality of life of all the female students and compare their answers to those of the male students. This could involve lots of students, and it would be nearly impossible for you to interview or observe all of them.

You probably would not be able to include all of the student **population** in colleges and universities in the United States because contacting all of them would be time consuming and cost too much money. Therefore, the next step is to decide how to select a **sample** that is **representative** of the population you have in mind. This is not as simple you might think because one of the goals is that your sample must *accurately* reflect the larger population so you can **generalize** about the population you are studying. For example, let's say you want to conduct a study of college students. You have found that the college students at your particular school have an average age of 21. Fifty-one percent of them are female, and they have an average income of $8,000 a year. So, you want to collect data on the students and visit a computer programming class in the evening to hand out your survey. You find that of the 40 students you surveyed, 80% were male, the average age was 35, and the average income was $40,000 a year. Does this sample represent your college population? No. You must decide what sampling method is appropriate for the research you are conducting. In this chapter you will learn about two types of sampling methods, probability sampling and nonprobability sampling.

PROBABILITY SAMPLING

Probability sampling is designed to allow a determination of how likely the members of the sample are to be representative of the population from where they are drawn. In other words, the researcher decides which segment of the population will be used for the project in order to accurately portray the parameters of the larger population. The most common way of accomplishing this is by **random selection. Randomization**, or **random selection** means that every subject in the population has the same chance of being selected for the sample, and therefore, the sample group should possess the same characteristics of the larger population. There are a number of ways to randomly select your sample. **Simple random sampling** is a procedure that generates numbers or cases strictly on the basis of chance. Selection could be as simple as rolling the dice and getting heads or tails. You can also use phone numbers as a way of randomly selecting numbers with the help of a computer and **random-digit dialing**. Random-digit dialing is most useful because if a phone number is no longer in service or no one is home, then the program automatically replaces that number with the next random number.

Systematic random sampling is just a little different from the simple random sample method. In this type of sampling every nth element is selected from a list after the first element is randomly selected within the first n cases. This type of sampling is convenient when the population elements are arranged consecutively. To use this type of method you must first randomly select the first number to be sampled. Then you must decide on your **sampling interval** where the total number of cases in the population is divided by the number of cases required in the sample. So, if you have 500 students in your population and you want 50 students to be in your sample, your sampling interval would be 10. Next you would count using your sampling interval from the first case and every nth case is included in your sample.

Stratified random sampling uses information that is already known about the total population before sampling. This makes the sampling process more efficient. To begin, all elements of the population are distinguished based on their characteristics. This forms the **sampling strata**. Next, the elements are sampled randomly within the strata. For example, if your school is 3/4 women and 1/4 men, then your sample should look the same way. Your sample is a **proportionate stratified sample** if each stratum is represented exactly in proportion to the population. It is a **disproportionate stratified sample** if it varies from the population.

Cluster sampling is used when a sampling frame is not available; however it requires more information before sampling than the previous methods do. Clusters are naturally occurring elements of the population. Thus, city blocks would be clusters for sampling people who live in cities and businesses would be clusters for sampling employees. To begin, you must draw a random sample of clusters, which requires a list of businesses or city blocks. You then draw a random sample of elements within each cluster. If you are interested in a cluster sample of employees, you would first record the addresses of all businesses and then you could separate them into categories such as the following:

Category	Number	Percentage
North	469	20.8
South	738	32.8
East	653	29.0
West	392	17.4
Total	2252	100

Next you must decide how large a sample you want. If you decide to use 100 businesses in each category, you would use a simple random selection within each category to come up with your sample.

As you already know, your project is well designed if the sample represents the population from which it has been selected. But **sampling errors** can occur. A sampling error is the difference between the characteristics of a sample and that of the population. The less

dents during the pilot-test stage reported using the "mostly truthfully" option when they intended to answer all items truthfully but were uncertain about the answer to a small number of items, such as the inability to recall exact dates or numbers of drug use episodes. The protocols were consistent with recommended protocols to improve validity of self-reports of drug use recommended by an advisory panel on validity issues convened by the National Institute on Drug Abuse.[21]

Results

A total of 20,629 students in grades 5–12 participated in the study, with an overall response rate of 98%. Gender distribution yielded almost equal numbers of male and female subjects, and grade distribution fairly represented statewide enrollment levels at each grade: fifth grade, 12%; sixth grade, 12%; seventh grade, 16%; eighth grade, 15%; ninth grade, 12%, 10th grade, 14%; 11th grade, 12%; and 12th grade, 8%. Proportions represented in the sample provided a standard error of 0.3%. The true proportion for each reported variable falls within [+ or −] 0.6% (two standard errors) of the reported proportion, with a 95% confidence level.

To substantiate consistency of the self-reports, a correlation coefficient of reported use for various drugs on a five-point Likert scale was calculated comparing reported levels of use the past year with use the past month. The correlation coefficient was calculated at [+ or −] 0.83, which was statistically significant at $p < .01$.

Items relevant to this study asked students to report how many times in the past year and the past month they used various drugs. Prevalence proportions of reported drug use by 8th, 10th, and 12th grade students, with national comparison data from the 1991 National High School Survey[3] (the most recent national comparison available) are presented in Tables 1 and 2. These grades were selected for presentation because they are the only grades for which comparable national comparison norms exists. As the data in the tables indicate, substantial proportions of Indiana students at each grade level reported use of most drugs the past year and the past month at rates in excess of rates reported by the national survey, with prevalence rates for all drugs except inhalants increasing by grade level. The most frequently reported drugs used by students included alcohol, cigarettes, smokeless tobacco, marijuana, inhalants, amphetamines, and tranquilizers. Reported rates of use for prescription drugs (amphetamines, tranquilizers, and prescription narcotics) by Indiana students greatly exceeded rates reported nationally.

To examine the relationship between smoking behavior and use of alcohol and other drugs, students' reported smoking behavior (as shown in dose-dependent tables) was cross-tabulated with reported alcohol and other drug use and with reported instances of binge drinking (drinking five or more servings of alcoholic beverages on a single occasion in the two weeks prior to the survey).

Data in Table 3 show the dose-dependent relationship between increasing levels of cigarette smoking and increased frequency of binge drinking. Reported rates of binge drinking by Indiana students substantially exceeded national comparisons at all three grade levels: 20.6% to 12.9% at 8th grade; 29.2% to 22.9% at 10th grade; and 37.6% to 29.8% at 12th grade. The cross-tabulation of pooled data for grades 5–12 shows a powerful relationship between heavy smoking and heavy drinking, tested by the chi-square statistic, which was

TABLE 1. ANNUAL USE OF TOBACCO, ALCOHOL, AND OTHER DRUGS BY INDIANA STUDENTS IN GRADES 8, 10, AND 12, WITH NATIONAL COMPARISONS PERCENT OF STUDENTS REPORTING USE AT LEAST ONCE IN PAST YEAR

	8th Grade		10th Grade		12th Grade	
	Ind	Natl	Ind	Natl	Ind	Natl
Cigarettes	41.8	NC	48.7	NC	54.3	NC
Smokeless tobacco	22.8	NC	27.1	NC	30.8	NC
Alcohol	57.2	41.0	71.8	72.3	79.1	77.7
Marijuana	10.5	6.2	19.7	16.5	23.7	23.9
Cocaine	1.9	1.1	3.5	2.2	4.8	3.5
Crack	1.5	0.7	1.9	0.9	2.7	1.5
Inhalants	13.7	9.0	9.2	7.1	7.9	6.6
Amphetamines	10.4	6.2	15.0	8.2	14.5	8.2
Tranquilizers	11.2	1.8	12.2	3.2	11.0	3.6
Prescription narcotics	5.2	NC	7.6	NC	6.7	3.5
Psychedelics	3.7	1.9	7.8	4.0	9.3	5.8
Heroin	1.4	0.7	1.8	0.5	2.3	0.4
Steroids	2.6	1.0	2.8	1.1	2.6	1.4

Ind. = Indiana Survey,(2) 1992; Natl. = National Survey,(3) 1991; NC = Not collected

TABLE 2: MONTHLY USE OF TOBACCO, ALCOHOL, AND OTHER DRUGS BY INDIANA STUDENTS IN GRADES 8, 10, AND 12, WITH NATIONAL COMPARISONS PERCENT OF STUDENTS REPORTING USE AT LEAST ONCE IN PAST MONTH

	8th Grade		10th Grade		12th Grade	
	Ind	Natl	Ind	Natl	Ind	Natl
Cigarettes	24.8	14.3	31.3	20.8	36.2	28.3
Smokeless tobacco	15.6	6.9	18.2	10.0	21.7	NC
Alcohol	35.1	25.1	47.1	42.8	56.1	54.0
Marijuana	6.7	3.2	11.8	8.7	14.4	13.8
Cocaine	1.1	0.3	1.9	0.7	3.1	1.4
Crack	1.1	0.3	1.1	0.3	2.0	0.7
Inhalants	7.4	4.4	4.8	2.7	3.9	2.4
Amphetamines	6.6	2.6	7.5	3.3	7.5	3.2
Tranquilizers	7.0	0.8	6.4	1.2	5.3	1.4
Prescription narcotics	3.3	NC	3.7	NC	3.2	0.1
Psychedelics	2.2	0.8	4.7	1.6	5.6	2.2
Heroin	0.4	0.3	1.1	0.2	1.8	0.2
Steroids	1.7	0.4	1.6	0.6	2.1	0.8

Ind. = Indiana Survey,(2) 1992; Natl. = National Survey,(3) 1991; NC = Not collected

significant at p > .01. Rates reported by all categories of smokers were substantially higher than those reported by nonsmokers, with 39% of 159 students who reported using two or more packs of cigarettes per day also reporting at least 10 episodes of binge drinking in the two weeks prior to the survey, compared with fewer than 1% of nonsmoking students.

The relationship of reported smoking behavior with use of alcohol and other drugs the past year reveals smokers are much more likely than nonsmokers to use all drugs listed. The likelihood of using the other drugs increased with the frequency of cigarette smoking. Use by nonsmokers of drugs other than alcohol and smokeless tobacco was almost nonexistent, and reported use rate of alcohol by nonsmokers was one-third the rate reported by one-pack-a-day or more smokers. Reported rate of smokeless tobacco use by nonsmokers was one-seventh that reported by one-pack-a-day or more smokers. Comparisons of use rates for all drugs were statistically significant at p < .01, using the chi-square statistic, with the ratio of increased risk for one-pack-a-day or more smokers ranging from about 10:1 for inhalants to more than 30:1 for marijuana, cocaine, heroin, and psychedelics.

To examine the relationship among students' perceived risks, perceived peer approval/disapproval, gender, grade level, ethnic background, or reported frequency of episodes of adverse consequences due to their drug use, as predictors of their use of alcohol and other drugs, a step-wise multiple regression analysis was used. The perceived risk component consisted of a seven-item belief subscale related to perceived risk of physical or other harm from drug use. Items were placed on a four-point Likert format ranging from "no risk" to "great risk." Reported frequency of episodes for adverse consequences from use of alcohol and other drugs was measured on a 10-item Likert-type scale asking students to report frequency of use-related events such as hangovers, missed school, or poor test performance.

To examine the relationship of age at first cigarette use, perceived risk, perceived peer approval/disapproval, with frequency of cigarette smoking the past month, data were subjected to multiple regression analyses. The regression model produced a multiple R of 0.50, and R square of 0.25, indicating 25% of the variance in student cigarette use can be explained by age at first use, perceived peer approval/disapproval, and perceived risk.

The stepwise multiple regression, using students' perceived risk, gender, grade level, and ethnic background as predictors of drug use the past month produced a regression model with a multiple correlation coefficient of 0.22. All four variables were statistically significant. However, the perceived risk variable contributed the most as a predictor of drug use with a multiple correlation coefficient of 0.18. A stepwise multiple regression to predict frequency of reported episodes for adverse consequences from alcohol and other drug use, using perceived risk, gender, grade, and ethnic background as stepwise variables, produced a multiple correlation coefficient of 0.36, again with the perceived risk variable having the strongest predictive value with a multiple correlation coefficient of 0.27.

Discussion

Previous studies[7,8] reported increased rates of illicit drug use related to frequency of cigarette smoking by high school seniors and inferred that cigarette smoking by children and adolescents can act as a "gateway drug," use of which increased the likelihood of using illicit drugs.[9–16] This analysis of data from the 1992 Survey of Alcohol and Other Drug Use by Indiana Students confirmed that among students in grades 5–12, cigarette smoking is a powerful predictor for use of alcohol and other drugs and that the relationship is dose-responsive. Compared to other frequently identified[17] predictors of illicit drug use (perceived risk of physical or other harm, or perceived peer approval/disapproval of use), self-reported cigarette smoking appears to be a better predictor of both alcohol abuse and of illicit drug use. Students reporting use of one or more packs of cigarettes per day were three times more likely to use alcohol, seven times more likely to use smokeless tobacco, and 10–30 times more likely to use illicit drugs than were students who never smoked.

Some studies suggest cigarette-smoking youth may be more likely to take risks of all types, and that this risk-taking/rebelliousness, not smoking itself, is the cause of the illegal drug use.[15,16] One study linked cigarette smoking with early age of sexual intercourse and with failure to make timely use of contraceptives, supporting the risk-taking hypothesis.[18]

Regardless of whether the relationship between cigarette smoking and the use of other drugs is causal or descriptive, parents, physicians, teachers, and others who work with children and adolescents should be aware of the powerful predictive value that cigarette smoking, in particular daily use of one or more packs of cigarettes, has in identifying alcohol abuse and use of illicit drugs. Since cigarette consumption at that level is difficult to conceal, due to physical signs such as the odor of smoke, stained teeth and fingers, and "smoker's cough," cigarette smoking by children and adolescents may provide the first warning sign of involvement with alcohol or other drugs and should alert adults to look for additional evidence of drug involvement.

Five of the 10 most frequent causes of death for adolescents in some way relate to alcohol and other drug use, and cigarette smoking is the leading cause of preventable death in the United States. Prevention of tobacco, alcohol, and other drug use is a key health promotion strategy. By recognizing the role cigarette smoking plays as a predictor of other drug use, community leaders, school administrators, school board members, parents, teachers, and health professionals can better assist adolescents in avoiding exposure to several leading causes of death and disability.

Further, it seems that perceived risk, perceived peer approval/disapproval, and age of first use are associated statistically with quantity and frequency of cigarette smoking in grades 5–12. Health education curricula should recognize the importance of students' perceptions of risk and peer approval/disapproval as of paramount importance in their approaches to alcohol, tobacco, and other drug abuse prevention.

References

[1.] Bailey, W. J., Sizemore, J. D., & Greene, S. 1991. *Alcohol and other drug use in Indiana: The Indiana Prevention Resource Center Survey—1991.* Bloomington, IN: Indiana Prevention Resource Center.

[2.] Bailey, W. J., Torabi, M. R., Majd-Jabbari, M., et al. 1992. *Alcohol and other drug use by Indiana Children and Adolescents: The Indiana Prevention Resource Center—1992.* Bloomington, IN: Indiana Prevention Resource Center.

[3.] Johnston, L. D., O'Malley, P.M., & Bachman, J.G. 1992. *national high school senior survey of alcohol and other drug use, preliminarydata—1991.* Washington, DC: National Clearinghouse on Alcohol and Drug Information.

[4.] Tobacco use among high school students United States, 1990. MMWR. 1991;40:617–619.

[5.] Torabi, M. R., Majd-Jabbari, M., Plaford, G., Seffrin, C., Ellis, N.T., & Wood, M. 1991. Prevalence of selected factors associated with drug abuse among high school students. *Wellness Perspectives: Research, Theory and Practice,* 7(4):65–75.

[6.] Ellis, N. T., & Torabi, M. R. 1992. *The Indiana student health survey.* Bloomington, IN: Dept of Applied Health Science, Indiana University.

[7.] Johnston, L. D., O'Malley, P. M., & Bachman, J.G. 1987. *National trends in drug use and related factors among american high school students and young adults, 1975–1986.* Washington, DC: National Institute on Drug Abuse, 248–255. U.S. Dept of Health and Human Services publication (ADM) 87–1535.

[8.] Johnston, L. D. 1986. Prepared testimony regarding cigarette advertising and its likely impact on youth, Subcommittee on Health and the Environment of the House Committee on Energy and Commerce. *Report of the Hearings of July 18 and August 1, 1986, Advertising of Tobacco Products.* Washington, D.C.: U.S. House of Representatives (Serial No 99–167), 860–886.

[9.] Kandel, D. B., Yamaguchi, K., & Chen, K. 1992. Stages of progression in drug involvement from adolescence to adulthood: Further evidence for the gateway theory. *J Stud Alcohol,* 53:447–457.

[10.] Fleming, R., Leventhal, H., Glynn, K., & Ershler, J. 1989. The role of cigarettes in the initiation and progression of early substance use. *Addictive Behavior,* 14:261–272.

[11.] O'Donnell, J. A. 1979. Cigarette smoking as a precursor of illicit drug use. In Krasnegor, N. A., (Ed.), *Cigarette Smoking as a Dependence Process,* Washington, D.C.: National Institute on Drug Abuse; 30–43 US Dept of Health, Education and Welfare publication (ADM) 79–800; NIDA Research Monograph No 23.

[12.] O'Donnell, J.A., & Clayton, R.R.. 1982. The stepping stone hypothesis: Marijuana, heroin, and causality. *Chemical Dependency,* 4:229–241.

[13.] Voss, H. L., & Clayton, R. R. 1987. Stages of involvement with drugs. *Pediatrician,* 14:25–31.

[14.] Yamaguchi, K., & Kandel, D. B. 1984. Patterns of drug use from adolescence to young adulthood: II. Sequences of progression. *American Journal of Public Health,* 74:668–672.

[15.] Yamaguchi, K., & Kandel, D. B. 1984. Patterns of drug use from adolescence to young adulthood, III. Predictors of progression. *American Journal of Public Health,* 74:673–681.

[16.] Gee, M. S. 1987. *Longitudinal correlates of hard drug use.* Presented at 67th Annual Meeting of the Western Psychological Association, April 23, Long Beach, CA.

[17.] Bachman, J. G., Johnston, L. D., O'Malley, P. M., & Humphrey, R. H. 1988. Explaining the recent decline in marijuana use: Differentiating the effects of perceived risks, disapproval, and general lifestyle factors. *Journal of Health and Social Behavior,* 29:92–112.

[18.] *National Household Survey on Drug Abuse: Main Findings—1990*. 1991. Washington, DC: National Institute on Drug Abuse; US Dept of Health and Human Services publication (ADM) 91–1788.

[19.] *Healthy People 2000: National Health Promotion and Disease Prevention Objectives*. Washington, DC: US Public Health Service, 1990. U.S. Dept of Health and Human Services publication (PHS) 91–50212.

[20.] Rouse, B. A., Kozel Richards L. G., eds. *Self-Report Methods of Estimating Drug Use: Meeting Current Challenges to Validity*. Washington, D.C.: National Institute on Drug Abuse; 1985. U.S. Dept of Health and Human Services publication (ADM) 88–1402; NIDA Research Monograph 57.

[21.] Zabin, L.S. 1984. The association between smoking and sexual behavior among teens in U.S. contraceptive clinics. *American Journal of Public Health*, 74:261–263.

REVIEW QUESTIONS

1. Describe the three-stage purposive/quota cluster sampling procedure used in this project.

2. What were the findings?

3. What would have happened if the researchers decided to use a different sampling method? Describe another method and project what the results would reveal.

ALCOHOLICS ANONYMOUS AND THE USE OF MEDICATIONS TO PREVENT RELAPSE: AN ANONYMOUS SURVEY OF MEMBER ATTITUDES

Robert G. Rychtarik, Gerard J. Connors, Kurt H. Dermen, and Paul R. Stasiewicz

---

The purpose of this study was to systematically assess the attitudes of Alcoholics Anonymous (AA) members toward the newer medications used to prevent relapse and to assess their experiences with medication use, of any type, in AA. The researchers used media solicitations and snowball sampling techniques to gather 277 AA members who were surveyed anonymously about their attitudes toward the use of medication for preventing relapse and their experiences with medication use of any type in AA. Do they address ethical issues that came up in their research?

Rychtarik, R. G., Connors, G. J., Dermen, K. H. & Stasiewicz, P. R. 2000. Alcoholics Anonymous and the use of medications to prevent relapse: An anonymous survey of member attitudes. *Journal of Studies on Alcohol*, 61(1): 134–138.

Members of Alcoholics Anonymous (AA) are often assumed to have strong negative attitudes toward the use of medication for alcohol problems. A common view is that AA members believe the alcoholic, to recover fully, must achieve sobriety solely on his or her own without reliance on another drug. Anecdotes about alcoholic clients stopping antipsychotic, antimanic, or other medications at the urging of AA members, often with adverse consequences, are legend in the alcoholism treatment field. Unfortunately, we were unable to find any systematic data on AA members' attitudes toward medication use. Data on the extent to which AA members discourage medication use also are lacking. In the only report we could find, Mason et al. (1996) note that a "small number" of depressed alcoholics stopped desipramine early because of "conflicts" with the AA philosophy.

Official AA literature (Alcoholics Anonymous, 1984) advocates that "no AA member play doctor" and advises members against telling others to throw away pills. Concern remains, however, that participation in AA or other self-help groups could result in conflict over the use of medications and interfere with substance abuse treatment (Freed and York, 1997; Rao et al., 1995). This concern has become more salient with the introduction of new medications for the prevention of relapse (e.g., naltrexone). Research to date suggests that these medications may significantly decrease relapse rates among alcoholics (O'Malley et al., 1992; Volpicelli et al., 1992), but compliance is essential (Volpicelli et al., 1997). If AA members are encouraged to stop taking the medication, their risk of relapse could increase, undermining any medication benefit. The potential impact of negative AA medication attitudes is large. The dominant treatment philosophy in the United States is based on the 12 Steps of AA and encourages AA affiliation as an essential part of recovery.

The purpose of the present study was to assess systematically (1) AA members' attitudes toward the use of medication for preventing relapse, (2) members' inclination to advise a fellow member to stop the medication and (3) members' exposure to AA pressure, either personally or on others, to stop taking a medication, no matter what type.

Method

Participants were among 304 individuals in the Buffalo, NY, area responding to newspaper advertisements seeking AA members for an anonymous phone survey of members' attitudes and opinions. Three callers declined participation; one caller terminated the interview prior to providing opinion data. An additional 23 callers were eliminated from the sample because they had not attended an AA meeting in the last 3 months. The final sample of 277 was a mean ([+ or −] SD) age of 50.64 [+ or −] 11.93 years and averaged 13.88 [+ or −] 2.33 years of education; 62% were men and 94% were white (4% black). On average, participants had attended AA for 12.87 [+ or −− 9.24 years and had attended an average of 36.30 [+ or −] 31.43 AA meetings over the past 3 months. A majority (66%) had been AA sponsors. Geographically, participants were drawn from AA meetings throughout the Buffalo metropolitan area.

A daily, except Saturday, newspaper advertisement was placed in the major city newspaper over a 2–week period. The advertisement solicited the help of AA members for a brief anonymous phone survey of members' attitudes and opinions. No further mention of the purpose of the survey was noted. Callers responding to the advertised phone number were told that the survey would take about 5 minutes. They were then advised that the survey would ask about their AA attendance and their opinion about a newly approved medication which reduced urges to drink among alcoholics in the early stages of recovery. Callers were told that the survey was neither promoting nor discouraging use of the medication; instead, the survey was requesting the caller's open, honest opinion. Callers were also informed that no identifying information would be obtained. Those callers agreeing to participate were then administered a brief structured interview by one of 10 trained research staff asking demographic, AA attendance, opinion and experience questions. Interviewers had received instruction in interview administration procedures and were provided standard responses to potential respondent queries. Upon completion of the survey, the caller was asked to tell other AA members about the survey and to encourage them to call.

Measures

Demographic. The participant's age, race (coded 0 = nonwhite, 1 = white), gender (0 = female, 1 = male) and years of education were obtained.

AA attendance. The reported number of years since the caller's first AA meeting and the number of meetings attended in the past 3 months were recorded. The latter variable was positively skewed and subsequently transformed using a square root transformation. The participant was also asked whether he or she had ever been an AA sponsor (0 = no, 1 = yes). Finally, the participant was asked for the general geographic area (e.g., town, section of the city) where he or she usually attended meetings. Common divisions within the Buffalo metropolitan area were used to divide the area into seven regions.

The proportion of the total sample within each geographical area ranged from 12% to 16%. The geographic measure was used to assess whether AA members' opinions about medication varied by area. In particular, this measure provided for an indirect assessment of possible differences in member attitudes across different AA meetings. We chose not to ask callers for specific information on the name or location of their most frequently attended meeting(s) to avoid the potential for identifying callers at specific meetings with the demographic data collected.

Medication opinion measures. Participants were instructed to listen while the following short story was read to them:

> Joe is an alcoholic. He has begun treatment for his problem at a local outpatient program, and has a counselor who sees him regularly, and he also has started attending AA. The treatment program's doctor has prescribed a medication for him that will help to reduce his urges to drink during the first six months of his recovery. The medication is not addicting, it is not habit-forming and it will not alter his mood.

Upon completion of the story, the caller was asked a series of questions. First, the caller was asked to choose, on the following 5-point Likert scale, the response that best described his or her thoughts about Joe's use of the medication: (1) it's a good idea, (2) it might be helpful, (3) not sure or don't have an opinion, (4) don' t like the idea but it's ok for him to try it, or (5) don't like the idea and think he should not take it. The caller was then asked whether he or she would recommend that Joe stop taking the medication (0 = no, 1 = yes) if he or she were Joe' s sponsor or learned of the medication use during the meeting.

AA and medication experience: The caller was then asked whether he or she, or someone known to them, had ever been discouraged by AA members from taking a medication that a doctor had prescribed (no matter what type; 0 = no, 1 = yes). Those participants responding affirmatively were asked to describe the medication used. In addition, the participant was asked whether he or she, or the other person, had continued taking the medication (0 = no, 1 = yes). Finally the time in years since the last such incident was recorded. A square root transformation was used on this latter variable to reduce positive skew. Medication type was subsequently coded into the following categories: antidepressants, pain medication, anxiolytics, disulfiram, lithium, antipsychotics, naltrexone, other unspecified mood altering medications and medications of other types.

Results

Opinion about medication for preventing relapse. Of the sample, 53% reported use of the medication was either a good idea (20%) or might be a good idea (33%), while 13% reported not knowing or not having an opinion; 17% reported not liking the idea but said it was all right for the individual to use it; an additional 17% reported not liking the use of the medication and believing the individual should not take it. However, only 12% said that as a sponsor or AA member they would recommend a member stop taking the medication.

General medication experiences and AA. Almost a third (29%) of the sample said they had personally been encouraged by other AA members to stop taking a medication. An additional 20% said that they knew only of others encouraged to stop a medication, while 1.8% were missing data on this variable. The mean ([+or –] SD) for the last occurrence of such pressure was 5.89 [+ or –] 6.93 years ago (median = 2.5 years). The medication categories and the percentage of these participants and others discouraged from using them were as follows: antidepressants (36%), pain medications (20%), anxiolytics (14%), lithium (6%), antipsychotics (2%), naltrexone (2%), disulfiram (7%), other unspecified mood altering medications (3%) and other medications (11%). Among participants who said they knew of someone else who had been discouraged from using a medication there was a high degree of uncertainty over whether the individual had continued to use it. Outcome results are therefore limited to the 77 participants who said that they themselves had been encouraged by an AA member to stop using a medication and for whom data on subsequent medication compliance was not missing. Of these participants, 69% said that they had continued taking the medication despite being encouraged to stop; 31% said they had stopped using the medication at the encouragement of AA members.

A higher number of AA meetings attended in the last 3 months was associated significantly, but to a small degree, with a more negative opinion toward use of relapse-preventing medication (r =. 16, n = 277, p = .007). Among callers personally experiencing some pressure to stop a medication, those who actually stopped also tended to have less favorable attitudes toward the medication (r= –.28, n = 77, p = .013) and were somewhat more likely to recommend that it be stopped (r = –.23, n = 77, p = .044).

Predictors of opinion about relapse-preventing medication. The set of demographic variables did not contribute significantly to the prediction of opinion toward the medication ([R.sup.2] change = .01; F = 1.01, 3/273 df, NS). AA attendance variables did contribute significantly ([R.sup.2] change = .03; F = 4.14, 2/271 df, p = .02). In the full model (model R = .20; F= 2.28, 5/271 df, p = .047), only number of meetings attended significantly contributed to the prediction of participants' opinions ([Beta] = .18, t=2.87, 271 df, p = .004). Those attending more AA meetings in the past 3 months were more likely, to a small but significant degree, to have less favorable attitudes toward the use of the medication. Neither demographic nor AA variable sets contributed significantly to the prediction of whether one would recommend that another member stop taking the medication (full model [chi square] = 8.40, 5 df, NS).

Predictors of general medication experiences. As a set, demographic variables contributed significantly to the prediction of having personally been discouraged from using a medication, of any type, by AA members or knowing of others who had been discouraged (improvement [chi square] = 8.09, 3 df, p =.04). Only age, however, contributed significantly in this step of the model (unstandardized B = -.02, Wald Statistic = 4.20, 1 df, p = .04, odds ratio [OR] = .98). AA attendance variables also contributed significantly beyond that of demographic variables (improvement [chi square] = 6.29, 2 df, p = .043). Older individuals were less likely, while members who had been sponsors were more likely to report having experienced pressure to stop a medication (overall model [chi square]= 14.38, 5 df, p = .01). No variable was significantly associated with personally having stopped using a medication in response to AA encouragement (overall model [chi square] = 5.78, 5 df, NS). Data on the years since the last occurrence of pressure to stop a medication were available from 130 (92%) of those exposed to pressure on either themselves or others. Both demographic ([R.sup.2] change = .22, F = 11.64, 3/126 df, p = .000) and AA attendance variables (R2 change = .08, F = 7.08, 2/124 df, p = .001) contributed significantly as they were entered into the prediction of years since the last episode. Only age contributed significantly among the demographic variables as they were entered ([Beta]= .46, t = 5.78, 126 df, p = .000). In the final full model (R = .55, F= 10.49, 5/124 df, p = .000), age, sponsorship history and meetings attended in the past 3 months contributed significantly to the prediction of the number of years since the last incident occurred. Younger participants reported more recent experiences ([Beta] = .35, t = 4.29, 124 df, p = .000) whereas those individuals who had served as a sponsor reported the last incident to have occurred more years ago ([Beta] = .27, t = 3.31, 124 df, p = .001). Individuals who attended more meetings over the past 3 months said that the last incident had occurred more recently ([Beta] = -.18, t = −2.22, 124 df, p = .028).

Discussion

We found little evidence to support the concern that individuals who take one of the newer medications to prevent relapse and who attend AA will be subjected to strong pressure to stop taking the medication. Though some pressure to discontinue medications of various types does occur in AA, more than two-thirds of individuals in the current sample who were encouraged by fellow members to stop a medication resisted the pressure and continued to take it. Still, a medication noncompliance rate of 31% among those personally pressured to stop a medication is a concern and deserves further study.

Although the sizes of effects were small, the results do suggest that more frequent AA meeting attendance increases the likelihood of being exposed to and incorporating somewhat more negative medication attitudes. Perhaps because of their assistance to other members, sponsors also appear more likely to have personally or vicariously experienced pressure to stop a medication, although less recently. These individuals, based on their experience, may have learned to minimize pressure by either keeping those they are responsible for off medication in the first place, instructing them to remain silent about medication use, or steering them to meetings whose members are more supportive of medication use. Though the direction of causality is unclear, the results also suggest that individuals susceptible to pressure from other members to stop a medication may have had less favorable attitudes toward medication use to begin with. The finding highlights the importance of assessing client medication attitudes when medication is part of the treatment plan. Finally, generational differences also appear to play a role. Among individuals who had been exposed to some pressure, those younger had experienced it more recently than did those older. Older individuals were also less likely to report ever being exposed, perhaps reflecting the greater availability of medications today than in the past.

Anecdotally, many participants in this survey said that, because medication designed for preventing relapse might help, they would not tell someone to stop taking it. Frequently they said anything that would help the individual achieve sobriety was worth trying. This philosophy is consistent with Chapter 5 of Alcoholics Anonymous (1976), which advises that one should be willing to go to any length to resolve a drinking problem (i.e., "Half measures avail us nothing." p. 59). Incorporating this philosophy when medication is used within 12-step programs could prove beneficial for improving medication compliance. The current results also suggest that careful assessment of medication attitudes is important in identifying individuals at risk for subsequent noncompliance. In addition, education and direct skill training should be studied as ways to inoculate individuals to both subtle and overt efforts by other members to stop appropriately prescribed medication.

A distinctive feature of the present study was the use of the media to recruit AA members. Ogborne (1993) noted the potential of media advertisements for this purpose but few studies have used it. Media recruitment offers several advantages over other methods for soliciting AA members. First, as Ogborne suggested, the method maintains respect for the traditions of AA. Members' anonymity is maintained and the research does not require involvement or permission of one or more AA groups. Second, the method allows for sampling from a wider range of AA groups and members than is possible when in-person recruitment methods are used. Studies that rely on clients in or discharged from treatment appear to sample only from a select group and do not sample those members with long periods of sobriety and involvement in AA who are not in treatment. In the present study, it was particularly important to sample from this latter group since these individuals would likely have a significant influence on newcomers to the fellowship.

Media recruitment of AA members, however, has limitations. Specifically, the sample in the current study consisted only of those self-selecting to call in response to the advertisement or calling after having been told of the study by a previous caller. The extent to which the sample population typifies all individuals attending AA is a concern. The pattern of demographic and AA attendance characteristics of the current sample, however, was comparable to that found in the random sample survey of 7,200 AA members conducted by AA World Services (Alcoholics Anonymous, 1997). That sample was somewhat younger (44 years of age) than the current sample, but the racial (86% white) and gender (33%) compositions were comparable. In addition, the higher educational status of the current sample appears consistent with the large proportion of members in the national survey reporting relatively high occupational levels. Meeting attendance in the national survey was also nearly identical to that of the current study (i.e., averaging more than two meetings per week). Overall, the comparability between the present sample and the larger random sample of AA members adds credence to the generalizability of the current results.

Nevertheless, other participant selection factors may have been operating to influence the nature of the population sampled. Further research in this area is needed, including longitudinal research on the experiences of individuals attending AA while taking relapse-preventing and other medications. Over-sampling of racial minority groups also appears needed in this line of research to examine potential racial differences in opinion and experiences. Finally, evaluating the medical appropriateness of either continuing or stopping the medication use reported in the sample was not feasible. Though many medications listed by participants have no addictive properties, other medications could be problematic. In the latter case, some judicious advice from fellow AA members to discuss the medication with a physician would be appropriate.

Other limitations of the current study should be noted. First, the sample recruited was predominantly one of relatively long-term AA members. Still, we felt this sample was most appropriate for the goals of the study since these individuals were likely to have the most conservative view of medication use and also the most influence. Second, a nonalcoholic comparison group was not surveyed. The results provide no data on the attitudes of AA members relative to those of the general population or of treatment-seeking samples with no AA experience. Third, we did not assess the proportion of the total sample using a medication while attending AA. So, we do not know the percentage of respondents on a medication who experienced pressure to stop. Fourth, we did not attempt to distinguish callers according to whether they were advertising responders or snowball responders. Differences in the characteristics and opinions of these two samples may exist. Fifth, the complete anonymity procedures used, though a strength, also precluded us from implementing safeguards to prevent multiple interviews of the same person. Sixth, we did not assess inter-interviewer reliability. The interview, however, was very brief, standardized and administered by trained research staff. Under these circumstances, error from inter-viewer variability would appear to be low.

To summarize, this study did not find strong, widespread negative attitudes among AA members toward the newer medications for preventing relapse. Some discouragement of medication use, however, is experienced in AA meetings. While most AA members appear to resist pressure to stop a medication, a need exists, when medication is used, to integrate it within the philosophy of 12-step treatment programs. Research into effective ways of helping individuals resist pressure to stop appropriately prescribed medication is also needed as are surveys of member attitudes toward other targeted medication types (e.g., antidepressants).

References

Alcoholics Anonymous. 1976. *The story of how many thousands of men and women have recovered from alcoholism*, 3rd ed., New York: Alcoholics Anonymous World Services.

Alcoholics Anonymous. 1984. *The AA member: Medications and other drugs* (brochure), New York: Alcoholics Anonymous World Services.

Alcoholics Anonymous. 1997. *1996 membership survey*, New York: Alcoholics Anonymous World Services.

Freed, P. E., & York, L. N. 1997. Naltrexone: A controversial therapy for alcohol dependence. *Journal of Psychosocial Nursing and Mental Health Services,* 35: 24–28.

Mason, B. J., Kocsis, J. H., Ritvo, E. C., & Cutler, R. B. 1996. A double-blind, placebo-controlled trial of desipramine for primary alcohol dependence stratified on the presence or absence of major depression. *JAMA* 275: 761–767.

Ogborne, A.C. 1993. Assessing the effectiveness of Alcoholics Anonymous in the community: Meeting the challenges. In Mccrady, B. S. & Miller, W. R. (Eds.) *Research on Alcoholics Anonymous: Opportunities and alternatives*, New Brunswick, NJ: Rutgers Center of Alcohol Studies, pp. 339–355.

O'Malley, S. S., Jaffe, A. J., Chang, G., Sshottenfeld, R. S., Meyer, R. E. & Rounsaville, B. 1992. Naltrexone and coping skills therapy for alcohol dependence. *Archives of General Psychiatry,* 49: 881–887.

Rao, S., Ziedonis, D., and Kosten, T. 1995. The pharmacotherapy of cocaine dependence. *Psychiatiatric. Annals.* 25: 363–368.

Volpicelli, J. R., Alterman, A. I., Hayashida, M., & O'Brien, C. P. 192. Naltrexone in the treatment of alcohol dependence. *Archives of General Psychiatry,* 49: 876–880.

Volpicelli, J. R., Rhines, K. C., Rhiner, J. S., Volpicelli, L. A., Alterman, A. I. & O'Brien, C. P. 1997. Naltrexone and alcohol dependence: Role of subject compliance. *Archives of General Psychiatry,* 54: 737–742.

REVIEW QUESTIONS

1. What type of sampling method was used for this study? Why was it used rather than random sampling?

2. How did they find their respondents? Who were their respondents?

3. Do you think the sample was representative of all AA members? Did it need to be?

PART III ■ MODES OF OBSERVATIONS

■

Chapter 8: Experimental, Survey, and Evaluation Research

What you have learned up to this point are the foundations of social science research. In the next few chapters you will learn about various modes of gathering data. Research can be separated into basically two types: **quantitative** and **qualitative**. Quantitative analysis, which you will be learning about in this chapter, is where the observations are given some sort of numerical representation. Qualitative analysis, which you will learn more about in the following chapters, is where observations are not quantified and where words, pictures, descriptions, or narratives are used as data.

To begin, you will learn about **experiments**, which are best used for topics where the researcher needs to control and explain the phenomenon being studied. Experimental design can be classified into three main types: true experimental design, quasi-experimental design, and double blind experiments. The **true experimental design** is where the researcher controls some variables while manipulating the effects of other variables. As you have learned in previous chapters, the variables used in an experiment are the independent variable and dependent variable. Therefore, the independent variable is the variable to be manipulated, while the dependent variable tells you if the independent variable had any effect on the dependent variable.

Let's say you want to conduct an experiment to determine the affect of exercise on heart rate. You could hypothesize that the more a person exercises the higher his or her heart rate. It sounds reasonable, but now you need to test this to see if your hypothesis is true. You will use only female students who are between the ages of 18–21 and will randomly assign half the females to receive the stimulus (the exercise) in the **experimental group.** The other half of the sample will not receive the stimulus and are in the **control group**. You will randomly assign the women by having them number off 1 and 2. Those who are designated number 1 will go into one group and the women designated number 2 will go into the other group. This is a true experiment because you randomly assign the subjects to one group or the other to reduce the variation between the experimental and control group and to make sure each and every subject has an equal chance of getting into each group. All true experiments have a **pretest,** which measures the outcome variable before the treatment has been given ,and a **posttest** to measure the outcome of both groups after the treatment has been given.

This experiment can be illustrated by using a series of symbols commonly used to describe experimental designs:

R= random assignment to either the experimental or control group

O= represents an observation or a measurement of the dependent variable

X= those who are exposed to the experimental stimulus or the independent variable

Therefore, this experiment would look like this:

R 01	X	O2 Experimental Group
R 01		O2 Control Group

In this particular experiment the dependent variable (O) is the heart rate, which is measured at point one (pretest). The subjects in the experimental group then begin to exercise (X) while the control group doesn't. Then the heart rate of each subject is measured again at point two (posttest) to see if there is a difference between groups.

A **quasi-experimental design** uses some of the same elements that the true experiment uses and even resembles a true experiment in some ways. However, in a quasi-experimental design the researcher has little control over the exposure or non-exposure of the subjects to the independent variable. There is no random assignment; however, there is a comparison group. For example, let's say you wanted to investigate the effects of sex on anti-social behavior. The groups, boys and girls, would already be preset. You cannot change their sex. You have two groups and pretest them all to document any anti-social behaviors. Then you would put half the boys and half the girls into two different treatment groups. Suppose members of one group receives money every time they went one hour without hitting someone and members of the other group receive reprimands every time they hit someone. At the end you would conduct a posttest to see which treatment had an effect on the boys and which treatment had an effect on the girls.

So, this quasi-experiment would look like this:

Boys 01	X1	O2 Treatment A: Money
Boys 01	X2	O2 Treatment B: Reprimand
Girls 01	X1	O2 Treatment A: Money
Girls 01	X2	O2 Treatment B: Reprimand

One of the most common types of quasi-experimental design is the **time series design,** which involves a series of repeated measures that are followed by the introduction of the experimental condition and then another series of measures.

For example, in this type of design the experimental group would look like this:

O1 O2   O3   O4   X   O5   O6   O7   O8

It could be concluded in this type of design that the independent variable produced some type of effect if the changes in the dependent variable remain after repeated observations.

A **double blind experiment** is most often used in medical experimentation. The point of a double blind experiment is to make the subjects believe they are receiving a drug and often a **placebo**, or fake drug, is given to the control group. The idea is to observe the improvements or behaviors of the subjects after they have received either the placebo or the treatment. I will give you an example. My son needed his wisdom teeth pulled—if you have had it done, you know it can be painful. His dentist was participating in a study on painkillers and gave my son the option of participating in the study. He agreed and after his teeth were pulled, when he began to feel pain, he was given a drug. Neither the dentist nor my son knew whether he was given the real drug or the placebo. But then he was asked to rate his pain for a specific amount of time. If the pill didn't relieve his pain, then he told the nurses and the dentist, rated it on the survey, and he was given drugs that they knew would work. So, not only did he get to participate in a study on drugs, he made money for having his teeth pulled. Not bad deal, huh?

Survey research is best used for topics where the researcher asks questions and learns about the attitudes or behaviors reported by the respondent. Surveys are probably the "most frequently used mode of observation in the social sciences and the most common method reported in the *American Sociological Review* (Babbie, 1995:256). Surveys have become a popular way of conducting research because they are versatile, efficient, and generalizable. While a survey is not good for testing your entire hypothesis, it certainly can enhance your understanding of a particular social issue. Surveys are efficient because the data can be collected from a large number of people. Surveys can be sent out in the mail, given out at a mall, or conducted on the telephone. One of the largest surveys is the U.S. Census, where the government tries to obtain information about every person in the United States. Surveys are often the only way to obtain information about groups of people and therefore a good way to generalize about the entire population.

Basically two types of questions are used in surveys. A close-ended question is one that provides the respondents a fixed set of answers to choose from. An open-ended question is where the respondents formulate their own responses. So, if the question asked is "What is your marital status?" a close-ended question could give 4 possible answers for the respondents such as married, widowed, single, or divorced. If the question were "What is your race?," there are so many possibilities to choose from it is often easier to leave a blank and allow the person to fill in their response.

Designing a questionnaire is not always as easy as you might think. To begin, you must go back to your hypothesis, and let your independent and dependent variables guide the questions you ask of your respondents. Remember that you are trying to figure out if the independent variable has some effect on the dependent variable. So, let's say you believe that the more education a person has, the higher his or her salary will be. The independent variable is education and the dependent variable is salary. You could just ask two questions: How many years have you been in school? And how much money do you make? However, would that be enough and could you be sure that education is really what had an effect on the salary? Since other variables might actually have an effect on your dependent variable, you really need to make sure you are capturing the extraneous variables, which are those variables that are not objects of the research. So, what other things can effect how much money a person makes in their job? Age, marital status, sex, and experience could all have an effect on the dependent variable, just to name a few. Therefore you must come up with questions that address those variables.

What kind of question could you ask that would capture your dependent variable? The question "How much money do you received annually from your job(s)?" would capture it. You can leave a blank for an open ended question where respondents can write in their response, or you can give them some choices such as <$10,000, $10,000–$20,000, $20,000–$30,000, and so on. Are there any other questions that would capture the dependent variable? Well, then you must go onto the independent variable. A question that would capture the independent variable would be "What is the highest grade you have completed in school?" Some examples of questions that would capture the extraneous variables include these:

1. What is your sex?

    Male _____

    Female _____

2. What is your age? _____

3. What is your marital status?

    Married _____

    Divorced _____

    Separated _____

    Widowed _____

    Single _____

I am sure you can come up with some other variables as well that could effect your dependent variable. The point is that you need to have questions that can capture all of the variables you can think of that could affect the dependent variable in any way. If your questions have nothing to do with the variables, take them out.

Questionnaires should also be neat and well constructed. Make sure you check for grammar and spelling. If you received a questionnaire that looked terrible you might not have any desire to take time to fill it out. There are also a few ways to distribute questionnaires. A self-administered questionnaire is where the respondent receives the questionnaire, fills it out on his or her own, and returns it to the researcher. Mail distribution and return is probably the most common type of distribution and one of the least expensive methods. This is where you send the questionnaire through the mail, with a self-addressed stamped envelope so your respondents can return their completed questionnaire without any expense. If the cost for the respondents' participation is low, the response rates will be higher. According to Babbie (1995), a response rate of 50 percent is adequate, 60 percent is good, and 70 percent is considered very good. The response rate can increase with follow-up mailings sent out a few weeks after the original questionnaire. One follow-up mailing can increase the response rate by an additional 20 percent, and a third follow-up mailing can add an additional 10 percent to the response rate.

Because the Internet and the World Wide Web have exploded in the last few years, more and more surveys are being conducted online. The number of individuals who have access to the Internet has grown to 81 million Americans in early 1999. Only about 90,000 Americans had Internet access in 1993. This is an increase of about 900 percent in 6 years. It is projected that by the year 2000 there will be 230 million Internet users worldwide (The United States Internet Council, 1999). More and more individuals will therefore have access to online surveys.

Online surveys can be set up on a Web site with a lot of fanfare to make them appealing to the potential respondents. It seems like everytime I log onto a Web site there is some sort of survey. Surveys can also be distributed and retrieved via e-mail. This tends to save time and money for all involved.

Evaluation research is widely used to measure the effectiveness of a program, poli-cy, or a specific way of doing something. Evaluating is common and we all do it. Think back to the last test you took. After the test was completed, what did you think? Did you think, "I should have studied more," or "I really get nervous with multiple choice tests," or "I think I passed the test, but just barely"? You were evaluating yourself.

Evaluation research is very similar to experimental research. Although the goal of basic research is to understand the social world, evaluation research is designed to evalu-ate the effectiveness of various types of programs in order to measure whether or not the program is working.

Social programs tend to address social problems such as homelessness, drinking and driving, and HIV/AIDS prevention. Because public policy and funding for social programs tend to be dependent upon the need for the program and its success in helping those who use the program, it is important to be able to evaluate it. Many federal granting agencies are even starting to require that social agencies have an evaluative researcher involved in the project from the beginning to make sure that the effectiveness of the program can be well documented. Suppose you are interested in reducing the rate of teen automobile fatal-ities, and you believe that developing a program to encourage teens not to drink and drive would be effective. You can obtain information about fatalities in your area, then after many months of putting the program together and presenting it to high school students in the area, you want to see if it reduces the number of fatalities. You can also develop a survey asking students about their drinking and driving patterns before the program and retest them after the program to see if their behaviors changed.

REFERENCES

Babbie, E. 2001. *The practice of social research* (9th ed). Belmont, CA: Wadsworth.

United States Internet Council, 1999. State of the Internet: USIC's report on use and threats in 1999. [ONLINE] http://www.usic.org/

INFOTRAC COLLEGE EDITION SUGGESTED READINGS AND DISCUSSION QUESTIONS

1. Using InfoTrac College Edition, enter the term "random assignment" and see what types of experiments you find. Pick five of the articles that interest you and go through them to see if you can determine what method of random assignment the researchers used to place their subjects in either the control or experimental group.

2. Type the word "experiment" and your particular discipline into InfoTrac College Edition. So, if you are a social work major, type "experiment and social work." What kinds of experiments are being done in your discipline? Can you figure out the independent variable, dependent variable, and the hypothesis?

3. Locate a sociological journal of our choice on InfoTrac College Edition. Look at the ar-ticles in at least two editions. What methods were used in each article? How many used experiments and how many used surveys?

Intraoperative Progress Reports Decrease Family Members' Anxiety

Jane S. Leske

In this study, the authors used a four-group, quasi-experimental posttest design. They wanted to examine the effects of the current medical standards of perioperative nursing care, attention, and two types of intraoperative progress reports (i.e., in person, telephone call) on family members' ratings of anxiety during their relatives' elective surgical procedures.. The researchers believed, rightfully so, that surgery can be anxiety provoking to the family members of the surgical patient. Leske and her colleagues believed, and tested whether or not the treatment and attention the family received prior to and during surgery would have different outcomes.

Surgery is an anxiety-producing situation for family members, especially during the time their relatives are in the O.R.[1] Research findings suggest that families want to be involved in the care of their ill members[2] but that anxiety interferes with their ability to provide this care. In addition, family members' anxiety may be transmitted to their ill relatives.[3]

Patients are being discharged "sooner and sicker," requiring their family members to assume increased responsibilities for immediate postoperative care. If family members are extremely anxious, they are unlikely to use information provided by perioperative staff members effectively or to ask appropriate questions during discharge teaching sessions.[4] Previous research suggests that in-person intraoperative progress reports are a beneficial perioperative nursing intervention to reduce family members' anxiety.[5] Further study is needed to evaluate the efficacy of various types of intraoperative progress reports and different methods of providing these reports to surgical patients' family members.

Background of the study

The waiting period during surgery is the most anxiety-producing time of the entire perioperative experience for patients' family mernbers.[6] Previous researchers have documented that some psychoeducational interventions (e.g., education, orientation of family members to intensive care units) reduce family members' anxiety.[7] Family members who received such interventions reported fewer fears and coped better with stress.[8] Published anecdotes suggest that after receiving intraoperative progress reports, family members described feeling more assured, having more appreciation for staff members' caring behaviors, and experiencing an increased sense of control and a reduction in stress and anxiety.[9]

In an earlier study, I examined the effects of intraoperative progress reports on family members of patients undergoing elective surgical procedures. I compared the state anxiety scores, mean arterial pressures (MAPs), and heart rates of family members who received no

Leske, J. S. 1996. "Intraoperative Progress Reports Decrease Family Members' Anxiety." *AORN Journal,* 64 (3): 424–435.

progress reports and family members who received in-person intraoperative progress reports. Family members who received the in-person intraoperative progress reports experienced significantly less anxiety than family members who did not receive this intervention.[10]

In a more recent three-group quasi-experimental study, I sought to determine whether the information provided in the intraoperative progress reports or the attention from a supportive person was the factor that reduced family members' anxiety. I compared the state anxiety scores, MAPs, and heart rates of family members who received either no progress reports, in-person intraoperative progress reports, or attention from a supportive person. The family members who received the in-person intraoperative progress reports had significantly less anxiety than family members in the groups who received no intervention or attention.[11]

Other nurse researchers have studied the effectiveness of providing information to patients' family members through telephone calls. Their results also suggest that family members who receive telephone calls report less anxiety than those who do not receive this intervention.[12]

These studies have demonstrated that providing information as an independent perioperative nursing intervention reduces family members' anxiety. Questions about the types and modes of information-giving interventions remained unanswered and prompted the current study.

The purpose of this study was to examine the effects of current standards of perioperative nursing care, attention, and two types of intraoperative progress reports (i.e., in person, telephone call) on family members' ratings of anxiety during their relatives' elective surgical procedures. This study was, in part, a replication and extension of the studies described previously.

Significance of the Study

Perioperative nurses must continue to incorporate humanistic approaches into their care of surgical patients and family members while dealing with tremendous technologic advances in surgical procedures and equipment. Previous nursing research has documented that family members may be more anxious than patients during the perioperative period. Anxiety-reducing nursing interventions may decrease family members' anxiety and improve the help they can provide to their ill relatives. These interventions, however, require further development and testing.

The following assumptions were fundamental to the purpose and design of this study.

1. Surgery is a source of anxiety for patients' family members.

2. Family members have important needs for anxiety relief during the intraoperative period.

3. Family members are able to describe their anxiety through self-report mechanisms.

The research question that guided the study was: "Is there a significant difference in reported anxiety among family members who receive either standard care, in-person intraoperative progress reports, an attention protocol, or telephoned intraoperative progress reports from perioperative nurses?" My hypothesis was that surgical patients' family members who received the in-person or telephone-call intraoperative progress reports would describe less anxiety than family members who did not receive these interventions (i.e., received the standard care or the attention protocol).

I developed the following operational definitions for this study.

- *Anxiety*. The emotional reaction evoked by a stressful situation, which produces physiologic changes secondary to sympathetic arousal (e.g., increased blood pressure and heart rate, anxiety-indicating responses to the S-Anxiety portion of the State-Trait Anxiety Inventory [STAI] Form y).

- *Attention*. A protocol checklist delivered approximately halfway through the patient's surgical procedure. This checklist, which required approximately five to 10 minutes to read, provided an overview of hospital routines and waiting room procedures.

- *Elective surgery.* All planned surgical procedures of a nonemergent basis.

- *Family member*. The surgical patient's adult blood relative, spouse, or significant other who waits in the hospital during the patient's surgical procedure.

- *Intraoperative progress report*. A protocol-driven progress report that was designed to relay information in person or by telephone call to family members approximately halfway through a patient's surgical procedure. The progress report lasted five to 10 minutes and followed a specific outline.

- *Standard care.* No intraoperative progress reports or attention protocol provided.

Anxiety is characterized by subjective, consciously perceived feelings of apprehension and tension that are associated with autonomic nervous system arousal. A three-stage cognitive appraisal of the anxiety-producing situation is essential to this psychological theory of stress. During the primary appraisal, an individual makes a distinction about the significance of the situation. The situation may evoke a variety of emotions depending on the presence and degree of the identified threat. The extent of an individual's sympathetic nervous system activation also depends on his or her interpretation of anxiety. The secondary appraisal is the process by which the individual evaluates his or her coping responses and options. Reappraisal is a change in the individual's original appraisal that results from new information or feedback from the environment. Within the context of most stressful encounters, information and emotions are combined for large portions of the cognitive appraisal process. Anxiety, however, threatens the integrity of an individual's cognitive system during the reappraisal process

Study Design

I used a four-group, quasi-experimental posttest design to compare the effectiveness of intraoperative progress reports in decreasing family members' anxiety. I compared family members' state anxiety scores, MAPs, and heart rates that were measured approximately halfway during their relatives' surgical procedures after providing the intervention (i.e., progress reports, attention protocol). I conducted the study during a six-month period at one community hospital located near a major metropolitan area in the Midwest.

Sample. I used power, effect size, and significance level to compute the sample size required to demonstrate significant results. Power is the probability of rejecting the null hypothesis (i.e., that intraoperative progress reports would not affect family members' anxiety). Effect size is a measure of how incorrect the null hypothesis is (i.e., how strong the effect of the independent variable [intervention] is on the dependent variables [anxiety measures]). I established the level of significance based on a formulation of the desired statistical power (i.e., .80), medium effect size (i.e., f = .25), and a significance level of .05. I determined that a sample size of 45 family members in each group would be sufficient to test the study hypothesis.[19]

All adult family members of patients having elective surgical procedures at this hospital during the six-month study period were eligible to participate. Their relatives' surgical procedures needed to last at least 30 minutes (i.e., from the time of incision) for progress reports to be clinically feasible. Family members had to be available in the waiting room during surgery; identify themselves as family members of these patients; be able to speak, read, and understand English; and be at least 18 years of age.

Measures. I measured family members' state anxiety scores using the S-Anxiety portion of the STAI Form Y. This self-report scale evaluates qualities such as current feelings of apprehension, tension, nervousness, and worry. The reliability and validity of this inventory are well documented. The S-Anxiety portion of the STAI Form Y consists of 20 statements to which I asked family members to respond. In their responses, they rated their feelings of anxiety while waiting for their relatives' surgical procedures to be completed. The responses to each statement are scored on a Likert-type scale, ranging from "not at all" anxious (i.e., one) to "very much so" (i.e., four). Examples of statements on this scale include "I feel calm" and "I am worried." I summed the response numbers for each statement and obtained scores that were in the formed range for this scale (i.e., 20 = low anxiety to 80 = high anxiety). The Cronbach's alpha coefficient for this study was .94, indicating a high degree of reliability.

I measured family members' brachial blood pressures using a noninvasive portable monitor with automatic oscillometry. I calculated each family member's MAP manually using this formula: 1/3 (systolic blood pressure – diastolic blood pressure) + diastolic blood pressure. I chose MAPs as the dependent variable because diastolic blood pressure is more constant than systolic blood pressure during most of the cardiac cycle and is a good estimate of arterial blood pressure. I used the pulse oximeter mode of the same monitor to determine family members' heart rates.

Each day during the study period, I numbered the scheduled surgical patients, drew numbers randomly from a hat, and selected two or three patients. I then asked the family members of these selected patients to participate in the study and did not limit the number of family members per patient who could participate. I ensured that the waiting periods of participating family members did not overlap so that potential interaction between patients' family members would not be an intervening variable (i.e., an alternative factor that affects the independent or dependent variable and over which the researcher has no control). I obtained written consent from all family members who participated.

I used a four-stage sampling procedure, assigning the first 50 family members to the control group (i.e., group one), the next 50 family members to the in-person progress report group (i.e., group two), the next 50 family members to the attention group (i.e., group three), and the final 50 family members to the telephone-call progress report group (i.e., group four). I chose this sampling method to maximize the probability of having equivalent groups and to prevent the interaction of family members in different groups.

Group one. Family members assigned to the control group received no nursing intervention because the standard of perioperative nursing care for patients' family members did not include intraoperative progress reports, When a patient's surgical procedure was approximately 50% completed, I asked his or her family members to fill out the S-Anxiety portion of the STAI Form Y and a demographic information form. After the family members completed these forms, the research assistants or I measured family members' MAPs and heart rates while they were seated.

Group two. After I completed data collection from all 50 family members in group one, I randomly selected 50 additional family members to be in the in-person progress report group. When a patient's surgical procedure was approximately 50% completed, a perioperative nurse came to the waiting room and provided the patient's family members a 5- to 10–minute progress report that followed a previously published protocol. The nurse informed the family members of the patient's physiologic status, that the surgical procedure was approximately 50% completed, that the patient would be transferred to the postanesthesia care unit (PACU) after surgery, that the family members would be notified when the patient was being transferred from the PACU to the postsurgical unit, and that they could visit the patient after he or she was in the postsurgical unit.

The nurse who gave the report avoided mentioning specific time frames. After family members received the in-person intraoperative progress report, they completed the S-Anxiety portion of the STAI Form Y and a demographic information form, and research assistants or I measured the MAPs and heart rates in the manner described previously.

Group three. After I completed data collection from all 50 family members in group two, I randomly selected an additional 50 family members to be in the attention group. When a patient's surgical procedure was approximately 50% completed, a research assistant verbally gave family members a protocol checklist. This checklist, which required 5 to 10 minutes for the research assistant to read, provided an overview of hospital routines and waiting room procedures. This "attention" session provided family members with the same amount of contact time as family members in the intraoperative progress report groups received. After receiving the attention protocol checklist, family members completed the S-Anxiety portion of the STAI Form Y and a demographic information form, and research assistants or I measured their vital signs in the manner described previously.

Group four. After I completed data collection from all 50 family members in group three, I randomly selected an additional 50 family members to be in the telephone-call progress report group. When a patient's surgical procedure was approximately 50% completed, a perioperative nurse called the patient's family members from the OR and provided a 5- to 10-minute progress report. The format and basic content of this report were identical to the in-person progress report provided to family members in group two. After family members received the telephone-call intraoperative progress report, they completed the S-Anxiety portion of the STAI Form Y and a demographic information form, and research assistants or I measured the MAPs and heart rates in the manner described previously.

Family members in all groups completed the S-Anxiety portion of the STAI Form Y and a demographic information form, received the interventions, and had their vital signs measured in the privacy of a conference room near the general waiting room area. When the patients were in the PACU. I obtained information about the patients' surgical procedures from their intraoperative records.

Sample Demographics

Two hundred family members of 150 surgical patients participated in this study. Three additional family members (i.e., one selected for the control group, one for the in-person intraoperative progress report group, one of the telephone-call intraoperative progress report group) declined to participate.

Family member profile. The 200 family members ranged in age from 18 to 80 years (mean [M] = 47.5 years, standard deviation [SD] = 14.75 years). Sixty-four percent of the family members were female. Family members described their relationships to the patients as spouse (45%), parent (28%), child (15%), significant other (9%), and sibling (3%). Family members' educational preparation ranged from eight to 24 years (M=.12.7 years, SD = 2 years). Eighty-nine percent of the family members had previous experience waiting for family members during surgery. I did not collect data on family members' racial or ethnic backgrounds or religious preferences.

Patient profile. The patients ranged in age from one to 90 years (M= 46.3 years, SD = 24.15 years). Fifty-six percent of the patients were females. The patients were scheduled for a variety of surgical procedures: general (28%), orthopedic (27%), otorhinolaryngologic (13%), ophthalmologic (13%), gynecologic (12%), urologic (4%), neurosurgical (2%), and thoracic (1%).

Seventy-seven percent of the patients received general anesthesia, but some had local anesthesia (11%), regional blocks (4%), IV conscious sedation with local anesthesia (4%), epidural anesthesia (3%), or spinal anesthesia (1%). Sixty-one percent of the patients were scheduled as outpatients, but some were morning admissions (33%) or inpatients (6%). The actual surgical procedures lasted from 30 to 620 minutes (M= 103.27 min, SD = 71.95 min).

Findings

Before comparing data from the four groups, I examined all demographic variables to ensure the equivalence of the groups. There were no significant differences among the groups for any of the demographic variables except duration of surgical procedure (F $[3,196]$ = 7.09, P < .001). The mean surgical procedure durations were 78.38 minutes (SD = 36.71 min) for the control group, 99.46 minutes (SD = 48.79 min) for the in-person intraoperative progress report group, 129.29 minutes (SD = 117.81 rain) for the attention group, and 109.06 minutes (SD = 55.48 min) for the telephone-call intraoperative progress report group. Duration of surgical procedures was not related to the dependent variables (i.e., STAI-S scores, MAPs, heart rates), so I did not use it as a covariate in the analysis.

Results

Family members in the in-person progress report group reported lower anxiety scores (F $[3,196]$ = 16.46, P < .001) and had significantly lower MAPs (F $[3,196]$ = 8.60, P < .(X)l) and heart rates (F $(3,196)$ = 3.31, P < .05) than family members in the control, attention,

TABLE 1 CONTROL GROUP (GROUP ONE) ANXIETY MEASURES

Measures	Range	Mean	Standard Deviation
State-Trait Anxiety Inventory Form Y S-Anxiety scores	20 to 66	43.42	12.58
Mean arterial pressures (mm Hg)	74.90 to 118.41	101.63	11.04
Heart rates (beats/min)	52 to 99	74.78	10.88

TABLE 2 IN-PERSON INTRAOPERATIVE PROGRESS REPORT GROUP (GROUP TWO) ANXIETY MEASURES

Measures	Range	Mean	Standard Deviation
State-Trait Anxiety Inventory Form Y S-Anxiety scores	21 to 51	28.56	7.10
Mean arterial pressures (mm Hg)	77.16 to 104.40	90.89	6.60
Heart rates (beats/min)	60 to 88	71.44	5.99

TABLE 3 ATTENTION GROUP (GROUP THREE) ANXIETY MEASURES

Measures	Range	Mean	Standard Deviation
State-Trait Anxiety Inventory Form Y S-Anxiety scores	20 to 60	37.30	12.32
Mean arterial pressures (mm Hg)	78.80 to 126.36	97.36	11.03
Heart rates (beats/min)	57 to 99	75.84	10.36

TABLE 4 TELEPHONE-CALL INTRAOPERATIVE PROGRESS REPORT GROUP (GROUP FOUR) ANXIETY MEASURES

Measures	Range	Mean	Standard Deviation
State-Trait Anxiety Inventory Form Y S-Anxiety scores	20 to 59	35.70	9.65
Mean arterial pressures (mm Hg)	73.76 to 128.37	97.08	12.95
Heart rates (beats/min)	62 to 98	77.00	9.20

and telephone-call report groups. In addition, family members in the in-person and tele-phone-call progress report groups had anxiety scores (t (2,98) = –4,21, P <.001), MAPs (t (2,98 = –3.01, P < .001), and heart rates (t (2,98) = –3.58, P <.001) that were significantly different from each other. Tables 1 through 4 summarize these results,

Discussion

The purpose of this study was to replicate, in part, major findings of my previous research. I obtained similar results in this study. Family members who received the in-person intra-operative progress reports recorded significantly less anxiety than family members in the control, attention, or telephone-call report groups. The control group's mean anxiety score of 43.42 was much higher than the normal sample mean of 35 that the authors of the tool reported, and the inperson report group's mean anxiety score of 28.59 was much lower than the normal sample mean reported by the authors of the tool. The mean anxiety scores of the attention and telephone-call progress report groups approximated the normal sam-ple mean.

Family members in the in-person progress report group reported lower anxiety scores than family members in the telephone-call progress report group. It was apparent that tele-phone-call reports or attention reduced family members' anxiety more than no intervention, but providing in-person intraoperative progress reports was the most beneficial intervention.

Normal MAP is approximately 93 mm Hg The MAP ranges in all four family-member groups contained the normal value. The MAPs in the control, attention, and telephone-call progress report groups were above the normal value, whereas the MAPs in the in-person progress report group were below the normal value. Adult heart rates normally range from 60 to 80 beats per minute.In this study, family members in all four groups had heart rates in the normal range, but the mean rate was lowest in the in-person progress report group.

The results of this study also confirm previous findings that family members of acute-ly ill patients are highly anxious. Family members in the control group reported higher anxiety levels than those reported by patients undergoing coronary artery bypass graft (CABG) procedure, patients undergoing cardiac catheterization procedures, mothers of hospitalized children, significant others of patients undergoing CABG procedures, and family members who were learning cardiopulmonary resuscitation techniques because they had relatives with cardiac disease. The high degree of anxiety in the control group is alarming considering the lack of intraoperative nursing interventions directed toward fam-ily members of surgical patients.

The majority of patients in this study underwent ambulatory surgery procedures, which is not an unusual finding. In 1992, more than half the surgical procedures per-formed were outpatient surgical procedures.

Previous research has suggested that the presence of a caring person during surgery waiting periods is as effective as providing information in reducing family members' anxi-ety. Other researchers have reported that emotional support is more effective than providing detailed information in reducing patients' preoperative anxiety. The results of this study sug-gest that in-person provision of information reduces family members' anxiety more than emotional support, presence of a supportive person, or telephone-call progress reports.

The control group's anxiety scores, MAPs, and heart rates support individuals' pri-mary appraisals of the waiting period during surgery as being anxiety producing, The reductions observed in these anxiety measures in the in-person intraoperative progress report group suggest that interventions may provide the coping option that family members need during the secondary appraisal process. Information provided by inperson intraoperative progress reports appears to decrease family members' anxiety, supporting the study hypothesis.

Other nursing intervention studies have shown that specific information, when provided to patients with high preferences for information, and general information, when provided to those with lower preferences for information, result in improved patient outcomes (e.g., length of hospital stay, coping ability The progress report protocol used in this study can be considered general information tailored to each specific surgical patient. The relationship between family preferences for specific or general information and patient outcomes needs to be explored in future studies.

Further research may determine reasons for the lack of perioperative nursing interventions directed toward surgical patients' family members. In-person intraoperative progress reports appear to be a beneficial nursing intervention for family members, but the cost effectiveness of such an intervention remains to be determined. Whether the information should be provided by a professional perioperative nurse or other individuals is unclear. The beneficial effects of family members' reduced anxiety on patient outcomes also requires investigation.

The sample size for this study was adequate, and the sample was selected randomly. The lack of a pretest measure, however, may require further research to examine causality in the effects of intraoperative progress reports on family members' anxiety. The results of this study can be generalized only to family members of patients undergoing elective surgical procedures. More research needs to be conducted to determine if similar results are obtained from perioperative nursing interventions directed to family members of patients undergoing emergency, major, or diagnostic surgical procedures.

Using research findings as a foundation for perioperative nursing practice may change nurses' attitudes about surgical patients' family members. In the current consumer-oriented health care climate, implementing new interventions (e.g., in-person intraoperative progress reports, family-focused perioperative nursing care) may make a difference in a facility's surgical market share. The benefits of nurse-family member interactions during the intraoperative period should not be underestimated. Adequately assessing family members' anxiety and appropriately intervening to decrease the stress associated with surgical experiences have important implications for perioperative nursing practice. .

References

1. Kathol, D. K. Anxiety in surgical patients' families, *AORN Journal*, 40 (July 1984) 131–137; M. C. Silva et al. Caring for those who wait, *Today's OR Nurse,* 6 (June 1984) 26–30.

2. Raleigh, E. H., Lepezyk, M., & Rowley, C. Significant others benefit from preoperative information, *Journal of Advanced Nursing,* 15 (August 1990) 941–945.

3. Sigsbee, M., & Geden, E. A.Effects of anxiety on family members of patients with cardiac disease learning cardiopulmonary resuscitation, *Heart & Lung,* 19 (November 1990) 662–665.

3. K. Frederickson, Anxiety transmission in the patient with myocardial infarction, *Heart & Lung,* 18 (November 1989) 617–622.

4. J. A. Reider, Anxiety during critical illness of a family member, *Dimensions of Critical Care Nursing,* 13 (September/October 1994) 272–279.

5. J. S. Leske, Effects of intraoperative progress reports on anxiety of elective surgical patients' family members, *Clinical Nursing Research,* 1 (August 1992) 266–267; J. S. Leske, Effects of intraoperative progress reports on anxiety levels of surgical patients' family members, *Applied Nursing Research,* 8 (November 1995) 169–173.

6. Silva et al, Caring for those who wait, 26–30; Raleigh, Lepezyk, & Rowley, Significant others benefit from preoperative information, 941–945.

7. Kathol, Anxiety in surgical patients' families, 131–137; Silva et al, Caring for those who wait, 2630; Raleigh, Lepezyk, & Rowley, Significant others benefit from preoperative information, 941–945; C. W. Chavez & L. Faber, Effect of an education-orientation program on family members who visit their significant other in the intensive care unit, *Heart & Lung,* 16 (January 1987) 92–99.

8. Reider, Anxiety during critical illness of a family member, 272–279; T. M. Davis et al, Preparing adult patients for cardiac catheterization: Informational treatment and coping style interactions, *Heart & Lung,* 23 (March/April: 1994) 130–139.

9. R. Eldridge, Surgery progress reports: Support for cardiac surgery patients' families, *AORN Journal,* 40 (August 1984) 241–246; R. Craig, D. Cioni, & C. Morrison, The forgotten: Families of your surgical patients, *Journal of Post Anesthesia Nursing,* 1 (August 1986) 170–174; S. G. Donnell, Coping during the wait: Surgical nurse liaison program aids families, *AORN Journal,* 50 (November 1989) 1088–1092; J. S. Mitiguy, A surgical liaison program: Making the wait more bearable, *MCN: American Journal of Maternal Child Nursing,* 11 (November/December 1986) 388–392.

10. Leske, Effects of intraoperative progress reports on anxiety of elective surgical patients' family members, 266–267.

11. Leske, Effects of intraoperative progress reports on anxiety levels of surgical patients' family members, 169–173.

12. M. J. Johnson & D. I. Frank, Effectiveness of a telephone intervention in reducing anxiety of families of patients in an intensive care unit, *Applied Nursing Research,* 8 (February 1995) 42–43; A. W. Keeling & P. D. Dennison, Nurse-initiated telephone follow-up after acute myocardial infarction: A pilot study, *Heart & Lung,* 24 (January 1995) 45–49.

REVIEW QUESTIONS

1. What were the independent and dependent variables in the experiment? What was the hypothesis?

2. Explain the four-group, quasi-experimental posttest design used in this study.

3. What were some of the limitations of this study?

LET YOUR FINGERS DO THE TALKING: SEX ON AN ADULT CHAT LINE

Diane Kholos Wysocki

Research on the Internet has increased during the past 5 years at an amazing rate. What hasn't increased quite so quickly is the ethical and methodological discussions about conducting this type of research. In this article, the researcher used a computer bulletin board to investigate the sexual interaction between people who met online. An interactive questionnaire was used to gather demographic information, information about general computer usage, and the respondents online sexual behavior. This study shows how easy it is for some people to answer personal questions online rather than offline, and it suggests that computers might increase respondent participation and willingness to answer sensitive questions.

Interpersonal relationships have changed at a dramatic rate during the late 20th century, with the advancement of technology and the emergence of the "information society" (Ryan, 1997). As a result, the ways in which people develop interpersonal relationships have changed, allowing them opportunities to explore new ways of social interaction (Marx, 1994; Turkle, 1995; Porter, 1997).

The increased availability of technological products such as computers, modems, computer bulletin boards (BBS) and the Internet, along with their declining prices (Van Dijk, 1993) have had a dramatic affect on social life as we have known it (Adamse and Motta, 1996). While in the comfort of home or office, social networks are increased (Wysocki, 1996), new online communities created (Rheingold, 1993; Marx, 1994; Stone, 1995; Turkle, 1995; Schwartz, 1996; see also Porter, 1997) individuals have met their spouses/partners (Morgan, 1993; Sanz et al., 1994) and even fulfilled their deepest sexual fantasies (Tamosaitis, 1995; Goldstein, 1996; Hamman, 1996a; Lubove, 1996).

The purpose of this paper is twofold: to examine how and why individuals participate in sexually explicit computer bulletin boards; and to see if sex on-line is a way of *replacing* face-to-face relationships or a way of *enhancing* them. This analysis focuses on the social construction of love and sexuality and uses a sexually explicit computer BBS that I have called *Pleasure Pit*[1] as the source for contacting individuals who combine their technological abilities with their sexual desires. Specifically, this project focuses on how one sexually explicit BBS operates, what types of people use it, what kinds of activities are available for the participants, why individuals participate in *sex* on-line, and how those sexual behaviors are accomplished without face-to-face interaction.

---

[1] *The name of the BBS has been changed to protect the identity of both the users and the owners.*

Wysocki, D. K. 1998. Let your fingers do the talking: Sex on an adult chat line. *Sexualities,* 1 (4): 425–452.

Sex On-Line

It has been suggested in the mass media that the computer, via e-mail, chat mode and BBS is *the place* to go for on-line "sexual" relationships (Elmer Dewitt, 1995; Adamse and Motta, 1996; Kornbluth, 1996). Sex via the computer can develop through the interactive sharing of fantasies, looking at sexually explicit photographs and/or sharing similar sexual interests (Bright, 1992; Rheingold, 1993; Childs, 1994; Bloom, 1995; Hamman, 1996b; Brophy, 1997). According to one source, more than 50 percent of all on-line communication is related to sex (Childs, 1994), and sexually explicit BBS with names like *Kinknet, ThrobNet* and *StudNet,* are geared to all kinds of variations of sexual pleasure. On the Internet, the lists of sexually explicit BBS are extensive, have active user participation and are very lucrative, with one service making over $500,000 a month (Anonymous, 1997a). Similarly, in one Web site file chat (or Internet Relay Chat—IRC) rooms were separated into those rated G—for users of all ages; R—not recommended for those under 18; and X—for those who are over 18. The site has between 800 and 1000 users on it at any given time. Within each of the sections there are different chat rooms for people to meet other individuals. The G-rated section has 7 chat rooms, the R-rated has 16 chat rooms, and the X-rated was the most active with 41 chat rooms that included *The House of Pain* for those interested in bondage and S & M, *The Sex Shop* for those interested in sex toys, and *The Locker Room* for gay men (Personal observations, Feb. 1998).

In *net.sex,* Nancy Tamosaitis (1995: 2), a journalist who writes about electronic communications and who spent time investigating sexual BBS, states that "cybersex" refers to "looking for a partner to exchange erotic e-mail with, or to meet live for steamy sessions on the IRC (Internet Relay Chat) area." Finding people who participate in cybersex is not difficult and Tamosaitis found that individuals who use sexual BBS report they are more comfort able telling secrets on-line, having on-line sexual encounters, and "cheating" on their spouses with someone they have "met over the BBS." Similarly, John Richards (1994) states it is impossible to tell how many sexually explicit BBS there are; however, in a poll by *Boardwatch Magazinethe* second and third choices of best BBS are sexually explicit and geared towards adults.

In October 1995, an on-line sexual survey was created by the Inter-Commerce Corporation. By June 1997, a total of 20,791 respondents had participated in the survey and reported that being on-line *enhanced* their sexual behaviors (InterCommerce Corporation, 1996). The top reasons respondents gave for participating in sex on-line was that it was "a benign outlet for sexual frustration . . . It has made me more open-minded . . . Promotes honest communication . . . Promotes safe sex . . . [and] has improved my sex-life." Other respondents believed cybersex helped their marriages and discouraged adultery. While information about the exact number of people who use the computer for sexual activities and information changes constantly, it is becoming recognized that if you want sex, it is only a keyboard away.

Gaining Access to Pleasure Pit

To learn about the sexual relationships people have developed over computers, I located the name and telephone number of a BBS through a computer newspaper offered free of charge in a computer store. The BBS was located in a Midwest U.S. city and called *Pleasure Pit.* Previous research has suggested that gaining entry to a new research setting could be difficult. Gaining access to this BBS, however, was easy with the help *of gate-keepers* or, in this case, the systems operators (SYSOP) (Berg, 1998). Originally I logged onto *Pleasure Pit* and explained to the SYSOPs that I was a sociologist interested in using *Pleasure Pit* to collect data. I was unprepared for the enthusiastic response I received and was invited to meet the SYSOPs and learn how the BBS was run.

When an individual first signed onto *Pleasure Pit,* he or she was required to give their correct name, address, and phone number to the SYSOPs. Before the user was given full access to the BBS, the SYSOPs checked to make sure the individual trying to gain access was not a minor by calling the home telephone number. If the number given by the user was not correct, BBS access was denied.

That first night, even as I was learning about the BBS, one of the SYSOPs wrote a message for all users to see that said,

> There will be a female here at the Pleasure Pit office to do interviews with any-body who happens to be on-line . . . she is doing research on BBS relationships and is interested in what happens to your inhibitions when you're on the key-board (we know what happens to them). Watch for more info on her activities. I may call your voice to set up a voice interview with her. If you volunteer you will be first called and you husband types (with spouses not into this) be sure to let me know that you do or don't want a call.[2]

During that same evening I placed my questionnaire onto *Pleasure Pit.* Using a door-ways[3] questionnaire program, each question gave the respondent the option of either choosing one of the multiple-choice answers or writing text if they wanted to give a more detailed answer. When the respondent completed a question and hit "enter," the program automatically moved to the next question. The *Pleasure Pit* programmer made it very easy for me to collect the data from my home computer. Every few days I would call *Pleasure Pit* from my home and then download the answers given by the respondents. At that time I would separate the respondent's name from the questionnaire and then give each ques-tionnaire a number to ensure confidentiality.

The SYSOPs and I tried a few more approaches to gain more involvement in my study. First, the SYSOPs told users once again that there was a questionnaire on-line from a sociologist who needed help and told them how to locate the questionnaire. Second, my presence was advertised on *Pleasure Pit when* people first signed in,[4] and there was also a

---

[2] It was never my desire to do voice interviews for this project. Rather, I wanted to see how I could get by collecting all of my data, which included both interviews and questionnaires, on-line. I was able to accomplish this for the entire project.

[3] This is a program that allows a user to access other programs. In this case, tile questionnaire pro-gram allowed me to make multiple choice or open-ended answers and would automatically go on to the next question when the respondent finished with the question that was being answered.

[4] This also helped cover any ethical issues that might have come up due to the nature of this study. Everyone knew as soon as they logged on, that I was '"urking" around and what I was doing. At the time I was conducting this study, which was part of my doctoral dissertation (Wysocki, 1996), col-lecting data on-line was very new to most people, especially University institutional Review Boards. It was decided that if a respondent took part in either an on-line interview or answered my questionnaire, they were giving consent. No one ever complained to the SYSOP or myself about my presence on the BBS as a researcher.

flashing notice saying I was the CO-SYSOP of an on-line relationship conference. Respondents—predominantly males—began to contact me immediately.[S] In order to attract more women, the SYSOPs sent a notice from me to the 122 registered females and couples on *Pleasure Pit.* The note said:

> To All Female Users of Pleasure Pit BBS.
>
> I am a graduate student at UC Santa Barbara. I am doing my Ph.D. dissertation on the relationships people develop over computer bulletin boards. I have placed a questionnaire in the Questionnaire menu (it is number 6) and I am CO SYSOP in Conference 36. People have been responding, however, I haven't heard from many women. Please help me by taking the time to answer my questionnaire. If you have any questions contact me on this board. Just address it to Diane. Or you can contact me on the Internet (address given) or Prodigy. (address given). All of your answers are confidential. Thanks Diane

Women began to contact me immediately and were quite willing to help by answering my questions.

Interviewing subjects on-line was very easy. *Pleasure Pit* users saw, my requests for respondents and contacted me. If they were willing, we would get into chat mode on *Pleasure Pit* where we could type back and forth to one another in real time. Otherwise, I would e-mail some questions to the respondent, who would then e-mail the answers back. The best part about doing "interviews" on-line was that I could capture[5] what was being written and I would automatically have it transcribed. Many of the respondents were more than willing to answer my questions and truly liked the idea of being "interviewed online" and talking about their cybersexual experiences.

Who Uses Pleasure Pit?

A total of 133 usable questionnaires were collected in this study. Questionnaires were discarded only if the respondents did not answer the demographic questions or if I had reason to believe they were not serious. I discarded two questionnaires because, after I examined them, I found they were from children who managed to gain access to the BBS.[6]

The amount of time the *Pleasure Pit* respondents had been using online bulletin boards of any kind varied from the first time to 15 years with a mean of 2.61 years. The hours each respondent spent on any BBS each day ranged from 1 minute to 12 hours a day, with a mean of 1.63 hours, with the majority (97%), having spent 5 hours or less a day on-line. This is consistent with other projects that have found users to spend 3 or more hours a week (Anonymous, 1997b). The respondents who used *Pleasure Pit,* and who communicated with other people on-line, said they talked with up to 100 different people

---

[5] I used the program TELIX to call *Pleasure Pit* and to capture what was being said. The procedure is simple: all I needed to do was hit Alt L on my keyboard, give the file a name, and it would automatically download.

[6] In this case I brought my feelings to the attention of the SYSOP, who checked out their phone numbers and found that they were actually children, who were using the computers at their high school to call this sexually explicit BBS.

each week for pleasure, but on average they communicated on-line regularly with 13.31 people in a week. The majority *(72%)* communicated with less than 20 different people.

The individuals who used *Pleasure* Pit were predominantly male *(77%),* which might be expected because, overall, more men use computers than women (Sanz et al., 1994). The respondents ranged in age from 19 to 62 years and were relatively young with the average age of all of the respondents being 35.2 years, and the majority (94.30%) under the age of 50. Reported ethnicity was mostly white (89.9%). Regarding religion, 22%said they were Catholic, 25% said they were Christian, 4% said they were Jewish, and the rest did not answer the question. Over 50% of the respondents stated religion had no influence in their lives. About half of the respondents were married, 30.28% stated they were single, and over 51& reported having up to three children. A total of 71% stated they were heterosexual, 22% reported they were bisexual, and only 4% stated they were homosexual. Only 3% reported themselves to be transgendered or transsexual. Most of the respondents worked, with 70% having a full-time job. Only 2% were retired, and the rest worked part-time, were students, unemployed, homemakers, or volunteers. The majority of the respondents in this sample reported having had a college education. Only 18 percent reported a high school education or less. Of the *Pleasure Pit* users in this sample, 22 percent declined to say how much money they made, but the majority (52%) of these respondents stated they made $39,999 or less a year.

Motives for On-Line Sexual Activity

Five basic reasons were reported by the respondents of this study for using sexually explicit BBS. As shown in Figure 1, the reasons most commonly given for taking part in sex on-line were the need for anonymity, time constraints in their personal lives, the ability to share sexual fantasies with other people, the ability to participate in on-line sexual activity, and the opportunity to meet other people with similar sexual interests.

Anonymity. As expected, respondents stated they participated in sexually explicit BBS because they were able to take on whatever persona they liked from within the comfort of their own home or office. According to Stone (1995: 84): "our commonsense notion of community and of the bodies from which communities are formed take as starting points, among others, that communities are made up of aggregations of individual 'selves' and that each 'self is equipped with a single physical body . . . [however, computers] place the 'I' without whose coupling to a physical body there can be no race or gender, no discourse, no structure of meaning . . . [it is] about negotiating realities."

In other words, individuals using computer BBS have the opportunity to be whoever they want to be because the computer "provides ample room for individuals to express unexplored parts of themselves" (Turkle, 1995:185). The users can take on a different identity and portray themselves as that person or persons. If they are too shy and/or are unable to be comfortable meeting people face-to-face, the computer provides the physical barrier and anonymity that enables the users to meet new people and communicate from a distance.

According to Goffman (1963), when individuals possess attributes that discredit them in the eyes of others, it can greatly affect their self concept of themselves and the way they interact with other people. The anonymity of the BBS is one way in which individuals can

Figure 1. Motivations For Using Sexual Computer Bulletin Boards

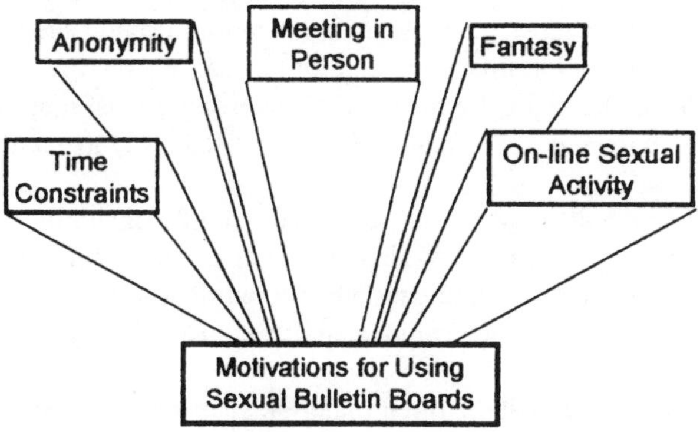

conceal themselves to avoid receiving the negative reaction of others. The computer provides the perfect shield against stigma. A single male wrote that since he was shy, e-mail "provided a curtain to hide behind." Some respondents, especially women, mentioned they felt they were fat and undesirable in person. On the BBS, they stated they felt completely different; they felt young, wanted, slim, and sexual.

Too many time constraints. Another reason respondents stated they used sexually explicit BBS was due to the many time constraints in their lives. Some mentioned they had very little time in their busy schedules to pursue friendships or sexual contacts on a face-to-face basis. Traditional face-to-face relationships of any kind develop through a pool of "eligibles" who are involved in the close proximity to one another (Michael et al., 1994). However, there are many constraints to finding a person with similar sexual ideas and desires within close social net works. According to Michael et al. (1994: 153) it is "difficult to find a sexual partner who, right off the bat, has the same sexual preferences as you have. If you desire anything but vaginal sex or, perhaps, oral sex, it will be hard to find a partner with your tastes." The respondents in this study stated the same thing. They believed it took too much time and was almost impossible to meet people with similar sexual interests and therefore the computer was the best way to handle this dilemma. A 41–year-old married man said he uses e-mail and BBS to meet people for sex because of the "immediacy of sexual conversation. Real life sexual relationships require a lot of small talk first." Paula, a single female who said she was in a face-to-face relationship with a man, considered the BBS as the "preliminary foreplay leading to real sex with swinging heterosexual couples who are real and sensitive." Paula was interested in trying new sexual behaviors, such as having sex with other couples, engaging in sex with women, and watching other people having sex. Paula believed she would not have found couples who shared her similar interests if she had not been on-line looking for sexual sharing.

Sharing sexual fantasies. The views most commonly held about sex are formed at a very early age and are dependent upon the dominant views held by groups we associate with and society as a whole (Rubin, 1990). Any sexual activity that is not heterosexually oriented and geared towards reproduction traditionally has been considered to be against the ideal norms of society (D'Emillio and Freedman, 1988), which makes it difficult for some to share sexual fantasies and interests with those in the face-to-face world. David stated he would never be the type to go to bars hoping to find some kind of (sexual) action, but wanted a friend with whom he could talk and have sex. He also said he had some sexual fantasies he was unwilling to share with his wife and had found the BBS was a safe way to ask for what he was really interested in.

Of the 72% of respondents who stated they had a spouse or significant other, only 20% had told their partner about their use of sexually explicit BBS. Often the users stated they *would not* or *could not* tell their significant other about their sexual fantasies. *Pleasure Pit* provided an outlet for them that they could keep private from those closest to them.

On-line sexual behavior. Sexually explicit material, such as videos, books, or magazines, are just a few of the outlets for people to find out about new sexual acts and develop new fantasies and ideas. Traditionally, this material has been geared toward the heterosexual male and has included scantily dressed or nude women in all kinds of poses or sexual acts; now sexual material has been made available for people with all kinds of sexual interests. Reading stories and looking at sexually explicit pictures typically has been known as "material to masturbate by." Whereas masturbation used to be considered dangerous and apt to "destroy both the body and the mind" of the individual (D'Emillio and Freedman, 1988: 69), it is currently taught as an accepted practice and takes place on a regular basis for many individuals (Michael et al., 1994).

With all this in mind, it should be no surprise that computers, e-mail, and various BBS have provided outlets for people interested in fulfilling their sexual fantasies. It is easier than meeting someone face-to-face and trying to decide if that person would experience the same sexual interests. For instance, if two people meet on a BBS conference for bondage, they already know that each has some interest in that kind of sexual activity and are able to divulge their fantasies early in the "relationship." If they like one another, they could then act out their sexual fantasy on-line.

On *Pleasure Pit,* one of the most common ways sex on-line happened was that the individuals went into chat mode and in "real time" typed out a fantasy with each other or a group of people. The sex act was accomplished by typing out in detail what each person could be doing to the other. Nate, a man who is getting married and whose significant other knows about his on-line escapades, stated he had sex on-line and loved it." It began with "me and this lady talking and she then called my computer, and we told each other what we looked like and then we started with . . . well, what we wanted to do with each other and then acted it out with words." Some commented they learned more about what their cyber partner wanted sexually because they were more willing to talk about their sexual needs and desires than with their face-to-face partners. Sex on-line, therefore, provided a place to practice what could be done later on in person.

Meeting *the sexual fantasy person of your dreams.* Meeting the perfect sexual partner is not always easy. If individuals were looking for someone who could fulfill their sexual fantasies off-line, they needed to be able to meet someone who expressed similar sexual interests. It was also difficult for most people to discuss sexual fantasies with someone rice-to-free   face-to-facebecause it meant risking rejection (Culbert, 1968). Normally

Figure 2. Initial Meetings -Face-to-Face vs On-line Interactions

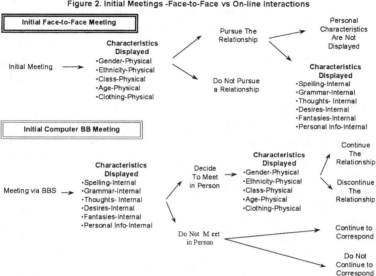

when individuals meet each other face-to-face, the meeting follows a fairly straightforward path, as shown in Figure 2. At the initial face-to-face meeting, physical characteristics, such as gender, class, ethnicity, and age are shown because the individuals are in close spatial proximity and the bandwidth is greater. These characteristics have been found to be very important variables in the continuation of face-to-face relationships (Cameron et al., 1977). If the relationship is continued, then the individuals involved take their time learning about the internal characteristics of one another while often putting on a *facade,* or *frontstage* appearance that could mask their true problems, feelings, or emotions (Goffman, 1959), thus making the sharing of sexual desires difficult.

On the other hand, relationships that develop over BBS appear to be much easier for people. They are able to get to know one another without inhibitions and share their sexual fantasies with their on-line partners. They meet on "conferences" where they are more likely to have similar sexual interests. Sexually explicit BBS discussions tend to move very quickly since both people divulge their fantasies early in the "relationship." The main difference between the greater and narrower bandwidth is that the individuals can create detailed images as part of their interaction with one another (Stone, 1995). If they like one another, they can act out a sexual fantasy on-line while typing in detail the images they are trying to portray about their sexual situation. In this way, the users also acquire clues about the individual backgrounds by way of their writing, grammar structure, and the internal characteristics. In other words, their *backstage identity* is shown at a much faster rate (Goffman, 1959).

After meeting on-line and finding they have similar sexual interests, the individuals decide whether to meet one another face-to-face. If they meet, the physical characteristics are then revealed (as shown in Figure 2), and the individuals decide whether to continue or discontinue the relationship based on the physical characteristics they display. If they decide not to meet one another on a face-to-face basis, they still have the option of continuing to correspond via computer. The computer BBS ultimately gives individuals more options than face-to-face meetings, and the respondents in this study who have met one another in person say that when they got to know one another by their internal characteristics first, then physical characteristics did not matter as much. In other words, finding someone who in fantasy is sexually compatible can be more important in the relationship than looks, age, sex, and ethnicity.

Many of the respondents stated they were quite willing to meet and have sex with another willing partner either over BBS or in person if the chance arose. Over 57% stated they had already met someone face-to-face with whom they became involved as a result of meeting through *Pleasure Pit*. Most stated the experiences went well for them. Sometimes, when individuals have met face-to-face after spending time in cyberspace, there was disappointment, which usually was the result of one or both parties not having told the truth about themselves. Most often the lies were about physical appearance. One single man, who had met with people off-line, said he had one sexual relationship that "was a bust if you will forgive the choice of words." Another man who now is divorced found "a couple of the people just weren't my type for whatever reason!," but never really said what his type was. One man was very uncomfortable when meeting his on-line friend because she brought her child to the meeting. Regardless, disappointment does not seem to stop these respondents front trying once again to meet someone with whom they may be sexually compatible.

Discussion

In conclusion, this study of adult sexual relationships over a sexually explicit BBS found people used it for many different reasons. The most common reason given was that the respondents had specific fantasies and desires that were not being fulfilled in their relationships off-line. Some of the respondents stated they did not have the time it took in off-line relationships to get to know one another and see if they have similar sexual interests. It became much easier to go to a "conference" set up for specific pleasures and know that the people participating in that "conference" have some interest in the subject or they probably would not be there.

The anonymity of the BBS also seemed to be an attraction to many of the users. They felt they could be more open and direct without having face-to-face interactions. Many stated they could say things to other people about their sexual needs and fantasies that they would not think of saying to someone they knew face-to-face or even to their spouse or significant other. Computer BBS just seemed to make self-disclosure much easier, and therefore reversed the order of the relationship. When people first meet in face-to-face relationships they look at the character of the individual to see how they are displayed (clothing, ethnicity, class), and then they decide whether to continue. In on-line relationships, the order is reversed. Once the BBS users had developed a relationship on-line, even if it was relatively new, the people involved sometimes met to have "real" sex. Ultimately, individuals got to know each other much better and quicker, based on actual characteristics. Rather than face-to-face relationships being replaced by computers, file the computer BBS has worked as a way of enhancing the face-to-face relationships in some cases. Often the ultimate goal of meeting on-line for many individuals on this BBS was to meet in person. Therefore, the BBS and face-to-face encounters work together in a common enterprise to enhance interpersonal relationships.

References

Adamse, Michael and Motra, Shcree (1996) *Online friendship, chat-room romance and cybersex.* Dearfield Beach, CA: Health Communications.

Anonymous (1997a). Internet sex sells, *Computerworld* 31(9): 59.

Anonymous (1997b) Users admit to spending three or more hours a week online, *Emedia Professional* 10(2): 25.

Berg, Bruce (1998) *Qualitative research methods for the social sciences.* Boston: Allyn & Bacon.

Bloom, H. (1995) Love with the proper stranger: Wrapped in the cloak of anonymity, people bare more than just their souls. In *Net guide: The guide to the internet and on-line services,* pp. 24–26. New York: Random House Electronic Publishing.

Bright, Susie (1992) *Susie Bright's sexual reality: A virtual sex world reader.* Pittsburgh, PA: Cleis.

Brophy, Beth (1997) Saturday night and you're all alone? Maybe you need a cyberdate, *U.S. News & World Report* 122(6): 60–62.

Cameron, Catherine, Oskamp, Stuart, & Sparks, William (1977) Courtship American style: Newspaper ads, *Family Coordinator, 26(1):* 27–30.

Childs, Matthew (1994) Lust online, *Playboy* (April): 152–153.

Constable, George (1990) *Understanding Computers.* Alexandria, VA: Time-Life Books.

Culbert, Samual Alan (1968) The *interpersonal process of self-disclosure: It takes two to see one.* New York: Renaissance Editions.

D'Emillio, John, & Freedman, Estelle (1988) *Intimate Matters: A history of sexuality in America.* New York: Harper & Row.

Elmer Dewitt, Phillip (1995) On a screen near you: Cyberporn, *Time* (3 July): 38–45.

Giddens, Anthony (1990) *The consequences of modernity.* Cambridge, UK: Polity.

Goffman, Erving (1959) The *presentation of self in everyday life.* New York: Doubleday.

Goffman, Erving (1963) *Stigma: Notes on the management of spoiled identity.* Englewood Cliffs, NJ: Prentice Hall.

Goldstein, A.I. (1996) Cybersex leaves me limp, *Forbes* 158(13): 104–107.

Hamman, R. B. 1996a. *Cyborgasms: Cybersex amongst multiple-selves and cyborgs in the narrow-bandwidth space of America Online chat rooms,* unpublished MA Thesis, Department of Sociology, University of Essex.

Hamman, R. G. (1996b) The role of fantasy in the construction of the online other: A selection of interviews and participant observations from cyberspace, [Online]: *http://www.socio.demon.co.uk/fantasy. html*]

InterCommerce Corporation (1996) Sex net, [Online]: *http://www. Survey.net/sex1.htmL*

Kantrowitz, Barbara (1994) Men, women & computers, *Newsweek* (16 May): 48–55.

Kornbluth, Jesse (1996) You make me feel like a virtual woman, *Virtual City* 1(2): 5758.

Lubove, Seth (1996) E-sex (virtual dreams interactive striptease service), *Forbes* 158(14): 58–60.

Marx, Gary (1994) Fragmentation and cohesion in American society. In Russell Dynes & Kathleen Tierney (eds.) *Disasters, collective behavior, and social organization.* Newark, NJ: University of Delaware Press.

Michael, Robert, Gagnon, John, Laumann, Edward, & Kolata, Gina (1994) *Sex in America: A definitive survey.* New York: Warner Books.

Morgan, Curtis (1993) Cybersex, *Miami Herald,* (22 Aug.): A1, A4.

Porter, D., ed. (1997) *Internet culture.* New York: Routledge.

Phlegar, Phyllis (1995) *Love online: A practical guide to digital dating.* Reading, MA: Addison-Wesley.

Rheingold, Howard (1993) *The virtual community: Homesteading on the electronic frontier.* Reading, MA: Addison-Wesley.

Richards, John (1994) Editor's Notes, *Boardwatch Magazine (April/May) 8.*

Rubin, Lillian (1990) *Erotic wars: What happened to the sexual revolution.* New York: Farrar, Straus & Giroux.

Ryan, Alan (1997) Exaggerated hopes and baseless fears: Technology and the rest of culture, *Social Research,* 65(3): 1167–1191.

Sanz, Cynthia, Shaw, B. & Young, S. (1994) Where love has gone, *People* (21 Feb.): 40–43.

Schwartz, John (1996) The American dream, and email for all, *Virtual City,* 1(2): 44–49.

Sheppard, Nathaniel (1995) Cyber Jerks, *Denver Post Magazine,* (26 Mar.): 6–7.

Stone, Allucquere Rosanne (1995) *The war of desire and technology at the close of the mechanical age.* Cambridge, MA: MIT Press.

Tamosaitis, Nancy (1995) *Net. sex.* Emeryville, CA: Ziff Davis.

Turkle, Sherry (1995) *Life on the screen: Identity in the age of the Internet.* New York: Simon & Schuster.

Van Dijk, Jan (1993) Communication networks and modernization, *Communication Research,* 20(3): 384–407.

Wysocki, Diane Kholos (1996) *Somewhere over the modem: Interpersonal relationships over computer bulletin boards,* unpublished Ph.D. dissertation, Department of Sociology, University of Santa Barbara.

REVIEW QUESTIONS

1. How was the questionnaire administered in this study? Would there have been a better way?

2. Do you believe people who answer surveys online, especially about sensitive subjects would be more honest than those who respond offline?

3. What were the findings?

The Longitudinal Effects of a Rape-Prevention Program on Fraternity Men's Attitudes, Behavioral Intent, and Behavior

John D. Foubert

One of the ways in which researchers use surveys is to evaluate existing programs. In this study the author evaluated a rape-prevention program that was designed exclusively for men. The program was set up to reduce male's acceptance of rape myths with the desire to reduce the likelihood of future raping and sexually coercive behavior. This project was designed to see if the program worked.

Rape and other forms of sexual assault have been repeatedly shown to be pervasive throughout the United States. The now-famous study by Koss et al[1] reported that more than one in four college women in a nationwide sample from 32 colleges and universities reported at least one experience after her 14th birthday that met the legal definition of rape or attempted rape. More recently, the U.S. Centers for Disease Control and Prevention surveyed more than 4600 college students at 136 institutions and found that 20% of college women reported having been forced to have sexual intercourse at some point in their lifetimes.[2]

Given the pervasiveness of rape, effective methods for decreasing its frequency are urgently needed. Although many studies have been conducted to assess the impact of rape-prevention programs on men's attitudes,[3] research on the affect of such programming on men's behavioral intent to commit rape and on sexually coercive behavior is very limited.[4]

College fraternity men are one group who have received attention in the research literature on sexual violence. O'Sullivan[5] found that fraternity members committed 55% of the gang rapes reported on college campuses between 1980 and 1990. Research has also shown that fraternity members have more rape-supportive attitudes[6] and are more sexually coercive than other men.[7]

In a comprehensive review of rape-prevention programs published during the past 20 years, Lonsway[3] noted the recent rise in popularity of programs targeting all-male audiences. She added that "because all-male programs offer the greatest promise in truly reaching the potential of rape prevention, such programs offer particular interest for future intervention and evaluation."[3 (p.242)] Several authors suggest that lower levels of defensiveness are elicited by all-male programs and that stronger programmatic effects are found in all-male (as opposed to coeducational) programs.[4, 8–11] All-male programs that use peer educators have been found to be particularly effective in the context of rape prevention.[10,12]

Foubert, J. D. 2000. The longitudinal effects of a rape-prevention program on fraternity men's attitudes, behavioral intent, and behavior. *Journal of American College Health*, 48 (4):158–163

Foubert and Marriott[9] described an all-male peer education approach that was shown to lead to a significant decline, sustained over 2 months, in rape myth acceptance among men in fraternity pledge classes.[10] We found that, immediately after participating in a program called "How to help a sexual assault survivor: What men can do," participants experienced a 55% drop in acceptance of rape myths as measured by the Burt Rape Myth Acceptance Scale.[13] Two months later, a significant 32% decline remained from rape myth levels shown on the pretest. In a further study of this program, the initial phase of the present study found that fraternity men's behavioral intent to rape significantly declined immediately after the program presentation.[14] Among the 20% of men who indicated some likelihood of raping before participating in the program, 75% reported a lower likelihood of raping after the program. Until the Foubert and McEwen [14] study, only Schewe and O'Donohue [4] had reported an impact on men's intention to commit rape.

Before the present study, the longest sustained change in acceptance of rape myths reported by a rape-prevention program in the research literature was 2 months.[10,15] The longest change in likelihood of raping was restricted to the day of the workshop.[4,14] In the present study, I assessed the impact of an all-male rape-prevention peer education program on participants' acceptance of rape myths, their likelihood of raping, and their sexually coercive behavior during an academic year (7 months).

Method

I tested the following hypotheses, using posttest and follow-up scores as the criterion measure:

- Program participants will experience a significant decline in likelihood of raping and in rape myth acceptance immediately after the program, relative to their pretest scores.

- Program participants will experience a significant decline in likelihood of raping and in acceptance of rape myths 7 months after the program in comparison with their pretest scores.

- When levels of sexual coercion are compared between program participants and a control group, follow-up scores will indicate that program participants committed less severe acts of sexual coercion during the 7 months after the program.

After receiving approval from the university human subjects review committee, all 23 fraternities at a mid-Atlantic public university were asked whether they would be willing to participate in the study. Eight fraternities (35%) agreed to do so. I randomly assigned 4 of the volunteer fraternities to participate in the program; their members constituted the experimental group (n = 109). The control group (n = 108) consisted of members of the 4 fraternities that did not participate in the program.

Within each group, I randomly assigned 2 fraternities to pretest and posttest conditions and randomly assigned 2 other fraternities to the posttest-only condition. Of these 217 participants assigned to the conditions, 145 completed all parts of the study required of them, resulting in a return rate of 67% (see Table 1).

The mean age of the 145 participants was 20.33 years (SD = 1.23). Members of the experimental group were overwhelmingly White (91%), with an additional 2% African

TABLE 1 PARTICIPANTS IN A CAMPUS RAPE-PREVENTION PROGRAM FOR FRATERNITY MEN, SHOWING TIME OF MEASUREMENT

	Time measured			
	Membership	Pretest	Posttest	Follow-up
Condition Group	N	n	n	n
Experimental Group				
Pretested				
Fraternity 1	41	28	28	20
Fraternity 2	36	31	31	23
Posttest only				
Fraternity 3	21		16	10
Fraternity 4	50		34	17
Control Group				
Pretested				
Fraternity 5	15	14		12
Fraternity 6	43	32		23
Posttest only				
Fraternity 7	16			10
Fraternity 8	34			30

American/Black, 4% Asian American or Pacific Islanders, 2% Hispanic/Latino/Chicano, and 1% listed as "other." At the time of the April data collection, 3% were 1st-year students, 41% were sophomores, 35% were juniors, and 21% were seniors.

Instruments

The Burt Rape Myth Acceptance Scale. I used the Burt Rape Myth Acceptance Scale to assess belief in rape myths; Bun defined the term rape myth as "prejudicial, stereotyped, or false beliefs about rape, rape victims, or rapists." [13 (p.217)] Scores at the higher end of this 19 to 133 scale range indicate stronger agreement with beliefs that correlate with sexually coercive behavior. The internal consistency for this scale was .87 on the pretest, .85 on the posttest, and .82 on the follow-up. Validity is supported by research showing that high scores correlate significantly with adversarial sexual beliefs (r = .40) and that men who report a higher likelihood of raping endorse more rape myths (r = .59).[11]

To assess behavioral intent to rape, I used Malamuth's [16] question: "If you could be assured of not being caught or punished, how likely would you be to rape?" Participants answered this question on a scale from not at all likely (1) to very likely (5). Malamuth reported that men who reported a higher likelihood of raping also reported higher levels of anger, aggression, and a desire to hurt women.

The Sexual Experiences Survey. The Sexual Experiences Survey (SES)[17] asks respondents to indicate their most serious level of sexually coercive behavior, ranging from coerced fondling to forced intercourse. The internal consistency of the SES among 143 male introductory psychology students was .89. Koss et al [1] found that 93% of male participants in their validity study of the SES reported the same information on a survey as in an interview.

Design and Procedures. The pretested experimental group completed the dependent measures immediately before they saw the 1-hour program in September 1997. As soon as the program ended, they completed the dependent measures for the posttest. I administered a follow-up, using the same measures, in April 1998. Posttest-only participants completed the dependent measures after the September 1997 program and again in April 1998. The pretested control group completed the dependent measures in September 1997; the posttest-only control group did not do so. All control group participants completed a follow-up administration of the dependent measures in April 1998, the same as the experimental group.

I modified the instructions for the SES [17] on the follow-up to ask participants whether they had committed any of the sexually coercive behaviors since completing the initial survey in September 1997. Participants did not attend any other rape-prevention programs during the academic year in which the study took place. In an attempt to prevent order effects, I randomly sequenced the different scales within the individual surveys.

Treatment. The experimental group participated in a 1-hour program during the beginning of the fall semester in their respective fraternity houses. Four male peer educators presented the program titled "How to help a sexual assault survivor: What men can do" to each audience. The program opened by setting a nonconfrontational tone, indicating that participants would be taken through a workshop designed to help them assist women in recovering from a rape experience.

After a disclaimer, an overview, and a basic review of rape definitions, presenters told the audience that they would be viewing a videotape that described a rape situation. This tape, produced by the Seattle Police Department, described a male police officer being raped by two men. At the conclusion of the video, peer educators processed the video as an act of violence (not sex) and drew parallels from the male police officer's experiences to common experiences of female rape survivors. Participants were then taught basic skills on how to help a woman recover from rape.

Next, the men were encouraged to communicate openly in sexual encounters and to help change societal norms that condone rape. After the presenters responded to questions, they noted that if the 1 hour in which the program took place was an average hour in the United States, 99 women would have experienced rape, attempted rape, or sexual assault.[18] I have described the program fully elsewhere.[19]

Results

Hypothesis 1 was that program participants would experience a significant decline in the likelihood of raping and in rape myth acceptance on the post program test (immediately after the program) relative to the pretest.

Hypothesis 2 was that program participants would experience a significant decline in likelihood of raping and rape myth acceptance on the follow-up (7 months later) relative to pretest scores. Hypotheses 1 and 2 were both confirmed.

Program participants had significantly higher levels of rape myth acceptance (p < .001) and likelihood of raping (p [is less than] .05) before the program than they did immediately afterward. These lower post program levels remained statistically unchanged over the 7-month academic year. Thus, when pretested rape myth acceptance (p [is less than] .01) and likelihood of raping (p [is less than] .05) were compared with follow-up scores, significant declines remained. Dependent measures in the control group did not change significantly across the three testing occasions, F(2, 33) = .32, p = .73.

Hypothesis 3, that levels of sexual coercion would be lower in the experimental group than in the control group at the follow-up, was not confirmed. Levels of sexually coercive behavior reported by the men who saw the program were statistically equivalent to those of nonparticipants (M = .46, SD = 1.6 for participants, compared with M = .35, SD = 1.5 for those who did not see the program).

Comment

My primary objective in conducting this study was to determine how an all-male sexual assault prevention peer education program affected fraternity men. Results showed that the program significantly lowered the men's reported likelihood of raping for an academic year of 7 months. Furthermore, I saw definitive evidence that the program decreased the men's belief in rape myths over a 7-month academic year. However, the results of this study did not show that those who saw the program behaved differently.

During the past 2 decades, researchers have had little success in identifying programs that lower men's acceptance of rape myths and their likelihood of raping.[3] Fewer still have been able to produce lasting declines in these areas.[3] Previously, two studies described programs in which significant declines in rape myth acceptance remained for up to 2 months.[10,15] The present study extended that interval to 7 months. In addition, only two previous studies were ever successful at changing men's intentions of committing rape. In each case, lack of follow-up precluded confirmation of the changes beyond the day of the program.[4,14] My present study showed that the program I used led to significantly lower likelihood of raping immediately after program participation as well as 7 months later.

The likelihood of raping did not differ significantly for the two treatment groups at follow-up. At least three factors may account for this. First, the control group began with a statistically equivalent, yet lower, level of likelihood of raping than the experimental group. Thus, the experimental group would have needed a much stronger decline in likelihood of raping to drop significantly below the unchanged control group. Second, this lack of a significant difference between groups could result from the analyses computing within-subjects effects being more statistically powerful than analyses comparing between-subjects effects.[20] Third, it could also be that the number of participants in each condition was too small to show a significant difference.

When studying the impact of the program evaluated in the present study, Foubert and Marriott[10] suggested that an improvement in rape myth acceptance of a pretested, untreated control group might have been a result of pretest effects from taking the Burt Rape Myth Acceptance Scale. A similar pretest effect was shown by Fonow et al.[15] The present study clarified this issue by pretesting only half of both the program and the control groups. Contrary to my expectations, statistically equivalent levels of rape myth acceptance were reported on the posttest and the follow-up, regardless of whether participants were pretested.

Despite the encouraging findings in attitude change and likelihood of raping, changes in sexually coercive behavior were not demonstrated. It is possible that sufficient information was provided and enough empathy with rape survivors was built for participants to change their attitudes and behavioral intent to rape, but the intervention was not enough to change behavior. Behavioral changes may also necessitate an intervention that is more comprehensive than the one-time program I used in this study. In addition, 7 months may not have been enough time to wait for sufficient sexually coercive behavior to occur for an evaluation of meaningful and significant differences between the control and experimental groups.

Another possible explanation is that the program itself influenced how participants answered the questionnaire at follow-up. Program participants learned how to define rape and how to determine whether they had a partner's consent during a sexual encounter. The control group did not have the benefit of learning this material. Therefore, the control group was less able to identify their behavior as sexually coercive because their understanding of how consent and coercion were defined was not clear. The experimental group was exposed to an educational program in which these concepts were taught.

The lack of a behavioral difference in the present study may have indicated different levels of knowledge of what rape, consent, and coercion are; what a woman means when she does not want to do something sexual; and what is meant by the use of physical force. The men who saw the program may have been more likely to identify their behavior as coercive or nonconsensual when it happened because they were better educated in knowing how such behavior is defined. The men who were in the control group may have been less likely to know that their behavior was nonconsensual. Thus, they may have been less likely to report it as such.

This study had several limitations, the first and most important of which is selection bias. Participants were members of a specific population on a campus (fraternities) and were members of chapters that volunteered to participate. Most fraternities did not participate; about one third of the campus fraternities volunteered. Student affairs staff members confirmed that the fraternities that volunteered were similar to the fraternity population at large in terms of policy violations and reputation, but the low rate of participation is a major concern.

In addition, not all members of individual chapters participated throughout the study. Differences between fraternity men and other men, fraternities that participated and those that did not, members of chapters who attended the program and those who did not, and members who completed the final follow-up and those who did not must be taken into consideration. These serious limitations must be noted when interpreting the results of the study. These findings, therefore, must be viewed as preliminary. Still, given the longitudinal nature of the study, it is noteworthy that 67% of the original participants completed it.

Sample size is another limitation. The number of participants I used provided enough statistical power for significant results to emerge on attitudes and behavioral intent. It is likely, however, that not enough participants were involved to detect meaningful differences in behavior. Also, given that only 9% of the participants in the present study were ethnically non-White, the results may not be relevant for non-White students.

These initial findings have several implications. First, this study suggests that educating men about rape in the context of an all-male, peer education "How to help a sexual assault survivor" program may be effective in changing men's beliefs in rape myths and their reported likelihood of raping. However, the program was not shown to change actual behavior. In view of the lack of effective means for eliciting changes in attitudes and behavioral intent to rape, I believe that further study and use of this approach, perhaps combined with other approaches, may lead to future findings of behavior change.

Several implications for promising areas of future research are suggested by the results of this study. One area of inquiry would be an exploration of different ways of measuring the program's impact on sexually coercive behavior. A larger and more representative sample of program and control group participants assessed over a longer time interval might reveal a behavioral difference.

Additional research could also attempt to combine programmatic approaches to determine whether interactive effects occur. For example, participants might be exposed to a victim-empathy program, as in the present study, and to a program focusing on defining consent in a sexual encounter, such as the one evaluated by Earle [12] and designed by Berkowitz.[8]

Conclusions

This study suggested that the program I evaluated elicited the longest change in attitudes and the longest change in the likelihood of raping found in an evaluation study of a rape-prevention program for men. Although the findings are preliminary and the conclusions are tentative, they suggest that the programmatic approach I used in the present study is worthy of future research. It could also be used by educators who are seeking to work toward the goal of creating campus environments where no more rape occurs. The research literature awaits proof of behavioral changes resulting from a rape-prevention program.

References

[1.] Koss, M. P., Gidyez, & C. A., Wisniewski, N. 1987. The scope of rape: Incidence and prevalence of sexual aggression and victimization in a national sample of higher education students. *J Consult Clinical Psychology,* 55:162–170.

[2.] Douglas, K. A., Collins, J. L., Warren, C., et al. 1997. Results from the 1995 National College Health Risk Behavior Survey. *Journal of American College Health,* 46(5):55–66.

[3.] Lonsway, K. A. 1996. Preventing acquaintance rape through education: What do we know? *Psychology Women Quarterly,* 20:229–265.

[4.] Schewe, P., & O'Donohue, W.1993. Rape prevention: Methodological problems and new directions. *Clinical Psychology Review,* 13: 667–682.

[5.] O'Sullivan, C. 1991. Acquaintance gang rape on campus. In Parrot, A., & Bechhofer, L., eds. *Acquaintance rape: The hidden crime.* New York: John Wiley, 140–156.

[6.] Schaeffer, A. M., & Nelson, E. S. 1993. Rape-supportive attitudes: Effects of on-campus residence and education. *Journal of College Student Development,* 34:175–179.

[7.] Garrett-Gooding, J., & Senter, R. 1987. Attitudes and acts of sexual aggression on a university campus. *Sociological Inquiry,* 59:348–371.

[8.] Berkowitz, A. D. 1994. Men and rape: Theory, research, and prevention programs in higher education. San Francisco: Jossey-Bass.

[9.] Foubert, J. D., & Marriott, K. A. 1996. Overcoming men's defensiveness toward sexual assault programs: Learning to help survivors. *Journal of College Student Development,* 37:470–472.

[10.] Foubert, J. D., & Marriott, K. A. 1997. Effects of a sexual assault peer education program on men's belief in rape myths. *Sex Roles,* 6:257–266.

[11.] Hamilton, M., & Yee, J. 1990. Rape knowledge and propensity to rape. *Journal of Research in Personality,* 24:111–122.

[12.] Earle, J. P. 1996. Acquaintance rape workshops: Their effectiveness in changing the attitudes of first year college men. *NASPA Journal,* 34:2–18.

[13.] Burt, M. R. 1980. Cultural myths and supports for rape. *Journal of Personality and Social Psychology,* 33:217–230.

[14.] Foubert, J. D., McEwen, M. K. 1998. An all-male rape prevention peer education program: Decreasing fraternity men's behavioral intent to rape. *Journal of College Student Development,* 39:548–556.

[15.] Fonow, M. M., Richardson, L., & Wemmerus, V.A. 1992. Feminist rape education: Does it work? *Gender and Society,* 6:108–121.

[16.] Malamuth, N. M. 1991. Rape proclivity among males. *Journal of Social Issues,* 37:138–157.

[17.] Koss, M. P., & Gidyez, C.A. 1985. Sexual experiences survey: Reliability and validity. *Journal of Consultant Clinical Psychology,* 53:422–423.

[18.] Maguire, K., & Pastore, A. L. *Sourcebook of criminal justice statistics.* Washington, DC: US Dept of Justice; 1995.

[19.] Foubert, J. D. 1998. *The Men's Program: How to successfully lower men's likelihood of raping.* Holmes Beach, FL: Learning Publications.

[20.] May, R.B., Masson, M.E., & Hunter, M.A. 1990. *Application of statistics in behavioral research.* New York: Harper & Row.

REVIEW QUESTIONS

1. How many different hypotheses the author had in this study? What were they?

2. Explain the program that was being evaluated and why?

3. What methods were used in this study? Discuss the sample and the limitations of the study.

Chapter 9: Field Research, Narrative Analysis, and Interviewing

The first thing you need to do before conducting most research is to look at the world around you. What do you see? I bet if you think about it, you have been a researcher for a long time without even realizing it. You might have even made some observations and come to some conclusions about the various things you see around you. Well, we all do.

Let me give you an example. I like to go to auctions. I originally didn't know that I liked auctions. When I first moved to Nebraska, I needed furniture. Friends told me about an auction where I would find really great deals. So, every Wednesday night I would go to the auction wearing my backpack, and I watched what was going on around me as I graded my students' papers. I had never been to an auction before and found that many things were happening. Auctions aren't just about buying furniture and other items. People in the audience socialized and appeared to know each other. The men working the front tables, who showed the merchandise, had different methods of holding items and talking about the items depending on what the item was and how much money they wanted to receive as a bid. They were putting on a show for the audience. Everyone seemed to have a different way of bidding on items. Some would scratch their nose, others would lift their hat, some would pull on their ears and for some, the bid was so subtle it was impossible, at least for me, to even see. I soon realized by watching and paying attention that there were many other things happening at the auction that I never would have known about without observing the behaviors for months.

Fieldwork can also be called **ethnography** or **participant observation.** This type of observation is just "let's hang out" and watch what happens around us, which can be fun. But watching and participating in the auction also helped me develop questions about auctions, such as the rituals, socialization, and economic systems that take place within an auction. Field researchers can explore all kinds of situations. Let me give you some examples. Tamotsu Shibutani (1978) was a research assistant at the University of California's Evacuation and Resettlement Study who had observed the evacuation of the Japanese into resettlement communities. Shibutani became part of Company K, a unit in the U.S. military during World War II. Company K had some problems such as rampant absenteeism, insubordination, violence and protests, along with very bizarre behavior portrayed to the people outside of the unit. However, because Shibutani (1978:vii) was on the inside, he could view the behaviors through the "eyes of the participant," so he was able to chronicle "one of the more disorderly units in United States military history and form a sociological generalization concerning the process of demoralization" among the members of Company K. Collecting data in this type of environment isn't always as easy as you might imagine. Shibutani wrote his notes and sent them through the mail almost daily to his friends and relatives who kept them for him until after his term in Company K ended.

In another study, Mitch Duneier (1992), a young white man, spent time in Valois "See Your Food" Cafeteria on Chicago's South Side for four years while he was a graduate student at the University of Chicago. He began to notice a group of poor, working-class black men who congregated at a table that became known as "Slim's table." Over the years he got to know the men, observed their behaviors, found out about their lives and listened to their troubles. He was able to refute stereotypes by spending time with Slim, a car mechanic who was more or less the respected master of the table where the diners met once or twice a day for their 45 to 90 minutes a meal. Duneier also observed Slim, an elderly white diner, who substitututed Bart as his father figure and cared for him. The diners formed a moral community that transcended the roles and images commonly shown about black men and as a result, Duneier was able to discredit many of the previous studies on Black men that often generalized about working-class Blacks, but from essentially middle-class researchers' points of view. This study helps to confirm the inaccuracies about Black stereotypes that are shown in the popular media, and Duneier was only able to accomplish this by spending time in the field with these men.

Being a participant observer has some drawbacks, however. How much of your participation can influence the activities and behaviors of the people you are studying? While observing is an important aspect of field research, you must also take notes. How do you do it? The field notes must provide extensive descriptive detail about the situation you are observing. **Jotted notes**, which are written in the field, are short and meant to trigger your memory for a later time. **Direct observation notes** involve the researcher writing the notes soon after leaving the field. These notes should be detailed, with concrete information and sayings from the respondents. Maps and diagrams should also be included in the notes. For instance, William Whyte (1955:13), in his book *Street Corner Society: The Social Structure of an Italian Slum*, watched what took place on a street corner in a slum district known as "Cornerville." This city was inhabited almost exclusively by Italian immigrants and their children. The area was known as a problem part of the city, but many in the cityfeared Cornerville was home to corrupt politicians, poverty and crime. Since the only way to gain knowledge about Cornerville was to live there and participate in the activities, Whyte did exactly that. One of the first things Whyte does is describe in detail the history of of Doc's gang called The Nortons. To show the status of the individuals involved he diagramed The Nortons during the Spring and Summer of 1937. The diagram looks like this:

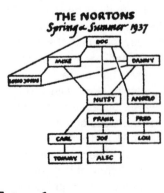

Since we can't be on that street corner, the information shown to the reader by the researcher is terribly important. It needs to be very specific, have as much detail as you can, and be as accurate as possible.

INTERVIEWING

Observing will help you determine what types of questions to ask your respondents when you **interview** them. If a specific place or situation is new to you, as the auction was for me, then observing for a few months allows you the ability to understand the situation in a very different way than if you had just decided to start asking questions of people. While a **questionnaire** involves written questions that are given to the respondents through the mail, e-mail, Internet, or in person, an interview involves the interviewer asking the questions and recording the answers given.

When you go into the field to collect data and observe what is going on, you have the opportunity to gather a rich set of data and ask questions of the people you are studying. Interviews in the field are usually unstructured, as in-depth as possible, and informal. Interviewing is also interactive and is different than the survey research we have previously discussed in that it is more intensive because of the thoroughness of the questioning. Intensive interviewing relies heavily on open-ended questions to develop a comprehensive view of the respondents' behaviors, attitudes, or actions.

Follow-up questions or probes allow the researcher to consider the subjects' answers and ask for clarification. What happens if you question a subject regarding their feelings about a new homeless shelter and the subject responds, "I don't like the new homeless shelter"? A follow-up question might be "Why don't you like it?"

NARRATIVE

Very few mainstream research methods books mention narrative or oral history as a way of collecting data. According to Reinharz (1992), this oversight appears to be because mainstream social scientists tend to find little value in studies that are subjective. Furthermore, there is little training and discussion about this method in most research methods classes.

Sometimes called oral history or biographical work, narrative is a way of listening to the voices of those who are being studied and is a way of uncovering "hidden histories, contesting academic androcentrism, and reinstating the marginalized and dispossessed as makers of their own past" (Miles & Crush, 1993:84). Narrative research is also used to analyze documents, to reanalyze previously published oral histories from a different perspective, to identify empirical patterns, and to examine groups quantitatively (Reinharz, 1992).

According to Reinharz (1992:133), "The researcher's purpose is to create a written record of the interviewee's life from his/her perspective in his/her own words." Boetcher Joeres and Laslett (1993) state that personal narratives are a way of studying the problems of women [and men] from all cultures and walks of life. Telling their histories is a way to pay tribute the people being studied.

REFERENCES

Boetcher Joeres, R. E., & Laslett, B. 1993. Personal narratives: A selection of recent works. *Signs,* 18(2): 389–392.

Duneier, M. 1992. *Slim's table: Race, respectability, and masculinity.* Chicago: University of Chicago Press.

Miles, M., & Crush, J. 1993. Personal narratives as interactive texts: Collecting and interpreting migrant life-histories. *Professional Geographer,* 45(1): 84–95.

Reinharz, S. 1992. *Feminist methods in social research.* New York: Oxford University Press.

Shibutani, T. 1978. *The derelicts of company K.* Berkeley: University of California Press.

Whyte, W. F. 1965. *Street corner society: the social structure of an Italian slum.* Chicago: University of Chicago Press

INFOTRAC COLLEGE EDITION SUGGESTED READINGS AND DISCUSSION QUESTIONS

1. Look up the article "Phenomenological and participatory research on schizophrenia: Recovering the person in theory and practice" (Article A20988886) in InfoTrac College Edition. What problems did the researcher have while doing the participatory research?

2. Locate the article "The margins of underdog sociology: Implications for the West Coast AIDS Project" (Article A19178123). In this article the researchers discuss the problems associated with going out into the field to collect data. Is there another method they could have used to gather data from the same population? Why or why not?

IMAGES OF CRIMINALS AND VICTIMS

E. I. Madriz

Two complementary qualitative methodologies—focus groups and in-depth interviews—were used in this article to explore women's fear of crime. The major argument in this piece is that women's fears are exacerbated by stereotypical images of criminals and victims. The stereotypes actually emerged during the participants' narratives and might not have become apparent if a survey had been used. Listening to women's voices became the key to finding out about their true fears.

Madriz, E. I. 1997 Images of criminals and victims. *Gender and society,* 11(3), 342–357.

The literature on fear of crime considers it "paradoxical" that women have higher levels of fear of crime, even though their levels of victimization are lower than men (Clemente & Kleiman, 1977; Ortega & Myles, 1987; Stafford & Galle, 1984; Warr, 1984). Feminist scholars, however, have reported that women's fear is the result of living with a variety of acts of aggression, many of which are not recorded in the criminal statistics. Because the majority of these acts of intimidation and violence against women are committed by male assailants—many of whom are known to the victim—female fear is fear of male violence (Gordon & Riger, 1991; Kelly, 1991; Russell, 1985; Stanko, 1990, 1993).

This article advances the view that female fear is exacerbated by images and representations of crime contained in the prevailing ideology of crime (Hall et al. 1978). This ideology is shaped by popular images about what is criminal, who is more likely to commit a crime and who is more likely to become a victim, what are the connections between criminals and victims, where and when is a crime more likely to occur, and what are the best ways to control or prevent crime. These representations reflect "attitudes so deeply embedded in tradition as to appear natural" (Reiman, 1995, 6), affecting women's—and men's—lives in a myriad of ways: restricting leisure and professional activities and teaching what crimes to fear, where and when to be afraid, who is dangerous, and who is safe.

Feminist literature identifies a diversity of ways in which women's lives are coerced (Gardner 1995; Carlen 1994; Hanmer & Saunders 1984; Russell, 1982, 1984, 1985; Smart, 1995; Stanko, 1985, 1990). Some studies deconstruct the discourse of femininity used in the informal and formal control of women. They focus on the "proper" role for women and men, the definitions of deviance and criminality as they relate to women, and the disciplining and policing of girls' behaviors (Cain, 1989; Chesney-Lind, 1995; Faith, 1993; MacKinnon, 1993; Rafter, 1990) Barbara Ehrenreich and Deirdre English (1978) focus on the public/private dichotomy, which identifies the home as a "safe haven" for women. Such division has resulted in major misunderstandings in the study of women as victims of criminal behavior. Although stereotypical images of crime and fear of crime focus on violence occurring in the public sphere, studies on domestic and intimate violence show that women's victimization most often occurs in private (Stanko, 1993).

Fear of crime is one of the most oppressive and deceitful sources of informal social control of women. The images and representations that shape Americans' fear of crime and appear in everyday narratives are translated into a familiar discourse filled with stereotypical images of offenders, victims, and their interconnectedness. Our images of "ideal criminals" (Christie, 1986)—or those individuals who are more likely to be given the status of criminal—are consistent with a traditional ideology of crime: Criminals are poor, minority men; uneducated; psychotic; or, more recently, immigrants.

Current representations of crime also contain images of victims and of the connections between victims and offenders. "Ideal victims" (Christie, 1986, 18) are those who, when affected by crime, are more frequently given the "legitimate status" of victim. Images of criminals and victims are intertwined. As Christie (1986, 25) points out, "the more ideal a victim is, the more ideal becomes the offender." Representations of ideal criminals and ideal victims mold our apprehensions and feed our anxieties, shaping the content of the everyday discourse on crime (Humphries & Caringella-MacDonald, 1990).

Images of nonideal victims are also an important element in the social construction of the fear of crime. Lisa Frohmann's ethnographic study on the prosecution of sexual assault crimes (1991) shows how prosecutors' decisions to reject or accept cases are oriented, among others, by factors related to the relationship between the victim and the offender and the victim's behavior and her personal life. Women who are assaulted by offenders known to them and who violate appropriate codes of behavior, such as being on the streets at night or being alcohol and drug users, are more likely to be considered nonideal victims and are frequently discredited by prosecutors.

Sally Merry (1981), in her book *Urban Danger: Life in a Neighborhood of Strangers,* explains how fear of crime among White, Black, and Chinese residents in a racially mixed neighborhood in Philadelphia contributes to divisions among groups along racial lines. Crime is an "idiom" that serves to legitimize the fear of strangers and unknown persons. As racial and ethnic networks share information about crime, they influence residents' presumptions of who is safe and who is dangerous.

I advance the thesis that images of criminals and victims reinforce racial divisions, increasing the disparity between men and women as well as among people from different socioeconomic backgrounds. My major argument is that popular representations associated with safe and dangerous situations, harmless and menacing individuals, and "good" and "bad" victims reinforce overlapping hierarchies of power, amplifying social distances among different groups and severely limiting women's daily activities.

This study examines popular images of criminals and victims in a group of women of different ages, races, and socioeconomic backgrounds. It focuses on the ways in which the social location of women affects these images. This study also explores the possibility that those women who hold qualities that match popular representations of the ideal victim will report a more heightened awareness to crime than those who do not fit such images.

Methodology

Between the fall of 1994 and the summer of 1995, I conducted 18 focus groups and 30 in-depth interviews in New York City and surrounding suburban areas with White, African American, and Latina women of different ages. The women were from different socioeconomic backgrounds: from a group of homeless African American teenagers in Manhattan to a group of White upper-middle-class women in the suburbs of northern New Jersey and upstate New York. There were a total of 140 participants in the study.

These complementary qualitative methodologies are aimed at gaining access to the way women construct and express their views about images of crimes, criminals, victims, and their interconnections. The in-depth interviews and the focus groups lasted between one and two hours each. The questions were included in a discussion guide. The guide was flexible enough to listen to the language of the women, allowing the discussion to move in a direction that was meaningful to the participants while keeping a certain structure to permit comparison between the groups. The groups were homogeneous in terms of age, race, gender, and socioeconomic background. From the total sample of 140 participants in the focus groups and in-depth interviews, 43 were White, 38 African American, and 59 Latina (Black, White, and mixed women of Latin origin). The age distribution was 47 teenagers (ages 13–19), 62 adults (ages 20–59), and 31 seniors (60 and older). The sample, therefore, overrepresents the number of women of color and teenage women. This was intentional because most studies on fear of crime underrepresent these groups, and very few even consider teenagers and Latinas. Thus, it was critical to give special attention to these women.

The individuals were recruited through contacts with community organizations and institutions in New York and northern New Jersey. In general, I contacted a person who organized the groups. The participants in the groups were women affiliated or related to organizations such as soup kitchens of alternative high schools. The sample, therefore, is one of availability and convenience, recruited through a revised process of snowballing (Morse, 1992).

Findings

Images of Typical Criminals. Several themes emerged from the participants' responses. First, it became evident throughout this study that, regardless of the race and socioeconomic background of the women, the images of criminals are strongly racialized, with Black and Latino men being uppermost in the fears of most women. During a discussion with a group of White middle-class college students in upstate New York, Gloria,(1) one of them, said,

> Oh, I just feel bad. I feel that anything that comes to my mind when you ask that question is . . . [hesitantly], I think of a thin, tall Black man. I know that it is a stereotype that is in the media, but that is the image that comes to my mind.

Gloria's words reflect the deep influence of these images. As an educated woman she understands that those are stereotypical representations of criminals. Being aware of these stereotypical images, however, does not resolve the problem: It is still the first portrait that comes to her mind. These images were not only reported by White women. Gladys, a dark-skinned Latina woman, said, "I am afraid of Black and Hispanic people and they are my people." African American women described similar feelings to that of White and Latina women. For example, Meredith, one of the participants in a discussion group, said, lowering her voice, almost whispering,

> I feel ashamed by saying this, but the image that comes to my mind when I think about criminals is that of a brother.

Another participant in the same group, Mary, a 26-year-old college student, recounted vividly what happened during the aftermath of a shooting in the Long Island Rail Road.(2) Her story exemplifies the way she believes the media portray images of Black men accused of committing crimes as inhuman, creating a racialized and objectified image of criminals.

> I am talking about what happened in the Long Island Rail Road with . . . what is his name . . . Colin Ferguson. The image that the media presented is that he is an animal, a monster . . . The next day I took the same train. You should have seen how people were looking at each other very strangely, in fear . . . You know that they were reading about it, you know that they are conversing about it. People in their coffee shops were talking about it . . . But, it was like . . . a racial division. In my school, the White professors, they were in their coffee shops talking about it. It affected them in a certain way. And it affected me and my friends who are Black in a different way . . . The day it happened I read the whole story and I thought . . . oh God, now every time a Black person enters in the damn trains all the Whites are going to go OOOOOOOHHHHHH! Here we go again! This

crime was horrendous, and yes, Ferguson is a Black man. But the way the media presented it was something that separated the races.

A second image that emerged was that of criminals as animalistic, as savages or monsters. Lombrosian images of offenders as prehuman have been a persistent theme in the literature since biocriminological theories emerged in the 19th century. These images were particularly evident among White middle- and working-class senior women. Kathy and Rose, two White women in their late 70s who live in the suburbs of northern New Jersey, shared with other members of the focus group:

> To me, the image of a criminal is that man . . . that monster, who shot all those people on the train and then made his own defense. That is the most scary thing of all . . . Because you know that people like Ferguson are mentally unbalanced and people on drugs are also mentally unbalanced . . . Most criminals are unbalanced. There is no way that you can reach at them . . . when the people are mentally disturbed, they do not know what they are doing.

Kathy and Rose's words reflect a multifaceted image. First, criminals are insane or "unbalanced." This was a very common theme among the participants who, on several occasions, used similar words to describe criminals: monsters, crazy, insane, mad, maniac, nuts, cracked, bizarre, weird. Second, criminals are out of control. The victim is completely helpless and at the mercy of these "mentally disturbed" persons. The representation that Kathy and Rose used was one of a mass murderer, Colin Ferguson. This image contrasts with the reality of crime. From the criminal statistics, we know that mass murders, such as the one committed by Colin Ferguson, are an extremely rare occurrence (Fox & Levin. 1994). When these events occur, however, the media bombard and saturate readers and viewers with reports about the incident, re-creating images of atavistic criminals. Politicians also jump on the bandwagon of the moral panic that such events provoke, promising a frightened public that if we had voted for them, this would have never occurred.

Comparable images were depicted by some of the participants, who described criminals as hanging around with other criminals or "in bunches," as Isabel, an elderly Latina woman who lives in lower Manhattan, said. "Ten, twenty, thirty, they are always together." "Yes, like in a pack," Gloria, another Latina woman, responded. This Darwinian representation is another piece in the mosaic of fears of several participants, who mentioned being afraid of Black and Latino teenagers who dress as "gangstas" and hang out in groups como animals (like animals), as one Latina participant remarked.

A popular theme that was also mentioned, particularly by elderly White working-class women, was that of criminals as immigrants, more specifically, new immigrants. Gene, Pat, and Pam, three elderly working-class White women who live on the lower East Side of Manhattan, shared their views with the group:

> The whole problem is the kind of people that you have in this country today. When my parents came . . . that type of person was different. Now, we have people that do not have respect for themselves and that is the whole problem. They are the ones that commit all the crimes. They just want to come to our country and live on welfare. They do not want to work. All they want is to live off of us. That is why they commit crimes. They are too lazy to work. Extending our arms to everybody. Come here and we'll feed you! [lifting her arms toward the ceil-

ing]. That's why we have so much crime. Golden shrine. . . Do you know? Wrong! That is the whole problem.

This emotional depiction of criminals presents in a "package" several intertwined racialized and class images: Criminals are "new immigrants"—a code word for dark-skinned immigrants—and are lazy, poor, dirty, wanting to live off of others, garbage, on welfare, and do not respect anyone.

A fourth image of criminals presented by some participants was of people who lack any human compassion. Leida, a 30–year-old Latina participant, connected the word criminal to una persona mala (a bad person) or someone a quien no le importa nada ni nadie (who does not care about anything or anyone). Other women used similar expressions, reflecting on the common theme that criminals lack human sentiments, as Rafaele Garofalo, a contemporary of Lombroso, stated during the late 19th century (Void & Bernard, 1986, 42–45). Criminals are "cruel," "inhuman," "immoral," "evil" individuals. This imagery, in which oversimplified assumptions of someone as "good" and "bad" are constructed and transmitted, becomes part of public consciousness and is woven in a complicated tapestry of class, racial, and gendered images with notions of goodness and badness.

Horror stories with decapitated bodies and tortured victims were commonly narrated, mostly by White middle-class, young women. Sandra, a White middle-class junior college student, shared with the group her horror story:

> My biggest fear is to be randomly taken away and my body to be found in a forest or in a ditch, you know, and have my family saying: "I thought she just went to the store, but she never returned." You know . . . that is really scary. I mean, the very thought that any time I am walking anywhere, and some lunatic can take control of you and kill you and end your life like that. And, many times they rape and torture you before killing you . . . That is the worst.

I then asked Sandra, "How likely do you think that an incident like that can happen to you?" She responded, "I really do not know, but it seems very real to me." These gendered, horror-producing, mass-mediated images (Barak, 1994) portray criminals as cruel, inhuman, and violent men who are strangers. "Definitely I am afraid of strange men," a student told me. "A man can overpower you," another young woman said to the group, "but I can beat up another woman," she added.

Images of Victims. Images of criminals as minority, poor, on welfare, and immigrants are nothing new. Much less attention, however, has been given to stereotypical images of victims and their influence on women's fears. Although official statistics on victimization show that men are more likely to be the victims of any violent street crime—except rape—than women (Bureau of Justice Statistics, 1995a), the majority of the respondents—irrespective of their race, age, and socioeconomic background—said that women were more likely to be victimized: "women, of course," Jenny, a White woman in her early 20s, decisively voiced. A very small fraction of the women interviewed said that the gender of the victim did not matter; only a handful of mainly African American women said that men were more likely to be the victims of a crime than women. In a focus group of White middle-class women, Judith, a woman in her 20s, said that "the typical victim is for sure a woman." "Any story in particular?" I asked. Heather, another participant, responded,

What I have in mind is the group of women who were killed at the University of Florida a couple of years ago. Because my first group of friends had gone to college and I have quite a few friends at the University of Florida and . . . when I think of a victim I think about these women. Because there were four women in their college apartment, getting ready to start a new semester and a man living in the woods came into their home and brutally murdered them. And I think of them as the victims because they are the average American living in their house, unaware, unsuspecting about what can possibly happen to them, and just happened.

Heather's story is quite revealing for several reasons. First, from all possible images of victims, she chose to talk about a life situation that is quite similar to hers. This was a very typical response. Many of the stories shared by the participants were closely related to the life circumstances of the woman narrating it. Heather is a college student, as were the women at the University of Florida. Second, the image of the criminal perfectly fits the image of an "ideal criminal": a stranger—literally—living in the woods, probably unemployed and "weird." Third, the women in Heather's narrative fit the representation of the ideal victim: the average—a code word for White middle-class American women—involved in a very respectable activity: going to college.

Images of victims presented by a small fraction of participants reflected some specific situational disadvantages: being poor, women of color, and immigrants. An undocumented Latina, Elizabeth, shared a story that reflects well the isolation and vulnerability that she feels and its relation to her image of "the victim":

I heard an incident in the radio Latina about a woman who was killed in her apartment. She screamed for help and the neighbors heard someone screaming. But, they could not understand what she was saying because she was yelling in Spanish. She was 25 years old and she yelled and yelled for help and no one came. They should have come anyway, to see what was happening. But they did nothing.

The relationship among victimization, fear of crime, and being an immigrant has not been studied. The words of Elizabeth, however, give us a glimpse of the fears that immigrant women face. Separated from their extended families and their communities, Latina women feel especially debiles or vulnerable. Even if they yell for help, their cries are unheard because people cannot understand them. This is an extremely powerful and emotionally appealing representation in the minds of many Latina women. Several of them mentioned the language barrier in association with their fear of crime. Maria and Elena, two Latinas in their 30s, said,

Me da mucho miedo que alquien me trate de robar y que yo no entienda lo que ellos quieren (I am afraid of someone trying to rob me and that I cannot understand what they want from me). Esta idea me aterroriza porque me pueden hasta matar (This idea terrifies me because they can even kill me): Si, nosotras estamos muy limitadas, porque no sabemos la lengua (Yes, we are very limited because we don't speak the language). Si algo nos pasa no podemos ni pedir ayuda (If something happens to us we cannot even ask for help). El otro dia me robaron la cartera y, pues, que iba yo a hacer? Como no tengo ni papeles, me quede con la rabia (The other day they stole my purse, and what am I supposed to do? Since I don't have documents, I just kept my anger to myself). Ahora tengo mas miedo, pero me cuido mas (Now I am more afraid, but also more careful).

Undocumented women feel especially vulnerable because they cannot report their victimization incidents to the police for fear of deportation. Therefore, they must remain silent about the crimes committed against them at home and in the streets. As Elena suggests, this makes them more fearful and more cautious, limiting their lives even more.

Several younger women, especially African American and White teenagers, mentioned innocence as an important trait pertaining to the ideal victim. "To me victims are like little Pollyannas," Margaret, a White teenager, suggested during an in-depth interview:

I imagine a blond girl, like . . . from the Midwest, with a ponytail, naive, unaware, walking down the street in New York City, singing laralaralara.

Besides the innocence and candor expressed in the image of Pollyanna, Margaret chose the figure of a Midwestern girl or a "mainstream American girl": a White, kind, virtuous, and family-oriented young woman.

Although a handful of women reported that the race of the victim did not matter, the majority of participants, regardless of their race, age, and socioeconomic background, reported that White women were more likely to be the victims of crime than Black or Latina women. Criminal statistics indicate, however, that Black women are more likely to be victimized than White women (Bureau of Justice Statistics, 1995b). White middle-class women, however, match the image of the ideal victim prevalent in the hegemonic ideology of crime. "White women are more often victims because they do not know how to scream," said Melinda, an African American teenager. Yvette, another African American teenager, expressed her views: "The majority of the scared women are White, that is the truth." She said that White women look scared when passing by Black men and sometimes when passing by Black women "like us," she concluded. Because Yvette is a homeless teenager, the implication is that White women also feel scared of poor Black teenage women.

Latina teenagers expressed similar ideas. In a lively discussion in one of the focus groups in Brooklyn, New York, they remarked,

White women are more victims because they do not know how to fight. We do, we know how to take care of ourselves. This is why they do not mess with us. But White girls are afraid of everybody, of Latinos, of Blacks. This is why they are more victims. They have it worse.

White women fit more closely the gendered, racist, and classist concept of "femininity" (Klein, 1995). They are taught not to get involved in physical squabbles. Only "bad girls"—or poor girls of color—do. Images of victims contribute to the social definition of "good" and "bad" women. Good women obey the codes of behavior and do not fight. Therefore, they should stay in because they do not know how to protect themselves. Bad women do not follow those codes. Therefore, they have to fight to protect themselves.

The virtual absence of Black and Latina women as victims in the media (Benedict, 1992) influences fear of crime in several ways. In this study, white women expressed more frequently being afraid of crime than Black and Latina women. This difference was especially evident among teenagers, with White middle-class teenagers expressing more fear than Black and Latina teenagers. In addition, the image of a White woman as the ideal victim is closely related to the idea of "White womanhood" and the need to preserve it. Black and Latina women's virtue is not as important: They are nonideal or "worthless" victims, unless they share common qualities with White middle-class victims. To be recognized as victims, Black and Latina women have to show that they are better than the rest of their kind: better mothers, students, more religious, more virtuous, and so on (Madriz, 1997).

Another theme that was mentioned by a handful of participants was the relationship between victimization and the size of a woman. Jody, a 15-year-old woman, stated,

> I think the size has a lot to do with it. Tiny women, like me, are more likely to be victims. Especially tiny women who walk around looking as if they are totally out of it.

Short women match stereotypical images of weakness and vulnerability. Shortness and tallness have to do with qualities regarded as feminine and masculine in our culture. Cinderella had small feet, symbolizing her femininity. Songs in Spanish popular culture talk of small women, with cinturas y pies pequenos (small feet and waists) as the personification of the "perfect woman."

Although 75% of lone-offender violence and 45% of violence involving multiple offenders are perpetrated by someone known to the victim (Bureau of Justice Statistics, 1995b), a pervasive theme among women—irrespective of their social location—as that women were mainly victimized by strangers. Children were also represented as victims of random violence committed by strangers, although the reality is that many acts of victimization against them occur while in the hands of their parents or guardians. A study by Richard Gelles and Murray Strauss (1979), for example, showed that between 1.4 and 1.9 million children in the United States are victims of physical abuse by their parents every year.

Women as Victims Sexual Attacks. Most stories and images depicted by the participants made reference to women as victims of murders or sexual attacks, specifically rape, although a few mentioned sexual harassment on the streets as a form of victimization. Although women are victims of many other crimes—property crimes and other violent crimes, such as mugging and domestic violence—the depiction of women as predominantly victims of sexual attacks reproduces the idea that what is important about women is their sexuality (Faith, 1993).

Many of the stories shared by the participants in this study presented crimes as individual, bizarre cases of random violence, without considering in their analysis structural factors such as misogyny, patriarchy, or gender-based privileges. Indeed, a large number of women expressed a blaming attitude toward the victims. With very few exceptions, this attitude was more prevalent among White middle-class older women than among working-class young Black or Latina women. For instance, during a focus group with elderly middle-class White women, several of them expressed their feelings about women as responsible for their own victimization:

> This may be old-fashioned thinking too . . . what I have heard through the years . . . you take the young girls today. . . I think . . . oh! They are inviting trouble . . . look how some of them act when they are out on the streets . . . how they dress, leaving nothing to the imagination, and I only think about what my mama used

to say . . . you know they are looking for trouble. A decent girl should not dress like that. Yes, I agree. Especially in these days women use these tights, showing everything. And then they complain if men look or grab them or if they tell them something they don't want to hear. Especially some of the young . . . well, Black and Hispanic girls. They like to wear those very tight pants . . . or too short miniskirts. They look for it. Yes, I think they like the attention. And men, you know how they are . . . These women are inviting trouble.

These expressions not only reflect the idea that women who do not follow a certain dress code are to be blamed for the harassment and attacks that they receive, but they are also class and race based. In these images, most White middle-class women are considered to dress decently, but lower-class Black and Latina women are presumed to like showing their bodies, and they are considered "vamps." Therefore, if they are victimized, they are considered nonideal victims.

Young Latina and African American lower-class women were less likely to exhibit a blaming-the-victim attitude. They were also more likely to express their belief that a woman has the right to dress the way she wants. Clara, an African American teenager, was emphatic in her assertion that "we are not harming anybody, you know . . . I dress the way I want," she concluded. Other expressions used by Latina teenagers were "a woman has the right to dress the way she wants," "men dress the way they want, no?" or "no matter the way you dress, men harass you anyway, so why bother?" Middle-class White and African American teenagers, however, were more cautious in expressing their belief that, "although women should dress the way they want, men follow girls that dress as a hooker," Melinda, an African American teenager, claimed.

Discussion and Conclusions

Although it is clear that women do not have unified images of criminals and victims, some common themes were reported by the majority of the participants. Among others, there is the belief that there are attributes pertaining to ideal criminals and to ideal and nonideal victims. The participants' images summarized in Table 1 indicate the racialized, class, and gendered nature of these images.

Regardless of the race and socioeconomic background of the participants in this study, images of criminals are those of Black poor men, and images of victims are predominantly those of White middle-class women. Second, according to many of the participants, ideal criminals and ideal victims can be recognized by their physical characteristics. While ideal criminals are "weird," dirty, tall, and big, ideal victims look "normal," small, and tiny. Third, concurrent with the prevalent ideology of crime, criminals also differ from "us" morally or psychologically: They are dehumanized, immoral, animalistic, irrational, violent strangers—mainly murderers and rapists—who attack their victims randomly and in the streets. On the contrary, ideal victims are fragile, good, innocent, vulnerable women, unknown to the criminal and attacked—kidnapped, killed, or raped—unexpectedly.

A direct consequence of the dehumanized images of criminals is that they restrict any type of public empathy toward those who break the law. This lack of empathy favors a social

TABLE 1: IMAGES OF IDEAL CRIMINALS AND IDEAL VICTIMS REPORTED THE MAJORITY OF PARTICIPANTS

Ideal Criminals

Gender, race, and class	Male
	Blacks Latinos
	Poor, on welfare, lazy, "new immigrants"
Physical attributes	Look "weird," dirty Big, tall
Psychological/moral attributes	Bad, immoral, cruel, undeserving
	Animals, inhuman, irrational, insane
	Violent, out of control, alcoholics, insane
Relation criminal/ victim	Strangers to the victims
Characteristics related to the crime	Attacks randomly in the streets
	Violent predators
	Murderers and sexual criminals

Ideal Victims

Gender, race, and class	Female, children
	White
	Middle class, hard working average
American	
Physical attributes	Look "normal," dress properly
	Small, tiny
Psychological/moral attributes	Good, decent, deserving
	Innocent, naïve
	Passive, vulnerable
Relation criminal/ victim	Strangers to the criminal
Characteristics related to the crime	Unexpected victim
	Harmless victims
	Kidnapped, killed, tortured, raped

Note: Images of non-ideal victims were also reported by a handful of participants. These images are predominantly associated with poor young women of color who do not adhere to strict codes of behavior set for them.

climate in which more repressive policies directed toward criminals are sanctioned: tougher laws, the use of the death penalty, and opposition to rehabilitation and community programs.

Women's lives are not only controlled by images of ideal criminals and ideal victims but also by images of nonideal or undeserving victims. These are those women who do not follow appropriate codes of behavior: They dress provocatively or engage in behaviors considered inappropriate for women. Some of these images are mediated by the social position of the participants. For instance, as reported by White middle-class elderly women, representations of non-ideal victims are clearly associated with poor Black and Latina young women who do not follow appropriate codes of behavior set for women. Poor Black and Latina women, however, were less likely to express this blaming-the-victim attitude toward other women who break rigid codes of behavior set for them.

An important consequence of the stereotypical images of criminals and victims is that they explain, at least partially, why domestic crimes are not considered "serious crimes"—they do not fit prevalent images of ideal criminals and ideal victims (Christie, 1986, 20). Domestic crimes are often committed by someone known to the victim and in the "sacredness" of their home. They explain also why white-collar and political crimes are not usually considered "serious crimes." White-collar criminals do not match images of ideal criminals because they are often middle-class White "respectable" men (Sutherland, 1983).

These prevalent depictions of criminal and victim oversimplify and distort the reality of crime (Fattah, 1986). For example, popular representations of women as victims reinforce the belief that women have the monopoly on submissiveness and men on aggression, that men have control of the streets, and women belong in the home. In addition, prevailing images of White women as ideal or credible victims explain why crimes committed against women of color are not seen as "real crimes" (Estrich, 1987). Women of color do not fit classist and racist stereotypical notions of the ideal victim.

As this study shows, images of criminals and victims are not totally polarized. Situational disadvantages, such as being an immigrant and undocumented and not speaking English fluently, shape feelings of vulnerability and apprehension that heighten the expectation among some Latinas that they are more likely to be the victims of crime. Poor Latina women's views of victims are shaped by their social position: They are at the bottom of the gender, class, and racial hierarchies. In addition, they are immigrants and they don't speak English. Thus, their images and expectations are shaped by the concurrent disadvantages of Latinas.

Women's lives are controlled by images contained in the ideology of crime in different ways. First, images of the ideal victims reinforce stereotypical ideas of women as unable to defend themselves against cruel, inhuman, and insane predators. Men are stronger and more aggressive, and women are weak and passive. Second, images of ideal and nonideal victims have implicit a code of behavior (Hall, et al. 1978): avoid the streets, stay inside, avoid strangers, dress properly. This code of behavior teaches comportment deemed "respectable" for women and conduct acceptable for men, legitimizing gender differences in the name of "keeping you safe" and reinforcing the private = women/public = men dichotomy. Third, these images teach women that there are "dangerous" and "safe" men. In reality, the latter—husbands, boyfriends, and acquaintances—are more likely to victimize women. Fourth, these stereotypical images reinforce the "horror story syndrome" (Walker, 1985) by presenting images of women being tortured, mutilated, or raped as if they were commonplace, when the reality is that in statistical terms—these are rare occurrences. Fifth, images of women as predominantly victims of sexual attacks reproduce the idea that what is important about women is their sexuality (Faith, 1993). In the academic world, this has had the sum effect of pushing the research agenda on women predominantly toward only one set of crimes: sexual crimes. Finally, the representations of the ideal victims as White middle-class women imply that when Black and Latina women are victimized, they do not receive the same sympathy and credibility that is granted to White female victims because they do not match images of the ideal victim.

Notes

(1.) The names of the participants have been changed to protect their anonymity and confidentiality.

(2.) In December 1993, Colin Ferguson, a Caribbean immigrant, opened fire against commuters on a Long Island railroad car in New York, killing 6 people and wounding more than 12 before he was subdued by some passengers. This crime is a good example of the representation of the "ideal criminal" because Ferguson is a Black man, and most of his victims were white.

References

Barak, Gregg. 1994. Between the waves: Mass-mediated images of crime and justice. *Social Justice* 21:133–147.

Benedict, H. 1992. *How the press covers sex crimes: Virgin or vamp*? New York: Oxford University Press.

Bureau of Justice Statistics. 1995a. Criminal victimization 1993. In *National crime victimization survey*. Washington, DC: U.S. Department of Justice.

Bureau of Justice Statistics. 1995b. Violence against women: Estimates from the redesigned survey. In *National crime victimization survey*. Washington, DC: U.S. Department of Justice.

Cain, M. 1989. *Growing up good: Policing the behaviors of girls in Europe*. London: Sage.

Carlen, P. 1994. Gender, class, racism and criminal justice: Against global and gender-centric theories, for postructuralist perspectives. In *Inequality, crime and social control*, G. S. Bridges & M. A. Myers (eds.). Boulder, CO: Westview.

Chesney-Lind, M. 1995. Girls, delinquency and juvenile justice: Toward a feminist theory of young women's crime. In *The criminal justice system and women: Offenders, victims and workers*, B. Raffel Price & N. J. Sokoloff (eds.). New York: McGraw-Hill.

Christie, N. 1986. The ideal victim. In *From crime policy to victim policy,* E. A. Fattah (ed.). New York: St. Martin's.

Clemente, F., & M. B. Kielman. 1977. Fear of crime in the United States: A multivariate analysis. *Social Forces* 56:2.

Ehrenreich, B., & D. English. 1978. *For her own good: 150 years of the experts' advice to women*. New York: Doubleday.

Estrich, S. 1987. *Real rape*. Cambridge, MA: Harvard University Press.

Faith, K. 1993. *Unruly women: The politics of confinement and resistance*. Vancouver: Press Gang.

Fattah, E.A. 1986. *Towards a critical victimology*. New York: St. Martin's.

Fox, J.A., and J. Levin. 1994. *Overkill, mass murder and serial killing exposed* New York: Plenurn.

Frohmann, Lisa. 1991. Discrediting victims' allegations of sexual assault: Prosecutorial accounts of case rejections. *Social Problems* 33:213–226.

Gardner, Carol Brooks. 1995. *Passing by: Gender and public harassment.* Berkeley: University of California Press.

Gelles, R., & M. Strauss. 1979. Violence in the American family. *Journal of Social issues* 35:15–39.

Gordon, Margaret T., & Stephanie Riger. 1991. *The female fear: The social cost of rape.* Urbana: University of Illinois Press.

Hall, S., C. Critcher, T. Jefferson, J. Clarke, & B. Roberts. 1978. *Policing the crisis: Mugging, the state and law and order.* New York: Holmes & Meier.

Hanmer, J., & S. Saunders. 1984. *Well-founded fear: A community study of violence against women.* London: Hutchinson.

Humphries, D., & S. Caringella-MacDonald. 1990. Murdered mothers, missing wives: Reconsidering female victimization. *Social Justice* 17:71–89.

Kelly, Liz. 1991. The continuum of sexual violence. In *Women, violence and social control*, Jalna Hartruer & Mary Maynard (eds.). Atlantic Highlands, NJ: Humanities Press International.

Klein, Doris. 1995. The etiology of female crime: A review of the literature. In *The criminal justice system and women: Offenders, victims and workers*, B. Raffel Price & N. J. Sokoloff. New York: McGraw-Hill.

MacKinnon, C.A. 1993. Feminism, Marxism, method and the state: Toward a feminist jurisprudence. In *Violence against women: The bloody footprints*, Pauline B. Bart & Eileen G. Moran (eds.). Newbury, CA: Sage.

Madriz, E. 1997. *Nothing bad happens to good girls: The impact of fear of crime on women's lives.* Berkeley: University of California Press.

Merry, S. E. 1981. *Urban danger: Life in a neighborhood of strangers.* Philadelphia: Temple University Press.

Morse, J. M. 1992. *Strategies for sampling. In Qualitative nursing research*, Janice M. Morse (ed.). Newbury Park, CA: Sage.

Ortega, S. T., & J. L. Myles. 1987. Race and gender effects on fear of crime: An interactive model with age. *Criminology* 25:133–152.

Rafter, N. H. 1990. *Partial justice: Women, prisons and social control.* New Brunswick, NJ: Transaction.

Reiman, J. 1995. *The rich get richer and the poor get prison.* Boston: Allyn & Bacon.

Rusell, D. 1982. *Rape in marriage.* New York: Macmillan.

Rusell, D. 1984. *Sexual exploitation.* Beverly Hills, CA: Sage.

Rusell, D. 1985. *The secret trauma.* New York: Free Press.

Smart, C. 1995. *Law, crime and sexuality: Essays in feminism.* London: Sage.

Stafford, M. C., & O. R. Galle. 1984. Victimization rates, exposure to risk and fear of crime. *Criminology* 22:173–185.

Stanko, E. 1985. *Intimate intrusion: Women's experience of male violence.* London: Unwin Hyman.

Stanko, E. 1990. *Everyday violence: How women and men experience sexual and physical danger.* London: Pandora.

Stanko, E. 1993. Ordinary fear: Women, violence and personal safety. In *Violence against women: The bloody footprints*, Pauline B. Bart & Eileen G. Moran (eds.). Newbury Park, CA: Sage.

Sutherland, Edwin. 1983. *White collar crime: The uncut version.* New Haven, CT: Yale University Press.

Void, G. B., & T. J. Bernard. 1986. *Theoretical criminology.* New York: Oxford University Press.

Walker S. 1985. *Sense and non-sense about crime: A policy guide.* Pacific Grove, CA: Brooks/Cole.

Warr, M. 1984. Fear of victimization: Why are women and the elderly more afraid? *Social Science Quarterly* 65:681–702.

REVIEW QUESTIONS

1. What type of methodology was used in this project? How did the researcher find the women she used in her sample?

2. Would a survey have been a better way of collecting the data for this study? Why or why not?

3. What were the ethical issues for the researchers?

THINKING THROUGH THE HEART

Ann Goetting

As you read this article by Ann Goetting, you will see that she uses narrative to find out about women who have successfully left abusive relationships. By listening to the stories of the women, Goetting was able to describe some very clear symptoms and patterns that take place in abusive relationships. It isn't enough to just listen to the voices of our respondents—it is important to learn from their experiences.

Goetting, A. 1999. Thinking through the heart. *In getting out: Life stories of women who left abusive men.* New York: Columbia University Press.

The Project in Development

This book *Letting Go: Life Stories of Women Who Left Abusive Men* (Goetting, 1999) is the product of an idea long in incubation, with antecedents reaching back into my youth. My father's unpredictable episodes of rage followed by fits of hollow kindness, in the daily context of condescension, trepidation, and humiliation, introduced me to battering before it had a name. No one in the household was spared my father's wrath, which continues to affect every member of my family today. The hardest part, as I see it now, was my inability to understand what it was all about. It was that ignorance that victimized me and rendered me powerless all those years. Later, as a family studies scholar and criminologist, I was drawn to the notion of studying and teaching about family violence. The knowledge and insights gained by that work provided the framework necessary to free me, to a great extent at least, from that childhood legacy of battering. It is that sense of liberation that inspired this book.   Battering thrives on ignorance and is snuffed out by understanding. I want everyone to understand battering because I want it to stop.

The project called for biographical accounts of American women that described the battering process from inception through exit. Diversity in terms of ethnicity, age, social class, religion, geographical region, sexual orientation, and general experience was a critical consideration. There was no intention to create a representative sample, because the goal was to demonstrate patterns and provide instructive cases rather than to generalize. Armed with this vision, I set out to find the women.

A nationwide call for participants to abuse shelters and other organizations and agencies sympathetic to battered women elicited a substantial response. Additionally, a personal search concentrating on my university and community yielded several participants. I first gathered basic background information from each woman and then shifted my attention to her battering and exit processes. My work was theory driven, always focused on the patriarchy and established patterns of battering and getting out. The texts I have created to tell women's stories combine information supplied by them-from autobiographical essays, diaries, newspaper and magazine articles, letters, and interviews—with my own interpretations. Their stories are filtered through me. I met with all except two of the participants, Lucretia and Raquelle, and in all cases I was invited into their homes. I wrote a story only when I was certain that I "knew" the woman well enough.

Early on, as I approached the third or fourth essay, the original concept of the project underwent dramatic revision. It was when I was preparing Colette's story that I knew for certain that I could not sterilize women's biographies by excluding critical dimensions that may at first blush seem unrelated to the subject at hand—battering.

I had read and heard Colette's heart-rending account of her treacherous childhood that culminated in the blood-drenched suicide of her clinically depressed mother. My image of Colette in the telling is frozen in time: visiting her on a cool summer afternoon in shaded, open sunroom, her clear-eyed candor and her serene style. A small framed black-and-white photo of her fashionably suited mother as a young Frenchwoman rested on a shelf nearby. Then, as Colette concluded the story of her own battering, I heard the tale of the death by car accident of Colette's only child at age six—with whom Colette had endured and escaped years of abuse. There were more framed photos on display to relay the significance of Michelle's life and death. Here was a woman's life story whose integrity should not be violated in the name of research on battering (Riessman, 993:4) . It is only in the context of Colette's story of her youth that her account of her battering rings true.

At that point the book in progress became a collection of life stories of women who had endured and safely left abusive men—not just stories of abuse and escape. The stories are more honest this way. They are stories packed full of women's issues and human issues: contextual knowledge at its best. The thematic link is the abuse and the getting out. I revised the biographies completed before Colette's, then went on to construct the rest contextually. So now the book teaches about childhood, good and bad alike; eating disorders; homelessness; clinical depression culminating in suicide; alcoholism; sibling relationships; baby smuggling; drug trafficking; homosexuality; motherhood; and adult child-parent issues. And it provides glimpses into Puerto Rico; Israel; Star Lake, New York; Wind River Indian Reservation; professional baseball; a Michigan outlaw militia; and the dreadful personal toll exacted by the United States involvement in the Vietnam War. When placed in context, issues surrounding battering seem neutralized and perhaps even dwarfed by the other life processes and events experienced by some of these women.

The construction of the biographies progressed at a brisk and even pace and without a hitch for one year beginning in February 1995. Each essay was a joint endeavor for me and the storyteller. I sent her my first draft, and from there we revised and refined together until we were both satisfied with the product. The women were allowed choice in revealing or suppressing first names and other identifying features. Some participated in the project as a gesture of liberation—a "coming out" of sorts. Their disclosure of their identity symbolizes their pride in having escaped a life of fear and oppression. Other women chose pseudonyms and withheld other specifics in order to protect family members. Using first names only, and leaving the real undifferentiated from the contrived, was my decision.

The stories are uneven. Some are eloquently expressed and nuanced exposes, while others are stilted by comparison. The variation in tone and texture reflects the uniqueness of the teller. Some women found comfort and even elation in the reflection process from their now safe spot, while others could barely tolerate remembering. Additionally, some women were basically more verbally expressive, articulate, and uninhibited than others. These variations produced detectable differences in the biographies, making an important contribution to understanding women's diversity. That women's lives cannot be packaged in some standard way is clearly evidenced by this collection. Nevertheless, every story is worth the telling, and each makes a unique contribution to the product of our combined efforts: a better understanding of battering and getting out and their consequences.

Ethnic diversity is an important part of this collection of life stories of battered women. A small but telling research literature apprises us of the enhanced problems that battered women of color face because of their minority status (Hendrickson, 1996; Mousseau & Artichoker, 1993; Bachman, 1992; White, 1995; Zambrano, 1985, 1994; Moss et al., 1997). Six women in this book—Sharon, Lucretia, Freda, Rebecca, Annette, and Blanca—are women of color, and their life experiences, when compared with those of White women, reflect reported differences between minority and White battered women. Themes of racism as well as sexism permeate the stories of these six women in predictable ways.

I have no war stories related to the production of this book; without exception, the women were generous, gracious, and patient teachers. This feminist project has made my journey to feminism well worth the trouble (see my autobiographical essay: Goetting, 1996).

The Truth about Biography

Concerns with accuracy have surrounded the literary form of narrative or lifetelling, including biography, for a couple of decades (Goetting, 1995). Do people tell the truth about their lives? The answer to that question is succinctly articulated by the legendary Cree hunter who traveled to Montreal to offer court testimony regarding the effect of the new James Bay hydroelectric scheme on his hunting lands. He would describe the way of life of his people. But when administered the oath he hesitated: "I'm not sure I can tell the truth . . . I can tell only what I know" (Clifford, 1986:8). We tell the truth pretty much as we know it, but that may not be someone else's "truth."

Some scholars of narrative speak of lifetelling as fiction. They claim that memory is faulty and leaves but a quiver of recognition of times past, which we then adjust into story. In that sense biography is "something made," "something fashioned"—the original meaning of fiction. The claim is not that life stories are false but rather that they are interpretations constructed around a string of imperfect recollections. These scholars point out additionally that lived experience is mediated by language, which is also imperfect. Often there are not words to accurately describe what has happened to us. Lived experience is further mediated by the context in which it is told. The version offered by Colette that day in her sunroom may be different in tone and texture from the version she told her current husband during their courtship years earlier. Biography, as a special form of narrative, further "distorts" the lived experience by adding the biographer's layer of interpretation to those of the storyteller. The perspective of the biographer can add a critical dimension to a story. My biography of Colette is surely different than would be, for example, O. J. Simpson's version of that same life. In sum, biography is not simply a "true" representation of an objective "reality"; instead, memory, language, the context of the telling, and the interpretations of both storyteller and biographer combine to create a particular view of reality. The counterpoint to lifetelling as fiction rather than truth is that it is truth if truth is properly defined. It is argued that in spite of inherent distortions, lifetelling does reveal truths. These truths do not disclose the past "as it actually was" by some arbitrary standard of objectivity; instead, they are reconstructed and, therefore, superior truths. We continue through our lifetime to interpret old events from new positions. Each time, we tell the story differently, and with each telling the story matures and gains depth. My story as a ten year-old of my father's rages was different than the story I tell today of the same times and incidents. From this perspective on truth, biography is better than having been there because it adds the element of seasoned consciousness to the original experience. In the words of Georges Gusdorf (1980):

In the immediate moment, the agitation of things ordinarily surrounds me too much for me to be able to see it in its entirety. Memory gives me a certain remove and allows me to take into consideration all the ins and outs of the matter, its context in time and space. As an aerial view sometimes reveals to an archaeologist the direction of a road or a fortification or a map of a city invisible to someone on the ground, so the reconstruction in spirit of my destiny bares the major lines that I have failed to notice, the demands of the deepest values I hold that, without my being clearly aware or it, have determined my most decisive choices. (38)

Our real concern with biography is not whether it is "truth" or "fiction" but what it can teach us about human feelings, motives, and thought processes. For example, in this book we are far less interested in knowing who hit or slapped whom how often than we are with knowing how a woman feels about being hurt by her partner, how she reacts and why. Biography does not supply us with verifiable truths; rather, it offers a special kind of impassioned knowing.

A final note on truth as it applies specifically to these biographies: certainly a curiosity about "his side of the story" is reasonable. Would these women's abusers tell the same stories about the relationship? Would they minimize or deny what they are accused of in these pages? First, it must be emphasized that we live in a gendered universe, where men and women are considered to be two distinct types of people and are treated accordingly. In that sense men and women occupy two different worlds and, in so doing, define and understand little, if anything, similarly (Tannen, 1990; Szinovacz, 1983). It is no surprise, therefore, that when researchers separate couples and inquire about shared activities and the dynamics of their relationship, those couples seem to describe two different relationships altogether (Szinovacz, 1983). It is that phenomenon that inspired sociologist Jessie Bernard (1972) to title her now classic essay of American marriage "Marriage: Hers and His." Battering is no exception to the rule. Two sound studies of couples in relationships where the woman is physically abused (one, from the United States [Szinovacz ,1983]; the other, Scottish [Dobash et al., 1998]) inform us that women report more types of violent victimization and in greater frequency than their male partners admit to. Furthermore, more women than men report injuries from the abuse and, again, women report higher frequencies. All in all, women perceive more violence in these relationships and tend to judge it as more serious. I suspect that the abusers of the women in this collection would tell very different stories and that they would minimize and deny the abuse of which they are accused.

Winning with Biography

Biography enjoys popularity among readers of every stripe. It offers privileged access to understandings of the human condition in all of its complexity. The life of the emotions, the life of the mind, the physical life, and the social life are told in context to produce a comprehensive whole. It is all there within easy grasp: the obscurities, the reasonings, the motivations, the passions. German sociologist Wilhelm Dilthey touts biography as the highest and most instructive form of knowledge about humanity (translated by Kohli, 1981:126). From that perspective the best way to truly understand a category of human experience, such as escape from battering, would be through examination of a diverse assemblage of biographies focusing on that experience—in this case life stories of battered women who got out.

In addition to providing a superior method of understanding the human experience, reading biography helps us make sense of our own lives by connecting us with others. It activates us to construct a benchmark against which to compare our own existence, thereby prompting us to rethink that existence. We continually test our own realities against such stories and modify our perceptions accordingly. In that way biography transforms us. In the process of this personal transformation, this reconceptualization of our life, we typically are comforted and sometimes elated by the newfound connections that inspired the journey. Finding people in situations comparable to ours who have discovered similar truths fortifies us with consensus and affirmation. We are no longer alone and vulnerable. Jane Tompkins (1989) tells it best:

I love writers who write about their own experience. I feel I'm being nourished by them, and that I'm being allowed to enter into a personal relationship with them, that I can match my own experiences with theirs, feel cousin to them, and say, yes, that's how it is. (170)

By delivering sensitive insight and inspiring a reinterpretation of life through human connectedness, reading biography can forge informed life change. The sociologist C. Wright Mills's promise of "the sociological imagination" (1959) instructs us that insights into social context can supply the resources necessary not only to understand one's own life but to at least partially control its outcomes. Similarly, social theorist Max Weber insists that humans can succeed only if "each finds . . . the demon who holds the fibers of his very life" (Gerth & Mills, 1946: 156).

It becomes apparent that reading biography can be personally rewarding and a joy to experience. It has the potential to nourish and fortify us and to propel us into a constructive path of personal renewal. Biography represents reason informed by passion, arguably the most powerful form of knowledge production. Robbie Pfeufer Kahn (1995) refers to that process as "thinking through the heart." The women whose stories grace these pages have generously and bravely embraced this process to one point of completion, many specifically in hopes that their stories would find, inform, soothe, and intelligently activate battered women. This book personifies "thinking through the heart."

References

Bachman, R. 1992. *Dealth and violence on the reservation: Homicide, family violence, and suicide in American Indian populations.* New York: Auburn House.

Bachman, Ronet, & Linda E. Saltzman. 1995. *Violence against women: Estimates from the redesigned survey* (NCJ—1 54348). Washington, DC: U.S. Bureau of Justice Statistics. August.

Bernard, Jessie. 1972. Marriage: Hers and his. *Ms.* December: 46–49, 110–111.

Clifford, James. 1986. Introduction: Partial truths. Pp. 1–26 in *Writing culture: The poetics and politics of ethnography,* James Clifford & George E. Marcus (eds.). Berkeley: University of California Press.

Dobash, Russell, Rebecca Dobash, Kate Cavanagh, & Ruth Lewis. 1998. Separate and intersecting realities: A comparison of men's and women's accounts of violence against women. *Violence Against Women* 4(4): *382–414.*

Gerth, H. H., & C. Wright Mills (eds. & trans.). 1946. *From Max Weber: Essays in sociology.* New York: Oxford University Press.

Goetting, Ann. 1995. Fictions of the self. Pp. 3–19 in *Individual voices, collective visions: Fifty years of women in sociology,* Ann Goetting & Sarah Fenstermaker (eds.). Philadelphia: Temple University

Goetting, Ann. 1996. Ecofeminism found: One woman's journal to liberation. Pp. 174–179 in *Private sociology: Unsparing reflections, uncommon gains,* Arthur B. Shostak (ed.). Dix Hills, NY: General Hall.

Gusdorf, Georges. 1980. Conditions and limits of autobiography. Pp. 28–48 in *Autobiography: Essays theoretical and critical,* James Olney (ed. & trans.). Princeton, NJ: Princeton University Press.

Hendrickson, Roberta M. 1996. Victims and survivors: Native American Womenwriters, violence against women, and child abuse. *Studies in American Indian Literatures* 8(1): 13–24.

Kohli, Martin. 1981. Biography: Account, Text, Method. Pp. 61–75 in *Biography and society: The life history approach in the social sciences,* Daniel Bertaux (ed.). Thousand Oaks, CA: Sage.

Mills, C. Wright. 1959. *The sociological imagination.* New York: Oxford University Press.

Moss, Vicki A., Carol Rogers Pitua, Pitula, Jacquelyn C. Campbell, and Lois Halstead. 1997. The experience of terminating an abusive relationship from an Anglo and African American perspective: A qualitative descriptive study. *Issues in Mental Health Nursing* 18: 433–454.

Mousseau, Marlin, & Karen Artichoker. 1993. *Domestic violence is not Lakota/Dakota tradition.* Sisseton, SD: South Dakota Coalition Against Domestic Violence and Sexual Assault. To obtain free copy, call 1-800-572-9196, or write P.O. Box 141, Pierre, SD 57501.

Pfeufer Kahn, Robbie. 1995. Interviewing the midwife's apprentice: The question of voice in writing a cultural ethnography of patriarchy. Paper presented at annual meetings of the American Sociological Association, Washington, DC.

Riessman, Catherine Kohler. 1993. *Narrative analysis.* Thousand Oaks, CA:Sage.

Szinovacz, Maximiliane E. 1983. Using couple data as a methodological tool:The case of marital violence. *Journal of Marriage and the Family 45:* 633–644.

Tannen, Deborah. 1990. *You just don't understand.* New York: William Morrow.

Tompkins, Jane. 1989. Me and my shadow. Pp. 169–178 in *Gender and theory: Dialogues on feminist criticism,* Linda Kauffman (ed.). Oxford: Basil Blackwell.

White, Evelyn C. 1995. *Chain chain change: For Black women in abusive relationships.* Seattle: Seal.

Zambrano, Myra M. 1985. *Mejor sola que mal acompanada: Para Ia Mujer Golpeada/For the Latina in an abusive relationship.* Seattle: Seal.

REVIEW QUESTIONS

1. How did the researcher gather her respondents?

2. Why does Goetting believe that narratives are "more honest?"

3. What is the "truth about biography?"

REFLECTIONS ON ORAL HISTORY: RESEARCH IN A JAPANESE AMERICAN COMMUNITY

Valerie Matsumoto

In this article Matsumoto describes how she interviewed more than eighty individuals. However, sometimes it isn't as easy as one might think to conduct interviews. Matsumoto talks about the problems that researchers sometimes have with collecting life stories and the "insider/outsider" dynamics that develop through the interview process.

I came to Asian American history and women's history through curiosity about my own family's past. I plied my parents and grandparents with questions: How did Obaachan and Ojiichan meet? Why did they come to the United States? What was it like growing up in Oakland? How did Uncle Dewey learn to hypnotize chickens? Why was Auntie Ritsu sent to a finishing school in Japan? And then there were the questions about "camp7"" a major reference point for my parents and their Nisei friends from as far back as I could remember. It was an evocative word, used as shorthand for many experiences I could not then fathom, catching only glimpses of tar-papered barracks, bleak deserts, young people packing suitcases to go to New York or Chicago. We would sit up late after dinner, drinking tea with old friends passing through town, telling stories. "Camp7" they would say, leaning back and shaking their heads, with a sigh. "Camp."

It was my mother who answered my questions, patiently explaining about the internment of Japanese Americans during World War II, recounting her family's trips, first to the Tanforan Assembly Center and then to the dusty Topaz Camp in Utah. How they could take with them only what they could carry; how after the war, they found that their stored belongings had been looted. I remember hearing about a woman who loved and rarely shared sweets, an expensive treat in camp. On some special occasion, she finally brought forth a box of chocolates she had been hoarding. When the box was passed around, everyone could see that the candies had become stale and wormy. Through my mother's shared memories, even this woman with the wormy chocolates became an engaging human linkage to the larger forces of history.

Recently I mentioned to my mother that a distant relative had expressed interest in hearing about her wartime experiences.

"Oh, it's too hard to talk about." she said.

"But you told me about it." I was surprised. "I didn't know you minded discussing it."

"You are my child, and you needed to know."

I preface my essay with this story because it underscores the kind of connection I have with a particular part of the U.S. past, the kind of gift oral history represents, and my own ignorance of the effort it took for my mother to share this with me. These kinds of lessons have been reaffirmed throughout the course of my research in Cortez, a small

Matsumoto, V. 1996. Reflections on oral history: Research in a Japanese American community. In Diane L. Wolf (ed.) *Feminist dilemmas in fieldwork*, Boulder, CO: Westview, pg 160–169.

Japanese American farming community in central California. In addition to examining institutional records, local newspapers, and other primary documents, in 1982 I conducted more than eighty tape-recorded oral history interviews. They ranged in length from one hour to six hours.

Interviewing three generations of men and women raised many questions about feminist operating principles in the field. The process provided rich, sometimes humbling, insights into cultural and generational assumptions and necessitated frequent reassessment of my relations with individuals and the larger community. In this essay, I focus particularly on the issue of control in interviewing and on consideration of "insider/outsider" dynamics.

What feminism means to me as a researcher is not only the concern for equal rights and access for women but the effort to be mindful of the historical inequities and struggles that have shaped the material conditions of ourselves and our subjects, female and male. This includes for me, as a Japanese American scholar, attention to the complexity of race and interethnic relations, critical elements in the landscape I study. It also means trying to cultivate an awareness of social stratification and privilege and the ways in which they may affect the process of oral history interviewing.

In these aims I have been influenced by my training as a social historian. An outgrowth of the scholarly reassessment catalyzed by the social movements of the 1960s and 1970s, social history has broadened the panorama of the U.S. past to include people previously ignored as historical actors: women, racial ethnic groups, members of the working class. The language of social historians in the 1970s and 1980s included "uncovering" and "reclaiming" buried pasts, writing not only history but "herstory," acknowledging discriminatory structures while emphasizing "resistance" to them. To these ends, historians drew on an increasingly wide range of primary sources, from material artifacts to probate records and census data. Oral history interviews, long a staple method for anthropologists, proved particularly useful for gaining access to the experiences of people who left few personal written records. Such interviews lent texture and color as well as substance to the broader frameworks delineated by documentary materials such as newspapers, internment camp publications, and organizational records. In Cortez I found a wealth of primary sources, the richest and most varied of which was oral history.

The relationship between the Cortez community and me has in some ways been an unusual one. Because of the community's origin in 1919 as a planned colony and its strong constellation of institutions, its members have a deep-rooted sense of themselves as a community and of the importance of their collective history. Fortunately for me, they had already begun seeking a scholar to write their history when I started trying to locate a receptive Japanese American settlement, preferably rural, to be the subject of my dissertation. Although their plans to commission a researcher dissolved in an internal disagreement over the form (book, photo exhibit, documentary film) the completed project ought to take, they welcomed me into their homes, directed me to local institutional records, and generously shared their time and perceptions of the past.

Two families, one Buddhist and one Christian, helped me set up most of the interviews. I tried to interview at least one or two members of each Cortez family. In addition to conducting interviews with people now living in Cortez and in surrounding communities like Turlock and Atwater, I also talked with people who had grown up in Cortez but had later moved to the San Francisco Bay area. All of the surviving Issei (first-generation immigrants) met with me, as did fifty-six Nisei (American-born second generation), and nineteen Sansei (third generation). In my interviews with the nine Issei, I was fortunate to have the interpretive assistance of their children and friends; despite the limitations, these joint interviews afforded me not only a window onto community dynamics in the pioneering period of the 1920s and 1930s but also an opportunity to observe Issei-Nisei relations in 1982.

Because of the general interest in my project, many people were willing to be interviewed. Nevertheless, I encountered a fair number who felt nervous about the prospect. Even those who readily agreed often said, "Oh, my life isn't very exciting. I haven't done much. But you should talk to my neighbor, s/he's really got a lot to say." While jotting down the name of the friend with a lot to say, I hastened to explain why the interviewee's perceptions were indeed important to my gaining a full, balanced view of the community's development.

I tried to demystify the process of the interview and to give the interviewee as much control over it as possible. Because I was often introduced to potential interview subjects at community events like the Boy Scouts' fundraising pancake breakfast or a Japanese American Citizens League installation banquet, people usually had a chance to meet me first. I had prepared a set of questions (three pages, single-spaced) that I sent to everyone who expressed interest so they could see exactly what would be asked. The questionnaire followed a life-history format, tailored to include Japanese immigration, farm life, World War II internment, and gender role expectations. I told them that any questions they did not want to discuss would be omitted from the interview.

Some oral historians prefer not to give questions in advance, arguing that doing so lessens the degree of spontaneity and candor of the interview. I believe, however, that more individuals would have hesitated to talk with me had they not seen the questions. Reading the questions ahead of time, with veto power, not only alleviated anxieties but also gave people the opportunity to locate photograph albums and newspaper clippings and to verify dates and events with relatives. Actually very few asked to have any questions omitted. The subsequent interviews were generally relaxed and comfortable. Nearly all took place in the subjects' homes, with the crackle of an almond-wood fire in the background and hot green tea at hand.

In a reversal of roles, I got a taste of being interviewed myself at the outset of each session. Usually this mini-interview consisted of questions about my family, education, and interests. Although I wanted the people of Cortez to feel at ease with me and believed that I owed them information about my own history and goals, the question of how much to disclose caused me some reflection. The preliminary information established certain common ground; my telling them that my grandparents had immigrated from Fukuoka Prefecture, settled in Oakland and Orange County, California, and were interned in the Topaz and Poston Camps enabled them to place me within a Japanese American context to which they could draw connections. Indeed, one of the Cortez Nisei and I learned, after he pulled out his family genealogical tree, that we might be distantly related!

Sometimes I worried that they might censor themselves or unconsciously weight their responses to suit my perceived inclinations. Of course, the kinds of questions I asked, the fact that I was interested in women's experiences as well as men's, and my status as a Sansei woman pursuing a doctorate in history suggested certain things to them (e.g., that I might be politically liberal and inclined to feminism). I reasoned that anyone truly uncomfortable with me for this or any other reason would decline an interview, as a few individuals did. But I tried to convey my respect for the interviewees' opinions by my body language, verbal cues, and follow-up questions. On occasion, subjects would (inadvertently) begin to turn the interview into a conversation by asking my opinion of issues like gender role change or national politics. I tried to let them know that I would be happy to respond afterward, but that I wanted the interview to reflect their thoughts and concerns.

Some emotional outpourings occurred for which I was unprepared, being trained as a historian rather than a psychologist. Although I had tried to give the interviewees enough control to avoid topics they did not wish to discuss, I had not expected that certain seemingly innocuous questions might open the floodgates of painful memories. One Nisei woman, when asked, "What was it like growing up here?" suddenly began to describe the brutality of her father toward her mother and how she had felt as a child. Tears rolled down her cheeks and she started to sob, as the words continued to tumble out. I was aghast, unsure how the interview had taken this turn and what it meant. As I handed her tissues and turned off the tape recorder, my own eyes damp, I worried that I had, however unwittingly, dredged up dark memories that might haunt her even more. I suggested that we stop for the day and was surprised when she shook her head and went on speaking. When this happened again during an interview with another woman who had carried painful memories of abuse as a domestic servant for more than forty years, unspoken, I began to understand the force of the need to tell.

After both of these incidents, I worried that negative psychological repercussions might result from the opening of doors catalyzed by the process of the interview. (These revelations usually came in the middle of the interview, during discussions of childhood and adolescence, the periods when most individuals have the least control over their lives. The interviews, ranging from two to six hours in length, usually ended with positive reflections on the most memorable occasions or happiest times experienced.) It was somewhat reassuring to observe that, when each interview was finished, although I felt leaden and depressed, the women seemed lighthearted and cheerful, one of them whistling as she bustled around her house. I hope that the act of telling me their experiences provided some measure of relief. Given the parameters of my relationship with the Cortez people, I did not feel I could suggest to anyone that they seek counseling, nor was I certain that it would be appropriate.

What then, from this perspective, was my role as an interviewer with feminist concerns? I had to consider this further when I was asked to interview two individuals. This constituted another role reversal of sorts, because usually I was the one asking. In one case, an Issei man living in a nearby town had missed being interviewed for a project sponsored by his own community. His family knew that he felt bad about this and so requested that I speak with him. He gave me not only a useful perspective on the historical relations between his community and Cortez but also an expanded sense of the significance of being interviewed.

In the second case I was asked to interview someone whose relatives were concerned about the effects of the pent-up childhood suffering caused by the World War II internment. They felt that it might prove beneficial for the person to relate these experiences and thought that talking to a non-family member might be easier. Although I was willing to conduct the interview (and did), I felt nervous about what results they might expect and stated this. I was relieved to learn that they did not anticipate a miraculous transformation, although they did believe that the act of telling might in some way facilitate healing.

These two interviews particularly made me aware that others might have their own needs with regard to the interviews, and that the process might affect them in ways that I had not imagined but had to take into consideration. What made this less daunting was the fact that no one wanted me to be a counselor. Listening attentively was what I could do and what seemed to be desired. There were days on which I returned to my home base feeling something like a traveling confessional, drained by the intensity of the interaction. However, I also felt deeply grateful to be able to see the past through the eyes of others. To share in this wealth of experience was both heady and humbling. Who is an "insider" in the context of such research? Who is an "outsider"? What does this status mean for the scholar? Carrying out interviews and documentary research in Cortez afforded a variety of vantage points from which I could consider these questions. From one perspective, I appeared to be an insider, as a third-generation Japanese American with rural roots and a grounding in Asian American history. I looked, sounded, and behaved very much like other Sansei from the community, and on several occasions was in fact assumed to be a Cortez family member or relative by Japanese Americans from nearby towns.

The two families who generously hosted me during my research visits also treated me "like family," providing me with food, lodging, and emotional support as well as trying to tell me about the dynamics of various relationships within the community. The women especially offered cues and insights; their training in detecting the motivations and needs of others, and their keen observation of emotional undercurrents, greatly facilitated my research. They alerted me to the tensions in families, in addition to identifying which individuals had disagreed with each other over various community issues (e.g., whether to build a community hall or a swimming pool; draft resistance and military service during World War II). They particularly made me conscious of the tremendous amount of work involved in maintaining balanced, cooperative relations in a small, tightly knit community.

My being perceived as a species of insider, by virtue of ethnicity and family background, certainly made it easier for me to gain acceptance in the community. I think interviewees felt more comfortable, resting on common understanding. However, sometimes they assumed that I knew more than I did. Because my family had, in my distant childhood, been involved with row-crop cultivation, and the Cortez farmers have specialized in orchards and vineyards, the agricultural practices that were a matter of second nature to them seemed mysterious to me. This led to a great deal of backtracking and pleas for elaboration during interviews. Even when taken aback by my ignorance, they patiently explained the seasonal round of work.

Although in some respects I was an insider, of course I was also an outsider. I did not grow up in Cortez nor did I have any connection with the community before I began the research. I did not have to do farm chores as a child. My family lived in a town on the Arizona-Mexico border, where there were few other Asian Americans. The second language I studied was Spanish, and it was not until I went to college that I had a chance to learn even a little Japanese. Visits to my grandparents in California and Utah provided glimpses of involvement in ethnic community through their church activities, fishing trips with Issei buddies, the Japanese-language newspapers they read in the afternoon, and the tofu and fish they bought from a regular peddler. Because I had been for a number of years the only Japanese American child in a predominantly Mexican American town, the Japanese American worlds in which my cousins, aunts, and uncles were rooted appeared immensely attractive. Part of my interest in studying a Japanese American community stemmed from this naïve fascination with the workings of ethnic networks and their meaning for those who participate in them.

One of the key lessons I learned through interviewing was that I wasn't the only one experiencing the tugs of being both an insider and an outsider. Regardless of how others perceived them, many individuals—especially women who had come to Cortez through marrying local men—felt that in some ways they were outsiders as well as members. Their discussion of the groups (ranging from handicraft clubs to civic organizations) to which they belonged, within and outside the community, and their place in the web of family ties made me conscious of the multiple affiliations they maintained. And I think my being from outside made it easier for them to talk about their relation to the larger group.

It is difficult for me to assess fully the impact of my own cultural upbringing on my interactions with the women and men of Cortez. On the surface, I possessed a degree of familiarity with certain aspects of food, commonly used Japanese words, the ongoing work of affirming ties and balancing obligation, and a shared history. This facilitated my exploration of their collective past. But it is harder for me to evaluate how much I responded to them as a Sansei woman seeking approval (mostly from elders) and trying to "fit in."

Working within the community as a Japanese American, I tried to follow the practices of social grace as much as possible, within the constraints of a limited graduate student budget. For example, this meant finding ways to convey my appreciation, especially for the hospitality of the two host families with whom I stayed alternately for seven to ten days at a stretch, making trips back and forth between the San Francisco Bay area and Cortez. Because they were farmers with bountiful kitchen gardens, I did not feel I could bring those staple offerings of Japanese American gratitude, fruit and vegetables. Instead I baked cookies, which met the criteria of being a consumable and appropriate token gift. (Fruit, *manju*—a Japanese confection, and cookies were the offerings of choice for two other Asian American women I know who have carried out Japanese American oral history projects.) I did not make this decision as a researcher considering the expectations of subjects, but rather as a Sansei woman conscious of the generosity extended to her and desirous of making some acknowledgment, however small. For the majority of the people who helped me, feeding me with history and okazu, many thanks and the completed dissertation manuscript were the only return I could make.

I have referred to myself as a "Sansei" because it was an important aspect of how I acted and was perceived within the community: as the grandchild of Japanese immigrants with a history much like that of the Cortez farmers. I also draw attention to my generational standing because it provides clues to my relational perspective on the Issei and Nisei, as well as my blind spots. Like many Sansei, I am more familiar with the world of the Nisei than of their parents, the Issei. Although I knew the outlines of their patterns of work and settlement and understood that arranged marriages were the custom among them and that relationships within the prewar family were in key ways different from those in the postwar period, conducting interviews in Cortez opened my eyes to generational differences I had missed.

One of the last questions in the interview particularly revealed the assumptions I had unconsciously made. I always ended a session with summing-up questions that reviewed the interviewee's life to date: "What was the happiest time in your life?" "If you had your life to live over, would you do anything differently?" "Is there anything I have not asked that you would like to add?" These questions seemed to work well. However, it became clear that one question to which Nisei responded readily posed problems of translation for the Issei: "What was the most exciting event in your life thus far?" The Nisei who translated for me struggled to ask this question. It became, "What was the most memorable event you experienced?" The fact that the question could not be asked in the same way in both languages made me aware of the nuances that I was missing in the Issei's responses, due to my lack of facility with Japanese. It also alerted me to differences in ways of perceiving and thinking about the world.

The responses to this question further underscored generational and cultural differences. Nearly all of the Nisei men and women said that getting married and the birth of their children were the most exciting events they had experienced. By contrast, the Issei did not cite these occasions. Instead, they talked about something that they had experienced alone, often linked with nature. For one Issei, it was a spiritual revelation; for another, it was seeing the sun setting behind Mount Fuji as his ship set sail for America. One woman described a night she still remembered vividly. She was working as a nursemaid for a Japanese consular official in Washington, D.C., from 1927 to 1930. Young and far from home, she felt lonely for her parents and familiar surroundings. One night when the diplomat and his wife were away attending a social function and all was quiet, she went outside by herself. She looked up and saw the beautiful full moon, and thought, "My mother and father in Japan may also be looking at the moon." Suddenly she felt connected to her family by the shining moon, and her loneliness disappeared.

For the Issei, whose marital partnerships were arranged by their parents, getting married meant crossing the threshold of adulthood but it did not include expectations of romantic love. Affection was viewed as an outgrowth of a relationship, not a prerequisite. The Nisei, however, who had giggled when their European American teacher gave a good-bye kiss to the husband who brought her to school, who had watched Clark Gable and Carole Lombard on the silver screen, had formed different hopes and dreams. Their attitudes about marriage reflected the norms of the larger U.S. society in the 1940s and 1950s. As a historian I understood and expected this, but somehow I was still surprised by the contrast in responses. I was much struck by how one generation chose events involving groups of people as "most memorable" and how another generation focused on individual experiences. Because there were so few surviving Issei, I was not able to proceed very far with this line of analysis, but it provided a salutary jolt to my thinking.

My relationship with the Cortez families did not end with the last interview. I have remained in touch with the two families—the Babas and the Yuges—who hosted me within the community; they have continued to keep me informed of local news. This has most often been, sadly, notification of the death of individuals I interviewed. These families have also served as intermediaries between me and the larger Cortez community, transmitting information back and forth.

I felt it was important for the community to have an opportunity to give feedback about the study. When I completed my dissertation in the fall of 1985, I sent several copies, bound and also looseleaf (so that people could easily make more copies). I told them that the manuscript would be further revised in preparation for publication and solicited their comments so that I could make changes. They were eager to see their history published and, with their usual efficiency, set up a network to facilitate the distribution of manuscripts for local review. A number of people sent tactful notes directing my attention to the misspellings of names and other such mistakes; two families returned helpfully marked copies. All of the suggestions I received related to the correction of factual inaccuracies (e.g., errors regarding maiden names and the number of miles between Cortez and Turlock). No one took issue with my interpretation; the only criticism that seeped back to me was someone's remark about how "scholarly" the dissertation was, which indicated, I think, that this person found the historiography a bit dry. The overall response was very encouraging. I am particularly grateful to the individuals who patiently read yet another draft.

As the manuscript progressed through revisions, and publication began to loom closer, like a long-awaited harvest, the Cortez families scoured their trunks and photograph albums for pictures that could be used as illustrations. Through another well-coordinated effort, they sent me nearly one-hundred photos of all sizes and ages, capturing community events and family milestones. Eleven were chosen for the book through a process of my indicating my wishes and the community's preferences to the production editor, who relayed these concerns to the press's art department, who then assessed the reproduction quality of the submissions.

Due to a series of factors including an auspicious coincidence and some delay in the publication of *Farming the Home Place: A Japanese American Community in California, 1919—1982,* a book party planned by the Cortez people for the fall of 1993 snowballed into a large community celebration in the spring of 1994. They decided, because 1994 would the seventy-fifth anniversary of the founding of Cortez, and because of the appearance of the book in 1994, to expand their annual community picnic into a reunion. Nisei and Sansei around the country responded enthusiastically; 600 people registered to attend the two-day event on April 30 and May 1, 1994. I was honored to be invited to be the guest speaker and to sign books (an academic author's dream).

I felt both excited and nervous as I drove through the San Joaquin Valley toward Cortez. It wasn't my first return trip, but I still worried: Would I recognize everyone I had met before? Would I remember names, and who belonged to which branch of which family? Would I feel like an awkward intruder at someone else's high school reunion? Insider/outsider anxieties resurfaced. I quickly discovered that many people returning to Cortez, or visiting it for the first time as inlaws and distant relatives, harbored similar uneasiness. My fears (and theirs, too, I think) soon evaporated in the warm outpouring of goodwill and affection. Nisei reminisced about childhood adventures and marveled at new farmhouses on short bus tours of Cortez. At the Japanese American Citizens League Hall, the community's all-purpose meeting place, parents and children clustered around an extensive photo exhibit, seeking familiar faces and telling stories. On the second day, families converged on the grounds of a local elementary school for the annual picnic. While Nisei and Sansei tossed horseshoes, played bingo, and watched a volleyball tournament, shrieking Yonsei (fourth-generation) children took part in games and races in which all participants won prizes. We ate hot dogs and beans. I happily signed many copies of *Farming the Home Place.* People I had heard about but never met came up to introduce themselves, providing more pieces for the sprawling historical jigsaw puzzle. The picnic ended with two traditional events: all children were issued water guns, with which they promptly and thoroughly drenched each other; and as parents carted away their dripping offspring, Nisei and Sansei men and women swiftly cleaned the grounds, packed up the food, and dismantled and hauled away tents, tables, and chairs. Everyone (including me) departed to continue smaller-scale family reunions throughout Cortez.

Doing research in the Cortez community taught me valuable lessons, as I emphasized in my speech at the evening banquet on April 30. The process made visible to me some of my own assumptions about generational perspectives, shaped as they are by gender, culture, and age. It gave me a chance to experience and observe the multiple layers of affiliation and difference that create insider/outsider identifications, and showed me how they vary according to context. Conducting oral history interviews caused me to reflect on the responsibility of the researcher to the subject, as well as on the meaning of being interviewed. And it has made me increasingly mindful of the gifts of trust and insight that sustain our work as scholars.

REVIEW QUESTIONS

1. What is "herstory?"

2. What does feminist research mean to this researcher?

3. Why do some oral historians prefer not to give questions in advance?

Chapter 10: Existing Statistics, Content Analysis, and Historical Data

You have learned in the previous chapters the various ways of collecting data and conducting research that are most common to social science researchers. In this chapter, you will learn about different types of research that do not involve your own data collection. Rather, in this chapter you will learn about three different types of research that involve using data that has already been collected by someone else.

The first type of research involves using **existing statistics** that may come in the form of numerical information, reports, and other official documents. Using existing statistics would be ideal for a project where the goal is to find out about information that has been collected by large bureaucratic organizations. Often this data is gathered for policy decisions or as a public service. Existing statistics can be used as supplemental data for any topic you are interested in. For instance, suppose you are writing a report about the positive aspects of private education. You may look for statistics that have been gathered by the Department of Education and find the differences in SAT and ACT scores between private and public high school students. In other types of research, it might not make sense for you to collect all of your own data from scratch. Using existing data can save you time, money, and energy. And at the same time, existing statistics give you a place to begin figuring out what you will be studying.

Using existing statistics is most appropriate when the researcher is interested in testing a hypothesis that involves variables that can also be found in reports by official agencies such as those that address economical, political, and social conditions. There is so much existing data available for you to look at that it can be mind-boggling. Much of existing data is free and can be found either on the Internet or in your library. Some examples of **primary existing data** would be the following:

- *Statistical Abstract of the United States*, which was published the first time in 1878, has been published annually since then. The *Statistical Abstract* is a compilation of official reports produced by over 200 U.S. government and private agencies. Many other governments publish similar reports. For instance, Canada produces the *Canada Yearbook* and New Zealand publishes *New Zealand Official Yearbook*.

- *Standard and Poor's Register of Corporations, Directors and Executives* lists over 37,000 U.S. and Canadian companies and provides information on the corporations, their products, officers, and sales figures.

- *Dictionary of American Biography* was first published in 1928 and updates information regularly. The *Dictionary* lists the careers, travels, and titles of publications by famous people.

- *Vital Statistics on American Politics* provides information on the campaign spending practices of every candidate for Congress. It details their primary and final votes, ratings by various political organizations, and a summary of the voter registration regulations by state.

• *The General Social Survey* (GSS) is a regular, ongoing study that has been conducted using personal interviews of U.S. households conducted by the National Opinion Research Center (NORC). The sample sizes for this project has been around 1500 for each of the 19 years the survey has been conducted. Each interview lasts about 90 minutes, and the data from this study would be beneficial if your project is in any of the following areas: Economic Studies, Education Studies, Epidemiology & Public Health Studies, Health Services Studies, Statistics & Methodology Studies, and Substance Abuse, Mental Health, and Disability Studies.

Here is another example. Let's say you were interested in conducting a project to investigate if the rates of HIV/AIDS is higher in some countries than others. To begin, you could go to the U.S. Census Web site at http://www.census.gov. Using their subject A–Z listing, you would look under A and find a section called HIV/AIDS then HIV/AIDS Surveillance, where you can find the HIV/AIDS Surveillance Data Base. From here you could find the HIV/AIDS prevalence rate of various countries and them compare (U.S. Census Bureau, 1999). You could then incorporate the U.S. Census data into own your research project and draw some of your own conclusions about some of the differences you find.

Existing statistics can also come from **secondary data**, which allows you to reanalyze the data from a previously collected survey. The primary focus for using secondary data is on the analysis rather than on the data collection. This type of data is used more frequently because it is inexpensive, it permits comparisons between individuals, groups, and nations, and it allows for replication. It also permits new research questions to be asked that were not asked in the previous study.

CONTENT ANALYSIS

Another type of research is **content analysis.** This involves quantitative measurement of the content of messages and communications being studied. In other words, content analysis is a technique for gathering and analyzing the content of where the researcher can study cultural artifacts to look for trends, patterns, and themes. There are a lot of cultural artifacts such as books, films, fashion, textbooks, and billboards that can be used in this type of analysis. The key to content analysis is that the data is not created for the purpose of the study, but rather the data are found the way they are and then studied systematically (Reinharz, 1992).

For instance, Brabant and Mooney (1997) were interested in sex role stereotyping in the Sunday comics. The researchers believed that while women's social positions had changed during the last 20 years, the media had not portrayed that change at all. Using studies conducted in 1974 and 1984 as guides, Brabant and Mooney collected cartoons in 1994 and analyzed each strip for the frequency or appearance of husbands and wives, where they were located (inside or outside the home), tasks they were doing, frequency of reading appearances, and whether or not the wives wore an apron. The researchers wanted to see if there was a difference in the way gender roles were portrayed between years. The authors found that even though male appearances inside the home increased, female appearances were higher than males over the three-time period. Furthermore, while women who wore aprons decreased over time, men were never pictured wearing aprons.

In another example, Kinnick (1998) compared the newspaper coverage of male and female athletes during the 1996 Summer Olympic Games. The profiles of athletes in five leading U.S. newspapers were examined for incidence of gender bias in reporting and photography. Although the study found evidence of gender bias for a number of criteria, female athletes were found to have received similar or more favorable treatment than male athletes, and no evidence of gender bias was found in terms of quantitative representation of female athletes or in the placement and prominence of stories. This study suggests that the coverage of female athletes has been improving.

Although items such as the Sunday comics or a photograph of a female athlete standing alone do not really mean to much to us, a content analysis has implications for the way people, items, or behaviors are portrayed to the rest of us.

Historical Research

The third type of research that you will learn about in this chapter is called **historical research**. History looks at past and present events, which can include diaries, graduation records, maps, religious artifacts, books, court transcripts, clothing, or photographs. While you might think that historical research is really only about gathering the facts about a significant event, such as a war in order to document it, historical method is not just gathering those facts, but interpreting them. Without the interpretation, there is no research.

The historical researcher makes an effort to go back as far as possible to the primary source. A **primary source** gives the direct outcome of specific events or experiences in someone's life. Let's say you want to research the life of women in the 1920s in a specific area, you would use primary sources such as newspaper clippings, diaries, and eyewitness accounts of the women's lives. You would want to give meaning to the lives of the women you are researching. Using the primary sources ensures the integrity of the study you are conducting.

Using **secondary sources** are just as valuable as the firsthand accounts of the events. Although the secondary sources are at least once removed from the primary sources, they can give you important information about the primary sources. Secondary sources can include bystanders who were not involved in an incident, but were given accounts by someone who was there. The main problem with secondary sources is how much trust you can put in the secondary sources understanding of the primary sources.

The main problems a researcher has conducting historical research is making sure that the data is reliable and valid. This is accomplished through authenticity and accuracy. **Authenticity** is also known as external criticism because it asks if the data are genuine or fake. It isn't always easy to tell if the document is truly a primary source. However, authenticity is established based on indicators such as the printing techniques used, the language, the writing styles, and when the document was established. **Accuracy**, also known as internal criticism, is concerned with the trustworthiness of the source. For instance, if you are investigating teen behavior in the 1940s and your source suggests that teens were promiscuous, would you find that trustworthy considering what you know about events during that period of time?

INFOTRAC COLLEGE EDITION SUGGESTED READINGS AND DISCUSSION QUESTIONS

Using InfoTrac College Edition, type in the words "Census data" to locate articles such as "Trends in Asian American racial/ethnic intermarriage: A comparison of 1980 and 1990 census data" (Article A20915052). There are many other articles that use sex, race, or religion as variables. Find 5 articles that use the Census data and address those variables. Explain how the researchers used the data. Was the data used for the entire study or was it just used to find out preliminary information?

REFERENCES

Boetcher Joeres, R. E., & Laslett, B. 1993. Personal narratives: A selection of recent works. *Signs,* 18(2): 389–392.

Brabant, S., & Mooney, L. A. 1997. Sex role stereotyping in the Sunday comics: A twenty year update. *Sex Roles*, 37(3/4): 269–281.

General Social Survey Data [ONLINE] http://www.norc.uchicago.edu/gss/homepage.htm

Kinnick, K. N. 1998. Gender bias in newspaper profiles of 1996 Olympic athletes: A content analysis of five major dailies. *Women's Studies in Communication*, 21(2): 212–228.

Miles, M., & Crush, J. 1993. Personal narratives as interactive texts: Collecting and interpreting migrant life-histories. *Professional Geographer,* 45(1): 84–95.

Posavac, E. J., & Carey, R. G. 1997. *Program evaluation: Methods and case studies.* Englewood Cliffs: Prentice Hall.

Reinharz, S. 1992. *Feminist methods in social research.* New York: Oxford University Press.

U.S.Census Bureau. 1999. Estimates of HIV-1 Seroprevalence [ONLINE] http://www.census.gov/ipc/www/hiv1.html

WHAT SOCIOLOGISTS DO AND WHERE THEY DO IT— THE NSF SURVEY ON SOCIOLOGISTS' WORK ACTIVITIES AND WORKPLACES

Robert J. Dotzler and Ross Koppel

In this article, data from the National Science Foundation Survey of Doctoral Recipients was used to investigate what sociologists do besides working in an academic setting. The researchers found that only 45.8% of Ph.D. sociologists actually teach sociology and that as a discipline other jobs that a sociologist could have, besides teaching are either ignored or dismissed. Rather than sending out a survey and asking sociologists what they do as a job, the researchers were able to use existing data that had been collected by the National Science Foundation, which saved not only time, but money.

Introduction

Sociologists' self-perceptions are inconsistent with the reality of their professional activities. The discipline *as taken for granted* sees itself primarily as professors teaching sociology. Recent data from the NSF survey of Ph.D. sociologists, however, reveal that this view is anachronistic and more wrong than right. Less than one-half of all sociologists—45.8%—teach sociology. The majority of our colleagues spend their days managing and administrating, conducting applied or basic research, teaching in areas other than sociology, and engaging in a wide range of tasks that are divergent from the traditional image.

We do not know why sociologists persist with a traditional, classroom-based image, but we do know that this image is profoundly consequential to the way sociologists interact with each other and with the larger society. As a discipline we tend to ignore or dismiss the *doing* of sociology in favor of the *teaching* of sociology or of theoretically focused research. As a discipline, we usually view sociology's use in society as something teachers do on the side—a perception that these data show to be false. Moreover, we argue that the perception is detrimental to the influence and role of sociology. Consider the role of the other sciences, both the social and the physical. Are their statuses and strengths *eroded or enhanced* by their practitioners? Are economists, biologists, psychologists, physicists, or anthropologists perceived as working primarily within the classroom? Sociology appears to be special in its adherence to a traditional image, despite its distorting and ultimately disempowering effects.

This report on sociologist's activities and types of employment is based on the 1995 Survey of Doctorate Recipients, which is produced every 2 years by the National Research Council under contract with the National Science Foundation. The survey was conducted the week of April 15, 1995, of all individuals with an earned doctorate. We were

Dotzler, Robert, J., and Ross Koppel. 1999. What sociologists do and where they do it—The NSF survey on sociologists's work activities and workplaces. *Sociological Practice: A Journal of Clinical and Applied Sociology,* 1(1): 71–83.

fortunate to obtain support and encouragement from NSF staff and contractors who devised many tables for this research.

We envision this article as the first of several that provide insight into our profession, our work lives, and our labor supply and demand. In future publications, we expand our analysis to include information on cohort effects (e.g., the great job dearth of the 1970s; see Koppel, 1993), quality! status of Ph.D. granting institutions, pay differences by employer type, gender, and region.

In this first analysis of the data we ask:

- What do sociologists do? What are the principal tasks and job descriptions?

- Where do sociologists work? What proportion are in academic institutions, in practice settings, in private industry, in not-for-profits?

- How do academic and practicing (applied) sociologists differ in their principal tasks?

A general caveat: It is probable that those in applied fields and in non-education institutions were more difficult to find and less likely to respond than sociologists in academe. Thus, we suspect, but cannot document, systematic underrepresentation of applied/nonacademic sociologists in all of the data presented here.

Most sociologists work in educational employment settings. However, as we shall see, many of those in educational institutions do not teach and, even of those who teach, sociology is not always the subject.

Table 1 gives us a sense of the size of the profession as well as the distribution between educational and noneducational employers for those with earned Ph.D.s up to age 76—a figure of 12,221. Of these, approximately five-sevenths (72.9%) work in educational institutions; about two-sevenths (27.1%) do not. The latter figure of 27.1% represents some 3300 Ph.D. sociologists working outside of educational institutions. Note that the data are weighted to reflect the actual number of sociologists in the profession. The actual sample size is 1300.

Before we review the analyses of tasks sociologists undertake, we briefly present a disaggregation of the findings on employer type.

Table 2 reflects the distribution for those employed by educational institutions. We can see that fully 83.7% of the almost 9000 Ph.D. sociologists working in educational institutions work in the traditional four-year college setting. Note that 6.5% of those in educational institutions work at "university research" jobs; medical schools represent another 3.5%. Precollege education occupies less than 1% of sociology's teachers.

Of the 3300 or so working in noneducational institutions (see Table 3), we see that about one-quarter (24.9%) are in private for-profit institutions; another one-quarter (25.3%) are in private not-for-profit institutions. Almost one-fifth (19.5%) are self-employed, and almost 30% work in government: state, local, military, and federal.

By combining Tables 2 and 3 (see Table 4), we get a sense of the great diversity of employment settings. Although educational institutions still predominate, a notable percentage of sociologists work in private, private not-for-profit, government, and self-employment settings.

We now shift focus from employer category to the more central question of principal job codes. Moreover, we examine these data for all sociologists (Table 5). We present the information for sociologists in education (left-hand column); sociologists in noneduca-

TABLE 1. TYPE OF EMPLOYER[A]

	Number	Percent
Educational institution	8,901	72.9%
Noneducational institution	3,310	27.1%
Total	12221	100%

[a]All data for Ph.D. sociologists employed during week of April 15, 1995; weighted 1995 SDR data. Actual sample size, 1300.

TABLE 2. TYPE OF EDUCATIONAL EMPLOYER

	Number	Percent
Precollege education	63.1	.08%
College		
2-year	406.2	4.6%
4-year	7451.3	83.7%
Medical School	313.9	3.5%
University research	579.9	6.5%
Other	87.1	0.9%
Total	8901.6	100%

TABLE 3. TYPE OF NONEDUCATIONAL EMPLOYER

	Number	Percent
Private for profit	823.8	24.9
Private not for profit	835.8	25.3%
Self-employed	614.2	19.5%
Government		
State and local	459.8	13.9%
Federal and military	512.7	15.5%
Other	63.6	1.9%
Total	3,309.77	100%

tional settings (middle column), and all sociologists combined (last column). These data are among the most powerful to emerge from this recent NSF survey of sociologists. They are based on the respondent's own classification of "best principal job code."

Look first at the left column, which comprises principal tasks for those employed by educational institutions: The leading category, not surprisingly, is teaching sociology

TABLE 4. TYPE OF EMPLOYER FOR THOSE IN EDUCATIONAL
AND NONEDUCATIONAL SETTINGS

	Number	Percent
Private for profit	823.8	6.7%
Private not for profit	835.8	6.8%
Self-employed	614.2	5.0%
Government		
State and local	459.8	3.8%
Federal and military	512.7	4.2%
Other noneducation	63.6	.5%
Precollege education	63.1	.5%
College		
2–year	406.2	3.3%
4-year	7451.3	61.0%
Medical School	313.9	2.6%
University research	579.9	4.7%
Other	87.1	.7%
Total	12,211	100%

(62.7%). This is followed by management (15%) and by sociologists teaching subjects other than sociology (16.3%). Sociologists as sociologists—presumably research and practice—is next at 4.6%. (We are obliged to use categories employed by the National Science Foundation's questionnaire and data reduction structure (cf. National Science Foundation 1995a, 1995b, 1996a, 1996b).

Look next at the middle column, which comprises principal tasks for those employed by noneducational institutions. We see that management and administration is the modal category, at 38%—almost two-fifths of the group. Sociologists (as researchers, policy experts, etc.) are another 17.1%. These are followed by "other social sciences," 8.6%; computer systems experts, programmers, and analysts, total 5.2%; clergy, 4.5%; entertainment, TV, and the arts, 3.9%; and judges/lawyers, 3.4%.

Now, we move to the data and column that we find most revealing—the combined or "both" column, on the right. The most significant finding is the fact that, when examined as a discipline, less than one-half—45.8%—of sociologists teach sociology. This is, we argue, a noteworthy and oft-ignored reality of our profession.

Other notable findings in this right-hand column include:

- It is striking that 20.3% of all sociologists work in management and administration. That is, slightly over one-fifth of all Ph.D. sociologists concern themselves primarily with coordination, administration, or management of organizations, government agencies, educational institutions, policy, etc.

- As we saw in the other columns, sociologists as "sociologists" comprise another 8% of the profession.

TABLE 5. BEST PRINCIPAL JOB CODE FOR SOCIOLOGY PH.D.S WITH EDUCATION EMPLOYERS, NONEDUCATION EMPLOYERS, AND BOTH TYPES OF EMPLOYERS[A]

	Education Employer (%)	Noneducation Employer (%)	Both
Clergy and other religious		4.5	1.2
Computer science programmers, analysts	0.2	5.2	1.8
Health workers	0.2	5.2	1.9
Artists, TV, public relations		3.9	1.0
Lawyers, judges	0.2	3.4	1.1
Management and administration	15.0b	38.0	20.3
Statisticians	0.2	3.3	1.0
Sales and service		4.2	1.5
Economists	.02	1.0	0.4
Psychologist and clinical		2.4	0.7
Sociologists	4.6	17.1	8.0
Other social scientist	1.0	8.6	3.1
Elementary education	0.2		0.1
Secondary-social sciences	0.2		0.1
Postsecondary teaching			
Sociology	62.7	45.8	
Assorted, not sociology	16.3		11.7
Social workers		1.8	0.5
Other occupations	0.2	1.5	0.4
Totals	100	100	100
(wt. N)	8.901.6	3,309.7	12,211

[a]Numbers do not equal 100% because of rounding, which is exacerbated by collapsing of cells.

- Teaching other social sciences in postsecondary educational settings totals 11.7% of all sociologists. This includes teaching of psychology, social work, health specialties, law, computer science, marketing and business, math, and education.
- Work in computer systems and programming occupies less than 2% of the profession.
- Note that very few are working as statisticians (1%), social workers (0.5%), and psychologists (0.7%).

These new NSF data allow us to extend the analysis of what sociologists do (Table 6). Specifically, the survey asked respondents about their primary work activity—a question that allows more nuanced responses than the previous question on "best principal job code." We present these findings for sociologists in noneducational institutions.

These data manifest the work of practicing sociologists, who apparently are occupied with conducting applied research, running institutions or agencies, advising clients

TABLE 6. PRIMARY WORK ACTIVITY OF SOCIOLOGY PH.D.S EMPLOYED IN
NONEDUCATIONAL INSTITUTIONS

	Number	Percent
Accounting, finance, contracts	170	5.1
Applied research	1,116	33.7
Basic research	74	2.2
Computer applications, programming, systems development	253	7.6
Development	120	3.6
Design	88	2.6
Employee relations	41	1.2
Managing and supervising	575	17.4
Production, operations, maintenance	3	0.1
Professional Services	354	10.7
Sales, purchasing, marketing, customer service, public relations	217	6.6
Quality or productivity management	27	0.8
Teaching	94	2.8
Other	177	5.4
Total	3,309	100

or colleagues, building computer systems, and making money (for the institutions, if not themselves).

- Fully one-third, 33.7%, are engaged in applied research as their *primary* activity.

- Managing, leading, planning, coordinating, developing, designing, and supervising occupies almost one-half of the work of nonacademic sociologists (48.1%), if we add: managing and supervising (17.4%); employee relations (1.2%); sales, purchasing, marketing, customer service, and public relations (6.6%); quality or productivity management (0.8%); professional service (10.7%); production, operations, and maintenance (0.1%); design (2.6%); development (3.6%); and accounting, finance, and contracts (5.1%).

We emphasize that the exact meaning of some of these categories has not been defined entirely to our satisfaction. As noted previously, we are dependent on the classifications established by the NSF survey. We understand, for example, that "professional service" refers to dealing with clients or performing professional sociological work. Thus, this category could easily be considered "applied research."

The questions reflected in the previous two tables required sociologists to select one major category to define their "primary work" or "best job code." Of course, our work lives often defy a single definition or single category. Often our work days or work weeks are too diverse to be reflected in one designation. The next table and set of comparisons address that reality. Table 7 (below) reflects the work at which the respondents spend 10 hours or more per week. As might be expected, the question, from which it is derived, allows multiple responses—reflecting the fact that there is more than one 10-hour period in a week..

TABLE 7. MAJOR WORK ACTIVITIES (10 HOURS OR MORE PER WEEK) OF SOCIOLOGY
PH.D.S IN EDUCATIONAL INSTITUTIONS, NONEDUCATIONAL INSTITUTIONS, AND BOTH

Work Activity	Education Employer (%)	Noneducation Employer (%)	Both (all, %)
Applied research	52.8	59.1	54.5
Management and administration	37.7	55.2	42.4
Employee relations	26.2	41.9	30.4
Computer applications	18.2	35.8	23.0
Accounting, finance, contracts	9.0	32.0	15.2
Sales, purchasing, marketing	7.1	31.3	13.7
Development	10.5	28.5	15.4
Professional services	17.3	26.8	19.9
Quality and productivity management	6.2	24.4	11.1
Design	5.9	23.5	10.6
Basic research	58.3	16.8	47.1
Teaching	90.5	15.2	70.1
Production, operations	0.6	3.5	1.3

Moreover, just as in the format for Table 5, we provide these data for sociologists: (1) employed in educational institutions, (2) employed in noneducational institutions, and (3) all sociologists (both groups combined). Thus, the left column shows the breakdown of major work activities for sociologists in education; the middle column shows the breakdown for sociologists employed by noneducational institutions; and the last column is for the combined population.

This table contains several powerful discoveries:

- The first row reveals that over 50% of those employed by both educational and noneducational institutions spend at least 10 hours or more per week of their time on applied research. Almost 53% of those employed by educational institutions spend at least 10 hours per week on applied research; the comparable figure for those with noneducational employers is 59.1%. This is a finding of signal importance. It reflects a central reality (versus the current image) of sociology as something other than pedagogy and supports the need for greater attention to sociological practice and the use of sociology in society.

- The second row illustrates the large role that management and administration occupies for *both* those employed by educational institutions and those who are not in educational institutions. "Management and administration" is a major job for almost two-fifths of academic and for four-sevenths of the nonacademic samples. Moreover, as we have seen in the previous analyses, if we add the time spent on accounting, employee relations, productivity management, development, etc., it appears that most sociologists are involved in several forms of management and supervision. This finding is consistent with the earlier tables and reflects a theme we have seen before.

- We are surprised by the differences in basic research. Almost three-fifths of those employed by educational institutions state that this is an important time allocation, whereas less than one-fifth of those who are not in educational institutions make similar claims. Frankly, we thought there would be more similarities between the two groups. Perhaps there is some normative pressure or ambiguity in definitions. Similarly, we were very surprised to see the noneducational institution employees spending almost twice as much time with computer applications as the educational employees. Perhaps academe is less digital than we thought or the nonacademic world is more high-tech than we supposed.

- Of course, teaching predominates among the educational employees, but we note that almost one in six noneducational institution employees is involved in teaching.

Implicit in several of the tables reviewed above is the question: why are some people in academe and others in practice? We do not have as complete an answer as we would wish, but we can address some elements of that question.

The NSF survey asked if one's current work is related to one's doctorate (Table 8). This is a question that must be examined in light of a heavy dose of cognitive dissonance. Nevertheless, the results are of interest. Note that, at this point, we have data only for those *not* in educational institutions. (Was the assumption that all those in educational settings are working in areas related to their doctorates?)

We find that even for those employed in nonacademic institution, slightly over two-fifths (41.1%) state their work is closely related to their doctorates, while another two-fifths (41%) report that their work is somewhat related. Thus, less than one-fifth (17.8%) state that their work is not related to their doctorates.

As we suggested above, there is much room for individual conceptual wiggling about what "related" means and the interpretations of both doctorate and current work. Nevertheless, over 82% of those not in educational settings claim their work is related to their doctorates. We await data on those in educational settings.

We are able to examine the reasons *why* work is not related to doctorate for those with noneducation employers. In the first of two tables (Table 9) more than one answer is possible: The major response is "job not available," although "pay/promotion" and "location" are also frequently noted. This is not a surprising finding.

The next table (Table 10) presents the findings where only the *most important* reason is allowed. We see the importance of nonavailability of a job in one's field. Note that "family," which was given in the earlier table, is not listed here.

Summary and Conclusions

Our major findings confront what we argue is a false and anachronistic image of what sociologists do. The data reported here, tabulated for this study by the National Science Foundation, reveal that most sociologists are not primarily classroom teachers of sociology. Moreover, even if we include all classroom-based sociologists in the analysis, most of the members of the profession spend most of their time working on applied research, administering and managing, advising on policy or programs, and dealing with computers, contracts, or clients.

TABLE 8. IS WORK RELATED TO DOCTORATE FOR THOSE EMPLOYED IN NONEDUCATIONAL INSTITUTIONS?

	Number	Percent
Closely related	1361.7	41.1%
Somewhat related	1356.8	41.0%
Not related	591.3	17.9%
Total	3309	100%

TABLE 9. IF WORK NOT RELATED TO DOCTORATE, WHY?

	Number	Percent
Pay and promotion	265	44.9
Working conditions	227	38.4
Location	264	44.7
Career change	205	34.7
Family	50	8.5
Job not available	332	56.3
Other	137	23.2

Note: More than one answer is possible.

TABLE 10. IF WORK NOT RELATED TO DOCTORATE, MOST IMPORTANT REASON FOR THOSE WITH NONEDUCATIONAL EMPLOYMENT

	Number	Percent
Pay and promotion	115	19.5
Working conditions	64	10.8
Location	14	2.3
Career change	54	9.1
Job not available	227	46.9
Other	64	10.8
Total	591	100

What we find is that a lot of sociologists are out in society practicing sociology. We suggest that this is a valuable activity both for our discipline and for society. Our concern is that our failure to reflect this reality within the discipline undermines our strength as a profession. How we understand what we do and how we present ourselves to others is consequential. (Need we recite W. I. Thomas's dictum?) Until very recently, however, the

American Sociological Association (ASA) devoted limited attention to the practice of sociology. We argue that the ASA and sociologists, for the long-term health and integration of the discipline, should devote more resources to the practice sector.

Our data address the reality and the image of sociology as a strictly university-based profession. We argue that the "use-value" of sociology is as meaningful as its "knowledge-value." Any reasonable understanding of the role of social sciences in society suggests that neither will flourish without the flowering of both. The rise of the "market" perspective and of the focus on a discipline's role in society, even within the walls of academe, calls for a better balance between "use-value" and "knowledge-value" within the discipline.

Contrary to the views of many (e.g., Halliday & Janowitz, 1992), these data indicate that a large number of Ph.D. sociologists work in roles very different from those of the college-based teacher/scholar. Our objective, however, is not to challenge academic sociology. We want to see it grow and flourish. Our argument is that it will grow and flourish best if the practice side of sociology is better cultivated and understood by sociologists across the board. The creation and expansion of jobs in the sociological practice sector depend in no small way on the university-based sociologist's understanding of and involvement with this sector. Equally important, the perceived and actual utility of sociology as a discipline is enhanced by sociological practice. Both academe and practice will benefit if sociologists are equipped technically and intellectually for work in practice. This will require a transformation of our current graduate programs.

We envision this article as the first of several that examines the NSF sociology Ph.D. dataset. We hope to provide insight into our work lives and into our labor supply and demand, cohort effects, pay differentials, quality/status of Ph.D.-granting institutions, gender, part- and full-time status, and region. We are negotiating with the NSF to obtain the dataset so that we can run multivariate analyses and can free the NSF staffers from their roles as intermediaries—although they have been both kind and helpful.

We hope that better information about what sociologists do will help all of us better understand, guide, and use our discipline in society.

References

Halliday, Terence, & Morris Janowitz (eds.). 1992. *Sociology and its publics: The forms and fates of disciplinary organization.* Chicago: University of Chicago Press.

Koppel, Ross. 1993. Looking for the "lost generation" in the wrong places. *ASA Footnotes,* May, 1993.

National Science Foundation. 1995a. *Guide to NSF Science and Engineering Resources Data, NSF 95-318,* Arlington, VA.

———. 1995b. *NSF Survey Instruments Used in Collecting Science and Engineering Resources Data,* NSF 95-317, Arlington, VA.

———. 1996a. *Selected Data on Science and Engineering Doctorate Awards, 1995.* NSF 96-303, Arlington, VA.

———. 1996b. *Characteristics of Doctoral Scientists and Engineers in the United States, 1993.* NSF 96-302, Arlington, VA.

———. 1997. Characteristics of Doctoral Scientists and Engineers in the United States, 1995. NSF 97-319, R. Keith Wilkinson. Arlington, VA.

REVIEW QUESTIONS

1. How is the data for the National Science Foundation Survey of Doctoral Recipient collected and how often?

2. What did the researchers find out from the survey they used?

3. Do you think they should have sent out their own survey, rather than having used the existing data? Why or why not?

AIDS AND THE MEDIA: A LOOK AT HOW PERIODICALS INFLUENCE CHILDREN AND TEENAGERS IN THEIR KNOWLEDGE OF AIDS

Diane Kholos Wysocki and Rebecca Harrison

While some might not think AIDS can affect children and teens, it does. Therefore, it is important to know what type, and the amount of, information children and teens are receiving about the disease. It is also important to know if they receive enough information to keep them from becoming infected. This research uses content analysis to find out if children and teen periodicals from 1982, when it became apparent that AIDS was a deadly disease, to 1989, when the data collection ended, actually gave children valuable information.

Acquired Immune Deficiency Syndrome (AIDS) was unknown before 1981. By the fall of 1987, however, the majority of America's public had at least heard about AIDS through some form of media (Goodwin & Roscoe, 1988). In a poll conducted *Newsweek,* 91% of those people who responded indicated that their awareness of AIDS was due to exposure given by the mass media. It is likely, then, that popular media such as magazines and television are shaping both the adult and adolescent view of AIDS.

Because researchers generally agree that media is an important source of public information (Goodwin & Roscoe, 1988), it becomes important to study how American media portrays AIDS. Of primary concern is how media influences our nation's children, whom without correct information could become a high-risk group for contracting Human Immunodeficiency Virus (HIV). The purpose of this study is to determine how popular magazines geared toward children and adolescents are reporting on AIDS, and what effect they might have in influencing a young person's current belief, knowledge, and attitudes.

The Risk of AIDS Among Adolescents

As of March 31, 1989, there had been 89,501 cases of AIDS reported in the United States (Centers for Disease Control [CDC], 1989). The CDC did not separate adult and adoles-

* Wysocki, D. K., & Harrison, R. 1991. AIDS and the media: A look at how periodicals influence children and teenagers in their knowledge of AIDS. *Journal of Health Education*, 22(1): 20–23.

cent cases of AIDS prior to 1986. Between 1986 and 1988, however, 335 adolescent cases of AIDS ranging in age from 13 to 19 years had been reported (Centers for Disease Control, 1989). These figures maybe conservative due to reluctance of high risk adolescents who are also drug abusers to seek medical attention. In addition, it is estimated that 21% of people currently diagnosed with AIDS are young adults between ages 20 to 29 (Tolsman, 1988). Because the virus frequently lies undetected for 8 to 12 years prior to diagnosis (Flora & Thoresen, 1988), these adults probably became infected during their teenage years. It seems, therefore, that a substantial number of adolescents are at risk for AIDS.

Reasons for this risk vary. Most commonly, sexual activity is the primary mode of HIV transmission among adolescents. In a 1986 Lou Harris poll conducted for Planned Parenthood, 57% of teenagers sampled reported having sexual intercourse by age 17 (Skeen & Hodson, 1987). In some communities the age of first intercourse was found to be as low as 12 years. An informal survey conducted by Renshaw (1989) in her Maywood, Illinois, clinic, found that of the 100 males and females sampled, the average age of first intercourse was 12.5 years and 14.5 years, respectively. In contrast, Zelnick and Shah's (1983) study found that the average age of first coitus experience was about 16 years old. Although studies vary as to the exact age of first intercourse experience, it is evident that this experience does frequently take place within the teenage years. In addition, although most of this early sexual behavior is between males and females, the Kinsey Institute has estimated that 4 in 10 adolescent males participate in some form of homosexual behavior. Brooks-Gunn, Boyer, and Hem (1988) believe that over 10% of adolescent males have had at least one homosexual experience. Thus, many adolescents maybe at risk for AIDS through both heterosexual and homosexual activity.

This risk is increased by the fact that few teenagers use protective measures such as condoms. A study done by Jaffe, Seehaus, Wagner, and Leadbeater (1988) found 46.2% of minority females between the ages of 13 and 21 never used condoms during vaginal intercourse and 74% never used condoms during anal intercourse. Sexually transmitted diseases such as chlamydia, syphilis, gonorrhea, and pelvic inflammatory diseases are found in highest numbers among teenagers 15 to 19 years of age, suggesting a high rate of unprotected activity (Brooks-Gunn, et aI, 1988). Sexual abuse and incest provide other avenues for HIV transmission to both young children and adolescents. Reports of abuse are steadily increasing and the rate of incestuous abuse among young females has quadrupled since the early 1900s (Russell, 1986). One study by Russell showed that of 930 subjects, 16% reported at least one incestuous experience before age 18 and another 12% before age14.

Another mode of HIV transmission within the adolescent population is sharing needles for intravenous drug use. Unfortunately, accurate statistics reporting the prevalence of teenage drug use are lacking. Miller and Downer (1988) estimated that 61% of seniors in high school have experimented with some kind of drugs for recreational purposes, and 1% of high school seniors have used heroin, with a much higher rate existing in inner-city areas. Other studies estimate that over 200,000 teens have tried injecting drugs (Brooks-Gunn, et al., 1988). It is likely that due to reluctance of adolescents to report accurately about such things as sexual activity and drug use, these estimates are low. Another concern is that some unknowingly will come into sexual contact with those that do inject drugs.

Additional possible sources of HIV transmission among adolescents are injecting steroids, sharing needles for piercing ears, tattooing, and becoming "blood brothers." Thus many behaviors place teenagers at risk for contracting AIDS.

Adolescents' Knowledge of AIDS

With so many adolescents currently at risk, AIDS education and awareness can be an important instrument to help prevent infection. Yet a 1986 survey that examined the existing AIDS education programs for the U.S. Conference of Mayors, found that only one-third provided any type of AIDS information. As a result, few adolescents have adequate knowledge about AIDS. Goodwin and Roscoe (1988) found that in their sample of 495 university undergraduates, 2 % (nine students) were very knowledgeable about AIDS, but two-thirds of the respondents possessed only moderate knowledge. DiClemente, Zorn, and Tenoshok (1986) looked at the level of AIDS knowledge, beliefs, and attitudes among 1,326 San Francisco adolescents, aged 14–18. Their findings showed that some knowledge of AIDS was present: 92% knew that one way of contracting AIDS was through intercourse, but 60% did not know that using condoms during intercourse can lower the risk of contracting AIDS. A Massachusetts study found even more discouraging results: 96% had heard about AIDS, yet only 15% of those who were sexually active were taking any precautions such as using condoms. In addition, the Massachusetts study found that many adolescents believed AIDS could be transmitted by kissing, sharing eating utensils, toilet seats, and donating blood. Studies such as these indicate that the AIDS information that adolescents receive is inadequate.

Adolescents, AIDS, and the Media

Current research suggests that AIDS is portrayed selectively by the media. The media, specifically popular magazines, have played a significant role in constructing and maintaining the view that AIDS is a "gay disease." Moreover, the mass media is judgmental in the way they portray the person with AIDS, showing primarily homosexuals, drug users, and prostitutes as the subjects of those media articles reporting on AIDS victims. By portraying people with AIDS as inherently different from adolescents, adolescents are given a false sense of security. As a result, they are at a greater risk for infection.

Method

For this study, we reviewed all periodicals (*n* = 79) geared toward children and adolescents, as identified in *Magazines for Libraries* and the *Children's Magazine Guide* under the sub-headings "teenagers" and "children." Of these 79 periodicals, a total of 13 had published articles pertaining to the subject of AIDS dating from January 1983 to April 1989, as shown in Table 1.

All articles were obtained except those contained in *Choices, Contact, Current Event,* and *Current Science.* These publications are not available in any libraries in the Phoenix Metro area, suggesting that they are minor publications with limited circulation. After reviewing the general content of each article, it was decided that even though *Rolling Stone* was listed under the subheading "teenagers," this magazine was not geared toward children and adolescents. For this reason, *Rolling Stone* was excluded from the analysis. This final sample consisted of 46 articles from eight periodicals (Table 2).

TABLE 1: FINAL SAMPLE OF ARTICLES

Current Health. Some Fact About AIDS. October 1988, p. 7.
Jack and Jill. Who Will Sit by Stevie? December 1988, p. 41.
Junior Scholastic. AIDS: The New Killer. October 16, 1987, p. 4.
Junior Scholastic. AIDS in America. March 25, 1988, p. 2.
Junior Scholastic. The Hidden Face of AIDS. March 25, 1988, p. 9.
Junior Scholastic. Epidemics in America's Past. March 25, 1988, p. 8.
Junior Scholastic. AIDS Around the World. March 25, 1988, p. 5.
Junior Scholastic. What You Should Know About AIDS. March 25, 1988, p. 6.
Junior Scholastic. What Do You Think About AIDS? May 20, 1988, p. 15.
National Geographic. Uganda: Land Beyond Sorrow. April 1988 p. 468–491.
Scholastic Update. AIDS: How Teenagers Are Meeting the Crisis. October 16, 1987, p. 17.
Scholastic Update. AIDS: Today's Most Deadly Challenge. April 20, 1987, p. 19.
Scholastic Update. AIDS: Working Together to Meet the Crisis. October 16, 1987, p. 5.
Scholastic Update. An AIDS Patients Fight for Life. April 20, 1987, p. 4.
Scholastic Update. Do AIDS Teens Have a Right to School. October 16, 1987, p. 27.
Scholastic Update. How Other Nations Cope with AIDS. October 16, 1987. p. 30.
Scholastic Update. Medicine's Race for a Cure. October 16, 1987, p. 22.
Scholastic Update. The Human Impact of AIDS: Four Cases of Altered Lives. October 16, 1987, p. 6.
Scholastic Update. The Sudden Spread of the AIDS Epidemic. October 16, 1987. p. 32.
Scholastic Update. What You Need to Know: The Lack of AIDS Information. October 16, 1987, p. 18.
Scholastic Update. Who Should Take the Test for HIV and Why? October 16, 1987, p. 21.
Scholastic Update. Who will Pay the High Cost of AIDS? October 16, 1987, p. 28.
Scholastic Update. Your Constitution: Is Disease a Legal Handicap. April 20, 1987, p. 12.
Scholastic Update. DataBank/Portrait of the Crisis. October 16, 1987, p. 4.
Scholastic Update. Mobilizing Against AIDS. October 16, 1987, p. 8.
Scholastic Update. What Our Top Doc Prescribes on AIDS. October 16, 1987, p. 10.
Scholastic Update. Four Teens on the Frontlines. October 16, 1987, p. 15.
Science World. A Ray of Hope for People with AIDS? January 12, 1987, p. 12.
Science World. AIDS and the Immune System. March 9, 1987. p. 5.
Science World. AIDS Update. January 15, 1988, p. 6.
Science World. AIDS Update: Report on AIDS. October 16, 1987, p. 21.
Science World. AIDS Update: Will There Be a Vaccine? September 18, 1987, p. 12.
Science World. AIDS: An Unknown Distance Still To Go. November 18, 1988, p. 18.
Science World. AIDS: The Facts. March 9, 1987, p. 9.
Science World. Home Tests of AIDS? April 7, 1989, p. 2.
Science World. Mosquito and AIDS. October 2, 1987, p. 19.
Science World. The Hidden Face of AIDS. March 25, 1988, p. 23.
Science World. The Virus Is Evolving Faster Than Anyone Expected. November 6, 1987, p.13.
Science World. What You Can Do About AIDS. November 18, 1988, p. 3.
Science World. AIDS Update: Will There Be a Cure? September 4, 1987, p. 19.
Science World. The Threat of AIDS. May 20, 1988, p. 20.
Seventeen. AIDS: An Up to the Minute Report. March 1988, p. 244.
Seventeen. Taking Action Against AIDS: The Story of Stacy and Ed. August 1988, p. 201.
Seventeen. We Must Protect the Rights of AIDS Victims—For Our Own Sake. October 1986, p.104.
Seventeen. What You Should Know About AIDS. November 1985, p. 24.
Teen. Teens & AIDS: What You Should Know. June 1987, p. 92.

TABLE 2. PERIODICALS THAT CONTAINED AIDS ARTICLES

Periodical	Number of Articles in Year							
	83	84	85	86	87	88	89	Total
Choices					2	3		5
Contact						1		1
Current Events			1	3	2	1		7
Current Health						1		1
Current Science			1	4	3	2	3	13
Jack. and Jill						1		1
Junior Scholastic					1	6		7
National Geographic						1		1
Scholastic Update					17			17
Science World					8	5	1	14
Seventeen			1	1			2	4
Teen					1			1

Note: Rolling Stone was listed as a teenage magazine, but we did not include it in this sample. Article are through April. 1989

Results

Extent of Coverage
Of the 46 articles used for this sample, no magazine published any articles on AIDS during 1983 and 1984. In 1985, one article was published. One article was published in 1986 and 27 in 1987. A decline was evident in 1988 with 16 articles published, and only one article on AIDS was published in 1989.

For analysis, each year was divided into four quarter. Articles within each quarter were then coded according to where they were placed in the magazine. Placement of articles was almost evenly distributed throughout all four quarters: 29% occurred within the first quarter, 29% in the second quarter, 16% in the third quarter, and 26% in the fourth quarter. Articles ranged in length from one-third of a page to four pages, with the exception of a 23 page pictorial essay in *National Geographic* In addition, *Scholastic Update* had one issue devoted entirely to AIDS. It was concluded that positioning and brevity of the articles suggest that magazines did not consider AIDS an important topic.

Basic Knowledge

Most of the articles covered basic information about AIDS. Fifty percent of the articles noted that AIDS is caused by a virus. Forty-four percent referred to AIDS as a virus that attacks the immune system, and 35% stated that AIDS is life-threatening or fatal. Two articles discussed the complexities of mutant RNA and its relationship to HIV, and four felt that AZT would eliminate some of the symptoms of AIDS. *Teen* Magazine was the only one to mention the symptoms of AIDS, such as severe weight loss, high fevers, and fatigue. The article, however, did not explain how to differentiate between the symptoms of AIDS and other illnesses. Thirty-three percent of the articles stated that AIDS could not be transmitted through casual contact. One-third explained that AIDS can be transmitted sexually, 40% wrote about intravenous drug use as a mode of transmission, and 30% simply stated that AIDS was transmitted through cuts or by blood. *Current Health* magazine suggested that "children are the least likely to get AIDSS and the few who did become infected, received it from their mothers.

Prevention

Most of the articles gave no information about how to protect one's self or others from contracting or transmitting AIDS, and the balance provided only minimal information. Only three articles said anything about safe sex. *Teen* discusses the importance of using condoms, but fails to explain how to put them on properly or where and what kind to purchase.

This article also suggested that readers avoid french-kissing. The November 1985 issue of *Seventeen* instructs readers to use a condom during vaginal or anal sex, avoid contact with semen during oral sex, and avoid french-kissing anyone in a high risk group. Three years later in March 1988, *Seventeen* suggested to readers that HIV does not live in saliva and that condoms are not 100% effective, reflecting scientists' growing knowledge of AIDS. Hotline numbers and information were given in only 16% of the articles. None of the articles mentioned that people are generally infected and capable of infecting others for 8 to 12 years before diagnosis. Only one article mentioned that it takes six months for the virus to appear in the blood stream after initial infection. This article did not, however, explain how someone might mistakenly think themselves not infected and therefore unable to transmit the disease during this time. Eight percent mentioned using condoms as a way of not transmitting the virus, while the benefit of using a spermacide such as Nonoxynol 9 was mentioned by only six%. Eight percent of the articles stated that people are not at risk if they practice abstinence, oral sex, or have only one partner, but none of the articles definded the term "abstinence," which would likely be unknown to most teens. Similarly, it was not made clear that serial monogamy could be a risk factor for AIDS, in that each time a person develops a new sexual relationship, that person is again potentially exposed to HIV infection even if the relationship remains monogamous for its duration.

Conclusion

It is indisputable that children and adolescents are at risk for AIDS. Behavioral changes in sexual activity promoted by accurate AIDS education is of paramount importance to reduce the risk of AIDS infection. Without accurate education from many sources, the necessary behavioral changes most likely will not occur. Appropriate education about AIDS should come from all possible sources, but especially from schools, parents, television, and magazines. As shown in this study, magazines geared toward children and teenagers are failing to provide a sufficient quantity and quality of information about AIDS. Children and adolescents who fail to get correct information will be unable to make sound choices about their lifestyles, and therefore will be unprotected against AIDS. Because media is the way in which children and adolescents get most of their AIDS information, media such as magazines and television must become more responsible in the information they provide to their young readers.

References

Brooks-Gunn, J., Boyer, C. B.. & Hem, K. (1988). Preventing HIV infection and AIDS in children and adolescents. *American Psychologist,* 43: 958–964.

Carroll. L. (1968). Concern with AIDS and the sexual behavior of college students. *Journal of Marriage and the Family,* 50: 405–411.

Centers for Disease Control. (1989). Update: Heterosexual transmission of Acquired Immunodeficiency Syndrome and Human Immunodeficiency Virus infection— United States. *Morbidity and Mortality Weekly Report,* 38: 423–433.

DiClemente, R. J., Zorn, J., & Tenoshok, L. (1986). Adolescents and AIDS: A survey of knowledge, attitudes, and beliefs about AIDS in San Francisco. *American Journal of Public Health,* 76: 1443–1445.

Flora, J. A., & Thoresen, C. E. (1988). Reducing the risk of AIDS in adolescents. *American Psychologist,* 43: 965–970.

Goodwin. M. P., & Roscoe, B. (1988). AIDS: Student's knowledge and attitudes at a Midwestern university. *Journal of College Health,* 36: 214–222.

Herber, M. (1987). *Living with teenagers.* New York: Basil Blackwell.

Jaffe, L. R., Seehaus, M., Wagner, C., & Leadbeater. B. J. (1988). Anal intercourse and knowledge of Acquired Immune Deficiency Syndrome among minority-group female adolescents. *Journal of Pediatrics,* 112 (6): 1005–1007.

Miller, L. & Downer, A. (1988). AIDS: What you and your friends need to know—A lesson plan for adolescents. *Journal of School Health,* 58: 137–140.

Renshaw. 0. (1989). Sex and the college student. *Journal of College Health,* 37: 154–157.

Russell. 0. (1986). *The secret trauma.* New York: Basic Books.

Skeen. P., & Hodson, 0. (1987). AIDS: What adults should know about AIDS (and shouldn't discuss with very young children). *Young Children,* 65–70.

Tolsman. D. (1988). Activities of the Centers for Disease Control in AIDS education. *Journal of School Health.* 58: 133–136.

Zelnick. N. I., & Shah, F. K. (1983). First intercourse among young Americans. *Family Planning Perspectives, 15*: 64–70.

REVIEW QUESTIONS:

1. Why wasn't the magazine *Rolling Stone* used in this analysis? Should it have been?

2. What other questions could the researchers have asked of the data?

3. Do you believe that if the same study were done now, the results would be different? Explain why or why not?

U.S. PRAIRIE AND PLAINS WOMEN IN THE 1920S: A COMPARISON OF WOMEN, FAMILY, AND ENVIRONMENT

Dorothy Schwieder and Deborah Fink

Interested in historical research, Schwieder and Fink investigated how rural women living in Iowa and South Dakota during the 1920s had significantly different experiences of their environments. The researchers used both qualitative and quantitative methods to compare the women in terms of their housing, access to water, childbearing, and family life.

An impressive body of scholarship on rural midwestern women has portrayed the Midwest as a homogeneous whole, at least from the perspective of women. Diaries, memoirs, and letters from rural midwestern women have shown them running poultry operations, canning garden produce, milking cows, and filling in where needed on the farm. Off the farm they constructed social networks with neighbors and family, served as the backbones of rural churches, and through civic activities helped form the core of rural communities. Much of what European American rural midwestern women did was similar to that done by their sisters in rural areas of western Europe. Without denying the many activities that rural women shared broadly, this paper makes the opposite point: even within the Midwest, given its several subareas with differing geographic conditions, the lives of prairie and plains women diverged markedly. Contrasting the conditions in the bordering states of Iowa and South Dakota, we establish differences between the prairie and plains environments in terms of farm women's work, their possibilities for socialization, and their economic resources. The contrasting mix of work, socialization, and leisure for women in the two areas produced not just a shade of variation, but a profoundly different rural experience for women.(1)

We use both qualitative and quantitative methods to delineate the contrast between the prairie and plains. Beginning with a general physical description of the two subregions and a discussion of settlement patterns, we then contrast early-twentieth-century narratives of a rural plains family in Lyman County in central South Dakota and a rural prairie family in Benton County in central Iowa. We compare the women of these families in terms of their housing, their access to water, their social spheres, their childbearing, and their economic resources. While comparing the narratives produces clear contrasts, these contrasts in themselves do not warrant conclusions about the broader social reality. Personal narratives provide rich detail and insight about small numbers of people, but they must be used with caution in delineating the broader picture. Those who have left detailed accounts of their lives are, for that reason alone, unusual. To establish a broader demographic context for these narratives, we use census data to explore the statistical parameters of the prairie-plains contrast. To do so, we compare demographic data from the 1920

Schwieder, D. & Fink, D. 1999. U.S. prairie and plains women in the 1920s: A comparison of women, family, and environment. *Agricultural History*, 73(2):183–197.

federal census from two townships in Lyman County, South Dakota, with two townships in Benton County, Iowa.(2)

Benton and Lyman Counties differed significantly in their geographical and environmental characteristics. Benton County is located in a part of Iowa receiving from thirty-two to thirty-six inches of precipitation per year; this placed the county in the prairie region of the state. Before white settlement, tall grass, sometimes as high as eight to ten feet, covered this area, with trees mostly along rivers and streams. Typically the topography of the prairie was gently undulating land, crisscrossed occasionally with rivers and streams. In effect, approximately four-fifths of the state lay in the prairie region where agriculture has generally been defined as intensive and where, with limited exceptions, farm families have produced substantial crops of corn, oats, hay, and hogs. Like farm families elsewhere, Iowans suffered from low market prices, particularly in the 1890s and 1930s, but crop production levels remained fairly consistent, particularly from 1900 to 1920.(3)

By contrast, Lyman County straddled the 100th meridian and lay within the Great Plains proper. Here, rainfall averages eighteen inches per year, placing the county at the upper end of the precipitation range (ten to twenty inches per year) for semiaridity. This rainfall, moreover, was unpredictable and yearly totals were subject to wide variations. In addition to the erratic rainfall, the plains environment was subject to extremes of heat and cold and strong winds that imperiled both crops and settlers.(4)

Because of marked differences in physical conditions, particularly rainfall averages, the settlement experiences in Benton and Lyman Counties have been substantially different. Benton County was organized in its present form in 1843; Lyman County, which had been a part of the Brule Indian Reservation until 1890, did not attract substantial numbers of white settlers until after 1900.(5)

Benton County shared the experience of most Iowa counties in that settlement moved across the state from east to west, in a steady, methodical manner. Five frontier zones emerged, the first in southeastern Iowa in 1833 and the last in extreme northwestern Iowa in the latter 1860s and 1870s. Benton County was located in the second frontier zone. Once settled, each zone experienced some out-migration, but in general, the entire state remained well populated from original settlement on.(6)

Lyman County's location within a more volatile geographical area led to a somewhat erratic settlement pattern. Unlike Iowa, with its steady, uniform settlement pattern, South Dakota's settlement reflected the extreme weather conditions peculiar to the plains. White settlers first arrived in the late 1850s in what eventually became southeastern Dakota Territory. In the 1870s discovery of gold in the Black Hills brought a rush of prospectors into the territory, but the agricultural, frontier really took place between 1878 and 1920. The first major migration of people into the central part of the state, known as the Great Dakota Boom, took place between 1878 and 1887, years of unusually high rainfall. In 1887 dry years had returned and drought conditions prevailed until 1897. Settlement in the central part of South Dakota (statehood was conferred in 1889) was semipermanent, however, as during periods of heavy rainfall, settlers moved further into the region to farm, and during times of drought, they retreated eastward.(7)

Typical of Dakota's boom and bust cycles, economic conditions improved after 1900, as farmers began to experience the Golden Age of Agriculture; one more time, thousands of settlers moved into the state, mostly into the area west of the Missouri River. Prosperity rested partly on more favorable weather conditions, which predominated until severe drought again appeared in 1910 and 1911. After 1911 a period known as the Second Dakota Boom took place, as agricultural conditions improved and continued through World War I. Although settlers in central South Dakota believed they could replicate the prairie farming patterns that many knew from Iowa, Minnesota, and other Midwestern states, they sustained this pattern for only a short time, eventually concentrating on wheat and cattle production rather than primarily corn production.(8)

In the 1890s Louise Jakobsen and Tinus Anderson arrived in Dakota Territory, a part of the large Norwegian immigration coming to take up land under the Homestead Act. Louise and Tinus had courted while in Norway and married soon after they arrived in Buffalo County, located in eastern South Dakota. In 1904, seven years after their marriage, the Andersons, along with three of Louise's nephews recently arrived from Norway, moved west across the Missouri River and relocated in Lyman County. The area was newly opened for settlement and probably the opportunity to acquire land through the Homestead Act influenced the decision to relocate. The move actually preceded the building of the railroad through Lyman County and the extended family members traveled the distance, some 120 miles, by covered wagon. Soon after arriving in Lyman County, the oldest of the nephews, James Jenson, and another recently arrived immigrant, Magdelena Amundson, were married in the Anderson home. Like the Andersons, James and Magdelena, or Maggie as she was always known, had courted in Norway and made plans to marry in the United States. The Andersons and Jensons then homesteaded adjoining quarter sections in Presho Township.(9)

For the next seventeen years, until Tinus Anderson returned to Norway in 1921, the lives of the Anderson and Jenson families were almost one and the same. Living across the road from each other, family members interacted on a daily basis. Tinus and James helped each other herd cattle from Buffalo to Lyman County in 1904. The two men assisted each other in constructing houses for their families. They traveled together to Chamberlain, some forty miles east, to buy lumber, and they traveled to White River, some fifteen miles south, to obtain tree branches for roofing the temporary livestock shelter. Louise and Maggie helped each other with domestic tasks and assisted each other during childbirth. The two families spent holidays together as well as traveling together to Presho to attend the Norwegian Lutheran Church, where all the Jenson and Anderson children were baptized. In her family history, Clara Jenson, the oldest child of James and Maggie, wrote that members of the two families particularly enjoyed listening to the phonograph owned by Emma Anderson, the oldest offspring of Louise and Tinus. Clara recalled that "the records were the cylinder kind and did we enjoy going to [the] Andersons to hear that." She also wrote that at Christmas time, "we always had a Christmas tree . . . and mother made all the Christmas goodies we shared with the Tinus Andersons and the George Jenson families."(10)

Life on the plains proved difficult. Initially, both families lived in one-room dwellings, probably best described as claim shanties. The year of their arrival, Lyman County experienced extreme drought, described as one of the driest years on record. For the next three years, rainfall was heavier than normal, but in 1909 rainfall decreased. That year the U.S. Weather Bureau recorded 3.5 inches of rainfall in the county. In 1915 the county received 30 inches of rainfall, but it was so cold that the corn did not fully mature and the hay was of poor quality.(11)

Even in years of above-average rainfall, securing an adequate water supply for both domestic and agricultural use was difficult. In her study of the West River country of South Dakota, Paula Nelson writes that "the search for water could become a dominating force in a homesteader's life." Nelson notes that on the plains, unlike areas to the east, many settlers "struggled for years to locate a dependable water supply on their claims, but without success."(12) Nelson cites the example of a Lyman County family, the Otto Dunlaps, who beginning in 1905 labored repeatedly but unsuccessfully to sink a well that would provide the family with a dependable water supply. Otto Dunlap finally built a stock dam that provided water for both livestock and household use. The Dunlaps had earlier lived on an Iowa farm with a good water supply, and they discovered life in South Dakota to be "very different." Unlike the Dunlaps, many families had to haul water from rivers and streams, sometimes fifteen miles away. To help offset the water shortage, settlers put out every available barrel and bucket to collect water when it rained.

Families settling on the plains experienced volatile weather when blizzards struck, often several times a year. Not only did bad storms occur in winter months, but frequently late in the spring. Only one year after arriving in Lyman County, on 8 May 1905, the Andersons and Jensons experienced a fierce late-spring blizzard. Cattle drifted before the wind from the Bad River in adjoining Stanley County into the western part of Lyman County, a distance of some thirty miles. Throughout the area, thousands of cattle, horses, and sheep perished. Residents soon discovered that "two good years out of five" for crop production meant they could probably survive. During many years of subaverage rainfall, physical tasks mounted as water had to be pumped or hauled for livestock, household use, and gardens.(13)

Louise and Tinus had two daughters and one son born in Buffalo County and one son born in Lyman County. The Jensons had four daughters and two sons, the first child born in 1905 and the last in 1911. While the four Anderson children were each born two years apart, the six Jenson children were born one year apart. No doubt, Louise Anderson's help with child care and household tasks was invaluable to Maggie Jenson during her confinements. As their families expanded, both the Andersons and Jensons added a room to their original dwellings.(14)

Even though the close kinship tie between the families made every phase of life easier to endure, along with thousands of other settlers on the plains, the Andersons and Jensons discovered that life there brought many hardships. While the two families lived only five miles from the nearest town of Presho, dozens of families in the county lived some twenty miles or more from the nearest community, making it difficult to market crops and livestock; the distance also meant greater social isolation. A Lyman County history containing the accounts of dozens of pioneer families refers frequently to the difficulty of reaching the nearest physician when family members became ill.(15)

For some fifteen years, the close relationship between the Andersons and Jensons, first in Buffalo County and later in Lyman County, continued. But in 1911, that relationship altered when Louise Anderson died from cancer. At the time, the four Anderson children were ages six, eight, ten, and twelve. Four years later, Tinus married Pauline Olson, an acquaintance from Norway who immigrated to Lyman County in 1915 at Tinus's invitation. The couple had two children and in 1921, at Pauline's insistence, the family returned to Norway. Although family accounts indicate that Tinus was reluctant to leave Lyman County, it is possible that the drop in farm prices in 1920, following the termination of government agricultural supports after World War I, helped convince him to give up farming in South Dakota. While Pauline and Tinus lived in Presho Township, their relationship with the Jensons was good, but apparently the two families did not enjoy the extremely close relationship that existed before Louise's death.(16)

Some four hundred miles to the east and some thirty-five years earlier, two other families put down roots near Atkins, Iowa. In 1868 Joseph Gongwer left Ohio and traveled west to Benton County, Iowa, to farm. Two years later he married a local woman, Martha Smythe; the couple had two sons, Ira and Archie, but only Ira survived to adulthood.(17) At about the same time, Belden and Carrie Smith migrated from New York State. They had married in 1865 and arrived in Benton County several years later. By 1870 they had purchased a farm located some four miles east of the Gongwer farm. The Smiths had one daughter, Daisy.(18)

Although farm families faced many difficulties in the post-Civil War years, farm life in Iowa had improved considerably since permanent white settlement began in 1833. By 1868, for example, Joseph Gongwer and the Smiths could travel west by railroad rather than covered wagon or stagecoach. When Gongwer and the Smiths arrived in southeastern Benton County, rapid settlement had been underway for about fifteen years, with the result that by 1870 not only did farms cover the landscape, but every part of the county contained numerous towns, complete with schools, churches, and community organizations.(19)

In 1901 Daisy Smith and Ira Gongwer married. Ira's parents had recently retired to Marion, and the newlyweds took over the 240-acre farm. The large farmhouse that Grandfather Gongwer built in 1885 had burned, but the farmstead also included a four-room house, which the young couple called home, later adding a kitchen and a second-floor bedroom. Fifteen years after their marriage, they added on another kitchen and built a separate summer kitchen, improving the home considerably. Daisy repeatedly told her husband that she disliked eating meals in the kitchen, so the 1916 addition meant the original kitchen became the dining room, complete with carpet, and the summer kitchen provided a place for cooking during warm weather, keeping both heat and smoke out of the main house. From the time of their marriage, Ira and Daisy enjoyed telephone service. In 1921, the family purchased a Fairbanks Plant, which provided electricity.(20)

In her role as an Iowa farm woman, Daisy Gongwer performed many traditional tasks. She raised chickens, baked the family's supply of bread, pies, and cakes, and planted and tended a large garden. She had separate rhubarb and asparagus patches, and her garden contained a strawberry bed and raspberry and blackberry bushes. The Gongwers also maintained an orchard containing apple and cherry trees. Daisy and Ira benefited considerably from the work of Ira's father who many years earlier had started the orchard and also the rhubarb, asparagus, and strawberry patches. Although the orchard required continual upkeep, that effort was considerably less than the initial planting and provided the family with an abundant supply of fruit. For Daisy, an important summer and fall task was canning the garden and orchard produce.(21)

The Gongwer family also provided most of their own meat supply. In the spring, they butchered five hogs and a beef cow. After processing, the meat was ground into sausage or packed into crocks and sealed with lard. The family milked several cows, and Daisy churned butter weekly. Although the family history does not include mention of refrigeration, they probably lowered their perishable foods into the well, located close to the back door of the house.(22)

While Daisy produced food mostly for family consumption, she also produced a surplus for commercial sale. Every week, traveling by horse and buggy, she went into Atkins to sell her butter, eggs, and cream, and occasionally chickens.(23)

Wash day was a weekly task dreaded by farm women. For Daisy the task was time consuming, but the work was less difficult than for her mother's generation. By the early 1900s many Iowa farm women, including Daisy, had washing machines powered by gasoline engines. With the well located close to the house, water needed to be hauled just a short distance to be heated in a boiler.(24)

While daily life on the farm meant long hours of hard work, threshing brought an excessive workload. Before automobiles became commonplace, threshers remained overnight at the farms where they worked. The farm women then not only had to provide sleeping quarters for the crew but also serve them breakfast and supper, as well as the noon meal. The host family, moreover, took lunch to the men in the field at both midmorning and mid-afternoon. Daisy's daughter, Ruth Gongwer Mumford, remembered her mother getting up at 3:30 A.M. to start food preparations for the threshing crew.(25)

The Gongwers enjoyed an active social life. Living only a few miles from Atkins, Daisy was able to go to town at least once a week. Daisy's daughter, Ruth, recalled the family taking part in school activities, particularly picnics and box socials, and being active in the nearby Fairview Methodist church. Ruth belonged to one of the earliest 4-H clubs in the area.(26)

Throughout her life as a farm woman, Daisy Gongwer worked long hours performing necessary domestic tasks and caring for her children. Like farm women everywhere, her tasks were numerous and often onerous. Yet, living in a commodious, fairly modern farm home and residing close to the nearest community, Daisy and her family experienced a comfortable, apparently prosperous, life that did not include many of the deprivations experienced by farm women living further west on the Great Plains.

Daisy and Ira, moreover, had started farming at a propitious time. Their marriage in 1901 coincided with the beginning of the most prosperous agricultural era in the country's history. The period from 1900 to 1914, known as the Golden Age of Agriculture, brought prosperity to rural Iowans who had already determined that the production of corn and hogs brought them the highest economic returns. As evidence of that proclivity, Iowa farmers typically produced more corn and hogs than any other state in the nation.(27)

The experience of the Andersons and the Gongwers allows for a close examination and comparison of living conditions in two families within the prairie and the plains in the early part of the twentieth century. While farm families everywhere needed to work hard and all experienced some isolation, the experience of families in Lyman County, South Dakota, points out that isolation there was far more pronounced than in Iowa. Given extreme weather conditions, Lyman County residents traveled to town less often and therefore took part in fewer social organizations.

Other aspects of farm life in the two regions also varied greatly. The Gongwer family, living in an area with approximately thirty inches of rainfall annually, had few concerns about moisture. Only in times of drought, such as in the 1930s, did Iowa farm women need to water their gardens. South Dakota farm women living in a semiarid region typically watered gardens every year, so gardening there took more time and effort than in Iowa. Wash day also differed for plains and prairie families. Daisy Gongwer washed clothes in a machine powered by a gasoline engine; Louise Anderson washed the family's laundry with a scrub board. Water for the Gongwers came from a pump outside the kitchen door. Louise Anderson's family carried water from a stock dam located some distance away.

Perhaps housing best delineates the differences between prairie and plains living in the first two decades of the twentieth century. The Gongwers from the beginning of their marriage enjoyed a comfortable, modern home complete with amenities such as a summer kitchen that brought a higher quality of life and made domestic work considerably less difficult. Tinus and Louise Anderson, typical of their neighbors in central South Dakota, lived in a two-room shanty on the plains. For Louise, not only was the home extremely crowded with four children, but the home contained not a single labor-saving device. The Andersons with four children and the Gongwers with one child underscored the fact that family size in Lyman County was typically larger than in the prairie region. In general, the experiences of the Andersons and the Gongwers suggest that South Dakota women's lives were more nearly circumscribed by a greater number of tasks performed under more primitive conditions, fewer social outlets, and greater isolation.

While case studies of the Anderson, Jenson, and Gongwer families provide a depth of information on farm women's socializing, childbearing, and living standards, census data provide insight into the breadth of the findings. Like case studies, census reports also give evidence relative to women's childbearing, their social lives, and their standards of living, but these statistics sacrifice personal details for statistical reliability and firmer generalizations about farm women's lives. Consideration of census reports of household size and composition, fertility levels, population density, and property values further underscores the significant contrasts between the experiences of farm women in the prairie region of Iowa and the plains region of South Dakota.

The 1920 federal census indicates both continuities and disjunctures between the lives of women in the prairie and plains regions of the Midwest. For the purposes of this study we have selected two central Iowa farming townships and two in West River, South Dakota. The Iowa townships, located in Benton County, are Homer and Bruce; the South Dakota townships, located in Lyman County, are Lund and Presho. These townships have significant cultural similarities. In all four townships, the majority (over 75%) of the population was native-born in 1920, and more were born in the state of residence than in any other state. Considering the birthplaces of the fathers as evidence of ethnicity, there was a German ethnic minority in Benton County, and a Norwegian ethnic presence and a small Dutch population in Lyman County. But the more salient cultural factor was the general trend of cross-country U.S. migration in the nineteenth century; most of the inhabitants of rural South Dakota and Iowa were migrants from eastern states or descendants of migrants. The largest number of immigrants arrived from countries in western Europe and the British Isles. Once in the United States, a sizable number of these immigrants crossed through the states of the Old Northwest before arriving in Iowa or South Dakota. In neither sample was there significant cultural influence from the South, the West, or from eastern or southern Europe.(28)

Although the South Dakota and Iowa townships were laid out on similar plans by ethnically similar groups, their populations differed in other ways. Each of the four townships were thirty-six square miles, or 23,040 acres, but in 1920 the Iowa townships supported approximately four times as many people and four times as many farms. Homer and Bruce had 104 and 97 farms respectively, while Lund and Presho each had 25 farms. Thus, the size of the farms differed significantly. The Iowa farms averaged 229 acres; the South Dakota farms averaged 922 acres, which was over four times as large as the Iowa farms. The larger number of Benton County farms, in turn, sheltered four times as many persons as did the South Dakota farms: the population of Homer and Bruce together was 1,011 in 1920 as compared to 253 in Lund and Presho.(29)

Also indicative of the distinct geographic and economic conditions was the substantially greater wealth tied up in the Iowa farms. Even though Benton County farms were only one-quarter the size of Lyman County farms, their average value was $44,807, as compared to $30,568 for the farms in Lyman County. The land and buildings of the Iowa farms averaged $196 dollars per acre in 1920 as compared to $33 per acre for the South Dakota farms.(30)

The differing farm sizes and population densities made concrete differences in the everyday lives of women. Compared to the Lyman County, South Dakota, women in 1920, the Iowa women of Benton County had more neighbors, they had closer neighbors, and they were closer to towns. In the Benton County townships there were 225 women over the age of twenty, compared to 45 in the Lyman County townships. This meant the possibility of a larger number of social contacts as well as the possibility of greater social diversity.(31)

The rural population of Benton County contained not just more people, but a diversity of adults, including extended family and hired workers as well as parents and children. The households of the South Dakota sample had more children and fewer adults than those of the Iowa sample. Approximately two-thirds of the households consisted simply of nuclear families in each area, but the remaining one-third of the households had different compositions. In South Dakota, the majority of the remaining households (70%) had no married couple in them, many of them consisting of single persons. In the Iowa sample (Benton County), the majority (80%) of the remaining households included nuclear families together with other relatives or hired hands. The households of the Iowa farms included sixty-eight individuals who were not listed as heads of households, spouses, or children of household heads; in Lyman County there were only six such individuals.(32)

Notwithstanding the greater incidence of single-person households in Lyman County, the average number of persons per household was approximately the same in the two samples. The reason for this is that the fertility of Lyman County women was nearly 50% higher than that of Benton County women (see Table 1). Consistent with previous comparisons of fertility in the prairie and the plains, the fertility of women in the sparsely populated rural plains was high. The farm women of South Dakota, being subject to more pregnancies and more childcare and having less adult assistance at hand, as a whole would have had less opportunity to define themselves as anything other than mothers. Part of the silver lining of motherhood was the harvest of familial relations including reciprocal assistance, as one's children grew beyond the age of total dependence. But in South Dakota the greater fertility did not result in more children remaining in their farm parents' homes through their teen years. Doubtless because of the tighter economic conditions and the hardship of plains farm life, children left home at an earlier age. The women of South Dakota were less likely than Iowa women to retain older children in their homes. In all four townships of the sample, a slightly larger number of older sons than older daughters

TABLE 1. FERTILITY RATES FOR BRUCE AND HOMER TOWNSHIPS, BRENTON COUNTY, IOWA, AND LUND AND PRESHO TOWNSHIPS, LYMAN COUNTY, SOUTH DAKOTA, 1920

	Married women Ages 15–44	Children Ages 0–4	Fertility rate
Bruce Township	92	79	859
Homer Township	78	67	858
Brenton County	170	146	859
Lund Township	16	20	1,250
Presbo Township	14	18	1,286
Lyman County	30	38	1,267

Note: In other words, in Bruce Township in 1920 there were .859 children aged zero to four years old for each married woman aged fifteen to forty-four. In Lyman County, there were 1.267 children aged zero to four for each married woman aged fifteen to forty-four. Fertility rate is defined as 1000 x (number of children ages 0–4 divided by the number of married women ages 15–44)

Source: Computed from manuscript population census schedules, 1920, Bruce and Homer Townships, Brenton County, Iowa, and Lund and Presho Townships, Lyman County, South Dakota.

remained on the farms, but Iowa youth of both sexes were much more likely to stay at home. On the Homer and Bruce farms there were forty-five daughters and sixty-nine sons over the age of fifteen, as compared to ten daughters and eleven sons over age fifteen in Lund and Presho Townships.(33)

Finally, there was a stark difference in the number of hired workers in the two counties. While Bruce and Homer farms had a total of twenty-seven persons listed in the census as hired workers, only one person in Lund and Presho was listed as being a hired worker. In terms of cooking and laundry, hired hands meant more housework, but in Iowa there were more women present to do this work. The presence of hired hands, moreover, made it less likely that farm women would be called upon to milk cows, do field work, or do other outside tasks. From the perspective of the 1990s, it is tempting to call women who did agricultural work liberated in comparison with women who did stereotypically women's work; but there is no evidence that an early-twentieth-century farm woman with a house full of small children would have sought to broaden her horizons by doing more outside farm work. More likely, she would have defined her "liberation" in terms of wider social contacts, more time for church and club work, and improved household equipment, all of which were more abundant in Iowa than in South Dakota.(34)

Within nuclear households, at least until the time that children could take over domestic tasks, one woman had to complete them all, thus not being able to concentrate on the tasks enjoyed most. Further, women who needed to complete a wide range of domestic tasks did not have much opportunity to develop greater proficiency in any given work area. For women within extended households, however, specializations were possible. With fewer children to care for and more people to share the work, Iowa women were without doubt under less pressure than were South Dakota women, who had more work to do and fewer hands to do it.(35)

The physical features of the prairie and plains account for major dissimilarities in the lives of the rural women. These dissimilarities can be considered in depth in detailed case studies or they can be observed in breadth in demographic data. While the types of daily tasks performed by women and men in the two areas were to some extent similar, they performed these tasks under markedly different conditions. Given the erratic weather conditions on the plains and the greater distances to be accommodated whether traveling to town or to the nearest neighbor, plains residents in South Dakota had to adjust to and accommodate a wider range of difficulties than did residents in the prairie region of Iowa. This is vividly present in the contrasting experiences of the Andersons and Jensons in Lyman County, South Dakota, and the Gongwers in Benton County, Iowa.

According to the federal census of 1920, farm size varied considerably between Lyman County and Benton County. Farms were farther apart in South Dakota; population was sparser. Households in South Dakota were less likely to contain the diversity of kinfolk and workers found in Iowa. South Dakota farm women spent a greater share of their lives bearing and rearing small children than did Iowa women, but they were less likely to have older children near them. As a result of contrasting physical environments, the lives of farm women in Lyman County, South Dakota, were profoundly different from those of farm women in Benton County, Iowa. While it is possible to generalize about some midwestern experiences, many aspects of farm women's lives are more clearly understood by considering the contrasts between the prairie and the plains.

Notes

(1) The following works have treated the Midwest as a homogenous region in regard to women's domestic activities: Katherine Jellison, *Entitled to Power: Farm Women and Technology, 1919–1963* (Chapel Hill: University of North Carolina Press, 1993); *Mary Neth, Preserving the Family Farm: Women, Community, and the Foundations of Agribusiness in the Midwest, 1900–1940* (Baltimore: Johns Hopkins University Press, 1995); Glenda Riley, *The Female Frontier: A Comparative View of Women on the Prairie and the Plains* (Lawrence: University Press of Kansas, 1988). Examples of works that have portrayed the plains experience as distinctive include Deborah Fink, *Agrarian Women: Wives and Mothers in Rural Nebraska, 1880–1940* (Chapel Hill: University of North Carolina Press, 1992).

(2.) We use the term "subregion" to denote that the Midwest is composed of three different geographical areas: the woodland region in the eastern Midwest, exemplified by Ohio; the prairie region in the center of the Midwest as represented by Iowa; and the plains in the western part of the Midwest as represented by South Dakota. See Dorothy Schwieder, *Iowa: The Middle Land* (Ames: Iowa State University Press, 1996), 36.

(3.) Schwieder, *Iowa: The Middle Land,* chaps. 3 and 8.

(4.) Herbert S. Schell, "Evolution of a Commonwealth," in *South Dakota: Fifty Years of Progress, 1889–1939,* ed. York Sampson (Sioux Falls, S.D.: Golden Anniversary Book Co., 1939), 9, 11.

(5.) Luther Hill, ed., *History of Benton County, Iowa* (Chicago: Lewis Publishing Company, 1900), 38–40; "Stars in Our Crown: A Brief Sketch of Each County in the

Sunshine State Prepared by the Federal Writers' Project Especially for this Book," in *South Dakota: Fifty Years of Progress,* 96–97. For the two most recent and comprehensive books on West River, South Dakota, see Paula Nelson, *After the West Was Won: Homesteaders and Town-Builders in Western South Dakota, 1900–1917* (Iowa City: University of Iowa Press, 1986); and Paula Nelson, *The Prairie Winnows Out Its Own: The West River Country of South Dakota in the Years of the Depression* (Iowa City: University of Iowa Press, 1996).

(6.) Schwieder, *Iowa: The Middle Land,* chap. 3.

(7.) Schell, "Evolution of a Commonwealth," 9–11.

(8.) Ibid.; Herbert S. Schell, *History of South Dakota* (Lincoln: University of Nebraska Press, 1968), 346–347.

(9.) Clara Jenson, interviews by Dorothy Schwieder, Presho, S.D., August 1985 and August 1986; Alma Muldoon, interview by Dorothy Schwieder, Nampa, Ida., August 1972; Nora Anderson, interview by Dorothy Schwieder, Presho, S.D., June 1998; *Early Settlers in Lyman County* (Pierre, SD: State Publishing Company, 1974), 98–99, 200–202. Louise and Tinus Anderson were the maternal grandparents of Dorothy Schwieder.

(10.) Ibid. George Jenson was a brother of James and a nephew of Louise Anderson. George had relocated in Lyman County along with the Tinus Anderson and James Jenson families.

(11.) *Early Settlers,* 58.

(12.) Nelson, *After the West Was Won,* 32–33.

(13.) *Early Settlers,* 101.

(14.) Ibid., 98–99, 200–202.

(15.) For examples of medical difficulties, see *Early Settlers,* 94, 95, 97, 98, 122; see also Clara Jenson interview, August 1986.

(16.) Clara Jenson interview, August 1986.

(17.) The authors wish to thank the staff of the Vinton Public Library, Vinton, Iowa, for making this material available to them.

(18.) Ruth Gongwer Mumford, interview by Ann Harrison, Benton County, Iowa, 1984, Tape I, pp. 1–3, Vinton Public Library, Vinton, Iowa. The material on the Gongwer family comes from an interview with Ruth Gongwer Mumford, conducted by Ann Harrison, for the Oral History Project conducted jointly by the Vinton American Association of University Women (AAUW), the Benton County Historical Society, and Benton County Cooperative Extension. The interviews focused on twelve women's experiences in Benton County.

(19.) Schwieder, *Iowa: The Middle Land,* 153–155.

(20.) Mumford interview, Tape I, pp. 29–30.

(21.) Ibid., Tape II, pp. 12–13, 16.

(22.) Ibid., Tape I, pp. 24–25, 27.

(23.) Ibid., Tape I, p. 28.

(24.) Ibid., Tape I, p. 23.

(25.) Ibid., Tape II, pp. 23–25.

(26.) Ibid., Tape II, pp. 4, 10.

(27.) Schwieder, *Iowa: The Middle Land,* 146–147.

(28.) Manuscript population census schedules, 1920, Bruce and Homer Townships, Benton County, Iowa, and Lund and Presho Townships, Lyman County, S.D. While the Andersons and Jensons lived in Presho Township, one of the Lyman County townships used for this study, the Gongwer family lived in Fremont Township in Benton County, rather than in either Bruce or Homer Townships. We would have preferred to have located an early-twentieth-century history of a farm family in either Bruce or Homer Townships, but were unable to do so.

(29.) Fourteenth Census of the United States: Agriculture, Iowa and South Dakota, 1920.

(30.) Ibid. Although both Homer and Bruce in Benton County and Lund and Presho in Lyman County had farms that were somewhat larger than the county averages, they reflected the general conditions in the two areas: for the whole of Benton County, farms averaged 168 acres, while Lyman County farms averaged 844 acres.

(31.) Manuscript population census schedules, 1920.

(32.) Ibid.

(33.) Ibid. Also see Deborah Fink and Alicia Carriquiry, "Having Babies or Not: Household Composition and Fertility in Rural Iowa and Nebraska,

1900–1910," *Great Plains Quarterly* 12 (Summer 1992): 157–168.

(34.) Manuscript population census schedules, 1920.

(35.) See Charlotte Perkins Gilman, *The Home: Its Work and Influence* (New York: McClure, Philips, 1903), for a discussion of specialization in women's domestic work. Gilman argues that the lack of specialization in women's lives, whereby each woman did a wide range of daily tasks as opposed to specialized work, hindered women's creative abilities and their development. Men, on the other hand, specialized in their work and therefore had experienced evolution to a higher social and economic plane.

REVIEW QUESTIONS

1. What methods were used in this study?

2. Who were the subjects used in this study?

3. What were the results of the comparison?

Explain in detail

PART IV ■ ANALYZING DATA

■
Chapter 11: An Introduction to Statistics

Now that we have talked about the foundations of research and the various methods you can use in a research project, you must learn what to do with the information you collect. In this chapter you will learn about **descriptive statistics,** which describe numerical data and can be categorized by the number of variables involved. For instance, **univariate** has one variable, **bivariate** has two variables, and **multivariate** has more than two variables.

RESULTS WITH ONLY ONE VARIABLE

Univariate statistics describe one variable. The two most common ways to describe the numerical data of one variable is with **graphs** or **frequency distribution**. Graphs have an advantage because they provide a picture that makes the results easier to comprehend. This graph shows the religions of the individuals in the study.

Religion of Students Bar Graph

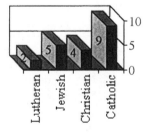

At the same time, a frequency distribution shows the exact numbers of the cases and the values that have been reported. The following is a frequency distribution. There is only one variable for both the graph and the table.

Religion	Frequency
Lutheran	2
Jewish	5
Christian	4
Catholic	9
Total	**20**

The primary goal is to accurately display the distribution's shape and to show how cases are distributed across the values of the variable. There are three features that you must be away of: central tendency, variability, and skewness that can be represented in either graphs or frequency distribution.

Central tendency is where your data is displayed in the form of averages. You may either use the mode, which is the most frequent attribute either grouped or ungrouped; the mean, which is the average, or the median, which is the middle attribute in the ranked distribution of observed attributes.

Let's suppose you are interested in looking at a group of children who range in age from 4 to 10, as shown in the following table:

Age	Number
4	3
5	4
6	6
7	8
8	4
9	5
10	2

The **mode,** which is also termed probability **average,** is the easiest way to measure because you look for the most frequent value. In our case of children, the mode would be 7-year-olds because there are 8 of them. If there were two groups that had 8 children in them, the distribution would be **bimodal.**

The **median** represents the middle value, or the point that divides the distribution in 50th percentiles. To accomplish this, you must find the middle value and have an equal number of cases above or below it. If there are an equal number of cases, then the median point falls between two cases and is computed by adding the values of the two middle cases and dividing by 2. Since you do not know the precise ages of the children, because the data is grouped, you need to find the middle numbers and divide them by 2 as shown in Table 1.

Sometimes the median is better because it is the middle score and reflects the point in the distribution above which half the scores fall and below which haft the scores fall.

TABLE 1: EXAMPLE OF THREE "AVERAGES"

Age	Number		
4	3		
5	4		
6	6		
7	**8**	Most frequent	Mode=7
8	4		
9	5		
10	2		

Age	Number		
4	3	4 x 3 = 12	
5	4	5 x 4 = 20	Mean = 6.91
6	6	6 x 6 = 36	
7	8	7 x 8 = 56	
8	4	8 x 4 = 32	
9	5	9 x 5 = 45	
10	2	10 x 2 = 20	
		221 total/32 cases	

Age	Number		
4	3	1–3	
5	4	4–7	
6	6	8–13	
7	8	14 15 16 17 18 19 20 21	
		7.06 7.19 **7.31** 7.44 7.56 7.69 7.81 7.94	Median = 7.31
8	4	22–25	**Midpoint**
9	5	26–30	
10	2	31–32	

The arithmetic average or the **mean** takes into account the values of each case in a distribution. The mean is computed by adding the value of all the cases and dividing by the total number of cases. You must be careful, though, because the mean value can be drastically affected by extreme scores and is not always the best indicator of the score distribution.

The central tendency is just one aspect of the shape of the distribution, is only one numbered summary of the distribution, and might not give you the total picture. Even though two distributions can have the same measures of central tendency, they can differ how they spread about the center. The problems can be mitigated if you report a summary of the **dispersion** of responses. One way to measure the dispersion is the **range,** which calculates the true upper limit of the distribution minus the true lower limit. In the case of the children, we know that the mean for the children is 6.91, but their ages range from 4–10. Another way to report dispersion would be through **interquartile range** (IQR). The IQR is the numerical measure that locate a particular value in a data set. More precisely, the pth percentile is the value that has p% of the data below 2nd $(1 - p)$% of the data. The IQR is $= Q_3 - Q_1$, and the IQR between Q_1 and Q_3 is 50% of the data. Thus IQR givers an idea how varied the data is—the bigger IQR, the larger variability.

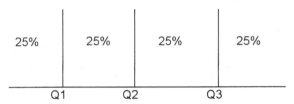

Here is an example. There are 2 classes of 12 students each and their scores on their exams are as follows:

Class 1 66 67 70 74 75 77 78 81 82 85 89 90

Class 2 50 58 61 66 70 77 78 82 89 93 95 96

For both classes, median is 77.5. However, by calculating the IQR for class 1 as follows,

$Q_1 = $ 3rd value + 4th value/2 = 70 + 74/2 = 72

$Q_3 = $ 9th value + 10th value/2 = 82 +85/2 = 83.5

We find the IQR = 83.5 – 72 = 11.5. For class 2

$Q_1 = $ 3rd value + 4th value/2 = 61 + 66/2 = 63.5

$Q_3 = $ 9th value + 10th value = 89 +93/2 = 91

The IQR = 91 – 63.5 = 27.5

So, even though the medians of the 2 classes are the same, by computing IQR we get an idea about the dispersion in the 2 data sets, Since 27.5 > 11.5 there is a greater variability in the second data set.

RESULTS WITH TWO VARIABLES

While a univariate statistic describes a single variable, the **bivariate** statistic tells you about the statistical relationship between variables. The purpose of bivariate statistics is to compare between groups. Let's say you want to explore the sex differences between students and whether or not they voted during the last election. Your independent variable is sex and your dependent variable is voting. To show the comparison, the table would look like Table 2.

We can tell by looking at the table that more men voted than women during the last election.

When you read a table or create a table there are certain things you need to consider:

TABLE 2: VOTING BY SEX

Voting	Men	Women
Yes	68%	56%
No	32%	44%
Total	100%	100%
	(496)	(362)

- A table should have a heading or a title that succinctly describes what is contained in the table.
- The original content of the variables should be clearly presented. The information is especially critical when a variable is derived from responses to an attitudinal question because the meaning of the responses will depend largely on the wording of the question.
- The attributes of each variable should be clearly indicated. Complex categories will have to be abbreviated, but the meaning should be clear in the table and the full description should be reported in the test.
- When percentages are reported in the table, the base upon which they are computed should be indicated. It is redundant to present all of the raw numbers for each category because these could be reconstructed from the percentages and the bases. The presentation of both numbers and percentages often make a table confusing and more difficult to read.
- If any cases are omitted from the table because of missing data, their numbers should be indicated in the table.

RESULTS WITH MORE THAN 2 VARIABLES

A **multivariate table** is one that has more than 2 variables. The same steps are used to read and create a multivariate table as in the bivariate table. The main difference is that you are looking for some type of explanation through the use of more than one independent variable. Let's say that you are interested in how many people voted in the last election by sex and their age. The table might look like this:

MULTIVARIATE RELATIONSHIP: VOTED IN LAST ELECTION, SEX, AND AGE

Voted in last election	Men	Women
Under 40	21%	30%
	(240)	(364)
40 and older	34%	50%
	(325)	(416)

The results indicate the more women voted in the last election than men and that more women who were over 40 voted than did those who were under 40. While fewer men than women voted in the last election, more men who were over 40 voted than did those men who were under 40. The following reading will give you a little more of an overview into how statistics is used in social science research. This is not meant to be a complete overveiw of statistical analysis, but just enough to wet your whistle until you learn more in class.

ELEMENTARY APPLIED STATISTICS: FOR STUDENTS IN BEHAVIORAL SCIENCE

Linton C. Freeman

Although Freeman wrote the book from which this chapter is taken in 1965, this material still provides a clear and concise explanation of statistics for students. As you read, notice how he explains the scales used in research.

The field of statistics can perhaps be best understood as a special language. And like any language, it allows us to think about things and to communicate our thoughts to others. It is not special in the sense that it will allow us to think or talk of anything different from what we can in our ordinary speech. It is special, however, in that it encourages us to talk in a more precise manner than we could in another language. It is this emphasis on precision that is the strength of statistics. If rigorous thought and precise communication are our aims, statistics is the language for us.

Like other languages, the language of statistics includes words and rules of grammar; these are the tools of a language. Statistics, however, is a limited language with a limited set of tools. In statistics we can talk only about the characteristics of things we can observe. Before the techniques of statistics can answer the questions put to them, they must be provided with data—with the raw materials of observation.

Some statistics require data of one sort, some another, but all statistics need data that are based on observations. This chapter will be concerned with an examination of the observational data required by all statistics and with the various kinds of observational data which are used by the several different statistics. Three forms of data will be discussed: nominal scales, ordinal scales, and interval scales. However, before we can examine specific types of data we must consider some of the general characteristics of all data that are useful for statistical analysis.

Variables

In any scientific study it is necessary that we observe and record some characteristic or characteristics of the world of our experience. We deal with things we see or touch or

Freeman, L. C. 1965. *Elementary applied statistics: For students in behavioral science* (pp. 3–16). New York: Wiley..

smell or hear; these things are all observable. But observability alone is not enough; they must also be capable of differing. If some observable characteristic of an object changes when it is observed again and again, or if it differs between one object and another, it is said to *vary*. In the language of the statistician it is called a *variable*. A variable, then, is an observable characteristic of something which is capable of taking several values or of being expressed in several different categories. Thus weight is a variable, for all objects do not weigh the same amount and a single object may change its weight from time to time. And age is a variable, and college grades, and strength and sex and speed and size and anything you can name which is (1) characteristic of objects or persons, (2) observable, and (3) differs from observation to observation. These, then, are the raw materials of statistical analysis. They are the data that constitute the subject matter of statistics.

Scales

If the data of a variable are to be put to use in a statistical analysis, they must be recorded in some systematic fashion. Each variable must be defined operationally; that is, it must be described in terms of the steps which are required in recording its changing values. Such a definition requires both a description of the characteristics to be observed and specification of the categories among which variation will be recorded. Statisticians often call this procedure of operationally defining variables *scaling;* the resulting descriptions are called *scales.*

In many, perhaps most, cases the scale of a variable will be dictated by common usage. Thus, in our society, the variable age is usually scaled in years, counting the first anniversary of birth as 1, the second as 2, and so on. Except for very young children, such a count is made in years, rounding not to the nearest whole year, but rather to the last anniversary passed. Thus a man who tells you he is 21, may have been born 21 years and 2 days earlier or perhaps 21 years and 362 days. We are already provided, therefore, with a standardized operational definition of age and a means of scaling that variable.

It is important to remember that the scale used to record a variable is not a part of the variable itself. The values taken by a variable are a part of its operational definition. Although some variables have generally accepted sets of values or categories, others, particularly in social science, have no well-established scales of measurement. These variables require that the investigator himself determine the categories among which they may be expected to vary. In studying a variable like social class, for example, one investigator might devise a scale which would yield three classes, say, upper, middle, and lower, but another investigator might specify four classes: upper, middle, working, and lower. Then, too, some variables, like popularity, might require that we start fairly fresh, without much precedent of common usage to go by, and work out an entirely new scale. A person's popularity might be scaled according to the frequency of his contacts with others, or by asking his associates their opinions of him, or in any number of ways. The important thing is to work out a rigorous way of defining a variable operationally before trying to launch into statistical analysis.

Constructing scales, then, is the outcome of operationally defining variables. And scales are necessary to provide data in any statistical study. However, scales are not all alike. They vary from extremely simple affairs consisting only of two unordered categories to quite complex devices including a long series of equally spaced classes starting from a real zero point. We shall discuss three of the most important types of scales.

Nominal Scales. The simplest scale consists of nothing but a set of categories. The basic operation of scaling consists of classifying observations into categories. Any two observations may be equal (in terms of the variable in question) and they are therefore classified into the same category, or they may be unequal, which leads to their classification into different categories. The categories therefore must be mutually exclusive and collectively exhaustive. That is to say, each observation can be classified only into *one* category of the set and each can *always* be classified into some one of them. Sex, for example, is such a nominal scale; all people can be classified into the category male or the category female, and no one may be classified as both.

Usually the classes in a nominal scale are named as they are in the preceding example. Sometimes, however, they are assigned numbers. Assignment of numbers to players in various positions in college football is an example of this practice. Some teams, for example, assign numbers 1 through 29 to quarterbacks, 30 through 39 to fullbacks, 40 to 49 to halfbacks, and so on. These numbers do not imply order; they are simply names which designate categories. Thus an end who wears number 87 is not any "better" or "higher" than a quarterback who wears 27. Eighty-seven merely indicates that its bearer plays a different position from the man who wears 27.

This example illustrates an important characteristic of nominal scales: although numbers may be used to designate classes, these numbers have very few of the usual attributes of numbers. They may not be added; two halfbacks with numbers in the forties do not equal one end with a number in the eighties. In fact, they permit no arithmetic operations at all. These numbers are merely labels for categories. Different labels designate different categories. The original labels may be exchanged for any other set providing that each is replaced by one and only one new label. They may be names (halfback, fullback, and so on) or numbers (40s, 30s, and so on) or even letters, but in any case no order is implied. These scales do not allow us to "measure" variation in any strict sense. Instead, variation is labeled—categories are named along with criteria for classifying observed cases into one or another category.

Many of the variables studied by behavioral scientists are of this nominal or classificatory type. A human ecologist may be interested in regions—say, Northern, Southern, Eastern, Western—and an anthropologist may be concerned with types of descent systems—matrilineal, patrilineal, bilateral—or a family sociologist with marital status—single, married, widowed, divorced. Each of these variables represents scaling at its simplest form where characteristics of objects are merely categorized into various classes.

In each of these examples, and in all nominal scales, observation leads to the classification of each case into one and only one of an unordered set of classes. There may be any number of classes from two on up, but every time they must be mutually exclusive and together they must permit the classification of any observable case. Because of this emphasis on classification alone, nominal scales are often called just *classifications*.

Many statistical writers use the word qualitative to describe nominal scales. They distinguish between these unordered or qualitative scales and scales which are ordered or quantitative. Essentially, however, this is just a distinction between two levels of strength or complexity of scale types. As we shall see, quantitative scales take more into account; they are simply more complex schemes for classifying observed data.

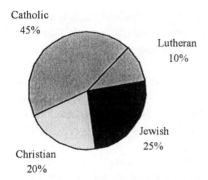

Fig. 1.1. A pictorial representation of a nominal scale—religion

Ordinal Scales. Like nominal scales, ordinal scales are made up of sets of mutually exclusive classes. Ordinal scales, however, possess one additional attribute: the classes form an ordered series. Whereas nominal scales only classify, ordinal scales classify *and order* the classes.

Suppose we are interested in scaling the variable "hardness" for three substances, say diamonds, glass, and wood. We may use "scratchability" as our criterion, and we should then attempt to scratch each substance with each of the others. We will probably find that the diamonds will scratch the glass and the wood and that they will be scratched by neither of these substances. And the glass will scratch the wood and the wood will scratch neither. Relative to hardness, then, we are able to establish a hierarchy—a rank ordering—in which the diamonds rank hardest, the glass less hard, and the wood least hard. In this example we should establish three ordered classes ranging from hardest to least hard.

Ordinal scales, then, establish an ordered series of classes. These classes may be named as in the preceding example (hardest, less hard, least hard), or they may be assigned numbers, which is the more common approach. Thus, diamonds rank 3 in hardness, glass 2, and wood 1. These numbers express the important attribute of order in such scales; they allow us to talk in such terms as "harder than," "higher than," or "more than." However, they do not imply how much harder, higher, or more. Diamonds are harder than glass, but on the basis of such a scale, we do not know how much harder they are. And we do not know whether diamonds are as much harder than glass as glass is harder than wood. Rank 3 is higher than either rank 2 or rank 1 in hardness, but we cannot assume that it is twice as hard as 2 or three times as hard as 1 or anything of that sort. Ordinal scales permit discussion of "moreness" or "lessness," but they make no assumptions as to how much more or less.

Since ordinal scales include a record of order, the labels assigned to their categories must preserve that order. Any labels may be used (new ones may be substituted for old) as long as the original order is preserved. This was done when we substituted the numbers 3, 2, 1 for the labels hardest, less hard, least hard, in the preceding scale. But we may, with equal legitimacy, name our categories 9, 4, and 1 or even 1285, 103, and 18. Because the magnitude of the differences among these values has no significance, any new values may be substituted as long as the order is not changed. This procedure is called an *ordinal* or *monotonic transformation.*

Pairs of observations on an ordinal scale, like those on a nominal scale, may be equal (that is, they may belong to the same class or category) or they may be unequal and therefore belong to different classes. If two observations represent different categories in an ordinal scale, either the first must be greater than the second or the second greater than the first. At no point may their order be ambiguous.

Anything which can be recorded in an ordinal scale can, of course, be simplified and treated as if it were not ordered. When we are not concerned with order, we can simply ignore it and treat ordinal data as if they were nominal. However, if we simplify our ordinal scale into a nominal form, we are often neglecting to use the information supplied by the index. So, in general, it is not wise to simplify a scale, for in doing so we are throwing information away.

Social class as measured by sociologists is an ordinal scale. It enables one to rank persons—to speak in such terms as "higher than" or "lower than," but never to answer how much higher. And attitude tests usually produce ordinal scales. We can talk of "more pro-" or "more anti-," but again the order is the end result; and we are usually unable to determine degrees of difference.

In conclusion, then, although nominal scales classify, ordinal scales classify and order. The ordinal scale provides us with a ranked series of mutually exclusive classes. These are often called simply *ranks.*

| Hardest 3 |
| Less Hard 2 |
| Least Hard 1 |

Fig. 1.2. A pictorial rep)resentation of an ordinal scale—hardness.

Interval Scales. Interval scales have all the qualities of ordinal scales plus one more. Not only do they provide an ordered series of classes, but the intervals between any two pairs of adjacent classes are equal. In this case the distance between 1 and 2 is the same as that between 8 and 9, 112 and 113, or between any two adjacent classes. Temperature as it is usually measured is an interval scale. The one degree between 700 and 710 is the same as the one between 890 and 900. This enables us not only to compare individual cases, but to talk about how many units more or greater one case is than another. We are not restricted to reporting merely that today is colder than yesterday as we would be if we used an ordinal scale; we can say that it is 13 colder.

To construct an interval scale it is necessary to establish some standard unit of measurement. For any two observations that are not equal, the degree of their difference must be expressible in terms of the standard unit.

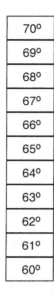

Fig. 1.3. A pictorial representation of an interval scale—temperature.

The units of measurement may, of course, be changed. A constant may be added to the number for each observation or each may be multiplied by a constant. Changes of this sort will affect neither the order nor the relative magnitude of differences in such scales; they are called *linear transformations*.

Interval scales are less common than the simpler forms in behavioral science data. However, we do deal with such variables as number of children and frequency of interaction that can be expressed as interval scales. Three children is the same increase over two as two is over one. And seven interactions is the same frequency less than eight as four is less than five. Some of these are even more complex forms of scales, but here they are all grouped together under the classification of interval scale.

We can also always simplify interval scales. A variable like height, for example, need not be recorded in the interval scale of feet and inches. It may be defined in terms of a pair of ranks; say everyone over 5 ft. 5 in. would be ranked as 2 (tall) and everyone below that figure as 1 (not so tall). Or to simplify further, even the notion of order may be dropped and the two categories can be treated merely as nominal categories.

This consideration points up the essential distinction among our three types of scales. Nominal scales classify—they can be visualized as sets of categories, each with a different name, which together exhaust the possibilities (Fig. 1.1). In ordinal scales, however, categories within the scale are ordered (Fig. 1.2). And the classes within interval scales are both ordered and equal in size (Fig. 1.3).

These distinctions are important in choosing statistics for the analysis of data.

The field of statistics has a long, but unearned, reputation for producing lies. It is altogether too easy to find a pair of items like the following:

Advertisement of the Sunny Dells Development Association, September 1, 1963:

Sunny Dells is a good place to live. The average family income in our town is $11,400 a year.

Pamphlet distributed by a reform political candidate, September 5, 1963:

Our taxes must go down if our town is to survive. Present rates are excessive when we stop to consider that the average family in Sunny Dells earns only $6800 per year.

Clearly, there is something wrong here. The typical family in Sunny Dells obviously cannot earn both $11,400 and $6800 a year. Can it be that one or both of these averages has lied?

The truth is not that statistics lie, but that liars use statistics. In a fact-minded culture like ours, the statistical argument has great appeal. The "average" can be determined by any of a half-dozen different procedures, and sometimes these will provide quite different results. The not too honest purveyor of statistics can take advantage of this situation and provide the consumer with an average which is not necessarily appropriate to the problem but one which is best designed to make his point. It is up to the consumer of statistics, therefore, to learn enough about the range of techniques that are available and their proper use to protect himself from this kind of statistical hard sell. A person who has a reasonably good grasp of the field of statistics will seldom be misled by the inappropriate use of a statistical technique.

The honest user of statistics must always keep one fact in mind: in some instances the use of one statistical procedure is appropriate; in others it is not. The choice of a statistic in a particular situation must be based on two considerations: (1) the nature of the available data and (2) the type of problem at hand. Chapter 1 discussed the kinds of data we might reasonably expect to encounter. This chapter will be concerned with the types of problems to which statistical analysis may be applied.

Three Jobs for Statistics

Hundreds of statistical techniques are available to the contemporary scientist or statistician. Of these, probably no more than twenty or thirty are used regularly in social science, but even twenty or thirty distinct techniques can be quite a confusing array unless they can be understood in terms of their uses.

Fortunately, for the user of statistics, most of the procedures we find can be roughly classified in terms of just a few basic applications. Social scientists generally confine their applications of statistics to three: (1) summarizing observations on a single variable, (2) describing association between variables, and (3) making inferences. Other applications may occasionally be found, but these three are the only ones that occur commonly in social science. They will be discussed in this chapter.

In general, people seem to be both neat and lazy. We express our inclination toward neatness by filing away everything we observe in a more or less orderly fashion in our minds or in our books. And the laziness shows when the filing system is examined, for instead of filing complete statements of our experiences, most of us are content with brief (and often not too accurate) summaries of the things that we know.

One of the primary activities of the social scientist, or of any person for that matter, is reporting things he has observed. "This is a hot day," we say, or "My class is small this year." Here, in each instance, we are describing one characteristic of one object. In the first instance, a day is the object, and its temperature is the characteristic. In the second, a group of students is the object, and their number the characteristic.

Usually, however, we are not concerned with describing a single case. Rather, we want to describe some characteristic of several objects. We might say something like, "Saturday and Sunday were both hot," or even, "Saturday, Sunday, Monday, Tuesday, Wednesday, Thursday, and Friday were all hot." Obviously, however, as soon as we try to deal with more than a few cases such a description becomes extremely cumbersome. Thus, instead of long-winded enumerations of all the days that seemed warm, we usually report merely that, "The week-end was hot," or "The whole week was a scorcher." We use a linguistic shortcut to summarize our experience.

In each of these examples we have used ordinary English to describe or summarize something we have observed. If our powers of observation are adequate, and if we have some facility with the language, we can communicate reasonably well in this fashion. A good deal of ambiguity, however, still remains. This is where statistical procedures come in handy. If we use statistical language, our communication can be less ambiguous. We can adopt scaling procedures and instead of saying "This is a hot day," we should say, "The temperature is 107 in the shade." And instead of "My class is small this year," we may report that "My class contains three students." Here the mode of expression suggested by statistical scaling obviously yields more precise statements and leads therefore to more effective communication.

When our observations are many, statistical techniques may be used to summarize them. Ideally, such a summary should be brief, and yet it should reflect, as much as possible, the sense of the original observations. An adequate summary should enable us to record and to communicate our observations.

There are many statistics which may be used to summarize observations. Among the most useful are those that belong to a set we call *averages*. There are many kinds of averages, but they are alike in that they all attempt to determine a typical observation to represent the entire distribution. So instead of "Last week was hot," we may say, "The average temperature was 88° last week." The latter statement is much more precise than the former.

If we calculate an average to summarize a particular set of observations, we are always left with the question of how satisfactorily it accomplishes that summary. The use of an average suggests a need for further information that will reveal just how typical this typical observation is. Statistics of this latter type are called *indexes of variation;* they help us to make judgments about the adequacy of our averages. We can, for example, think about two very different temperature patterns, each with an average of 88°. One week, let us say, fluctuates between 68° and 108°. The other week remains around 88°; it varies no more than 20 degrees one way or the other. An index of variation is used to summarize this pattern of change or difference. Together, an average and an index of variation provide a summary of a set of observations.

Many more examples can be given, but these should illustrate the point. The language of statistics is more precise than other languages; it allows us to make more accurate reports and summaries of the characteristics of things we observe.

Describing the Relationship Between Two Variables

A second aspect of communication involves the description of relationships or association. One of the primary aims of the social scientist is to reduce the apparent complexity of man's social life. If we look around us, we see that men differ in their attitudes, their values, even their conceptions of what is true and what is false. Sometimes they congregate in large cities, and sometimes they go off by themselves and live as hermits. They vote differently, earn different amounts of money by different means, and spend it in different ways. They worship different gods and follow different leaders. Some men conform to all the rules of their fellow men and others seem always unwilling or unable to restrain themselves. Men are strong or weak, kind or unkind, open or withdrawn; the range of behavior men exhibit seems almost limitless.

The social scientist, however, need not be intimidated by this seemingly endless range of variation. For he has found that the behavior of his fellows—like the behavior of stars or atoms or falling bodies—is not completely random and unpredictable. It is usually possible to specify conditions under which at least part of this variation disappears. When such conditions have been specified, a relationship has been established.

Among Eskimos, for example, persons differ with respect to their occupations. However, within the various age-sex statuses, the differences disappear almost completely. Mature men hunt, mature women prepare hides, and so on. Thus the variable, occupation, does not vary when the variable, status, is taken into account. The two variables are related; they are related in such a way that knowledge of one implies knowledge of the other, and our world is—in one degree—less complex.

Any description of relatedness between observable characteristics may be viewed as a matter of guessing. When we say that in Chicago the season and temperature are related, we are asserting that if we know the value taken by one of these variables, we can guess the value of the other more accurately than we can without such knowledge. If we are told that the temperature in Chicago is 92° on a certain day, we guess that the day occurred in summer. And if we are asked to guess the temperature of a winter day, we pick a figure in the twenties or thirties. Clearly, this relationship is not perfect; occasionally in January the thermometer has reached 68° and sometimes in August it has dropped to 37°· But such occasions have been rare; in general, the relationship holds.

There may be a very large relationship or a very small one, but if we can guess one variable from another at all, we have a useful knowledge. There is a very small relationship between smoking and lung cancer. Yet this relationship, small as it is, may be helpful in finally discovering the causes and cure of cancer.

From this discussion it is clear that we can describe and discuss relationships between variables in everyday English. However, as in describing a single variable, the lack of precision in our language places unnecessary restrictions on our discourse. Whereas in English we must say that this and that are highly related (or not so highly related), in statistical language we can affix a precise number to their relationship. This number tells us the exact degree of their relatedness—precisely how much a knowledge of one variable helps us in guessing the other. Using this statistical tool, called the *coefficient of association,* we can describe relationships in a rigorous fashion. So again, precision is our reward for using statistical language.

Inference

Thus far, our discussion has been confined to the role of statistics in helping us to describe and summarize things we have experienced. However, statistics can be useful also in generalizing from past experience, in making predictions about the cases we have yet to see.

Every day each of us makes a series of decisions based on generalizations of relationships we have perceived in the past. When we leave home in the morning, we may look at the sky and decide whether to wear a raincoat. We know that one attribute of the weather (whether the sky is overcast or not) has in the past often been related to another attribute (whether it rains or not), and we assume that this relationship will continue to hold. We do not then just arbitrarily decide to take or leave our raincoats (we do not toss a coin); instead we judge in terms of a generalization of our past observations of the relationship between overcast skies and rain. Similarly, our decision to go to college may be based on our prior knowledge of the relationship between amount of education and potential earning as it has applied to others. Here we predict that the same rule will apply to us. And our desire to avoid a course in statistics may result from our earlier perception that the amount of mathematics in a course is generally related to its difficulty.

In this manner we use our knowledge of a past relationship between things as a guide for future behavior. Whenever we have been able to guess one characteristic of something on the basis of our knowledge of another, we assume that the relationship will continue to hold. In effect, we look at a few cases and generalize from these to the cases we have yet to see. This procedure seems to serve as a useful general guide for behavior.

Clearly, however, some generalizations are better than others. That is, some of our predictions stand up in light of further observations, whereas others do not. Our grandmothers, for example, thought that the emotional experiences, good and bad, of a pregnant woman would be reflected in the physical and emotional makeup of her child. Generalizations of this sort are probably built on the occurrence of a chance case or two and they persist without further follow-up. Although this generalization is patently false, our common folklore is still full of such nonsense. We try to avoid generalizing on the basis of too few cases, and we try to make sure that the cases are typical. But our ordinary linguistic tools let us down. How few cases are too few? And how can we tell if those we have observed are truly typical of the whole set?

Again, statistical procedures are helpful. The procedures of statistics include some which are called *statistics of inference;* these are designed to help us answer the questions we have raised. Common sense tells us that the more cases we observe the more probable are our generalizations. These statistics tell us how sure we should be on the basis of any given number of cases. So again precision is the reward of the user of statistics.

Statisticians distinguish two types of statistics of inference: *estimates* and *tests of significance.* Estimates refer to direct generalizations of observations. The average income of college graduates, for example, is an estimate based on studies of some, but not all, college graduates. Tests of significance, however, are concerned with comparing our observations with some hypothetical state of affairs. We may guess, for example, that there is a relationship between education and income in America. It would be prohibitively expensive to try to study the whole population of Americans, but we could take a sample of that population. Suppose that for the cases in our sample we did find some relationship between education and income. A critic may argue that the observed relationship is peculiar to our sample—that if we had studied the whole population of Americans, no such relationship would have been indicated. A test of significance would enable us to determine the precise probability that such was the case. It would allow us to determine the likelihood of getting an apparent relationship in our sample if there were none in the population.

In both cases the basic problem is one of generalizing from observed data to the larger population of cases from which the observations were drawn.

Review Questions

1. Describe the 4 scales Freeman talked about in this chapter.

2   What scale would you use if your variable was social class?

3. What scale would you use if your variable was temperature?

Nothing New Under the Sun? A Comparison of Images of Women in Israeli Advertisements in 1979 and 1994

Anat First

First compared two studies that were done in 1979 and 1994 to see how women and men were portrayed in printed Israeli advertisements. As you read the introduction, watch for the variables. Would this be a univariate, bivariate, or multivariate study?

Gender Advertisements and Social Implications

Both critical theory and cultural studies emphasize the central role of advertising in the formation of our symbolic reality (Kellner, 1995; Goffman, 1979; Schudson, 1993). In Western culture, politicoeconomic reality and the symbolic reality presented by the advertising world are related. Kellner (1995) notes that "all ads are social texts that respond to key development during the period in which they appear" (p. 334). Goffman, in *Gender Advertisements* (1979), speaks of advertising as a world of "commercial realism" in which we are given "realistic" images of domestic life and male-female relationships, "in which the scene is conceivable in all detail . . . providing us with a simulated slice of life" (p. 15). Schudson (1993) describes advertising as "'capitalist realism' . . . [which] does not claim to picture reality as it is but reality as it should be—life and lives worth emulating" (p. 215). Both Goffman and Schudson emphasize reality within a specific culture as a site of reference for advertisements.

First, A. 1998. Nothing new under the sun? A comparison of images of women in Israeli advertisements in 1979 and 1994. *Sex Roles: A Journal of Research,* 38(11–12): 1065(13)

Goffman's *Gender Advertisements* (1979), a landmark volume on the depiction of gender in advertising, provided the theoretical framework for both studies. Goffman suggested that advertising conveys cultural ideas about each sex, sometimes in a subtle form, at other times more explicitly. He categorized gender "behavior displays" and the present study uses five of them: (1) Relative Size: "One way in which social weight—power, authority, rank, office renown—is echoed expressively in social situation is through relative size, especially height" (p. 28). (2) The Feminine Touch: "Women, more than men, are pictured using their fingers and hands to trace the outline of an object or to cradle or caress its surface . . . or to effect a just barely touching" (p. 29). Winship (1981) noted that women in advertisements are frequently represented in a "fragmented" way or "cropped" and signified by their lips, legs, hair, eyes or hands, which stand for the "sexual woman." (3) Function Ranking: "In our society when a man and a woman collaborate face to face in an undertaking, the man—it would seem—is likely to perform the executive role" (Goffman, 1979, p. 32). Function ranking can also be tested in terms of activity or passivity, and also, according to Schudson (1993) in terms of product prestige. (4) The Ritualization of Subordination: "A classic stereotype of deference is that of lowering oneself physically in some form or other of prostration. Correspondingly, holding the body erect and the head high is stereotypically a mark of unashamedness, superiority and disdain" (Goffman, 1979, p. 40), and (5) Licensed Withdrawal: "Women more than men, it seems, are pictured engaged in involvement which removes them psychologically from the social situation at large" (Goffman, 1979, p. 57).

The Analysis of Gender Advertisements

Previous studies have analyzed the changing nature of women's role portrayals in magazine advertisements. Sullivan and O'Connor (1988) found that current ads in some ways more accurately reflect the diversity of women's social and occupational roles more than do those of the 1960s and 1970s. Yet, in some professional magazines like medical journals the portrayals of women continue to be stereotyped and outdated (Hawkins & Aber, 1993).

Another perspective on the study of the portrayal of women emerges from research that views communication as "symbolic action" and advertising as commercial pictures that reflect "actual or putative leadership and symbolization of some structure or hierarchy or value presentable as central to society." (Goffman, 1979) Gender representation is a dominant feature of modern advertising, and it provides an ideal place to examine the encoding of cultural norms and value in ritualized format (Jhally, 1987).

Griffin, Viswanath, and Schwartz (1994) outline a persistent problem regarding the best method for analyzing advertising images: How do we designate and evaluate meaningful coding units? This methodical question is so central to the study of women in advertising that it provides a convenient way to discuss the extant body of research.

In Western societies, women constitute a sociopolitical minority even when they are the majority numerically. As a minority, women can be—and have been—studied in ways that parallel the research on other minority groups. Greenberg and Brand (1994) report that work on minorities and the media can be grouped into three major sets. The first counts the presence or absence of minorities in media. The second set consists of studies that attempt to assess the status and role of a minority. The third examines the extent to which the minority characters interact with majority characters. Research on women and the media can be similarly characterized by the types of analyses conducted (for example, see, Lazier & Kendrick, 1993). The current paper falls within this last set.

This paper integrates visual and content analysis utilizing a quantitative method, similar to Griffin et al. (1994) or Belknap and Leonard (1991). A comparison of two studies (in 1979 and 1994), it employs Goffman's (1979) categories in both studies and tested the frequency with which particular roles and symbols appear in different newspapers and magazines across those categories.

The Israeli Scene

Israel has often been perceived as offering women greater equality than do most Western nations. For example, the mandatory participation of Israeli women in military service is a practice that has drawn world attention. The fame of Israel's first woman Prime Minister, Golda Meir, has also contributed to that image (Rapaport, 1993). Yet in Israel, as in most modern Western democratic societies, the prevailing social outlook identifies women with the private sphere where they are responsible for the family and household, while men are associated with the public sphere, and are thus eligible for status in the labor market, in the army, and in politics. Israeli women's acceptance of these traditional identities has predisposed them toward roles centering on family affairs. The role of Israeli women in the family is constructed by two processes. The first is the fact that Israel is a "garrison state" and that women do not have a major role in this apparatus (Yishai, 1996). In reality female roles in the military are mostly nonessential and noncombat. The second process is related to the nature of Israel as a Jewish state, in which Jewish religious norms and laws apply to women, for example, marriage and divorce laws, which are inherently unequal in their application, are governed by the religious courts. Recently, however, women have gained greater access to several public fields formerly monopolized by men, particularly education and management. One effect of this growth has been to weaken the perception that only men are suited for activity in the public sphere and that the private sphere is the exclusive charge of women. These developments in the traditional sociocultural order have enabled women to become more involved in political activity, which has further contributed to systematic change in the country's social framework (Benjamin-Kurtz, 1996).

In 1978 a national committee(3) presented the results of its study of women and the mass media in Israel. Its conclusions included a critique of the portrayal of women in Israeli advertising. The committee found that advertisements in the Israeli media tended to present women in sexist, negative, and harmful images, often directly contradicting the idea of equality.

The original study of gender and Israeli advertisements presented here was conducted in 1979 (see First, 1981). Fifteen years later, in 1994, another study was conducting using the same methods of investigation and categories to look for indications of change in the representation of gender in advertising. This paper presents a comparison between these two time periods.

Methodology

The Sample. The combined sample from the study (1979) and the restudy (1994) consisted of 2,497 full-page or larger advertisements that appeared in prominent daily newspapers, women's magazines, and men's magazines in Israel in the given periods. This included 1678 advertisements collected during the twelve months of 1979 and 819 advertisements collected from January 1st to July 1st, 1994.

The sample of advertisements from women's magazines came from two sources—all the issues of *Na'amat* and *At* from the relevant periods. *Na'amat,* a women's political periodical owned and published by the largest women's organization in Israel, is affiliated with the Trade Union Federation and the Labor Party. *Na'amat* provided the sample with 51 advertisements in 1979, and with 20 more in 1994. *At* was the foremost commercial women's magazine in 1979, and at that time put forward some feminist views. In 1994, it was still a leading women's magazine. In 1979, 346 advertisements from *At* were included, with 88 more being sampled in 1994.

In 1979, 338 advertisements from all the issues of *Monitin*—a men's monthly magazine—were included. The magazine closed after several years, however, and we did not select another men's magazine to replace it in our 1994 data set, because none existed.

The sample also covered all the weekend newspaper advertisements, which had three sources. The first, *Ha'aretz,* is a morning paper widely read by government officials and other elites. *Ha'aretz* provided 381 advertisements in 1979 and 328 advertisements in 1994. In 1979, we also selected 572 advertisements from *Ma'ariv,* an evening newspaper that had the second largest circulation in Israel at the time.

The 1994 advertisements were drawn from another newspaper, however: *Yediot Acharonot,* then the most popular evening newspaper in Israel. The reason for changing newspapers springs from the fact that in 1994 *At* and *Ma'ariv* were owned by the same family, and so it was decided to substitute *Yediot Achronot* for *Ma'ariv* in the 1994 study. *Yediot Acharonot* contributed 383 advertisements to the 1994 study.

These figures indicate that the studies tested the whole population of Israeli advertisements over the given periods. The analysis that follows, however, concerns only those advertisements that depicted at least one adult human being. In 1979, 746 advertisements portrayed at least one adult, whereas 628 did so in 1994. That is, at least one adult appeared in only 1374 out of 2497 advertisements.

The Coders. The content of the sampled advertisements was coded by two trained individuals who worked independently. The coders were given a codebook that defined and delineated visual and textual categories based on Goffman's work, and they were engaged in a discussion about what was and was not included in each category.

In 1979, the analysis was undertaken by two coders, a man and a woman, aged 3040, with some academic education. In 1994, it was performed by two other judges, also a male and a female, aged 25–30, students in the Department of Mass Communication and Journalism at the Hebrew University of Jerusalem. The reliability ($p < .05$, CR > 1.96) of the coding process in 1979, as well as in 1994, was tested by means of the model presented in Singer (1964). In both studies there was a little disagreement between coders, but when a disagreement did arise, discussions were held until consensus was reached.

Coding Units. Drawing heavily on Goffman's work, both studies used five behavior groupings. It is noteworthy that in the 1979 research there was a disagreement on the category "relative size" and it was not included in that study. The categories are not necessarily mutually exclusive.

- *Relative Size.* This category was determined by comparing the height of parties pictured in the advertisements. The results of this comparison were coded using a scale from one to four: (1) the man is shown as taller than the woman in an exaggerated manner, (2) the man is reasonably taller than the woman, (3) the man and woman are of the same height, and (4) the woman is shown as taller than the man in an exaggerated manner.

- *The Feminine Touch.* The feminine touch was measured by pictures involving the use of the whole body or only one part of it (fingers, the face, legs, lips); self-touching; cradling the object; using provocative body positions; and relevance of the exposed part of the body to the product.

- *Function Ranking.* To capture this variable, the professions were coded and were rated using Hartman (1979) and Krous and Hartman's status scale (1993), which ranks employment status in Israeli society.

- *Licensed Withdrawal.* Types of facial expression were coded indicating that the individual is not completely absorbed in the immediate reality presented in the advertisement. These included the following expressions—fear, shyness, anxiety, plus turning one's gaze away from another—all of which show a loss of control.

Findings

Overall, we found that in printed advertisements in Israel, women were and still are depicted as sex objects, parts of their body are used to highlight advertisements' headlines, and they are displayed in various forms of subordination, although there was a change for the better regarding some aspects of function ranking between the two periods. There were two major differences between the studies. The first was the increased number of men in the advertisements. The second was the increased number of women performing behavior displays that turn them into sex objects. It seems that those who produce the advertisements have not altered their basic conceptions about the behavior and symbolic meaning of women. Some changes have occurred, however, mostly concerning the prominence of features of the same behavior group, and in some cases the association of a number of those features with men as well as women.

Relative Size. A difference of height among the human figures depicted was found in only 14% of the 1994 sample (this variable was not tested in the 1979 sample). However, in most of the cases (10%), the men were taller in an exaggerated manner, men and women were in the same height in 3% of the cases, and women were taller than men in only 1% of the advertisements. Even though the incidence of relative size was sparse, when it did occur the stereotypical patterns emerged very clearly.

Feminine Touch. At least one feminine touch phenomenon occurred in almost all of the advertisements (90%) in both periods. As indicated in Table 1, the appearance of every behavioral aspect increased between the periods. For example, in 1979 women were shown touching themselves in 27% of the cases (out of 746 ads), and in 1994 this kind of behavior appeared in 52% of the ads (out of 628 ads). The percentages of men touching themselves

TABLE 1. PROFESSIONAL STATUS OF MEN AND WOMEN IN 1979 ADVERTISEMENTS VS.
1994 ADVERTISEMENTS (IN PERCENTAGES)(A)

	1979		1994	
	Women N = 83	Men N = 179	Women N = 77	Men N = 78
Low (1–3)	14	20	5	10
Average (4–6)	63	38	50	45
High (7–9)	23	42	45	45
Total	100	100	100	100

[a] The percentages are rounded 1979 chi-square 23.38, df 4, p [less than] 01; 1994 chi-square 36.11, df 8, p [less than] 01.

also grew between the periods (from 6% to 31%) but a significant gap (chi-square 37.885, df 2, p < 00) between the percentages of women and of men still remained in 1994.

In 1994, we looked at the relevance to the product of the appearance of a man or a woman in the advertisement and found that in only 40% of the cases was the appearance of an adult relevant. There was a significant difference (chi-square 21.404, df 2, p < 00) between the relevance of male nudity (31%) and of female nudity (49%).

Function Ranking. In the 1979 study, most of the women were presented in roles that were associated with average status: on the scale of nine levels, they ranked between four to six. Occupations at these levels include secretary, nurse, and saleswoman. However, in the restudy, women were represented equally in both average status (50%) and high status levels (45%), as shown in Table 1. A number of other differences were found in the depiction of men's and women's professions. Whereas in the earlier study men were represented twice as much as women overall, in the restudy both gender groups were equally represented and achieved the same percentages in the high status levels. The trend of over-representing men in low status occupations continued, although it decreased between the two studies.

Other aspects of function ranking were also analyzed in 1994. The first additional feature was activity versus passivity. We found that 71% of the men were depicted as active as against 54% of the women (chi-square 25.366, df 1, p < 00). The second feature was product price. Women were more likely than men to be associated with cheap products whereas men were more likely to be associated with expensive ones (chi-square 13.886, df 3, p [less than] 00).

Ritualization of Subordination. Overall, about 70% of the 1979 advertisements featured some aspect connected to the subordination of women, as opposed to 60% of the advertisements in the restudy. In both studies, there was a significant difference between women and men (1979, t = 17.67, m1 = 0.53, m2 = 0.23, p < .01; 1994 t = 3.57, m1 =

13.39, m2 = 12.25, p < 00). There is a major transformation over time regarding the kind of behavior that indicates modes of subordination. In the 1979 study, 15% of the women were depicted in an erect position, as opposed to 44% of the men. However, in the 1994 study, 73% of the women were portrayed in an erect position, compared to 68% of the men. This change recurs across several indicators of ritual subordination. For example, in the first study 38% of the women and 3% of the men were shown leaning backward, while in the restudy 16% of the women and 11% of the men were leaning backward. On the other hand, we rarely found women and men lying on the floor in the first study, yet in the restudy 15% of women and 7% of the men were shown lying on the floor. Additionally, the depiction of women in a "clownish" position doubled in 1994 (from 6% to 14%) while the percentage for men remained constant (8%).

In both studies, women were more associated than men with the kinds of smiles that testify to agreement. However, there is a difference in the depiction of men between the two studies. For example, in the first study we did not find a single man depicted with a smile that suggested embarrassment, while in the restudy, 5% of the men were smiling in an embarrassed fashion.

Licensed Withdrawal. In both studies women were more associated than men with the kinds of facial expression that testify to a situation of licensed withdrawal. The most interesting finding is the consistency of male expressions as shown in Table II. Significant change over time in the presentation of female expressions primarily concerns expressions of control, which doubled from the first to the second study. Also, the "other" category changed its character between the studies. In the study this category refers mainly to expression of passion while in the first study it applied to neutral expressions.

Finally, in both studies, no differences were found between the newspapers and journals examined with regard to our hypotheses.

Discussion

The title of this paper might suggest that nothing has changed over the years regarding the portrayal of women in Israeli advertisements. This contention was ratified. Both studies make clear that advertisements systematically portray women rather than men in situations where parts of their body are used to frame and promote the product. These features include the use of fingers, hands, face, lips, and other exposed parts of the body. However, in the restudy this tendency increased for both men and women, although the increase was especially marked for women. As regards occupational status. It was found in the first study that where such status was indicated, the distribution of men across occupational levels was significantly different from that of women. In general, more advertisements portrayed men as having an occupational status (or having an occupation at all) than portrayed women in that manner. There were more men than women at the upper and the lower levels of the status hierarchy, while at the middle levels the proportion of women was greater than men. This "landscape" had changed substantially by 1994. Women were depicted both as having professions and achieving the same status as men. The biggest change occurred at the highest status level. Women doubled their representation from 1979 to 1994, equaling men in the latter year. At first glance this seems like a major shift, but a deeper analysis shows that the changes were somewhat superficial. The advertisers altered part of the narrative of the relations of men and women, accord-

TABLE II. EXPRESSIONS OF MEN AND WOMEN IN 1979 ADVERTISEMENTS VS. 1994
ADVERTISEMENTS (IN PERCENTAGES)(A)

Expressions	1979 (N = 764)		1994 (N = 628)	
	Women	Men	Women	Men
Regret	4	0	1	0
Fear	6	3	3	3
Shyness	20	12	22	12
Control	29	79	57	78
Other	41	6	17	7
Total	100	100	100	100

[a] The percentages are rounded 1979 chi-square 16.21, df 2, $p < 01$; 1994 chi-square, 157.572, df 44, $p < 00$.

ing to changes in the makeup of the labor force in Israeli society, changes that had occurred in most Western democracies (for example, see Ferrante, Haynes, & Kingsely, 1988; Furnham & Biter, 1993). Effectively, the numerical representation of women had increased (to women's benefit), but the symbolic representation of women still demonstrated their inferiority.

This alteration can be read in relation to capitalist ideology overall. Testing other features of the social order, I found that men were depicted as active and women as passive. Moreover, the advertisers refer to women and men differently according to their ability to buy the product. While it seems that the occupations of the gender groups have been altered, women are still regarded as lacking money (they cannot allow themselves expensive products). Schudson (1993) claims that "there were various ways to find identity and placement in the larger world. Income was especially convenient because it provided a 'ranked identification' and consumer goods begin to be an index and a language that place a person in society and relate the person in symbolically significant ways to the national culture" (p. 158). Thus women were ranked in an inferior position to men.

The subordination of women remained steady over time. While gestures of subordination were more "graceful" in the first study, subordination became more obvious in the 1990s; women were found more often on the bed or on the floor. "Beds and floors provide places in social situations where incumbent persons will be lower than anyone sitting on a chair or standing. Floors also are associated with less clean, less pure, less exalted parts of the room" (Goffman, 1979, p. 41), and naturally lying on the floor or on a bed are expressions of sexual availability. These findings corroborate those of the "feminine touch" behavior group: that women were more represented as sexual objects in the 1990s than in the late 1970s.

Moreover, a greater number of advertisements depicted men rather than women in positions of control. The most important finding was that licensed withdrawal remained the same over the years.

There is more than one way to read these findings. One approach, which has been discussed above, already provides an overall perspective on the relations between men and women. It seems that women are still portrayed as sex objects and their depiction reflects subordination and a lack of ability to control most of the situations in which they are involved.

Another approach is to interpret this portrayal of gender with reference to advertisements as part of "capitalist realism" (Schudson, 1993). In capitalist society, citizens are turned into consumers. As Kellner (1995) suggests, "mass-produced goods and fashion are used to produce a fake individuality, a 'commodity self,' an image" (p. 336), and the depiction of gender in advertising serves to convert the individual into this product-image. Thus, when confronted with the problem of gender stereotypes, instead of transforming women from products into human beings, advertisers prefer to convert men themselves from human beings into products. This process can help us explain the increasing "use" of men as sex objects in advertisements. Additionally, that there were no differences among the magazines and the newspapers examined suggests, among other things (for example, the small size of Israel's population), that the name of the game is "capitalist realism," which is dominant in all print media.

In addition, we have to read our findings in an Israeli context. First we have to note that even though much public attention has centered on the issue of the portrayal of women in advertisements, not a lot has changed over the years. On the one hand, women are better portrayed according to their professions even in a situation of "hyperritualization" (Goffman, 1979), since they have achieved increased representation in different status levels of the labor market. On the other hand, women in 1994 were in worse shape according to the other behavioral aspects as demonstrated above.

Last, whereas researchers have found that some basic values have indeed changed in Israeli society between the 1970s and the 1990s (Adoni, 1995), the basic values and attitudes toward women are much the same, as manifested by the content of Israel's advertisements. I would stress that while some chauvinistic characteristics were reduced, the various subordination behaviors of women are still common; women are still seen as sex objects, and even in more provocative forms than in the past.

References

Adoni, A. (1995). Literacy and reading in a multimedia environment. *Journal of Communications, 45*, 152–172.

Belknap & Leonard (1991). A conceptual replication and extension of Erving Goffman's study of gender advertisements. *Sex Roles, 25*, 103–118.

Benjamin-Kurtz, G. (1996). Attitudes, perceptions and behavior patterns of men and women in the central committees of Israeli political parties. Thesis accepted for the degree of Doctor of Philosophy, Bar Ilan University, Ramat-Gan (in Hebrew).

Durkin, K. (1985). Television and sex role acquisition: Content. *British Journal of Social Psychology, 24*, 101–113.

Ferrante, C. L., Haynes, A. M., & Kingsley, S. M. (1988). Images of women in television advertising. *Journal of Broadcasting and Electronic Media, 32*, 231–237.

First, A. (1981). Presentation of men and women and sex stereotypes as they are reflected in printed advertisements. Thesis accepted for M.A. degree, Tel Aviv University, Tel Aviv (in Hebrew).

Furnham, A., & Bitar, N. (1993). The stereotyped portrayal of men and women in British television advertisements. *Sex Roles, 29,* 297–310.

Goffman, E. (1979). *Gender advertisements.* New York: Harper & Row.

Greenberg, B. S., & Brand, J. E. (1994). Minorities and the mass media. In J. Bryant & D. Zillmann (Eds.), *Media effects.* Hillsdale , NJ: Lawrence Erlbaum.

Griffin, M., Viswanath, K., & Schwartz, D. (1994). Gender advertising in the U.S. and India: Exporting cultural stereotypes. *Media, Culture and Society, 16,* 487–507.

Hartman, M. (1979). Prestige grading of occupations with sociologists as judges. *Quality and Quantity, 13,* 1–19.

Hawkins, J. W., & Aber, C. S. (1993). Women in advertisements in medical journals. *Sex Roles, 28,* 233–242.

Jhally, S. (1987). *The codes of advertising: Fetishism and the political economy of meaning in the consumer society.* New York: St. Martin's.

Kellner, D. (1995). Advertising and consumer culture. In J. Downing, A. Mohammadi, & A. Sreberny-Mohammadi (Eds.), *Questioning the media.* London: Sage.

Krous, V., & Hartman, M. (1993). Changes in prestige grading of occupations in Israel 1974-1989. *Megamot, 40,* 78–87 (in Hebrew).

Lazier, L., & Kendrick, A. L. (1993). Women in advertisements: Sizing up the images, roles and functions. In P. J. Creedon (Ed.), *Women in mass communication.* London: Sage.

Rapaport, G. (1993). *On feminism and its opponents.* Tel-Aviv: Dvir Publishing House (in Hebrew).

Schudson, M. (1993). *Advertising. The uneasy persuasion.* London: Routledge.

Singer, J. D. (1964). Content analysis of elite articulations. *Conflict Resolution, 8,* 425–485.

Sullivan, G. L., & O'Connor, P. J. (1988). Women's role portrayals in magazine advertising: 1958–1983. *Sex Roles, 18,* 181–188.

Winship, J. (1981). Handling sex. *Media, Culture and Society, 3,* 25–41.

Women Status. (1988). 18, Jerusalem: The Office of the Prime Minister, Adviser on the Status of Women (in Hebrew).

Yishai, Y. (1996). Myth and reality in gender equality: The status of women in Israel. M. Lissak & B. Kny Paz (Eds.), *Israel towards the Year 2000: Society, politics and culture.* Jerusalem: Magnes (in Hebrew).

REVIEW QUESTIONS

1. Why were two different years used in this study?

2. How was the information coded?

3. How many variables were in this study?

Glossary

A

accuracy   a measure of how trustworthy and accurate a historical data source is

agreement reality   things you consider real because you have been told they are real by other people and those other people seem to believe they are real.

anonymity   provided by research in which no identifying information is recorded that could be used   to link respondents to their responses

attributes   the characteristics of things or people

authenticity   the genuineness of historical data sources

authority   those who we believe just because we think they truly know about the subject because they are in a position of authority

average   a measure of central tendency represented as the mean, median, or mode

B

bimodal   a variable that has only two attributes

bivariate   two variables

bivariate statistic or analysis   Where the analysis of two variables are simultaneously used for the purpose of determining the empirical relationship between them.

Bogardus Social Distance Scale   a measurement technique that dtermines the willingness of the respodents to participate in social relations with other kinds of people in varying degrees of closeness.

C

census data   data collected by the government that gives the characteristics of the population

central tendency   summary of averages which include the mode, the arithmetic mean, or the median.

close-ended question   interview questions that have a clear and apparent focus and a clearly defined answer

cluster sampling   used when it is either impossible or impractical to compile an exhaustive list of elements that compose the target population

code of ethics   Guidelines set up by national organizations which guide our research endenvors and protect respondents from harm

concept   a mental image that summarizes a set of similar observations, feelings, or ideas explaining exactly what is meant by the term used

conceptualization   the process of specifying what is meant by a term

confidentiality   provided by the researcher where identifying information that could be used to link the respondents to their responses is only available to designated personnel

conflict theory   according to Marx, people are always in conflict for power

content analysis   a method used to study communications processes in magazines, television, or any other type of media

control group   a statistical or experimental means of holding some variables constant in order to examine the causal influences of others

convenience sampling   an available group of subjects

cross-sectional studies   a method of developmental research that is used to examine age differences rather than age changes in subjects

D

deductive reasoning   when reasoning moves from the general to the specific

dimensions   a specific aspect of a concept

dependent variable   a variable, or factor, causally influenced by another (the independent variable)

descriptive research   research that describes a phenomenon without any attempt to determine what causes the phenomenon

descriptive statistics   simple measures of a distributions central tendency and variability

direct observation notes   notes taken while watching the activities being

dispersion   the distribution of values around some central value, such as the average

disproportionate stratified sample   when a sample subpopulation is disproportionate to ensure there are sufficient numbers of cases from each for analysis

double-barreled question   a single survey question that actually asks two questions but allows only one answer

double blind procedure   an experiment where neither subjects nor staff who are delivering the experimental treatments know which subjects are getting the treatment and which subjects are getting the placebo

double negative questions   when the appearance of a negation of a questionnaire item paves the way for easy misinterpretation

E

ethics   guidelines for research where the researcher makes sure that all respondents have voluntary participation and they are not harmed

ethnocentrism   The tendency to look at other cultures through the eyes of one's own culture, and thereby misrepresent the other cultures

ethnography   the study of people at firsthand using participant observation or interviewing

evaluation research   research that evaluates social programs or interventions

exhaustive   a variable's attributes or values in which every case can be classified as having one attribute

existing statistics   where you obtain someone else's data and undertake your own statistical analysis

experiment   a research method in which variables can be analyzed in a controlled and systematic way, either in an artificial situation constructed by the researcher or in naturally occurring settings

experimental group   the group that receives the treatment in an experiment

experimental reality   things you know as real because you have had your own direct experience with

experiment   research that examines the cause and effect relationships through the use of control and treatment groups

explanatory research   research that seeks to identify causes or effects of the phenomenon being studied

exploratory research   research in which social phenomena are investigated without prior expectations in order to develop the explanations

F

feminist theory a theory that looks at inequality in race, gender, sex, and sexuality

field work   sometimes used as a synonym for ethnography, it describes the activity of collecting data in empirical research

follow-up questions   after having a question answered by a respondent, the interviewer asks another question to follow up with the first one

frequency distribution   numerical display showing the number of cases and usually percentage of cases that corresponds to each value or groups of values of a variable

functionalism   a theoretical perspective based on the notion that social events can best be explained in terms of the functions they perform and the contributions they make to the equilibrium of society

G

generalizability   the ability to draw inferences and conclusion from the data collected

graphs   a way of showing or displaying statistical answers

H

hypothesis   an idea or a guess about a given state of affairs, put forward as a basis for empirical testing

historical research   a methodology for examining how events that have occurred in the past affect events that happen in the present and in the future

I

independent variable   a variable, or factor, that causally affects another (the dependent variable)

index   a type of composite measure that summarizes several specific observations and represents some more general dimension

indicator   the end product of the conceptualization process where a specific set of indicators indicate the presence or absence of the concept we are studying

institutional review board (IRA)   a group of representatives who are required by federal law to review the ethical issues in all proposed research that is federally funded and that involves human subjects or can potentially harm subjects

interquartile range   the simplest measure of the dispersion is the range which determines the range of scores for the middle 50$ of the subjects

interview   a method of collecting data, similar to an oral questionnaire, that can be either structured and focused or informal and flexible

J

jotted notes   notes taken by the researcher during the research project

L

longitudinal studies   a method of developmental research that assesses changes in behavior in one group of subjects at more than one point in time

Likert scale   a method used in attitude scales that requires the individual to either agree or disagree to a set of statements using a scale

M

macrolevel analysis   analysis and theories that deal with broad areas of society such as the political or the economic system

mean   a statistical measure of central tendency, or average, based on dividing a total by the number of individual cases.

measurement techniques   includes the method of collecting data,   This can be a survey, interviews, or focus groups

median   the number that falls halfway in a range of numbers.   This is a way of calculating central tendency that is sometimes more useful than calculating a mean

mesolevel analysis   analyses and theories that deal with social groups or organizations, such as classrooms and offices

microlevel analysis   analysis and theories that deal with narrow or small aspects of social life, such as the differences in play between boys and girls.

mode   the number that appears most often in a given set of data.   This can sometimes be a helpful way of portraying central tendency

multivariate   where several variables are used and analyzed

multivariate table   a way of display the findings for more than two variables

mutually exclusive   a variable's attributes or values are mutually exclusive if every case can have only on attribute

N

nonprobability sampling   when the likelihood of selecting any one member of the population is unknown

O

open ended questions   interview questions that provide an opportunity for the respondent to respond in anyway they want

operationalization   specifying the operations that will indicate the value of cases on a variable

oral history   interviews with people about events they witnessed or experienced at some point earlier in their lives

ordinal scales   measurement that assigns only rank order to outcomes

P

paradigms   a fundamental model that organizes our view of something and tells us where to look for answers.   Sometimes is used interchangeably with the terms perspective and/or

participant observation (fieldwork)   a method of research widely used in the social sciences, in which the researcher takes part in the activities of the group or community being studied

personal troubles   troubles where the individual thinks the problems they are having are a reflection of only themselves

placebo   something that is used in place of the experimental stimulus to make the respondent think they have received the stimulus

population   the people who are the focus of social research

posttest the test given to subjects in a randomly assigned group after the end of the experiment

pretest the test given to subjects in a randomly assigned group prior to the beginning of the experiment

primary existing data original sources of information that is used in

primary sources documentation that is firsthand information.

probability sampling the type of sampling that is used when the likelihood of selecting any one member of the population is known

program evaluation see evaluation research

proportionate stratified sample where a uniform proportion of cases are drawn from each homogeneous group

public issues issues that the individual has no control over. They are because of society and more macro

purposive sample when a sample is selected on the basis of your own knowledge of the populiation based on the researchers own judgement and the purpose of the study

Q

qualitative research research methods that emphasize depth of understanding and the deeper meanings of the human experience and which are aimed at generating theoretically richer observations

quantitative research research that emphasizes precise, objective, and generalizable findings

quasi-experimental design done when groups are preassigned to treatments

questionnaire a set of structured, focused questions that employ a self-reporting, paper and pencil format

quota sampling a nonprobablity sampling procedure that is similar to stratified random sampling in that a particular stratum is the focus that ends when a specified number is selected

R

random-digit dialing where the computer automatically makes random telephone calls

random sampling a sampling method in which a sample is chosen so that every member of the population has the same probability of being included

range a measure of dispersion composed of the highest and lowest values of a variable in some set of observations

reliability the quality of measurement method that suggests that the same data would have been collected each time in repeated observations of the same phenomenon

representative sample a sample that "appears like" the population from which it was selected in all respects that are potentially relevant to the study.

research a way of answering a hypothetical question

research methods   The diverse methods of investigation used to gather empirical or factual material.   Different research methods exist.   Sometimes it is useful to combine two or more methods within a single research project.

S

sampling   studying a proportion of individuals or cases from a larger population as representative of that population as a

sampling errors   the difference between the characteristics of a sample and that of the population

sampling interval   the standard distance between elements selected in the sample

sampling strata   where all elements of the population are distinguished based on their characteristics

scale   a type of composite measure composed of several items that have a logical or empirical structure among them such as the Likert or Bogardus social distance scales

secondary data (sources)   analysis of data that has been collected by someone other than the researcher

simple random sampling   a method of sampling in which every sample element is selected only on the basis of chance through a random process

snowball sampling   a method of sampling in which the sample elements are selected as they are identified by successive informants or interviewees

social desirability   the appeal of the question being asked of the

stratified random sampling   a method of sampling in which the sample elements are selected separately from the population strata that are identified in advance by the researcher

survey a method of research in which questionnaires are administered to the population being studied

symbolic interactionism   a theoretical approach that emphasizes the role of symbols and language as the core elements of all human interaction

systematic random sampling   every kth element in the total list is systematically chosen for inclusion in the sample

T

theory   an attempt to identify general properties that may explain observed events. Theories form an essential element of all scientific works. While the theories tend to be linked to broader theoretical approaches, they are strongly influenced by the research results they help to generate.

time series design   a quasi-experimental design that consists of many pretest and posttest observations of the same group

tradition   need definition. appears in chapter 1

true experiment   an experiment in which the subjects are randomly assigned to an experimental group that receives a treatment or other manipulation of the independent variable and a comparison group that does not receive the treatment and whose outcomes are measured in a posttest

U

units of analysis   the level of social life on which a research question is focused
univariate   A single variable being studied

V

validity   the truthfulness or accuracy within the score of a test or interpretation of an experiment
variable   a dimension along which an object, individual, or group may be categorized, such as weight or sex
voluntary participation   when the subjects know about the study they are participating in and have made a voluntary decision to take part